The causes of crime

The causes of crime

New biological approaches

Edited by
SARNOFF A. MEDNICK
TERRIE E. MOFFITT
SUSAN A. STACK

Social Science Research Institute
University of Southern California

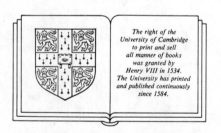

The right of the
University of Cambridge
to print and sell
all manner of books
was granted by
Henry VIII in 1534.
The University has printed
and published continuously
since 1584.

CAMBRIDGE UNIVERSITY PRESS

Cambridge
New York   New Rochelle
Melbourne   Sydney

Published by the Press Syndicate of the University of Cambridge
The Pitt Building, Trumpington Street, Cambridge CB2 1RP
32 East 57th Street, New York, NY 10022, USA
10 Stamford Road, Oakleigh, Melbourne 3166, Australia

First published 1987

Printed in the United States of America

Library of Congress Cataloging-in-Publication Data
The Causes of crime.
Proceedings of a NATO conference held on the
island of Skiathos, Greece, Sept. 20–24, 1982.
Includes index.
1. Criminal anthropology – Congresses. 2. Criminal
behavior – Congresses. 3. Sociobiology – Congresses.
I. Mednick, Sarnoff A. II. Moffitt, Terrie E.
III. Stack, Susan A.
IV. North Atlantic Treaty Organization.
HV6035.C38 1986 364.2′4 86–11778
ISBN 0 521 30402 4

British Library Cataloguing in Publication Data
The causes of crime: new biological approaches
1. Criminal behavior
I. Mednick, Sarnoff A. II. Moffitt, Terrie E.
III. Stack, Susan A.
364.2′4 HV6047

ISBN 0 521 30402 4

Contents

Contributors

Wouter Buikhuisen
Criminology Instituut
Rijkuniversiteit te Leiden
Garenmarkt 1a
2311 PG
Leiden, Holland

Douglas Carroll
Department of Psychology
University of Birmingham
Birmingham, U.K.

Robert Cloninger
Department of Psychiatry and
  Genetics
Washington University Medical
  Center
P.O. Box 14109
St. Louis, MO 63178

John F. Connolly
Psychology Department
University of British Columbia
Vancouver, Canada V6T 1W5

Deborah Denno
Center for Studies in Criminology
  and Criminal Law
University of Pennsylvania
Philadelphia, PA 19104

David P. Farrington
Institute of Criminology
Cambridge University
7 West Road
Cambridge CB3 9DT, U.K.

William F. Gabrielli, Jr.
Department of Psychiatry
University of Kansas Medical
  School
398th and Rainbow Blvd.
Kansas City, KS 66103

Irving Gottesman
Department of Psychology
University of Virginia
Charlottesville, VA 22901

Robert Hare
Psychology Department
University of British Columbia
Vancouver, Canada V6T 1W5

Barry Hutchings
Institute of Clinical Psychology
University of Copenhagen
Copenhagen, Denmark

Malcolm W. Klein
Department of Sociology and
  Social Science Research Institute
University of Southern California
University Park
Los Angeles, CA 90089-MC-1111

Sarnoff A. Mednick
Social Science Research Institute
University of California
University Park
Los Angeles, CA 90089-MC-1111

vii

Israel Nachshon
Department of Criminology
Bar-Ilan University
Ramat-Gan, Israel 52100

Mark A. J. O'Callaghan
Department of Psychology
Hollymoor Hospital
Northfield
Birmingham B31 5EX, U.K.

Dan Olweus
Department of Personality and
  Psychology
University of Bergen
N-5274 Bolstadoyri, Norway

Robert T. Rubin
Division of Biological Psychiatry
Department of Psychiatry
Medical Center
Harbor University of California,
  Los Angeles
Torrance, CA 90509

James H. Satterfield
California Child Study Foundation
5535 Balboa Blvd.
Encino, CA 91316

Daisy Schalling
Department of Psychiatry
Karolinska Sjukhuset
S-104 01 Stockholm, Sweden

Gordon Trasler
Department of Psychology
University of Southampton
Southampton S09 5NH, U.K.

Peter H. Venables
Department of Psychology
University of York
Heslington
York Y01 5DD, U.K.

Matti Virkkunen
Psychiatric Clinic
Helsinki University Central
  Hospital
Lapinlahdentie
00180 Helsinki 18, Finland

Jan Volavka
Department of Psychiatry
New York University School of
  Medicine
Manhattan Psychiatric Center
Ward's Island, New York 10035

Preben Wolf
Sociological Institute
University of Copenhagen
Linnesgaade 22
22 1361 Copenhagen K, Denmark

Preface

A minimal level of conformity is a prerequisite for civilized human inter-action. Although creativity and the flourishing of arts and sciences are stifled by *over*conformity, *under*conformity (or lawlessness) threatens the very existence of the individuals and structures that comprise civilization. The origins of both over- and underconformity must be better understood if human civilization is to be preserved and developed. Anything that contributes to such understanding must be nurtured.

At the turn of the century, biologically oriented speculation dominated the study of lawless human conduct. The speculations were inspired by Darwin's theory of evolution. In some instances, the mechanistic and coldblooded applications of this theory to social conditions produced an attitude toward human beings that smacked of immorality. Spencer's brand of social Darwinism, for example, suggested that the human species be improved by selective breeding and favored "shouldering aside the weak by the strong." Social Darwinism was extended to support aspects of colonialism, racism, and limitation of social welfare. In the 1920s, in the United States, this orientation provided the intellectual basis of dis-criminatory immigration laws. These laws contributed to the death of thousands who might have escaped Hitler's extermination programs. Hitler's master-race ravings are among the recent "biological" specula-tions of the causes of human social behavior.

Given this history, it is not surprising that men and women interested in social justice have a tendency to view with suspicion any new specula-tions or empirical investigations linking biological factors with human social conduct, especially crime among the underprivileged. Nor is it cause for wonder that they prefer to seek causes of crime among eco-nomic, social, and political factors.

There is little doubt about the relevance of these socioenvironmental agents. Nevertheless, for one small, but critical group of antisocial indi-viduals they explain relatively less variance than for other antisocial types; we refer to chronic offenders. The chapters in this volume indicate clearly that chronic offenders have certain biological characteristics that distinguish them from law-abiding citizens or infrequent offenders. As we discuss in the Introduction, chronic offenders comprise about 5% of males but commit well over 50% of crimes. This fact has critical implications in the field of crime prevention. Even a modestly successful intervention program with chronic offenders would have a marked effect on the level of crime in society. It would certainly not retard our progress in intervention to have a more complete understanding of the reasons for the deviant behavior of chronic offenders. This volume consists of reports and reviews of responsible, methodologically sophisticated investigations aimed at helping us learn more about these offenders.

We must not permit these honest research efforts to be ignored simply because in the nineteenth century Herbert Spencer twisted the theory of evolution to selfish, bigoted ends. Nor should this work be dismissed or suppressed in the fear that some evil politician will misuse it. A tool can be used in many ways; let us try to turn this sharp tool of knowledge to the correction of social injustice. Our cities, the strongholds of art, literature, music, and science, have decayed. Part of the reason for this decay is the fear of being assaulted or robbed. In many areas of many cities we have dropped below the level of societal conformity necessary for civilized human interaction. Understanding *all* the relevant characteristics of chronic offenders should be a high priority if we hope to control crime sufficiently to restore a minimal level of civilized interaction in our cities.

It is the conviction of the editors that the work reported in this volume represents a new beginning in criminological research.

S. A. M.
T. E. M.
S. A. S.

Acknowledgments

This volume reports the proceedings of a NATO conference held on the island of Skiathos, Greece, September 20 through 24, 1982. We thank Dr. Craig Sinclair for his very effective help with the administrative aspects of the program. NATO must be commended for committing resources to this type of scientific activity.

Mednick's work on this volume was supported, in part, by grants from the Netherlands Pure Research Foundation (Zuiver Wetenschappelijk Onderzoek) and the Danish Carlsberg Foundation. The National Bank of Denmark was kind enough to provide work space at Nyhavn 18, in Copenhagen. We thank Hr. Bjarne Weber for his assistance.

The production of the volume was also assisted by the staff and facilities of the Social Science Research Institute (Ward Edwards, Director), University of Southern California.

Introduction
Biological factors in crime causation: the
reactions of social scientists

Sarnoff A. Mednick

The XYY chromosome affair

The XYY chromosome episode may have been the most publicized criminological event of the century. Males usually have 46 chromosomes; two
of these are the sex chromosomes, one X and one Y. (XY is the notation
for this configuration.) The normal female sex chromosomes are XX; the
male sex chromosome is Y. In 1961 Sandberg, Koeph, Ishihara, and
Hauschka found a man with an extra Y chromosome (XYY). This man
was not especially aggressive or criminal, but, to some, the extra male
chromosome suggested the possibility of exaggerated maleness, aggressiveness, and violence. Indeed, following this discovery, chromosome
surveys were undertaken in some institutions for the criminally insane,
and the results seemed to suggest that XYY men were exceptionally
violent. The press presented descriptions of the crimes perpetrated by
some of these men that could have furnished material for a series of lurid
horror films. The popular press (and some scientific publications) began to
develop an image of a huge hulk of supermaleness, spurred on to aggressive, violent acts by his extra Y chromosome.

I am describing this phenomenon of the late 1960s and 1970s because it
is an outstanding example of a specific biological factor being linked causally to criminal behavior. The reaction of some social scientists to this
suggestion of a biological basis for criminal behavior was instructive. In
1970, two responses were published. Kessler and Moos (1970) dispassion-
ately and incisively surveyed the literature and noted that the mental
hospital findings were quite inconsistent. They were based on arbitrarily
defined, small samples. In response to this cogent criticism, several studies were launched that examined the behavior of the XYY males selected
from large representative populations. Among these studies was our research in Copenhagen, which involved the karyotyping of the 4,139 tallest
men selected from a total birth cohort. In this total population, the 12

1

XYYs we found were mildly criminal but not at all violent (Witkin et al., 1977).

Sarbin and Miller (1970) offered a different form of criticism of this possible biology–crime link. Their criticism was emotional and political. They made it clear that they were opposed to the possibility of "internal causality" in "the causes of crime," referring to the XYY research as "Demonism revisited." They implied that it was immoral or, at least, scientifically unethical even to consider investigating the possibility that a biological internal characteristic might increase the likelihood of an individual committing a crime. It was clear to them that researchers should be forbidden to study possible biological factors in crime causation; the proper study of crime should be restricted to social, economic, and political variables.

The adoption study

On May 25, 1984, Mednick, Gabrielli, and Hutchings published a report in *Science* indicating that adopted children were more likely to receive criminal convictions if their biological parents had received criminal convictions. (These results are reported in chapter 2.) A reporter who had read an advance copy of this article called the national legal director of the American Civil Liberties Union and described to him the results of the study. Without ever having seen the report, this gentleman made the following statement to the press: "I'll bet the study is full of holes."

The delinquency prevention project

In 1984 I proposed a delinquency prevention project to an agency of the Department of Justice. The project concerned the study of the sociological, psychological, and biological characteristics of the chronic offender. More specifically, the plan was to apply a set of well-researched assessment techniques to a large cohort of boys (about 2,000) who had been apprehended for the first time for a delinquent offense. We would then put this information aside and wait some years until some of the boys had begun to evidence chronic offending. We could then look back to our initial assessment and see whether among our predelinquent measures there was some combination of factors that distinguished the boys who later became chronic offenders. Such differentiating factors could be used to construct a predictive equation that would eventually be capable of selecting from among a cohort of first offenders those who would go on to become multiply recidivistic. It is, by now, commonly understood that a relatively small group of multiply recidivistic offenders (comprising only about 4% to 5% of males) account for the large majority of the crimes in a society, especially serious crimes. If we could reduce the level of crime among this very active group of youths, there would be a disproportionate reduction in the level of crime experienced by society. The small size of the group and their high level of crime would provide remarkable leverage for crime prevention of they could be identified early enough in their careers. The youths would benefit if society could pinpoint scarce social resources for helping them to succeed without being involved with crime.

There would be another important potential benefit of pursuing this line of research; those young offenders who were identified as *not* likely to continue in an active criminal career could be permitted to go home with a reprimand. This would minimize contact of the large majority of youthful offenders with the criminal justice system and greatly reduce the load on police, courts, and probation officers.

Could we successfully develop an instrument that would select those at high risk of becoming future chronic offenders? There have been many attempts to do so utilizing social and/or family measures. These attempts usually account for approximately 30% of the variance. There is excellent evidence that some biological factors are especially useful in distinguishing chronic offenders. (Biological variables do not do as good a job of differentiating one- or two-time offenders from nonoffenders.) If we added biological measures and the interaction of biological with social, familial, and psychological measures to the predictive battery, there would almost certainly be a great improvement in the percentage of variance explained (unless the biological variables were highly correlated with the social factors, which seems highly unlikely).

As mentioned above, a proposal for developing this type of predictive measure was indeed sent to the Justice Department. It received approval up to the highest echelons. Just before the paper work for the funding was completed, a Justice Department social scientist smuggled the proposal to a Washington columnist. In what seemed an intentionally distorted and misleading article, the columnist presented the project in a less than flattering light, referring to "voodoo tests" that "might strike the squeamish as something cooked up by the Nazis' Dr. Mengele." The "voodoo tests" mentioned in the article included the electroencephalograph, skin conductance, lateral dominance, and recording of minor physical anomalies. In response to this single inaccurate publication, the Justice Department immediately canceled funding for the project. It was made clear to me that the funding was canceled only because of the one article and perhaps the fear of possible additional publicity. Congress also responded; it passed legislation making it illegal for this agency to conduct studies involving biological or physiological measures taken on delinquents!

Why is there this unremitting prejudice among social scientists concerning the possibility that biological factors are partial determinants of behavior? One reason given is the supposed hopelessness and untreatability of genetic disorders. The same prejudice once existed among social scientists studying the origins of schizophrenia. At a professional meeting some years ago, I shared the podium with an eminent psychiatrist. I noted in passing, during my talk, that all reasonable workers in the field would bow to the accumulated evidence and acknowledge that genetic factors play some role in the etiology of schizophrenia. The eminent psychiatrist leaped to his feet and shouted that it was not true, and even if it were true he would never admit it because that would lead to a pessimistic attitude toward treatment. A similar stance is taken by some workers in the field of criminal justice. They fear that if a partial genetic etiology is found, public policy might adopt a "lock 'em up and throw away the key" attitude. They believe that if "the cause" is environmental then retraining is likely to be successful and treatment professionals will be more optimistic about the efficacy of treatment. I hesitate to accept this rationale, for several reasons:

1. Attempts to control or limit scientific inquiry have ultimately proved to be fruitless. Even highly centralized and controlling governments have not been completely successful in blotting out the spirit of free inquiry.
2. Even with current environmental assumptions, our treatments for offenders can hardly be described as exceptionally effective, nor are treatment professionals highly optimistic. It seems possible that a more complete understanding of the causes of criminal behavior (including biological factors) would hasten an improvement in our methods of treating offenders.
3. Understanding of the interaction of genetic and environmental factors in crime must inevitably lead to improvement of treatment and prevention. Consider phenylketonuria, a condition that caused a sizable percentage of the mental deficiency in society until its genetic–environmental etiology was detected. Children afflicted with this disease are born with an inherited intolerance for substances present in certain common foods. After birth, as they are exposed to these substances in their everyday diets, they gradually sink into severe mental retardation. The genetic contribution to the condition was discovered in the 1930s; the nature of the biological deficit was found in the 1950s. Now newborns are routinely tested for this condition. A diet excluding the dangerous substances means a relatively normal life for many of these children. In this paragraph I have simplified the complex problems involved in the treatment and prevention of phenylketonuria; the issues involved in the treatment and prevention of criminal behavior will almost certainly prove to

be even more complex. Despite this, it should be clear that partial genetic causation need not imply pessimism regarding treatment or prevention. Quite the contrary!

4. Some fear that if a partial biological etiology for criminal behavior were found, treatment would involve radical medical intervention including the administration of psychotropic drugs or even psychosurgery. This is simply not true. Treatment would not necessarily be medical or even biological. Baker and B. Mednick (1984) point out that "a number of environmental mediators have been shown to actually protect the biologically at-risk child against long-term deviant or less than optimal outcomes. Some of the mediators identified were high SES, low levels of family conflict, availability of counseling and remedial assistance" (p. 144). Baker and Mednick cite an extensive literature that clearly indicates that long-term negative outcomes for children suffering a variety of biological deficits may be totally or largely prevented by appropriate environmental intervention. Much of the research they cite pertains to perinatal injuries and consequent childhood cognitive deficit. To prevent cognitive deficits in children with biological damage, very early intervention is most successful. For the treatment or prevention of delinquency and criminal activities, however, our research suggests that stabilizing rearing conditions in early adolescence would produce optimal results. We found that children with certain biological deficits had an increased likelihood of becoming involved in delinquent acts. More careful examination revealed that if the adolescent period was spent in a stable family, the biological predisposition did not result in delinquency outcomes. Only in unstable family circumstances during early adolescence did biological factors seem to be criminogenic. (Unstable family circumstances in this case refer to a large number of changes in the adult constellations in the household.) These results imply that societal resources must be used to help stabilize rearing conditions of early delinquents. The state, however, cannot put itself in the business of policing marriages. Some potentially viable alternatives might exist. Ideas we have been considering include offering payment to appropriate unemployed or part-time-employed individuals to develop and maintain stabilizing relationships with adolescents with biological predispositions. Such individuals might be women without occupational training whose children are grown or active, interested retired couples. The important point is that the evidence indicates that biological deficits can be compensated for by appropriate environmental intervention.

Current evidence concerning biological factors

I have described emotional and political reasons for social scientists' failure to embrace the role of biological factors in criminal behavior. There is also a rational reason. This is simply that the evidence for the influence of biological variables is weak, consisting mainly of conjecture. For example, at about 11:30 a.m., many people feel a bit irritable because their blood sugar level is low. This led to the conjecture that hypoglycemia might be the basis of some violent outbursts. Pure conjecture! In chapter 16 of this volume Virkunnen takes this hypothesis from the world of conjecture to the universe of empirical test. In genetic research on criminal behavior much of the early research was based on methodologically questionable twin studies or, even worse, ideologically tainted studies from Nazi Germany. The more recent twin studies of the late Karl O. Christiansen and the remarkably convergent results of the independent adoption studies reported in this volume by Mednick, Gabrielli, and Hutchings (chapter 5) and by Cloninger and Gottesman (chapter 6) irrefutably support the influence of heritable factors in the etiology of some forms of antisocial acts. Because we can only inherit biological predispositions, the genetic evidence conclusively admits biological factors among the important agents influencing some forms of criminal behavior.

An important lack in this volume is a careful consideration of an integrated theory that links biological deviation with the learning or the development of antisocial behavior. Perhaps theory can be the central focus of a future volume.

References

Baker, R. L., & Mednick, B. (1984). *Influences on human development: A longitudinal perspective*. Boston: Kluwer Nijhof Press.

Edelberg, R., & Muller, M. (1977). The status of the electrodermal recovery measure: A caveat. Paper presented to the Society for Psychophysiological Research, Philadelphia.

Kessler, S., & Moos, R. H. (1970). The XYY karotype and criminality: A review. *Journal of Psychiatric Research, 7,* 153–70.

Mednick, S. A., Gabrielli, W., & Hutchings, B. (1984). Genetic influences in criminal convictions: Evidence from an adoption cohort. *Science, 224,* 891–4.

Sandberg, A. A., Koeph, G. F., Ishihara, T., & Hauschka, T. S. (1961). An XYY human male. *Lancet,* pp. 488–9.

Sarbin, T. R., & Miller, J. E. (1970). Demonism revisited: The XYY chromosomal anomaly. *Issues in Criminology, 5,* 195–207.

Witkin, H. A., Mednick, S. A., Schulsinger, F., Bakkestrom, E., Christiansen, K. O., Goodenough, D. R., Hirschhorn, K., Lundsteen, C., Owen, D. R., Philip, J., Rubin, D. B., & Stocking, M. (1977). Criminality, aggression and intelligence among XYY and XXY men. In S. A. Mednick & K. O. Christiansen (Eds.), *Biosocial bases of criminal behavior* pp. 165–88. New York: Gardner Press.

1 Some cautions for the biological approach to crime causation

Gordon Trasler

Criminology and penology are historically, and (I believe) necessarily, interdisciplinary studies. There have been times when one discipline has claimed the central role, or even a monopoly, in explaining crime, only to be supplanted by another with similar claims. It is now abundantly clear, however, that the complex phenomena of crime and delinquency are not amenable to explanation in terms of a single discipline: There are social, psychological, and physiological correlates of persistent criminality, and these demand explanation within the framework of the relevant discipline. This is an uncomfortable state of affairs, because most criminologists are specialists who are trained to work within their parent disciplines and inadequately informed about the state of other fields of scholarship. But we ignore the activities of our colleagues with different specialties at our peril – that is to say, at the risk of wasting time and energy on poorly defined issues. We must constantly be glancing across at our fellow criminologists from other disciplines to see what they are doing, how their empirical studies are progressing, and what changes are taking place in the theoretical frame in which they are working, for if we do not do this, we shall inevitably discover that we have been laboring away at some problem that others have abandoned or redefined. Paradoxically, although the nature of the questions each of us asks is constrained by our parent discipline, developments in other disciplines may render those questions trivial or pointless. I shall try to give examples of this. It is one of our weaknesses that many of us are so immersed in the intricacies and complexities of our own native disciplines that we have neither time nor sufficient understanding of sister disciplines to grasp fully the implications of such developments for our own work in criminology.

My first example concerns the gradual recognition, since the 1960s, that "official delinquents" and known criminals do not by any means comprise the whole population of people engaged in crime and delinquency and may in some respects be unrepresentative of such people. I refer to four strands of research with which most criminologists will be familiar. First, self-report studies, such as those conducted by Christie, Andenaes, and Skirbekk (1965), Elmhorn (1965), Gold (1966), Belson (1975), West and Farrington (1973, 1977), and Hindelang, Hirschi, and Weis (1981), have been consistent in showing that a surprisingly large number of adolescents are involved, from time to time, in minor theft, damage, and other offenses. Occasional lawbreaking is not, as we once supposed, confined to a minority of deviant individuals; on the contrary, it is so widespread that it must be regarded as a normal feature of adolescence in very large segments of Western society.

Second, studies of police practice in relation to the decision to record an offense or to overlook it, to charge or merely to reprimand the offender, and to pursue suspicions by interrogation or not to do so show that each of these decisions operates selectively to exclude a number of individuals from certain groups and categories, but not others; the consequence is that those against whom criminal convictions are recorded do not constitute a representative sample of people known by the police to have committed offenses. As Gold (1970) demonstrated in his study in Michigan, the very small subset of young people committed to custodial institutions is not typical of young offenders, or even of young recidivist offenders.

Third, studies of the behavior of victims show that many crimes (not only trivial thefts, but some quite serious assaults, robberies, and frauds) are not reported to the police, even in relatively ordered, law-abiding communities in Western Europe and North America (Clinard, 1978; Sparks, Genn, & Dodd, 1977). There are also, of course, certain categories of offenses – notably shoplifting and malicious damage to property – that do not normally feature in police records or in crime statistics unless the culprit is caught in the act. This seldom happens, though we do know, from estimates of stock losses and maintenance costs, that minor crime of this sort takes place on an enormous scale and must involve a very large number of people.

Fourth – and this point is of a rather different kind – we must question the extent to which the inhabitants of recidivist prisons are representative of persistent offenders with substantial criminal records. An interesting study by Petersilia, Greenwood, and Lavin (1978) made an important distinction between intensive and intermittent offender types (those who are "continually engaged in crime . . . committed to a criminal lifestyle, and . . . careful about avoiding arrest" and those who commit crimes irregularly, with less care and little planning). They estimated that "the average intensive offender committed about ten times as many crimes as the intermittent offender, yet was five times less likely to be arrested for any one crime. Once arrested, the intensive offender was also less likely to be convicted and incarcerated" (p. 118). We are clearly not entitled to regard recidivist prison inmates as a representative sample of persistent serious criminals.

These four strands of research, taken together, have far-reaching consequences for the ways in which psychologists may legitimately investigate the relations between personality and criminality. Until a few years ago it was usual for psychologists to make comparisons between groups of incarcerated offenders (prisoners, inmates of young offender institutions, etc.), described as "criminals" or "delinquents," and groups of apprentices, students, or servicemen, who were usually referred to as "noncriminal" or "nondelinquent" controls. It is now evident that such comparisons are doubly misleading. Offenders in custody are not representative of criminals in general, or even of persistent criminals, but constitute a special, highly selected subset of that minority of offenders who are apprehended, charged, and convicted. On the other hand, control groups of people at liberty are virtually certain to include some individuals who have in fact committed crimes. This is true even in those rare studies in which the investigators have had the wit, patience, and resources to check the records of all their "controls" for official criminal convictions, for we know that only a minority of crimes result in convictions.

Difficulties of this kind are sometimes brushed aside with the comment, "All that may be true, but the fact remains that offenders in custody are likely, on average, to have committed more, and more serious, crimes than people at liberty." That is a comforting thought, but there is no reason to think that this is the case. Reference has been made to the small percentage of the criminal population that is highly recidivistic and that accounts for a very large proportion of offenses. Although the existence of such a group has been part of the "received doctrine" of criminology since the publication of Wolfgang's pioneer studies in Philadelphia (Wolfgang, Figlio, & Sellin, 1972), it is a proposition that should be interpreted with considerable caution. As Blumstein (1979) pointed out:

Any stochastic sequence of events with a non-zero probability of termination after an event will inevitably result in a distribution of sequence lengths. In criminal-career terms, this implies that someone in a cohort has to have committed the most crimes in the cohort, and that person will, of necessity, account for a disproportionately large number of crimes. Or more generally, since every statistical distribution has to have a right-hand tail, the group of "chronic offenders" who comprise the right-hand tail will necessarily account for a disproportionately large number of offenses. The critical question is whether the members of that group are distinguishably different. Certainly they have different records in retro-spect, but the same can be said of winners and losers in any chance process.

This does not necessarily mean, of course, that the characteristics of those who appear in the tails of the distribution may not be different from those of people in the middle of it, but it does warn us that strikingly different frequencies of arrests or convictions in a career may, in some indeterminable proportion of cases, be due to the extremely chancy oper-ation of the law enforcement system. When the risk of being arrested after a burglary is no more than one chance in 10, the distinction between the man with 20 convictions and the man with three is less impressive than might at first appear to be the case. Nor can we escape from a further difficulty: that the behavioral characteristics we wish to study, such as extraversion, aggressiveness, recklessness, and so on, may have played some part in the selective process that results in some offenders, but not others, being sent to custody. Such distorting effects clearly pose a spe-cial problem for investigators concerned with the biological, physiologi-cal, or genetic correlates of criminality. There is also a possibility that the personality measures we employ are sufficiently affected by the condi-tions in which the measures are made as to invalidate comparisons be-tween people in custody and those at liberty.

This point applies, of course, to work already completed, and one is dismayed to see how much of the evidence on which we have relied is vulnerable to such criticisms. To take a single example, the well-known theory of H. J. Eysenck (1977) contained in his book *Crime and Personal-ity* rests on some robust assertions about the connections between extra-version and criminality. Eysenck argues that the low level of cortical arousal that is said to be characteristic of extraverts has two conse-quences: Extraverts develop classically conditioned responses slowly and with difficulty, and so have trouble acquiring a conscience, and they are hungry for excitement, are sensation seekers, readily seduced by the temptations of the big cities. The evidence for the association between extraversion and "official" criminality is by no means persuasive, how-ever and it is based mainly on comparisons between incarcerated offender groups of various kinds and nonincarcerated controls or (what is not quite the same thing) published norms. In their review of the empirical under-pinning of Eysenck's theory of criminality, Farrington, Biron, and LeBlanc (1982) list 14 studies that compare prisoners and institutionalized delinquents with control samples. In five of these the incarcerated groups showed a higher mean extraversion score than the controls; in four, they had a lower mean extraversion score; and in the remaining five studies the findings were equivocal in relation to extraversion. Differences between samples were almost always slight; as the authors point out, "even when the delinquent group is significantly high on extraversion, this seems to be primarily a case of very small differences in very large samples." For example, S. B. G. Eysenck and H. J. Eysenck (1974) reported that the mean extraversion score of 13.64 for 2,070 prisoners was significantly higher than that of 13.24 for 2,442 controls. It is possible, as Eysenck has suggested, that being in custody inclines respondents to understate their extravert tendencies; as he puts it, "questions relating to party-going or social intercourse may be rather meaningless" when one is in prison. That may be so, but it has also been suggested that, in the drab conditions of prison, criminals may be tempted to depict themselves as the fun-loving, high-living heroes of popular fiction. It is impossible to resolve this question, because all of the available data come from studies of incarcerated criminals.

Another fundamental change of perspective in criminological research – especially of research with a biosocial emphasis – stems from the realization of the transient or temporary nature of much delinquency and the observation that many, and probably most, of those who have engaged in criminal activities during their adolescent years cease to do so when they reach adulthood. We have, of course, been aware for a long time that the highest incidence of criminal convictions occurs among youths in their late teens and that the frequency of convictions begins to fall off fairly sharply in the early twenties. Recent self-report studies of unrecorded crime show a similar trend: Those whose delinquencies have escaped the notice of the police tend to give up delinquent patterns of conduct as they reach adulthood. But the significance of this phenomenon escaped us, or rather we misinterpreted it, because we still clung to the belief that criminality of all kinds was primarily a characteristic of persons, a disposition to dishonesty or violence that was rooted in some abnormality or developmental deficit and that therefore would persist unless it was modified or restrained by treatment or deterrence. According to this view, the fact that many young people cease to commit offenses in their late teens and early twenties reflected the success of the criminal justice and penal systems in dealing with them; the few who persisted, becoming adult recidivists, were the failures of the system, the "hard core" of highly criminal individuals who failed to respond to available methods of treatment.

We have gradually arrived at the realization that there are no grounds for believing that the criminal justice and penal systems are effective in treating or restraining criminality. Ceasing to be a delinquent must be in some sense a spontaneous thing, a process of maturation or of adaptation to the different circumstances of adult life (see Trasler, 1979). There is an interesting parallel between "spontaneous desistance" from delinquency, as it is sometimes described, and "spontaneous recovery" in neurotic illness. As Eysenck (1952) pointed out in his well-known paper on the effectiveness of psychotherapy, it is all too easy to assume that, whenever a patient gets better while undergoing treatment, it must be the treatment that made him better. Many untreated neurotics recover in due course, and the same seems to be true of many active, but undetected adolescent delinquents in our society.

The simplest, and (in my view) the most convincing, explanation of spontaneous desistance from adolescent crime is one that concentrates on the satisfactions of delinquent conduct – as Skinner would put it, the reinforcers that maintain such behavior – during adolescence but cease to do so when the individual becomes an adult. Much teenage crime is fun – fun because it is risky and exciting, but expecially because it is a social activity, usually carried out in small groups of two or three youngsters and strongly reinforced by peer-group approval, the enjoyable camaraderie of a collective adventure in an otherwise rather boring and unsympathetic world. As they grow older, however, most young men gain access to other sources of achievement and social satisfaction – a job, a girlfriend, a wife, a home, and eventually children – and in doing so become gradually less dependent on peer-group support. What is more to the point, these new life patterns are inconsistent with delinquent activities, and (in that sense) the individual grows out of delinquency.

There is nothing in the least subtle about this account of the course of events (indeed, I notice with alarm that it might be described as common sense), but it is surely less improbable than the belief that our uncertain and clumsy system for catching, punishing, and treating young offenders has somehow succeeded in remedying a defect in them that would otherwise have destined them for a life of crime. However, the notion that adolescent delinquency (but not necessarily adult crime, for reasons too involved to be discussed here) is to a considerable degree situation dependent, a response to social and environmental reinforcers and cues, poses problems for those (such as Eysenck, Mednick, and myself) who have regarded conscience as the key mechanism in restraining people from behavior that is contrary to laws, mores, and other social rules and have explained criminality mainly in terms of inadequacies in the function of conscience. The essential characteristic of conscience is that it is largely or entirely situation independent; it is an internalized system of values and proscriptions (or "inhibitory responses") that is little, if at all, affected by cues in the immediate environment. There are, moreover, good grounds for arguing that the essentials of conscience are laid down in the early years of dependent childhood, so that the later development of conscience consists in the elaboration and refinement of its cognitive superstructure, whereas the affective mechanisms on which it is based, which provide its motivational mainspring, remain largely unchanged.

I am not sure that I would now defend quite that view of conscience, and I may not have adequately represented Eysenck's view, but I am fairly confident about the essential point – that what we now know about spontaneous desistance from delinquency compels us to modify, at the very least, single-mechanism conscience models of law-abiding behavior and criminality in order to make room for situational adolescent crime. We have little defense, I think, against Clarke's (1977) charge that, in our preoccupation with the personal attributes of offenders, we have neglected the roles of cues and reinforcers that are external to the individual, in eliciting or inhibiting criminal actions. I believe that it is possible to devise a modified, two-stage scheme that would meet some of the difficulties that have arisen, but I will not attempt to sketch it now; my present purpose is simply to argue that these developments in penology have substantially redefined some of the problems to which conscience theories were addressed and so have forced psychologists to reconsider their theories. If they had not done so, they would have been left wrestling with criminological irrelevancies.

There has been a resurgence of interest in biological explanations of criminality, fostered by the publication of some methodologically highly sophisticated studies of the genetic inheritance, brain chemistry, and psychophysiology of certain groups of persistent offenders. This research has been most competently reviewed in Mednick and Volavka (1980), Moyer (1976), Hare and Schalling (1978), and Jeffery (1979). In particular, the twin studies of Christiansen (1977) and, even more emphatically, the cross-fostering studies of Hutchings and Mednick (1977) and Crowe (1975) have established a strong case for the thesis that the disposition to get into trouble with the law is, in some sense, partly inherited. Whether the mechanism of inheritance is genetic or social remains a question, and a very important one. That the effect of this mechanism is to influence, rather than independently to determine, whether the individual becomes criminal does not seem to be in doubt; it is clear that the social environment plays a substantial part in this matter. What has to be explored is whether, and how, genetically transmitted characteristics are implicated.

The classical method of the statistical geneticist – the estimation of heritability – cannot satisfactorily resolve this question. The reason is straightforward: Where heritable characteristics are invested with social meaning, so that physical attribute and social advantage or handicap are closely linked, it is not feasible to distinguish the biological from the social effect. For example, in a society that places multiple handicaps on people who have a particular kind of skin pigmentation, occupational failures will have, on the face of it, a high degree of heritability and in other respects will exhibit all the features of a genetically transmitted characteristic; yet what is being transmitted in this case is a biological characteristic that society has endowed, perhaps quite arbitrarily, with a significance that has nothing to do with nature. I use this illustration because it is tempting to speak as if the demonstration of a high degree of heritability, in the statistical sense, were proof that the behavioral characteristic is the direct, biological expression of what is carried by the genes. For example, H. J. Eysenck and S. B. G. Eysenck (1976) use heritability estimates for "psychoticism," measured by a self-descriptive questionnaire, in this way; they conclude that the characteristic of psychoticism has a genetic basis and is a main cause of psychopathic behavior, psychotic illness, and criminality. This seems very unsatisfactory; if we are to make suggestions about the biological bases of criminality, we have to indicate what it is that is genetically transmitted – not simply that something exhibits a pattern of incidence that is consistent with familial transmission – and the essential stipulation is surely that whatever it is must clearly be relevant to the transactions between the individual and his social environment that issue in criminality or in conformity (or "law abidance," as Mednick calls it).

There have traditionally been two kinds of solutions to this problem: Either one can look for abnormal drives or appetites or a biologically based disposition toward violence (i.e., for evidence that the individual is driven by impulses too strong to be restrained), or alternatively one can try to find some characteristic that impedes the learning of social conformity and the development of self-restraint. The difficulty with the first solution is that it seems to make sense only of certain rather unusual kinds of persistent criminality. There is now substantial evidence that extremely aggressive animals can be produced in the laboratory by selective breeding, that abnormal aggressiveness and frequent episodes of what appears to be extreme rage can be induced in laboratory animals by surgical intervention, local stimulation of the brain, and pharmacological manipulation (Ginsburg, 1979). Although research with human subjects is restricted by ethical considerations, it is well established that brain tumors and epilepsy may lead to uncontrollable outbursts of rage and acts of extreme violence in human beings. There is no denying the assertion that some acts of criminal violence, such as homicide or other physical assaults, can be directly traced to brain dysfunctions and that some persistently violent offenders owe their aggressive characters to some accident of genetics or disease (Goldman, 1977; Moyer, 1976, 1979). There is also persuasive evidence that such pathological aggressiveness can often be controlled by the administration of appropriate drugs; some would argue that surgical ablation, as in amygdalectomy, can also be effective.

Let us consider the significance of such observations for criminological explanation. They feature prominently in discussions of the biological aspects of crime, as evidence that one cannot satisfactorily explain crime without taking such things into account. Here, however, one must make a distinction that may appear to be trivial but is surely important. It can be put most simply by saying that, whereas psychology is committed to explaining violent and aggressive behavior, and sociology is undoubtedly in the business of accounting for deviant social conduct, criminology is concerned only with the conditions in which people break the criminal law – why they are not restrained or deterred by the elaborate system of control that consists of statutes, courts, policemen, penalties, and deterrents. Some crimes involve aggression, and some acts of aggression are criminal; others are not. It is difficult to conceive of a more violent act than the dropping of the second atomic bomb on Nagasaki or the attack on the Iranian Embassy by the British Special Air Service, but in both cases those who acted did so legitimately, in accordance with the prevailing laws. However interesting the problem of how they could act as they did, it is not a criminological question; it is a question for psychology. Criminology is concerned with crime – breaches of the criminal law – and so with criminal violence, not with legitimate violence. It is mainly for this reason that we are obliged to go for the other kind of explanation, in terms of relative inability to learn to control or suppress those kinds of behavior our society forbids. To use Mednick's colorful terminology, in our culture at least, learning to behave appropriately means learning to inhibit "aggressive, adulterous and avaricious behavior."

Thus we are committed to the search for some sort of learning disability – difficulty in responding to the attempts of parents and others to inculcate appropriate restraints – that might be linked with some physiological characteristic under the control of the genes. Eysenck and Levey (1972) contend that this is "conditionability," that is, the capacity to respond to any kind of associative conditioning, which they believe to be a function of constitutional extraversion. However, extensive research generated by this proposal has failed to demonstrate a connection between persistent criminality and refractoriness to associative conditioning in general, and indeed it now seems very doubtful whether it is sensible to talk about "conditionability" as a unitary, general characteristic at all. Different sorts of learning and conditioning seem to make different demands on people: Those who are susceptible to one kind of conditioning may be unresponsive to another.

This observation focuses attention on what one has to learn in order to become a law-abiding person. As Mednick has pointed out, the principal task is to learn to avoid certain kinds of behavior – well-motivated behavior, the natural tendencies of human beings to seize the things and satisfactions they want and to react aggressively to those who frustrate them. Many years ago Hobart Mowrer suggested that avoidance learning was a special process in which parents, by expressing disapproval, caused their children to associate anxiety with these kinds of behavior – anxiety that could be dissipated only by breaking off the sequence of behavior before it actually issued in aggression or the act of taking someone else's possessions. According to this model, the dissipation of anxiety "powers" the avoidance: Rapid dissipation (or "reduction") of anxiety means effective, reliable avoidance, whereas people who, for some reason, dissipate anxiety rather slowly may be expected not to be very good at learning to avoid socially disapproved behavior.

This is the essential logic of Mednick's proposal, that the rapidity with which people dissipate anxiety may be the crucial variable and that it may reflect differences between one individual and another that are stable and unalterable and have to do with structural characteristics of their nervous systems. It is not difficult to see that such differences in brain functioning might well be genetically controlled. They are also potentially measurable; conventional psychophysiological methods of measuring electrodermal activity (i.e., changes in the electrical conductance of the skin) are believed to give a reliable indication of rates of dissipation of anxiety. Using these methods in a small pilot study, Mednick and his colleagues showed differences between men with records of criminal convictions and others with clean records, and (what is especially interesting) differences between individuals who subsequently got into trouble with the law and those who did not; moreover, there are some indications that such differences do have a hereditary basis. One might conclude that, although these findings are as yet very tentative and preliminary, they seem to point in the right direction.

There are, however, some formidable difficulties with this theoretical scheme. Studies of the "recovery limb" of the electrodermal response (i.e., the rate of dissipation of anxiety) do not monitor what goes on in the course of ordinary social behavior; the technique used is to elicit the response, using some kind of external stimulus, such as a loud noise. We assume that someone who shows rapid recovery in the laboratory will do so in the very different conditions of the real world, but we do not know that this is so. Perhaps more important, there is reason to suspect that recovery from a conditioned electrodermal response (which is, of course, the index implied by Mednick's model) may exhibit different characteristics from recovery from primary or directly elicited responses. There are also problems concerning the constancy of electrodermal recovery patterns across situations. For example, Levander, Schalling, Lidberg, and Lidberg reported in 1979 the results of a study that, in their words, "indicated a pronounced effect of situational variance or a low reliability: test–retest coefficients ranging from zero to 0.29." The picture is complicated by the effect of artifacts caused by peripheral consequences of immediately preceding elicited or spontaneous responses. Finally, there are now considerable doubts as to whether the "recovery limb" really is an index of anxiety dissipation. Edelberg, who initiated this line of research, now seems to be inclined to the view that the "recovery limb" has to do with differences in attention rather than anxiety or arousal as such (Edelberg & Muller, 1977). There are problems, too, with Mowrer's model of avoidance learning, on which the whole edifice is built: Although it is plainly true that anxiety induction is necessary to learn avoidance behavior – that is, in the acquisition phase – no one has succeeded in showing that anxiety and its reduction are necessary elements in subsequent performance of avoidance. It does not seem to be the case that maintenance of the habit of avoidance (and it is a very durable habit) depends on the triggering of conditional anxiety and its dissipation. So this model is in some trouble, despite the apparently promising empirical results.

There is, however, an intriguing alternative, which has been put forward by Gray (1975). He has shown that, at least in certain nonhuman species, the business of learning to inhibit behavior that has previously been punished is the function of a set of structures in the limbic system that are not involved in the same way in other kinds of learning. It is possible in animals, but not in humans, to monitor very accurately the functioning of this system and to interfere with it or to stimulate it artificially, so that we can be fairly sure that this really is a physical system that has a key role in the learning in which we are especially interested – that is, learning not to do things that have previously attracted punishment. This assumes, of course, that in gross terms the great structure of our brains discharges the same functions as the corresponding structures in the brains of animals, but this seems a reasonable working assumption.

Locating the structure is a small step forward, but it has yet to be shown that individual differences in the functioning of this system actually exist, as the theory requires, or, if there are such differences, that

they are genetically controlled. So there is a very long way to go before
we can claim to have a robust model. However, what we have is a set of
notions that are capable of generating some specific and precise research
into the psychological process and physiological mechanisms of avoidance learning.

All this seems remote from the problems of criminal behavior. What
makes it interesting, however, is that what Gray is concerned with at the
physiological level seems to parallel the processes that developmental
psychologists such as Walters, Parke, Aronfreed, Hoffman, and others
have investigated in the child laboratory, as "moral internalization and
the establishment of self-control." These investigators have concentrated
on the cognitive aspects of these learning processes, and they have indeed
shown that the development of conscience is an elaborate and protracted
process in which the nature of the cognitive structures that children build
for themselves to articulate their experiences of parental approval and
censure is extremely important. Yet this research has also shown that
affective components, in the form of expressions of disapproval, mild
punishment, or simply the temporary withholding of encouragement, are
important in the development of internalized controls. It is arguable on
existing evidence that the phenomena of passive avoidance learning and
the establishment of internalized controls do not merely exhibit resem-
blances, but are alternative perspectives on the same process.

The essential feature of "moral internalization" is neatly described in
this remark of Martin Hoffman (1977): "Most people do not go through
life viewing Society's moral norms as external, coercively imposed pressures to which they must submit. Though the norms are initially external
to the individual and often in conflict with his desires, the norms eventually become part of his internal motive systems and guide his behavior
even in the absence of external authority. Control by others is thus replaced by self-control." To put this in slightly different terms, what we
call "moral internalization" represents the establishment of a situation-
independent form of behavioral control, one individuals carry about with
them, as it were, that imposes on their conduct a consistency and a
relative indifference to many of the opportunities and provocations that
may arise in the circumstances in which they find themselves. What is
important here is that "internalized" controls, or conscience, constitute a
system that is in a sense prior to situational contingencies. They have an
orienting effect; they sensitize individuals to some signals in their immediate environments and cause them not to respond to (indeed, not to notice)
other signals.

Hoffman points out that the effect of moral internalization is that what is internalized comes to be part of one's own thinking, part of the way in which one sees the world, and thus part of the self-conscious activities of choosing among courses of conduct and deciding how to act. This seems to me a very important observation. One of the least satisfactory features of the notion of conscience as a conditioned reflex has been the implication that it constitutes a rival system to that presented by the contingencies in the immediate environment.

There are, I believe, some circumstances in which we can observe the effects of the absence of internalized control (as in "primary psychopathy") or its temporary erosion under the influence, for example, of alcohol (see Trasler, 1978a). We describe the results as uninhibited hedonism, impulsiveness, opportunism, heedlessness of others, or lack of feelings of obligation and of guilt. All of these expressions describe the behavior of individuals who are wholly responsive to the immediate contingencies. Their behavior seems both bizarre and pathological to us – certainly fickle and lacking in predictability; yet it is (paradoxically) adaptive behavior, since it represents an attempt to adjust to the here and now without reference to considerations or experiences that are prior to it.

This has some important implications for the control of crime. It has significance for the effectiveness and the limitations of deterrents and arranged contingencies in controlling antisocial behavior, and it draws our attention to the relative roles of internal, or situation-independent, controls and external, or situation-specific, elements in the control of deviant activity.

Finally, I shall discuss one more issue and one more example of the possibilities for misunderstanding and the value of keeping abreast of parallel developments in this untidy, multidisciplinary field of criminology. It has to do with the status of notions and segments of theory that we import into criminology from our native disciplines and occasionally from other people's – how we should regard them at the time of borrowing them and what their future relation should be to further developments in the field from which they have been taken. A good example is Mowrer's theory of passive avoidance. This theory was developed to make sense of some puzzling aspects of the behavior of laboratory rats in Skinner boxes and maze runways, and on the whole it seemed to do this rather well. Mowrer himself, who is that rare kind of psychologist, a laboratory scientist who keeps one foot in the field of clinical psychology, quickly saw the neat analogy between passive avoidance and human "conscientious" behavior, and that is how the notion of conditioned fear-mediated inhibition of punished behavior made its way into abnormal psychology and eventually into criminology. It arrived as an analogy; in certain respects the conscientious human behaves like the punished laboratory rat. It had heuristic value; we are now very familiar with the crucial variables governing the establishment and maintenance of passive avoidance in the rat, and it seems sensible to explore how far corresponding variables control conscientious behavior in people. It prompted experiments, notably those of Richard Walters and his colleagues in the child laboratory, on "resistance to temptation," which showed that, although some of the principles that control passive avoidance in the rat also hold for children, others have to be drastically modified because of the child's capacity to recognize and make use of principles and rules beyond the limited comprehension of the rat.

There is no doubt that the importation of Mowrer's theory has stimulated new ideas and new research in criminology and neighboring fields, notably studies of moral development in children and of parental behavior. It drew attention to the peculiarly important role of learning through punishment in our culture and to the predicament of those who, for some reason, are unable to do this. It stimulated a long series of investigations of the cognitive, affective, and psychophysiological correlates of psychopathy, which – though they did not help us much in the problems of managing psychopaths – taught us more about the optimal conditions for the development of conscience in more normal people.

What is the current status of the passive avoidance model in criminology? When we say, "Conscience is a conditioned reflex" – or more precisely, "Conscience is a system of conditioned reflexes" – is this merely an analogy? Do we just mean that conscientious people often behave rather like rats that have been trained, through punishment, to inhibit food-getting behavior? Or are we saying, "This segment of human behavior really is identical with the rat behavior that it resembles, because in both cases the CNS mechanisms implicated are the same, the paleocortex, the 'visceral brain' " – which is surely the equivalent of saying that conscience is nothing but a system of conditioned avoidance responses?

The question is important for several reasons. Contemporary psychologists are given to "reductionist" styles of thinking in two senses of that word. They prefer, for reasons of scientific parsimony, to account for behavior in the simplest possible terms and by reference to the so-called lower functions of the brain whenever possible; and they have a strong, if not always explicit, tendency to assume that, where there is a systematic relation between a physiological change and a change in behavior, that (and not the reverse) must be the direction of causation. If delinquents exhibit excessive slow-wave electroencephalogram activity, we naturally assume that this is, or is directly related to, the cause of their delinquency, and we seldom contemplate the possibility that indulging in delinquency, or the boredom often associated with delinquency, might influence EEG patterns in the peculiar conditions of the research laboratory. This disposition to regard physiological events as prior to behavioral ones is a rich source of conflict between psychologists and sociologists, who are often offended at what they consider the suggestion that moral behavior is no more than a sort of conditioned eyeblink. The curious history of the study of electrodermal recovery in criminals illustrates these largely unstated assumptions rather well. What began as a peripheral physiological indicator of central processes – what many people would regard as the "truly psychological" processes of attending and being curious – has been invested with a quite different meaning and has been given the status of a separate and superior means of access to the supposed physiological causes of behavior, which somehow exempts the investigator from paying further heed to what subjects are saying or believe themselves to be doing.

We must ask ourselves what happens to the borrowed segment of theory if, in its original context, it becomes necessary to abandon it, or at least to amend it. If, as Seligman and Johnson (1973) contend, Mowrer's two-factor theory of passive avoidance is no longer viable in accounting for rat behavior, because of new, contradictory experimental findings, does that mean we must dispense with it as an explanatory device in the psychology of human criminal behavior? If so, we are surely admitting that it is more than a suggestive analogy. If not, we must be acknowledging that it is only that: If this is our view, we are clearly not entitled to claim for such importations any tithe of authority or standing merely because they have proved useful in their original context.

Special problems arise when criminologists borrow theoretical notions from disciplines with which they are not themselves fully familiar. Their lack of acquaintance with the provenance of such notions, the context in which they were developed, and the assumptions on which they are based and their ignorance of the extent to which they are accepted by those who are more expert in the discipline from which they are drawn often result in unduly trusting and incautious enthusiasm for them. Other people's disciplines tend to appear more impressive, more certain, than one's own. For example, I think it doubtful that many of the nonpsychologists who have read Eysenck's lucid and persuasive account of the role of individual differences in conditionability in mediating criminality realize that the very notion of conditionability is fraught with difficulties and surrounded by much controversy among contemporary psychologists. There is dispute about what the term means: whether it refers to consistency in rates of acquisition and extinction of conditioned responses as between appetitive and aversive procedures, to consistency across response systems, or to consistent response to stimuli presented through different sense modalities. It is not clear whether all of these kinds of regularity, or only some of them, are essential to the notion of conditionability. What empirical evidence there is remains elusive and conflicting; the fact is that we are not yet sure whether this link in the theory is capable of bearing the considerable weight that has been placed on it. But criminologists trained and reared in disciplines other than psychology can hardly be expected to know this. It may be that psychologists working in the fields of criminology and penology have a particular duty to ensure that their colleagues do not have unreasonably high expectations of a psychological theory of this kind. I use this example because it is one with which I am familiar, but I am sure that it can be matched by others from each of the disciplines that comprise modern criminology. One thinks of catastrophe theory, the notion of "secondary deviance," the "accounting" method, chromosomal anomalies, victim-precipitated crime, overcontrolled aggression, econometric modeling; each of these labels represents a powerful idea or theory that has invaded criminology, showing much promise but also placing a duty on those with special expertise to acquaint their colleagues with the unresolved difficulties that any new approach inevitably has.

Such problems are prominent in contemporary criminology with the revival of biological and biosocial theories of criminality, bringing with them the prestige that seems to accrue from their origins in the developed, highly respected biological sciences. Those who advocate them seem to promise implicitly that our still weak and puny science, grafted on to such vigorous stock, will begin to grow apace. It is difficult not to be impressed by the elegance and precision of statistical genetics or the esoteric complexities of limbic system functioning. But the appropriate test of a theory is not its aesthetic quality, its plausibility, or even the extent to which it appeals to common sense, but the degree to which it enables us to explain, predict, prevent, and cure criminality.

References

Belson, W. A. (1975). *Juvenile theft: The causal factors.* New York: Harper & Row.
Blumstein, A. (1979). The identification of "career criminals" from "chronic offenders" in a cohort. Unpublished manuscript, Carnegie-Mellon University, Pittsburgh.
Christiansen, K. O. (1977). A preliminary study of criminality among twins. In S. A. Mednick & K. O. Christiansen (Eds.), *Biosocial bases of criminal behavior* (pp. 89–108). New York: Gardner Press.

Christie, N., Andenaes, J., & Skirbekk, S. (1965). A study of self-reported crime. In K. O. Christiansen (Ed.), *Scandinavian studies in criminology* (vol. 1). London: Tavistock.

Clarke, R. V. G. (1977). Psychology and crime. *Bulletin of the British Psychological Society, 30,* 280–3.

Clinard, M. (1978). *Cities with little crime.* Cambridge University Press.

Crowe, R. (1975). An adoptive study of psychopathy. In R. Fieve, D. Rosenthal, & H. Brill (Eds.), *Genetic research in psychiatry.* Baltimore, MD: Johns Hopkins University Press.

Edelberg & Muller (1977). The status of electrodermal recovery measure. Paper presented to the Society for Psychophysiological Research, Philadelphia.

Elmhorn, K. (1965). Study on self-reported delinquency among school children in Stockholm. In K. O. Christiansen (Ed.), *Scandinavian studies in criminology* (Vol. 1). London: Tavistock.

Eysenck, H. J. (1952). The effectiveness of psychotherapy. In H. J. Eysenck (Ed.), *Handbook of abnormal psychology* (1st ed.). London: Pitman Medical.

Eysenck, H. J. (1977). *Crime and personality* (3rd ed.). London: Routledge & Kegan Paul.

Eysenck, H. J., & Eysenck, S. B. G. (1976). *Psychoticism as a dimension of personality.* London: Hodder & Stoughton.

Eysenck, H. J., & Levey, A. (1972). Conditioning, introversion – extraversion and the strength of the nervous system. In V. D. Nebylitsyn & J. A. Gray (Eds.), *Biological bases of individual behavior.* New York: Academic Press.

Eysenck, S. B. G., & Eysenck, H. J. (1974). Personality and recidivism in Borstal boys. *British Journal of Criminology 14,* 385–7.

Farrington, D. P., Biron, L., & LeBlanc, M. (1982). Personality and delinquency in London and Montreal. In J. Gunn & D. P. Farrington (Eds.), *Abnormal offenders, delinquency, and the criminal justice system.* New York: Wiley.

Ginsburg, B. E. (1979). The violent brain: Is it everyone's brain? In C. R. Jeffery (Ed.), *Biology and crime.* Beverly Hills, CA: Sage.

Gold, M. (1966). Undetected delinquent behavior. *Journal of Research in Crime & Delinquency, 3,* 27–46.

Gold, M. (1970). *Delinquent behavior in an American city.* Belmont, CA: Brooks/Cole.

Goldman, H. (1977). The limits of clockwork: The neurobiology of violent behavior. In J. P. Conrad & S. Dinitz (Eds.), *In fear of each other.* Lexington, MA: Heath.

Gray, J. A. (1975). *Elements of a two-process theory of learning.* New York: Academic Press.

Hare, R. D., & Schalling, D. (1978). *Psychopathic behavior: Approaches to research.* New York: Wiley.

Hindelang, M. J., Hirschi, T., & Weis, J. G. (1981). *Measuring delinquency.* Beverly Hills, CA: Sage.

Hoffman, M. L. (1977). Moral internalization: Current theory and research. In L. Berkowitz (Ed.), *Advances in experimental social psychology* (Vol. 10). New York: Academic Press.

Hutchings, B., & Mednick, S. A. (1977). Criminality in adoptees and their adoptive and biological parents: A pilot study. In S. A. Mednick & K. O. Christiansen (Eds.), *Biosocial bases of criminal behavior* (pp. 127–142). New York: Gardner.

Jeffery, C. R. (Ed.). (1979). *Biology and crime.* Beverly Hills, CA: Sage.

Levander, S. E., Schalling, D., Lidberg, L., & Lidberg, Y. (1979). *Electrodermal recovery time, stress and psychopathy* (Report from the Laboratory for Clinical Stress Research, No. 59). Stockholm: Karolinska Institute.

Mednick, S. A., & Volavka, J. (1980). Biology and crime. In N. Morris & M. Tonry (Eds.),

Crime and justice: An annual review of research (Vol. 2, pp. 85–158). University of Chicago Press.

Moyer, K. E. (1976). *The psychobiology of aggression*. New York: Harper & Row.

Moyer, K. E. (1979). What is the potential for biological violence control? In C. R. Jeffery (Ed.), *Biology and crime*. Beverly Hills, CA: Sage.

Petersilia, J., Greenwood, P. W., & Lavin, M. (1978). *Criminal careers of habitual felons*. Washington, DC: National Institute of Law Enforcement & Criminal Justice.

Seligman, M. E. P., & Johnson, J. C. (1973). A cognitive theory of avoidance learning. In F. J. McGuigan & D. B. Lumsden (Eds.), *Contemporary approaches to conditioning and learning*. Washington, DC: Winston.

Sparks, R. F., Genn, H. G., & Dodd, D. J. (1977). *Surveying victims*. New York: Wiley.

Trasler, G. B. (1978a). Relations between psychopathy and persistent criminality: Methodological and theoretical issues. In R. D. Hare & D. Schalling (Eds.), *Psychopathic behavior: Approaches to research*. New York: Wiley.

Trasler, G. B. (1978b). Review of *Crime and personality* (3rd ed.) by H. J. Eysenck. *British Journal of Criminology, 18,* 190–2.

Trasler, G. B. (1979). Delinquency, recidivism and desistance. *British Journal of Criminology, 19,* 314–22.

West, D. J., & Farrington, D. P. (1973). *Who becomes delinquent?* London: Heinemann.

West, D. J., & Farrington, D. P. (1977). *The delinquent way of life*. London: Heinemann.

Wolfgang, M. E., Figlio, R. M., & Sellin, T. (1972). *Delinquency in a birth cohort*. University of Chicago Press.

2   Watch out for that last variable

Malcolm W. Klein

Typically, theoretical approaches to the understanding and prediction of criminal behavior are concerned with four classes of variables. The first of these are precursors, or independent variables. The second are process, or intervening, variables. The third are outcome, or dependent, variables. Finally, theorists often attempt to place these etiological paths in contrasting settings by reference to context variables.

For instance, one might attempt to relate neurological deficits (independent) to violence (dependent) via the mediating processes of family control mechanisms (process) in cultures differing in their tolerance for violent behavior (context). Researchers find it difficult to give equal emphasis to each class of variable; indeed, we probably have fairly consistent, stylistic preferences for one or two of the four. This chapter is offered to those whose style of research has made them less familiar with the issues of the dependent variable in criminological research and theory.

The purpose of the chapter is to alert researchers, especially those approaching criminal behavior from backgrounds in other content areas, to a host of issues they will face when predicting delinquent or criminal outcomes. I have the impression, for instance, that systems analysts and operation researchers tend to assume that different systems are generally analogous and that "outputs" are therefore merely variations on a theme. To the extent that the criminal justice system is adversarial and deliberately noncollaborative, the systems analysts will be misled and their conclusions will be misleading.

Similarly, many clinical researchers make the assumption that crime – especially delinquency – is merely a manifestation or form of general symptomatology of mental illness or deviance. The assumption leads them to "overpsychologize" criminal behavior and to underestimate the normalcy of delinquency.

In much the same way, many biologically trained researchers tend to

25

overlook the differences that may exist among the concepts and associated behaviors indicated by such terms as violence, aggression, criminality, delinquency, antisocial behavior, and psychopathy. Common errors resulting from this confusion include the selection of inappropriate independent-variable measures and the prediction of too many "false positives."

For each of these cross-disciplinary travelers welcomed into criminological territories, the dependent variable may be their undoing. In a limited space, this chapter warns of a large number of relevant issues; the reader interested in greater depth of coverage of individual points can refer to more original sources, some of which are cited throughout the chapter. The present treatment covers five general areas:

1. Juvenile versus adult crime
2. Measurable dimensions of crime and delinquency
3. Alternative modes of measurement; self-report versus official records versus victimization
4. Definitional issues
5. Distributional patterns of crime and delinquency

Juvenile versus adult crime

Of the many matters that distinguish delinquency from adult crime, each of which bears directly on measures of those two sets of behaviors, we shall look briefly at five issues. The first and most obvious is that juveniles frequently commit certain acts not common to adults, and adults commit certain acts uncommon to juveniles. Leaving aside "definitional delinquency" – status offenses such as running away, truancy, and so on – which is *legally* discrete, a good example of an act common to juveniles is auto theft for pleasure rather than profit. In the United States we distinguish between "joyriding" and "grand theft auto." Juveniles far more often than adults steal cars for the quick thrill of possession and "cruising." Adults far more commonly steal a car in order to sell it or its parts.

For adults, a number of property offenses are fairly common but are not normally a reasonable option for juveniles. Among these are various forms of fraud, embezzlement, forgery, and fencing. Among the vices, juveniles simply do not have the same opportunities as adults for pimping, gambling, or international drug trafficking.

A second difference is well illustrated by the comments above on car theft. That is, quite often the explicit and implicit motivations for criminal acts have different emphases. Juveniles, it is generally believed, are more susceptible than adults to peer pressure or more greatly influenced by anticipated reactions to their peers (Erickson & Jensen, 1977; Klein,

1969). The juvenile act is said to be more expressive, the adult act more instrumental.

A third difference is the malleability of the behavior, or its sensitivity to sanctions of one type or another. The first detected acts, those for which we are first apprehended, are most likely to occur in the juvenile years when the response to police and court officials seems most likely to have its effect in either deterring or generating further criminal behavior (Klein & Mednick, 1982). This is a particularly important issue in biosocial research on deterrence, which must take into account the *learned or habituated* behavioral responses to sanctions whose effectiveness is to be related to neurophysiological predispositions.

So far, we have mentioned classes of juvenile–adult differences that derive principally from the perpetrator of the act, that is, behaviors, motivations, and sanction sensitivity of the actor. There are also differences stemming from those who *react* to the criminal behavior – the official agencies and the community. For instance, as our fourth juvenile–adult difference, consider the matter of community tolerance for illegal behavior and the community's willingness and ability to absorb it (Carter, 1968). There are major national differences as well; a number of European juvenile justice systems are activated for youths of age 15, whereas most states in the United States apply the justice system mechanisms to juveniles of age 10 or even younger. Generalizability of research carried out in nations and communities with markedly different tolerance and absorptive capacities will be inaccurate if these differences are not carefully noted.

By the same token, the fifth difference sometimes reflects community attitudes. The police and courts can vary widely in the acts to which they respond, in their options in responding, and in their discretion in responding to actors in terms of gender, ethnicity, and so on, in addition to age. Discretion in responding is more common in juvenile cases, and therefore cross-community differences in official rates are more common for delinquency than for adult crime. For example, one study of police arrest and release rates in 47 communities (Klein, 1974) revealed a range of release rates from 2% to 82%. This is a remarkable difference. But consider the implications if the decision to release or to arrest were in fact a determinant of future levels of criminal conduct; recidivism as measured by the perpetrator's *behavior* would reflect wide differences in official response beyond only individually determined recidivist predispositions (Klein, 1974, provides a case in point).

The same point can obviously be made about adult behavior, but in this case it may well be that court decisions and penal practices are more important. Because harsher sentences and more dramatic punishments are meted out to adults than to juveniles on the average, the impact of these will presumably be differentially effective (positively and negatively). Both incapacitation and the deterrence–rehabilitation dimension seem more applicable to adults than to juveniles once the effects of first sanctions are established.

All of the foregoing has a clear implication for researchers, no matter what their disciplinary preferences. Differences between the juvenile and adult outcome variables can be substantial with respect to types of behavior, motivations, sensitivity to sanction, tolerance of the community, and response of official agencies. Given these differences, lumping juvenile and adult dependent-variable measures together merely invites disaster. For the majority of cases, analyses of juvenile and adult crime must be carried out separately.

For those engaged in longitudinal studies that employ data on both sides of the age of majority, this is especially unpleasant news. It is not simply that juvenile versus adult is an additional variable (the sort of thing for which a dummy variable in regression analyses is an apt solution); the point is that juvenile and adult criminal acts are often *qualitatively* different. They are different in meaning, in process, in what they tell us about the actor and the actor's context. When I am assaulted tomorrow by an angry biologist who objects to my comments about his research, it will be an act very different, in nature and acceptance, from the assault I suffered at the hands of Johnny Young on the school playground when I was 10 years old. The alert researcher will take account of these age-related differences; as a victim, so shall I.

Measurable dimensions of crime

When we say there has been an increase or a decrease in crime, whether at the aggregate or the individual level, just what do we mean? Is it that the number of offenses has changed or that their seriousness has been altered or that the time between offenses is different or that the pattern of crime is different? These questions refer to different and, to a considerable extent, independent dimensions of crime. Documenting changes on any one dimension does not necessarily imply observation of change on another. We shall discuss five of the dimensions briefly.

1. Counting the *number* of offenses is more complex than it might seem. For instance, in the realm of official charges a single incident may often produce more than one charge (e.g., assault and possession of a deadly weapon) and more than one count on the same charge. Sometimes

it is not clear when one "incident" ceases and another begins: Does a half-hour lull in a domestic dispute lead to the recording of two charges of battery or one, or one charge with two counts? The answer to a question such as this is often determined at the discretion of the police or prosecution, not, unfortunately, at the discretion of the researcher. It should be noted, in addition, that this sort of issue is *never* addressed in self-report methodologies.

More crucial is the distinction between what I call *simple* recidivism and *multiple* recidivism. Simple recidivism merely refers to the number of persons in a sample or cohort who recidivate, regardless of how often. Multiple recidivism refers to the number of further offenses committed by the subset of the cohort that recidivates at all. Thus we ask in the first case how many people commit further offenses and in the second how many offenses each of these people commits. The two indices are logically and empirically independent, and which is employed may be of critical importance.

In a study of recidivism following random assignment of juveniles to diversion and nondiversion alternatives, we found that our conclusions differed depending on the measure used. Multiple recidivism was the more sensitive measure for a 6-month follow-up period, but simple recidivism better distinguished the outcome in the several experimental groups over a longer, 27-month follow-up period (Lincoln, Klein, Van Dusen, & Labin, 1982). Had we used the simple recidivism measure early, we might well have concluded that there were no differences, and the same might have been true had we used multiple recidivism for the longer follow-up.

2. Somewhat surprisingly, measures of offense *seriousness* have not proved to be as sensitive to change as have measures of number of offenses. Practitioners faced repeatedly with a failure to reduce recidivism have often suggested that they can nevertheless produce a reduction in the average seriousness of recidivist behavior. There is little empirical support for such a claim.

One reason for this is the rather consistent finding at both the juvenile and adult levels that most perpetrators do *not* manifest patterned crime, but rather involve themselves in "versatile" or "cafeteria-style" offense behavior (Farrington, 1979; Klein, 1982; Petersilia, Greenwood, & Lavin, 1977). If offenses are unpatterned, then logically there is little hope for consistent increases or decreases in seriousness, and this absence of increments in seriousness is indeed the common finding (Klein, 1971, 1982).

Still, seriousness measures continue to be applied in various research endeavors, so we should discuss the alternatives. Several forms of seriousness measures have been employed; it is important to understand that they are both empirically and conceptually different. The simplest is a dichotomous measure such as the FBI's distinction between Part I and Part II crimes. This is a comprehensive if simplistic approach; one weighs Part I offenses twice as heavily as Part II offenses. Yet a study by Blumstein (1974) showed this index to be just as sensitive for aggregated data as the far more complex Sellin and Wolfgang (1964) index. Conceptually, the FBI's index connotes little more than an agreement among relevant officials (many years ago) on the seriousness and reliability of various offense categories.

In contrast are those indices based on official responses to behaviors (e.g., arrest rates or prosecution rates). The notion here is that seriousness can be operationally defined by the rate at which officials decide to act on cases in which an option is available (there is a perpetrator; there is useful evidence). For example, the juvenile seriousness index of McEachern and Bauzer (1967) is based on the proportion of cases in each offense category for which court action was requested by the police. Here, the police, perhaps reflecting community attitudes, are the operational definers of seriousness.[1]

Another form of index, best exemplified by the Sellin and Wolfgang measure (1964), is based on the damage to persons or property resulting from the offense. Whether damage is assessed by ratings or by other means (dollar value, extent of injury), such an index differs in being victim-oriented rather than offender-oriented or related to justice system response. This is a very clear and meaningful conceptual variation that may not seem very pertinent to researchers concentrating on offender behavior per se.

A fourth approach is to use laypeople's judgments of seriousness (e.g., the Rossi, Waite, Bose, & Berk scale, 1974). Such a scale is conceptually less clear than other indices, because it does not explicate the *basis* for the judgments of seriousness (damage, fear, sanction levels, stereotypes, etc.), but it has obvious advantages: potential-victim orientation and, to judge from research to date, relative external validity across a wide variety of respondent categories. Seriousness, in this instance, is what most people say it is.

It seems clear, then, that one's choice of seriousness index must be related to some conceptual base. Each type of index carries a *meaning* with it; indices are not conceptually interchangeable, with decisions to be based on convenience alone. Yet convenience or practicality must also be considered. Some indices include more offenses than others. One may exclude status offenses, whereas another excludes "victimless" crimes. There is the related problem of information loss.

In evaluating the impact of a juvenile gang intervention program, a comparison of four indices was undertaken (Klein, 1971). In a measure of simple recidivism, loss of group members in the analysis ranged from zero using one index to 16% using another. On a measure of multiple recidivism, the range went from a loss of offenses of 1% to a loss of 50%! Choice of index, then, can be of immense practical significance; few of us can afford to lose half our data.

3.   The third dimension to consider is *time between offenses*. This is not a linear dimension; time between offenses decreases around the age peaks of offensivity and often increases following the institution of an intervention program. For juveniles in the United States, for instance, time between offenses is shortest around the age of 16. For any intervention program, one would expect rates of recidivism to be highest immediately following the program, because time between subsequent offenses increases thereafter. However, this might not reflect on the program at all if one used a multiple recidivism index, because *chronic* offenders *decrease* the time between subsequent offenses. Thus attrition from a program cohort becomes a critical problem, depending on the degree to which the program or its evaluators retain contact with the chronic offenders in the cohort.

If time between offenses seems a useful index, it must be recognized that it is less so for juveniles, because it is constricted by the age of majority. Whether this falls at age 16 or 18 or any other age, the cessation of strictly juvenile charges at that point forces statistical dependence between the time measure and a number-of-offenses measure; one might as well use the latter then.

Furthermore, at both the juvenile and adult levels, but especially at the latter, incapacitation through incarceration or other routes has a direct effect on time between offenses. One must be very wary of this issue of "street time" or time at risk, especially as it relates directly to seriousness of charges. If more serious charges are most likely to lead to prosecution and incarceration, they will also lead to greater time between offenses. The severity of this artifact problem depends on the offense severity and system response patterns in the population under study.

4.   The fourth concern is one to which we have already alluded, offense *versatility*. As noted earlier, most individual offense careers are relatively unpatterned. Whether measured by self-report or official indices, and whether tested by percentage of distributions, factor analytic techniques, transitional probabilities, or other procedures, the proposition of specialized offense careers has consistently failed to be supported (see Farrington, 1979, for a review of adult cases, and Klein, 1982, for a review of more than 30 reports on juvenile studies).

This situation has some obvious implications. Research directed toward one or a few categories of offenses – property crimes, vice, or drug use, for example – will be defeating its own purpose by missing much relevant behavior. Research purportedly identifying a pattern of specialization, such as status offenses or violence, absolutely must undertake cross-validation procedures. Research seeking consistent etiological processes related to one form of crime – violence, for example – must include other forms of crime as well in the dependent variable in order to determine whether the discovered precursors are specific to the crime (violence) or to a broader band of behavior. The theoretical conclusions can be drastically affected by *assuming* specialization. This illustration for violence would, I presume, be particularly pertinent to those with a biological orientation; they seem most interested in violent or assaultive behaviors as outcome variables.

5. The final dimension to be noted here is *chronicity*. As noted by Wolfgang, Figlio, and Sellin (1972), Hamparian, Schuster, Dinitz, and Conrad (1978), and an increasing number of other researchers, offense behavior is not equally distributed among offenders. A relatively small proportion of offenders contribute disproportionately to the level of delinquency and crime in any community or cohort. This is the fact that lends importance to the distinction between simple and multiple recidivism; one's choice of recidivism measure may rest in part on one's belief that research subjects will include chronic offenders.

Another implication concerns research on low-base-rate crimes, violence again providing a useful example. Given the versatility patterns, it follows that the more offenses recorded for an individual, the greater are the chances that these will include low-base-rate offenses including violence. It would be tempting, then, to suggest that chronic offenders are more violent or, in the case when a violent offense occurs early in one's career, that violent offenders will become chronic offenders (see Hamparian et al., 1978, for contrary evidence in a "violent" cohort). But this would be to turn an artifact into an etiological proposition.

A final point to be made about chronicity is that the existence of a small number of highly criminal offenders is sometimes taken as prima facie evidence that there are characterological or other individual precursors of chronic offending. The logic is poor; equally plausible explanations can be offered on the basis of labeling theory that these chronic offenders are the societal residue of cumulative differential handling and stigmatization. Until such time as research procedures are developed to assess such competing theoretical alternatives *at the same time,* we would do well to build our research paradigms without the assumptions of the dominance of either biological or social determinants of chronicity. A reasoned interactional approach in the meantime would not seem out of order (see Shah & Roth, 1974).

Official versus respondent reported crime

There are various sources from which reports of crime are taken in order to measure crime as a dependent variable. Occasionally, laboratory studies employ observational data. In studies of children, researchers may use parental and school reports. Typically, however, the source of crime reports has until recently been limited to the data recorded in official files of the police, court, and correctional agencies. More recently, self-report measures have come into vogue, as, to a lesser extent, have victimization reports. We shall look briefly at two major alternative sources of data (and error): official records and self-report measures. Victimization surveys are seldom of use for individual or cohort research in which the offender is the focus. They do not deal with "victimless" crimes and certain classes of crime victims (the young, the infirm, and victims of white-collar crime) (see Empey, 1982, and chapters 5, 6, and 7 for a useful review and summary).

Official records

There is something strangely satisfying in using official records as the source of offense data; the data are selected by others and therefore presumably not subject to our own biases, and they have a public "seal of approval" that seems to provide legitimacy or formal sanction. Yet official data are replete with problems for measuring individual behaviors beyond those inherent in any public recording enterprise. We shall consider just a few.

Official records seriously underreport criminal behaviors. Police records may contain notice of as few as 1 in 10 or 1 in 20 criminal acts. Court records are even more selective. Sometimes referred to as the "dark figure" of crime, the unreported offenses are simply lost data for researchers, and what *is* reported may be so little that room for variation across research subjects is simply not sufficient.

Furthermore, police data illustrate a second problem of level of contact with suspects. In most U.S. police departments, one can distinguish among street contacts (sometimes recorded, often not), arrests (custody or temporary detention), and bookings (permanent records, often with fingerprinting and "mugging"). Most research reports merely refer to *arrests,* assuming that this is a generally discrete and uniform behavior. It is not (Klein, Rosensweig, & Bates, 1975). Choice of level of contact implies, for the researcher, different levels of comprehensiveness, discretion, and uniformity of recorded acts taken from any single police department or court.

Official records taken from several jurisdictions (e.g., different police departments or different courts) should not be assumed to be of equal value. Agencies differ, both by policy and by practice, in their definitions, reporting, and recording. The more professional police departments tend to report and record more offenses. Court records are affected not only by intake procedures and trial procedures, but also by caseloads, record system personnel, and data retrieval options. Each of these may vary from court to court, yielding different likelihoods of specific individual data being uniformly available for research purposes.

Similarly, each jurisdiction may respond to different legal statutes, case law, and administrative interpretations that affect what does and does not get recorded. From curfew violations to rape, offenses are recorded (or not) in relation to these differences. Research over time also must recognize *changes* in statute, case law, and administrative interpretation. Longitudinal researchers seldom consider this problem, thus exposing their dependent-variable measures to possible noise and bias.

Crimes vary considerably in their reportability. Homicide has high reportability; blackmail and prostitution have very low reportability. There are various reasons for their wide variation; criminal acts differ in their secrecy and detectability, in the willingness of victims to report them for personal (e.g., rape) and financial (e.g., insurance reports of thefts) reasons, and in official discretion in recording them. Research that relies on official records but assumes that reports of different offense categories are equally valid estimates of the incidence of the offense behaviors will be masking differences of considerable magnitude, perhaps enough to alter research conclusions.

Finally, arrest and court dispositions often constitute a problem. In many agency data filing systems, dispositions are not uniformly recorded. This is especially true at the police level.

Variations in release (outright, in the custody of another, with informal probation), in further justice processing (filing of complaints or petitions, detention vs. nondetention), and in referrals (to probation or parole, to welfare, to community agencies, to other agencies such as immigration) may be important data for research purposes, especially for research deterrence. Unfortunately, most official records are less than satisfactory sources of detailed disposition data. Even when they are, researchers seldom recognize the value of disposition data.

Self-report measures

These inadequacies in official records have led to the development of self-report instruments. Respondents are asked to admit to offenses committed, usually being presented with a specified list of offenses, a limited time period (e.g. "over the past year," "since we last interviewed you"), and a limited number of response categories. Early work on self-report measures led to a plethora of scales and procedures in the absence of much worthwhile methodological investigation. More recently, however, extremely careful work has led to excellent technologies (e.g., Elliott & Ageton, 1980) and studies revealing surprisingly satisfactory reliability and validity (Gold, 1970; Hindelang, Hirschi, & Weis, 1981; Hirschi, Hindelang, & Weis, 1980).

The advantages of self-report over official sources of data on individual offenses are several. Each individual provides far more items than does his or her official record (if, indeed, there is an official record at all); the reporting biases of the agencies are avoided; differences in reportability are minimized; jurisdictional differences are minimized; and the research comes closer to the behavioral level of the delinquent or criminal act.

It is not surprising, then, that there has been a rapid increase in the use of self-report measures. Already, we have learned much from them concerning the prevalence, incidence, and distribution over categories of persons of behaviors previously thought to be far less common than we now know them to be. These measures have sharpened our understanding of the drawbacks of arrest and conviction records.

Still, there are problems. Serious offenses are most likely to be underreported in self-report studies (Hindelang et al., 1981). Respondent bias is a problem, especially in repeated interviews in which respondents have been alerted to the researcher's interests and can anticipate the next interview. It is often difficult for respondents to provide uniformly valid responses about arrests and dispositions; for example, a street contact may mean arrest to one but not to another. Most important, very little work with self-report methods has been done with adult cohorts.

As might be concluded from the foregoing, self-report indices can fairly be judged superior to official records for much research in offending patterns, especially at the level of *individual* offenders. But the choice and therefore the implications for research conclusions can be determined by practical matters. Among these are access to official records, the expense of self-report measures, attrition related to respondent willingness to participate, and the costs of repeated measurements over time. When possible, the use of both sources can be most illuminating (see Lincoln et al., 1982, for a case in point).

Definitions and analogs

What we mean when we refer to delinquency and crime requires some attention. As Hirschi and Selvin (1967, p. 185) noted, "How one defines delinquency determines in large part how one will explain delinquency." Are acts criminal only if there are specific laws prohibiting them? Curfew laws in some jurisdictions make one's presence on the street after ten o'clock a delinquent offense. In others, such delinquency is not possible because there is no such law. Is an arrest without a conviction a proper measure of crime as a dependent variable? What of "undetected" crime? Many of us have committed acts punishable by law without being apprehended. Should a "theory" of *crime* attempt to incorporate these? Or should theory and our research expand to include all violations of "conduct norms" regardless of legal statutes? Will antiriot and antiterrorist legislation add crowd behaviors and political protest to our list of offenses in the dependent-variable measures? Will decriminalization of the use of certain drugs justify excluding these categories from our measures?

In addition, there is the question of the proper *unit* of analysis. Should we study the act, the actor, or the response? The actor is usually the focus of longitudinal studies; such studies seek changes in individual patterns of offensivity. Individual acts, in contrast, suggest a more interactive approach, more the realm of the social psychologist than of the psychologist. A focus on the response – the arrest, disposition, conviction – forces the study of organizational factors, in which the actor becomes mere fodder in the sociologist's feed bin.

Every research study using delinquency or crime as an outcome variable makes these choices, but usually implicitly without recognition of the implications or consequences for theory. Definition of crime as a specifiable list of acts, legal or not, is perhaps the most common. Yet seldom does this research consider the situational determinants of the act, or its complexity: A robbery or an assault or the act of running away from home is in fact a complex set of behaviors highly influenced in form by the setting. Merely to count such acts as offenses is to overlook much of their meaning as behaviors.[2]

Definition of the variable by the response, however, raises problems of the biases and discretion of the responder (i.e., the police officer or judge). For instance, relabeling an act as one offense rather than another is a common police charging practice, just as is the plea bargaining so common in American courts. The charges in the official records are the altered ones, not necessarily the charges best reflecting the behavior of the offender.

Defining crime in terms of legal requirements imposes a host of nonbehavioral considerations. It forces one *not* to measure unadjudicated acts. It forces one to distinguish among suspects, arrestees, and convicted offenders. In addition, it requires an understanding of both the legal and the *lawmaking* processes seldom to be found among researchers in criminology.

Finally, defining crime in terms of the actor brings into account a number of useful individual variables but usually leads to a "trait" approach that bears little resemblance to the realities of crime. That is, it suggests a phenomenon of "criminality" analogous to intelligence or sociability or impulsivity, an assumption that fully overlooks the complexities of crime in its behavioral, legal, and social reaction senses.

I shall make one other point here – an arguable point but one that must be made. Those researchers who come to criminology from other fields understandably bring with them some stylistic ways of thinking. The example of mental health researchers serves the purpose well. Criminal behavior does not correspond in form, source, or definition to such other undesired behaviors as schizophrenia or psychopathy. For one thing, crime is far more "normal" behavior. It is usually far more rational or, at least, instrumental. It carries a very different set of meanings for those who respond to it. The discrete acts that are summarized under the term "crime" are very different in form from those generally referred to by psychiatric diagnoses. Researchers who hope to transfer their styles of conceptualization, their notions of etiology, and their research technologies from mental illness to crime are doomed to years of frustration.

Selected empirical tests: distributional patterns

If one adequately appreciates the complexities of crime and delinquency as dependent variables, the opportunity for useful theoretical development is obviously enhanced. If useful criminological theory emerges, there are numerous "facts" of crime that can be used to test the adequacy of that theory. I regret to report that most popular theories of crime fail to pass most of these tests (Klein, 1967). Still, in listing some of these, perhaps we can provide some sense of the breadth of problems that any developing theory of crime might consider.

Ecological and demographic patterns

The incidence of crime and delinquency is not distributed evenly among categories of persons. There are substantial differences between men and women for which biological, social, and organizational explanations have been offered. Less satisfactorily explained are differences between ethnic groups, social classes, and age categories. Because these kinds of differences are the most universally reported, it behooves anyone developing an etiological theory to take them into account. Theories developed in relatively classless societies or in societies with little ethnic variation are likely to seem naïve and narrow in nations more varied in their social makeup.

Temporal patterns

In similar fashion but less commonly recognized, there are patterned differences in the commission of criminal acts according to time. Day and night differences are at once obvious and yet almost never accepted as worthy of theoretical concern. There are seasonal trends, trends related to war and postwar years, trends related to periods of economic depression. It is through these temporal doors that some economic theorists have entered the criminological arena. Have the biological, psychological, and even sociological theorists declared such patterns meaningless or beyond their ken, or have they merely not recognized them? One suspects the latter: Nonrecognition is commonly the fate of contextual variables.

Differential offense patterns

Other patterns have been observed that have the same capacity of the others to challenge developing theories. For instance, gang delinquency is different in kind and quality from nongang delinquency (Cohen, 1969; Tracy, 1981), and gangs show different emphases in their criminal patterns (Short & Strodtbeck, 1965). Drug usage varies across populations and time periods. Crimes vary widely in the contributions of victims and victim–assailant relationships. There are differences in companionship patterns between juvenile and adult crime (Empey, 1982) and differences in companionship patterns among categories of offense (Erickson & Jensen, 1977; Klein, 1971).

Other differential patterns were mentioned earlier in this chapter (e.g., reportability), and others might be listed, but the point seems clear; crime and delinquency are multifaceted dependent variables. The most careful research and the most comprehensive and useful theory will be that which attempts to come to grips with more than a few of these facets. Demographic, temporal, and offense pattern differentials are as much a part of the dependent variable as are seriousness, incidence, and recidivism. It is the researcher who concentrates on *individual*-level etiology who is most likely to overlook these patterns, and it is therefore that researcher who must be most alert to their implications.

Conclusion

Lest it be thought that the foregoing constitutes a compendium of dependent-variable problems in criminology, it should be noted that other matters of consequence have not been discussed. We have not covered the newest form of crime measurement: victim surveys. We have not discussed aggregate- versus individual-level measurement and have thereby skirted issues of general versus specific deterrence theory. Omitted have been coverage of offenses committed during incarceration and problems associated with probation and parole revocations as recidivism measures. The compounded errors of aggregated, multiagency statistics such as those available from centralized government agencies (the FBI, the Home Office) have not received attention.

Nonetheless, enough problems have been advanced to betray any hope that the dependent variable in our research can be given less attention than its independent, process, and contextual partners in crime. There is nothing new in this litany of problems; the criminological literature is replete with examples both good and bad. This chapter, in documenting the litany, merely attempts to redress the balance among friends. In stepping deftly along the pathway to effective theory, we must not be so intent on each earlier step that we miss the last big one and tumble into the conceptual abyss below.

Notes

1 It should be noted that this index should not be used in evaluating police effectiveness. The program *actor* must be independent of the outcome defined.
2 Thus, for instance, justice agents *and* researchers often record only the most serious charge associated with a criminal incident. Convenience is selected over meaning.

References

Blumstein, A. C. (1974). Seriousness weights in an index of crime. *American Sociological Review, 39*, 854–64.

Carter, R. H. (1968). *Middle-class delinquency: An experiment in community control.* Berkeley: University of California, School of Criminology.

Cohen, B. (1969). The delinquency of gangs and spontaneous groups. In T. Sellin & M. E. Wolfgang (Eds.), *Delinquency: selected studies* (pp. 61–111). New York: Wiley.

Elliott, D. S., & Ageton, S. S. (1980). Reconciling race and class differences in self-reported and official estimates of delinquency. *American Sociological Review, 45*, 45–110.

Empey, L. T. (1982). *American delinquency: Its meaning and construction* (2nd ed.). Homewood, IL: Dorsey.

Erickson, M. L., & Jensen, G. F. (1977). Delinquency is still group behavior: Toward revitalizing the group premise in the sociology of deviance. *Journal of Criminal Law and Criminology, 68*, 262–73.

Farrington, D. P. (1979). Longitudinal research on crime and delinquency. In N. Morris & M. Tonry (Eds.), *Crime and justice: An annual review of research I* (pp. 209–348). University of Chicago Press.

Gold, M. (1970). *Delinquent behavior in an American city.* Belmont, CA: Wadsworth.

Hamparian, D. M., Schuster, R., Dinitz, S., & Conrad, J. (1978). *The violent few: A study of dangerous juvenile offenders.* Lexington, MA: Heath.

Hindelang, M. J., Hirschi, T., & Weis, J. G. (1981). *Measuring delinquency.* Beverly Hills, CA: Sage.

Hirschi, T., Hidelang, M. J., & Weis, J. G. (1980). The status of self-report measures. In M. W. Klein & K. S. Teilmann (Eds.), *Handbook of criminal justice evaluation* (pp. 473–500). Beverly Hills, CA: Sage.

Hirschi, T., & Selvin, N. C. (1967). *Delinquency research.* New York: Free Press.

Klein, M. W. (1967). *Criminological theories as seen by criminologists: An evaluative review of approaches to the causation of crime and delinquency.* Albany, NY: Governor's Special Committee on the Criminal Offender.

Klein, M. W. (1969). On the group context of delinquency. *Sociology and Social Research, 54*, 63–71.

Klein, M. W. (1971). *Street gangs and street workers.* Englewood Cliffs, NJ: Prentice-Hall.

Klein, M. W. (1974). Labeling, deterrence, and recidivism: A study of police dispositions of juvenile offenders. *Social Problems, 22*, 292–303.

Klein, M. W. (1982). *Delinquency specialization and versatility: A review of the evidence.* Los Angeles: University of Southern California (mimeo).

Klein, M. W., & Mednick, S. A. (1982). *Conceptual scheme for specific deterrence theory: Testing sanction sensitivity to early sanctions in the juvenile justice system.* Los Angeles: University of Southern California (mimeo).

Klein, M. W., Rosensweig, S. L., & Bates, R. (1975). The ambiguous juvenile arrest. *Criminology, 13*, 78–89.

Lincoln, S. B., Klein, M. W., Van Dusen, K. T., & Labin, S. (1982). *Control organizations and labeling theory: Official versus self-reported delinquency.* Bloomington: Indiana University (mimeo).

McEachern, A. W., & Bauzer, R. (1967). Factors related to disposition in juvenile police contacts. In M. W. Klein (Ed.), *Juvenile gangs in context: Theory, research, and action* (pp. 146–60). Englewood Cliffs, NJ: Prentice-Hall.

Petersilia, J., Greenwood, P. W., & Lavin, M. (1977). *Criminal careers of habitual felons.* Santa Monica, CA: Rand.

Rossi, P. H., Waite, E., Bose, C. E., & Berk, R. A. (1974). The seriousness of crime:

Normative structure and individual differences. *American Sociological Review, 39,* 224–37.

Sellin, T., & Wolfgang, M. E. (1964). *The measurement of delinquency.* New York: Wiley.

Shah, S. A., & Roth, L. H. (1974). Biological and psychophysiological factors in criminality. In D. Glaser (Ed.), *Handbook of criminology* (pp. 101–74). Chicago: Rand McNally.

Short, J. F., Jr., & Strodtbeck, F. L. (1965). *Group process and gang delinquency.* University of Chicago Press.

Tracy, P. E. (1981). *Subcultural delinquency: A comparison of the incidence and seriousness of gang and nongang member offensivity.* Philadelphia: University of Pennsylvania (mimeo).

Wolfgang, M. E., Figlio, R. M., & Sellin, T. (1972). *Delinquency in a birth cohort.* University of Chicago Press.

3   Implications of biological findings for criminological research

David P. Farrington

This chapter is not intended to be a detailed review of biological findings that have relevance to criminological research. Specific findings are reviewed in detail in this volume and elsewhere (e.g., Mednick & Volavka, 1980; Shah & Roth, 1974). This chapter was written at a more general level and argues that criminologists should not ignore biological variables. Instead, they should attempt to measure such variables in research projects and to investigate where they might fit into criminological theories. This chapter reviews some advantages and problems of including biological variables in criminology and considers why criminologists are often hostile to the idea of their inclusion.

The chapter is specifically concerned with the implications of biological findings for criminological *research* and so does not discuss their practical implications for the prevention of crime or the treatment of criminals. If some of the claims made by biological researchers are correct, there might be important implications for prevention and treatment. For example, Hippchen (1978) argued that biochemical findings could be combined with knowledge about sociopsychological factors to develop a more complete theory of criminal behavior, thus improving both prediction and treatment. He further argued that recidivism rates among prison populations could be reduced by between 25% and 50% by means of orthomolecular (biochemical) treatment. As someone impressed by the scholarly review of Sechrest, White, and Brown (1979), which concluded that "we do not now know of any program or method of rehabilitation that could be guaranteed to reduce the criminal activity of released offenders" (p. 3), I find this claim amazing. However, I am willing to be convinced by randomized experiments on biological prevention or treatment (see Farrington, 1982a).

Another topic this chapter does not review in detail is the problem of defining and measuring crime and delinquency, which arises in biological and nonbiological criminological research. This topic is reviewed in chapter 2. There are many obvious definitional difficulties. For example, crime and delinquency are heterogeneous concepts, covering behaviors as apparently diverse as theft, vandalism, violence against the person, drug use, and various kinds of heterosexual and homosexual indecency. Because the criminal law varies over time and place, the definition of an act as a crime also varies over time and place. Legal categories are usually so wide that they include acts that are behaviorally quite different. Legal definitions usually rely on the concept of intent, which can be established by legal procedures but which creates difficulties for social scientists (e.g., because of discrepancies between what people say and what they do).

The best solution to these problems, in my view, is to use behavioral rather than legal definitions of criminal and delinquent acts. For example, it should be possible to define shoplifting in behavioral terms even if a court would be needed to establish whether an act constituted shoplifting in legal terms. Similarly, the best solution to the problem of measuring crime and delinquency is to use systematic, direct observation wherever possible. For example, Buckle and Farrington (1982) observed and recorded shoplifting as it happened. Both official records and self-reports are biased measures of crime and delinquency, and other methods of measurement (e.g., the use of prisoners or institutionalized delinquents) raise even more problems. Biological and nonbiological criminologists have to grapple with the problem of definition and measurement of crime and delinquency more effectively than they have in the past.

Biological measurement in criminology

Biological findings are sufficiently promising to justify criminologists' attempts to measure biological variables in their research projects. Biological variables have several advantages over the social and psychological variables usually measured in criminological research. In particular, biological variables are usually measured on interval or ratio scales and are usually normally distributed. This means that parametric techniques such as multiple linear regression and path analysis can be used. In contrast, social and psychological variables are often measured on nominal or ordinal scales and, even when they are measured on an interval scale, often do not resemble a normal distribution. For example, in studying the relation between parental discipline and delinquency, parental discipline can be measured on a nominal scale (e.g., normal, lax, strict, or erratic; see McCord, McCord, & Zola, 1959). Delinquency can be measured as a dichotomy (delinquent–nondelinquent) or according to number of arrests, which will almost certainly have a J-shaped distribution.

Most criminological variables are essentially categorical and clearly violate the underlying assumptions (typically, normal distributions and interval scales) of the most popular statistical techniques. There are three ways of coping with this problem. One is essentially to deny that it exists, by claiming that such techniques as the product–moment correlation and the student's t test are so robust that they can be used with ordinal scales that are not normally distributed (see, e.g., Johnson, 1979, p. 98). It is true that some statistical tests give reliable results (e.g., reasonably accurate p values) with some violations, but in general researchers cannot be sure that their data, with their particular violations, will not yield misleading results.

The second is to try to avoid the problem by converting data to a form that resembles normally distributed interval scales, by combining a number of variables, and by using appropriate statistical transformations. One difficulty is that scores on the resulting variables may be difficult to interpret. Another problem is that, if the constituent variables are measured roughly, the conversion process may produce scales with a spurious impression of exactness and sensitivity. A better technique is to devise a measure and deliberately adjust its constituent items and scoring technique to produce something that looks like a normally distributed interval scale. This is, of course, the usual procedure in devising IQ tests. The normal distribution of IQs is an act of faith rather than an empirical result.

The third solution, which I have adopted myself, is to use statistical methods that are appropriate to the kinds of rough categorical data typically collected in criminological research. These methods, based on contingency tables, have many drawbacks. In particular, in the case of samples of the sizes I have been dealing with (400), the major multivariate technique of log-linear analysis can cope with only about six dichotomous variables at a time and correspondingly fewer variables with three or more categories. The use of this technique forces the researcher (a) to reduce the number of categories of each variable to a minimum, thereby losing information, and (b) to use some other method of reducing the large number of variables measured to the small number that can be dealt with by this technique.

The point is that, with the kinds of categorical data commonly collected in criminology, there is no ideal way of carrying out a large multivariate analysis. With biological variables that are measured on interval scales and are normally distributed, there are adequate techniques.

Another advantage of using biological variables is that it should be possible to measure them with less error than social and psychological variables. Furthermore, the reliability of measurement can be established more accurately, and indeed the concepts of reliability and validity can be used more effectively. The problem with a variable like parental discipline is that there is no yardstick by which it can be measured and no generally accepted units of measurement. There are yardsticks and measurement methods for biological variables such as heart rate and testosterone level.

Unfortunately, the sensitivity of measurement of biological variables can create difficulties in comparing these variables with social and psychological ones. A variable that is measured more accurately may have a stronger measured relation to an index of crime or delinquency than one measured less accurately, even when the underlying theoretical constructs are equally closely related to the construct of criminal or delinquent behavior. Strangely enough, the reverse may also occur, in which a more sensitively measured variable appears (to persons lacking statistical sophistication) to be less closely related to a dependent variable. For example, a difference in IQ between convicted and unconvicted youths of eight points has sometimes been dismissed as negligible or unimportant. West and Farrington (1973) reported an IQ difference of only six points between their convicted and unconvicted youths. However, they also showed that, when comparable categorical scoring methods were used, IQ was about as closely related to delinquency as was low family income and large family size. The point is that convicted and unconvicted youths differ significantly on many variables, but on a normally distributed interval scale, this difference often amounts to no more than half a standard deviation.

One reason for measuring biological variables in addition to social and psychological ones is that there are advantages in using multiple methods of measurement. In particular, it is then possible to argue that relations between empirical variables reflect underlying relations between theoretical constructs rather than common measurement biases. For example, if erratic parental discipline as reported by youths is significantly related to self-reported delinquency, this could mean either that discipline and delinquency are related or that youths who are willing to admit delinquent acts are also willing to admit other socially disapproved aspects of their lives. There would be less ambiguity if self-reported delinquency were related to parental reports of discipline. Multiple methods of measurement are also useful in establishing reliability and validity.

The major difficulties arising from the measurement of biological variables center on the disapproval of other criminologists (which will be discussed later) and the practical problems of biological measurement outside the laboratory. In order to carry out important research on biology and crime, it will be necessary to measure biological variables outside the laboratory and outside institutions, in conditions that are not optimal for this kind of research.

There are a number of reasons for this. As indicated earlier, I will not discuss in detail the undesirability of studying institutionalized samples. Briefly, however, institutionalized offenders are extreme groups, so comparisons between them and noninstitutionalized nonoffenders are likely to be misleading. Also, it is difficult to disentangle factors related to offending from factors related to the probability of offending leading to institutionalization and factors that are consequences of institutionalization. A major problem with laboratory research is that the people who are of most interest to criminologists – those who commit the most criminal acts – are also the most elusive and uncooperative to researchers (see, e.g., West & Farrington, 1977, p. 165) and hence the least likely to come to laboratories. Therefore, laboratory samples are likely to be deficient in the most frequent and serious offenders, unless special efforts are made to recruit these people.

The legal and ethical problems arising in biological research are likely to be greater than those arising in social–psychological research, especially if biological measurement involves physical interference or pain. In order to obtain legally effective informed consent, it may be necessary to explain in great detail all possible risks (however improbable) that are attendant on a procedure. This may lead to a low rate of participation in the research. Unless investigators are confident that social benefits will result from a project, it may be difficult to justify ethically the infliction of physical pain.

It is clearly more practicable to carry out biological research in the field, which involves little or no physical interference with people. It is difficult to imagine a field project involving the implantation of electrodes in the brain, for example. One of the most interesting projects was carried out by Witkin et al. (1976) in Denmark. Out of a target sample of 4,558 men greater than 6 feet tall, blood samples and buccal smears (to determine chromosomal constitution) were obtained for 4,139 (nearly 91%). Of the remainder, only 174 refused, and the rest were not contacted, in some cases because they had left the area. This shows what is possible in the way of biological research.

Biological research may prove to be more expensive than more common kinds of social research, because of the equipment, recording hardware, and biologically trained technicians that may be needed. Biological research in criminology may involve cooperation among researchers from different disciplines, as Shah and Roth (1974) advocated. This may well be a desirable development.

As with nonbiological research, the most adequate designs involve longitudinal studies and randomized experiments, in that order. Longitudinal studies are needed to establish basic relations between variables and to generate hypotheses concerning which biological factors lead to which social factors and vice versa. Randomized experiments are then needed to test these hypotheses, when this is practicable. There have already been some interesting longitudinal studies including biological variables (e.g., Magnusson, Duner, & Zetterblom, 1975; Mednick, Volavka, Gabrielli, & Itil, 1981; Wadsworth, 1979), and I shall discuss results obtained in another such project later. Future longitudinal studies must have more frequent measurement of a larger number of biological and nonbiological variables. Randomized experiments in criminology involving biological variables are not likely to be undertaken in the near future.

Biology and criminological theories

Biological variables are rarely included in criminological theories. It could be argued that the adequacy of criminological theories in predicting or understanding either the development of criminal tendencies or the occurrence of criminal acts would be improved by including biological variables. Whether this is true is not yet known, but it could at least be investigated. It would be desirable to develop and test theoretical models including biological and nonbiological variables. There could be an interaction between theory and empirical research in the kind of longitudinal survey discussed above, with the theory guiding the research and the results of the research leading to modifications in the theory.

A useful blueprint for a theory is that proposed by Clarke (1977). He stated explicitly that his model was designed to explain the occurrence of criminal events rather than the development of persistent offending, but I think that the model could be adapted to serve both purposes. Clarke proposed that the occurrence of a criminal event depends on (a) heredity (e.g., poor conditionability), (b) early environment and upbringing (e.g., inconsistent discipline), (c) criminal personality (e.g., impulsive), (d) socioeconomic and demographic status (e.g., young, male, unskilled), (e) current living circumstances (e.g., inner-city residence), (f) crises and events (e.g., loss of job), (g) the situation (e.g., a poorly lit street), and (h) cognitive and perceptual processes and motivational states (e.g., boredom). Clarke himself was rather doubtful about heredity and criminal personality, but it would be interesting to begin with this kind of blueprint and try to establish where biological factors should be included and how they are related to other factors.

An alternative approach would be to take a more specific theory, such as that proposed by Trasler (1962, 1978), linking criminal acts to autonomic underreactivity and child-rearing methods used by parents in different social classes and expand it. It seems likely that any theory of criminal persons or criminal events will have to include intrapersonal factors (e.g., biological ones), interpersonal factors (e.g., peer-group or family interaction), and larger social structural factors (e.g., poverty and unemployment). Apart from the fact that Trasler included biological variables, his theory has much in common with Hirschi's (1969) control theory, which (it will be argued later) has been one of the two dominant American theories of delinquency since the early 1970s. Both the Trasler and Hirschi theories are based on the premise that children have to learn socially conforming behavior. It would not be difficult to expand the Hirschi theory to include biological variables.

The other major American theory of delinquency has been the labeling theory popularized by Lemert (1972) and Becker (1963). Unfortunately, the antiscientific proponents of this theory have resisted attempts to test it, as Hirschi (1980) pointed out. Nevertheless, attempts have been made to test it empirically (e.g., Farrington, 1977). Labeling theory includes intrapersonal, interpersonal, and social structural factors, in arguing that changes in self-concept occur as a result of interaction with agents of social control and labeling by society. It would not be difficult to expand this theory to include biological variables.

In any theory, the problem is to specify linkages between theoretical constructs and to specify operational definitions of theoretical constructs. It seems likely that direct causal relations between biological factors and criminal behavior are comparatively rare. Occasional cases are quoted. For example, Moyer (1979) reported the case of a woman patient whose anger and aggressive tendencies could be turned on and off by the flick of a switch, because she had an electrode located in a neural system controlling aggression. However, in a general theory of criminal tendencies or criminal events, linkages are likely to be more indirect than this.

Theoretical linkages can be discovered and verified only by empirical research. There has been no shortage of attempts by sociologists to explain relations between biology and crime by reference to nonbiological variables. For example, Taylor, Walton, and Young (1973, p. 46) argued that XYY males tended to be convicted not because they committed a large number of offenses but because their excessive height, unusual appearance, and mental deficiency made them more likely than other lawbreakers to be arrested. It is also possible to explain relations between social variables and crime by reference to biological factors. For example, Kelly (1979) argued that biochemical factors might cause criminal behavior and then pointed out that biochemical factors were often caused by social factors such as cultural patterns of nutrition or prevailing distributions of power or social structure (connected, e.g., with lead pollution levels in cities). Therefore, relations between social structure and crime might be explained by reference to biological variables.

What is needed, as already indicated, is a theoretical model including all variables. It would then be possible to establish whether biological variables add to nonbiological ones in predicting criminal events or tendencies. This depends on whether the biological variables are measuring the same or different theoretical constructs (or are part of the same chain of theoretical constructs) as the nonbiological variables. For example, if low income produces poor nutrition, which produces some biological abnormality, which produces criminal tendencies, then measuring the biological variable might add little to the predictability of criminal behavior by low income alone.

Broadly speaking, a theoretical model could attempt to explain how different factors add to produce criminal acts or tendencies, as in a multiple regression equation, or to explain how different factors interact to produce criminal acts or tendencies, as in a hierarchical clustering technique such as predictive attribute analysis. Those who have advocated theoretical models including biological and nonbiological variables have usually given interactive rather than additive examples, as in the following statement by Shah and Roth (1974, p. 139):

Greater height and size, hyperactivity, and aggressiveness could, in interactions with particular environmental influences, facilitate patterns of behavior socialized into athletics, sports, aggressive business, or other careers; such characteristics could also become channelled into patterns of behavior that may have a high probability of being socially defined as criminal.

Mednick (1977b) also proposed an essentially interactive theory, in arguing that genetic and physiological factors were more important in explaining crimes by middle-class people, whereas economic and social deprivation were more important in lower-class crime.

Another issue is whether a theory should be designed to explain the majority of criminal persons or acts or only freak persons or acts. The XYY chromosome abnormality, for example, if it has any relevance to crime, can explain only a tiny proportion of persons or acts (Witkin et al., 1976). It may be possible, however, to propose a theory that explains a small proportion of persons who commit a large proportion of acts.

Wolfgang, Figlio, and Sellin (1972) reported that 6% of their youths accounted for 52% of all arrests, and Mednick (1977a) argued that it might be this small proportion of people who were especially deviant biologically.

Many urgent tasks face criminological theorists who are interested in developing models including biological and nonbiological variables. The first priority, in my view, is to explain obvious relations between crime and age, sex, and race. Less obvious and central variables can then be studied. Another priority, which is much more difficult because of its retrospective nature, is to explain why recorded crime has increased enormously in Great Britain and North America since World War II. This increase is often quoted as evidence against the use of biological variables, because it is often (implicitly or explicitly) assumed that biological variables are less easy to change than social ones. As already indicated, my first priority in terms of research method would be a longitudinal survey, and I shall now discuss some results from such a survey undertaken by Donald West and myself.

The Cambridge Study in Delinquent Development

The Cambridge Study in Delinquent Development is a prospective longitudinal survey of 411 males. Data collection began in 1961–2, when most of the boys were aged 8, and ended in 1980, when the youngest person was aged 25 years and 6 months. The major results of the survey can be found in four books (West, 1969, 1982; West & Farrington, 1973, 1977), and a concise summary is also available (Farrington & West, 1981).

At the time they were first contacted, all the boys were living in a working-class area of London. The majority of the sample was chosen by taking *all* the boys aged 8–9 who were on the registers of six state primary schools within a 1-mile radius of a research office that had been established. In addition to 399 boys from these six schools, 12 boys from a local school for the educationally subnormal were included in the sample in an attempt to make it more representative of the population of boys living in the area.

Almost all the boys were white Caucasian in appearance. Only 12, most of whom had at least one parent of West Indian origin, were black. The majority (371) were being brought up by parents who had themselves been reared in the United Kindgom or Eire. On the basis of their fathers' occupations, 93.7% could be described as working class (categories III, IV, or V on the Registrar General's scale), in comparison with the national figure of 78.3% at that time. This was, therefore, overwhelmingly a white, urban, working-class sample of British origin.

The boys were interviewed and tested in their schools when they were aged about 8, 10, and 14 by male or female psychologists. They were interviewed in the research office at about 16, 18, 21, and 24 by young male social science graduates. Up to and including age 18, the aim was to interview the whole sample on each occasion, and it was always possible to trace and interview a high proportion. For example, at age 18, it was possible to interview 389 of the original 411 (94.6%). At ages 21 and 24, the aim was to interview subgroups rather than the whole sample. The interviews with the youths at age 18 and later were fully tape-recorded and transcribed, making verbatim quotations possible.

In addition to tests and interviews with the youths, interviews with their parents were carried out by female social workers who visited their homes. These took place about once per year from when the boy was about 8 until he was 14 or 15 and in his last year of compulsory schooling. The primary informant was the mother, although the father was also seen in the majority of cases. The boys' teachers also filled in questionnaires about their behavior in school, when the boys were about 8, 10, 12, and 14. The vast majority of parents and teachers were cooperative. For example, at least 94% of teachers' questionnaires were completed at each age.

It was also possible to make repeated searches in the central Criminal Record Office in London for findings of guilt sustained by the boys, their parents, their brothers and sisters, and (in recent years) their wives. These searches continued until March 1980, when the youngest sample member was aged 25 years and 6 months. The criminal records of the youths who have not died or emigrated are believed to be complete from the 10th birthday (the minimum age of criminal responsibility in England and Wales) to the 25th birthday.

The major aim of this study was to investigate the development of crime and delinquency in English males, as well as its precursors and concomitants. The research was theoretically guided, but not by only one theory. The intention was to measure as many as possible of the variables that were alleged by existing criminological theories to be important in producing delinquent and criminal behavior. By measuring many variables from different sources, it was feasible to investigate the relative importance of variables and to study the importance of some after controlling for others. In nonexperimental research, it is desirable to measure as many variables as possible in order to avoid the argument that observed relations would not have held after controlling for certain unmeasured variables.

This research has often been criticized by British sociologists. Cohen (1974, p. 19) stated that "in methodology and conception this research goes no further than the extraordinary jumble of eclectic positivism that rendered the work of the Gluecks such an anachronism." Parker and Giller (1981, p. 236) dismissed it as a "metaphorical backwater," noting that the researchers "meticulously count, correlate and crosstabulate those very variables which the sociologists of deviance spent the greater part of their time disparaging." Such sociologists are openly hostile to systematic empirical research, preferring unsystematic participant observation with tiny samples. Their reports tend to be journalistic in style, and the major evidence for their conclusions consists of selected statements (not necessarily recorded verbatim) by juveniles. Such statements can be illuminating, but they must be coupled with quantitative information so that the reader can assess how typical they are.

Most information in our research was derived from interviews. The boys' parents provided details about such topics as family income, family size (also checked against school records), the social class of the family breadwinner, the parents' degree of supervision of the boy, and their child-rearing behavior (which was a composite variable reflecting attitude, discipline, and parental agreement). The boys provided details about their job histories and leisure habits, such as hanging about, drinking, and sexual activity. The boys also completed a large number of psychological tests and self-report questionnaires at different ages. As examples, nonverbal IQ was measured by the progressive matrices test, vocabulary by means of Mill Hill synonyms, and personality by the New Junior Maudsley Inventory (at 10 and 14) and the Eysenck Personality Inventory (at 16). The self-report questionnaires measured the commission of delinquent and violent acts, attitudes (e.g., to the police), and reported delinquent behavior of a boy's friends.

Ratings of the boys' troublesome and aggressive behavior in school, their truancy, and their school attainments were obtained from their teachers. Ratings of such things as troublesomeness, daring, dishonesty, and popularity were also obtained from the boys' peers when they were in primary school. The interviewers rated the physical appearance of the youths, including racial characteristics, wearing of glasses, nail biting, and hair length. Also, a small number of behavioral measures were taken by systematically giving the youths opportunities to smoke and to gamble part of their interview fee.

In addition to all these measures, some physical and biological variables were studied. The heights and weights of the boys without jackets and shoes were measured at ages 8, 10, and 14 by the psychologists working in the medical room of each school. They were scored according to the boys' percentile rankings in relation to frequency distributions obtained from normal samples, correcting for the exact age of the boy at the time of measurement. Grip strength was measured at age 10 using a dynamometer. It was used to identify probable mesomorphs among the boys whose weights were relatively greater than their heights.

This chapter concentrates on results obtained with a fourth variable, pulse rate, which was measured at age 18. Previous work (Davies & Maliphant, 1971) linked low pulse rates to low autonomic reactivity and suggested that there was an association between low pulse rates and bad behavior in school. In addition, parallel research by Wadsworth (1976) reported that violent and sexual offenders had low pulse rates. Pulse rate was measured in the present research with a pulsimeter, which included a pressure cup fitted over the right middle finger. The pulse was made visible by a needle movement across a dial, and this was counted using a stopwatch. The readings were taken toward the end of the interview (which lasted 2 hours on average) with the youth sitting quietly, resting his arm on a desk. The cumulative number of beats was recorded after 30 and 60 sec. If a youth moved, the procedure was recommenced. All youths except two (387 of 389 interviewed) had pulse rates measured, although in 23 cases the figure was based on the 30-sec reading.

Results

It had been expected that the frequency distribution of pulse rates would be approximately normal. Table 3.1 shows the actual distribution in comparison with a normal distribution (rounded to whole numbers) with the same mean (70.8) and standard deviation (10.0). The two distributions were not significantly different on a Kolmogorov–Smirnov test (maximum difference .0598 at the 69–70 level; .0691 would be significant at $p = .05$). However, they were significantly different on a ψ^2 goodness of fit test. Because of small expected values at the extremes, this was based on 20 categories, collapsing 50 or less, 51–54, 87–90, and 91 or more. The ψ^2 value came to 32.0 with 17 degrees of freedom (d.f.; in view of two estimated parameters), and it was significant at $p = .025$.

It can be concluded that the use of biological variables does not necessarily guarantee normal distributions, although the distribution of pulse rates is sufficiently near the normal one for parametric methods to be appropriate. The major deviations from the normal distribution come in

Table 3.1. *Frequency distribution of pulse rates*

Pulse rate	Frequency	Expected frequency (normal distribution)
48 or less	5	5
49–50	1	3
51–52	3	5
53–54	4	7
55–56	8	10
57–58	12	12
59–60	20	17
61–62	21	20
63–64	26	23
65–66	34	27
67–68	30	29
69–70	48	31
71–72	28	31
73–74	27	29
75–76	19	28
77–78	20	25
79–80	24	21
81–82	18	17
83–84	7	14
85–86	5	10
87–88	5	8
89–90	6	6
91–92	4	3
93–94	1	3
95–96	1	1
97–98	6	1
99 or more	4	1
Total	387	387

the categories 69–70 (expected 31, actual 48) and 91 or more (expected 9, actual 16). The former case may represent interviewer error. Given that the most common pulse rates were 70 and 71, it could be that the interviewers preferred to record 70 rather than 71 in doubtful cases.

Of the 387 youths who had their pulse rates measured, 5 were not at risk of being convicted up to their 25th birthdays, because they died or emigrated. Of the remaining 382 youths, 34 were first convicted between ages 10 and 13 inclusive, 35 at 14 or 15, 30 at 16 or 17, and 31 between ages 18 and 24 inclusive. Convictions were counted only if they were for offenses normally recorded in the Criminal Record Office, which are generally synonymous with "serious" or "criminal" offenses. For example, motoring convictions and public drunkenness were excluded, and the majority

Table 3.2. *Mean pulse rates*

Definition of group	N	Pulse rate Mean	S.D.
Unconvicted youths	252	71.4	9.6
First convicted at 10 to 13	34	69.5	8.1
First convicted at 14 to 15	35	68.2	9.2
First convicted at 16 to 17	30	68.7	11.5
First convicted at 18 to 24	31	72.5	12.8
Convicted of violence	32	67.7	9.1
Convicted six or more times	22	67.7	5.4

of convictions included were for thefts, burglaries, or taking motor vehicles. The mean pulse rates of youths first convicted at 10–13, 14–15, and 16–17 were slightly, but not significantly lower than the mean of the 252 unconvicted youths (see Table 3.2).

About a quarter of the convicted youths (32 of 130) had at least one conviction for violence. A youth was included in the violent group only if he had been convicted of an offense that must have involved violence against another person (such as causing grievous bodily harm) or if a police report said that he had used, or had threatened to use, physical violence against another person during the commission of an offense. The criteria for inclusion in this officially violent group were strict. Robberies that involved mere jostling or snatching were not counted, nor was carrying an offensive weapon without actually using it or threatening to do so. The 32 convicted violent youths had significantly lower pulse rates than the 252 unconvicted youths (mean 67.7 as opposed to 71.4; $t = 2.06$, $p < .05$). This essentially replicates Wadsworth's (1976) finding.

As in the longitudinal survey of Wolfgang et al. (1972), a small proportion of this sample accounted for about half of all the convictions. The 23 youths each with 6 or more convictions accounted for 230 of the total number of 468 convictions (see Farrington, 1981). All except one had pulse rates measured. Table 3.2 shows that their mean pulse rate (67.7) was the same as that of the violent youths, although it was not significantly different from the mean pulse rate of the unconvicted youths. (Twelve youths were in both the violent and "chronic" groups, and their mean pulse rate was 67.2.)

Table 3.3 shows the cumulative percentages of youths convicted at different pulse rates. It can be seen that those with a below-average pulse rate (70 or less) tended to have above-average conviction rates. If the sample is dichotomized into those with pulse rates of 70 or less and those

Table 3.3. *Percentage of youths convicted at different pulse rates*

| | | Percent convicted up to age: | | | |
Pulse rate	N	13	15	17	24
60 or less	52	7.7	17.3	32.7	40.4
61–64	45	6.7	20.0	26.7	37.8
65–68	64	12.5	31.3	39.1	45.3
69–70	47	17.0	23.4	29.8	38.3
71–74	55	10.9	18.2	23.6	27.3
75–80	62	0.0	4.8	11.3	21.0
81 or more	57	8.8	12.3	19.3	29.8
Total		34	69	99	130
Convicted					

with pulse rates of 71 or more, a significant difference is obtained (40.9% of 208 with below-average pulse rates were convicted, in comparison with 25.9% of 174 with above-average rates; corrected $\psi^2 = 8.84$, 1 d.f., $p < .005$). However, it is statistically invalid to choose a cutoff point to maximize a difference.

These results are reasonably satisfactory, but problems emerge when pulse rate is included in an analysis with all other variables. The majority of measured variables significantly differentiated between convicted and unconvicted youths. Furthermore, for the purposes of the main analysis, each variable was dichotomized into the "worst" quarter and the remaining three-quarters, wherever possible. There were various reasons for this. First, in order to compare variables, it was desirable that each should be measured equally sensitively (or insensitively). Second, in order to carry out log-linear analyses, it was desirable to have as few categories as possible for each variable. Third, the one-quarter/three-quarters split had been used from the beginning of this study because of the prior expectation that about one-quarter of the sample would be convicted and the desirability of equating the proportion of those predicted who were convicted and the proportion of those convicted who were predicted.

When pulse rate was dichotomized into the lowest quarter (64 or less) versus the remainder, it was not significantly related to any of the conviction measures. The analysis (described in Farrington, 1982b) focused on the prediction of convictions between the ages of 10 and 13, 14 and 16, 17 and 20, and 21 and 24. The four major independent predictors were economic deprivation (e.g., low family income), family criminality (e.g., convicted parents), parental mishandling (e.g., poor supervision), and school failure (e.g., low vocabulary). Low pulse rate was nearly significantly related to having convicted parents ($p = .053$) and poor parental supervision ($p = .053$).

The only variable (out of nearly 80 in the analysis) to which low pulse rate was significantly related was self-reported violence at ages 14 and 16 combined. This was based on the admission of seven violent acts (mostly describing street fighting; see Farrington, 1973). Unfortunately, the relation was in the opposite direction of that expected. Only 11 of the 100 with pulse rates of 64 or lower were among the 77 who admitted four or more violent acts, in comparison with 23.0% of those with higher pulse rates (corrected $\psi^2 = 5.96$, 1 d.f., $p < .025$). Therefore, pulse rates seemed to be negatively related to self-reported violence and positively related to convictions for violence. In view of the close relation between self-reported and official violence (see, e.g., Farrington, 1978), these results are surprising.

For completeness, the results for height, weight, and grip strength will be mentioned. Weight was not significantly related to convictions, and the youths identified as probable mesomorphs on the basis of grip strength were, if anything, less likely to be convicted than the remainder. However, low height at 8 to 10 and 14 was significantly related to juvenile convictions, especially those occurring at the earliest ages (10–13). Low height at 8 to 10 was also related to many other variables, notably low family income at 8, large family size at 10, poor housing at 8 to 10, low vocabulary at 10, poor parental supervision at 8, convicted parents at 10, and separations from parents up to 10. Low height at 8 to 10 did not predict convictions at 10 to 13 independently of troublesomeness at 8, poor housing at 8 to 10, Roman Catholic family at 8, and low IQ at 8 to 10 and hence was dropped from the analysis.

The problem in summarizing these results is that the findings depend on the analytic methods used. The rough tabular methods and the dichotomizing were dictated by the rough nature of many of the variables. If all variables had comprised normally distributed interval scales, more sensitive parametric techniques could have been used, and pulse rate, for example, might have proved to be more important. The key question is whether pulse rate, or any biological variable, is related to delinquency independently of nonbiological variables. The analyses carried out so far indicate that observed relations between pulse rate, height, and convictions may not hold independently of the more important variables of economic deprivation, family criminality, parental mishandling, and school failure. However, more research is needed to establish the precise linkages between biological and nonbiological variables.

Biology and criminologists

It is all very well to recommend that criminologists include biological variables in their research and theories, but this is unlikely to happen in practice. Both in Great Britain and in North America, criminology has been dominated by sociologists since World War II, and most of these sociologists have been hostile to research on biology and crime. In his edited collection *Taboos in Criminology,* Sagarin (1980) has summarized the present state of affairs:

In criminology, it appears that a number of views . . . have become increasingly delicate and sensitive, as if all those who espouse them were inherently evil, or at least stupidly insensitive to the consequences of their research. . . . Unpopular beliefs arouse people's ire, which they manifest in a variety of ways. . . . To question [accepted beliefs] is to risk jeers and hissing when the issues are discussed in public and a torrent of abusive letters when they are debated in print. . . . In the study of crime, the examples of unpopular orientations are many. Foremost is the link of crime to the factors of genes, biology, race, ethnicity, and religion. (Pp. 8–9)

In the same book, Gordon (1980) outlines some of the consequences of carrying out research on taboo topics (in his case, the relation between IQ, race, and delinquency). His work was rejected by the major American sociological and criminological journals and was eventually published in nonrefereed book collections and in journals outside the main arena (*Journal of the American Statistical Association* and *Journal of Mathematical Sociology*). With these journals, "it felt as though I were at last dealing with real scientists, persons who would allow some disturbing data a little breathing space instead of stifling them before they could receive exposure to other members of the discipline" (Gordon, 1980, p. 42). Gordon also reports the loss of an attractive job opportunity and that

I and others have also noted younger colleagues skirting controversial issues for fear of not receiving research funds or of otherwise damaging their careers. Senior colleagues often express what appears to be sincere agreement on many of these issues in private, but point out that it is foolhardy to take a position publicly. (P. 47)

The most influential theories of delinquency since the late 1960s have been the control theory of Hirschi (1969) and the labeling theory of Lemert (1972). Neither includes biological variables. Nor do more recent extensions of these theories (e.g., Elliott, Ageton, & Canter, 1979; Johnson, 1979). Johnson's statement is quite typical:

At the outset, the discussion is limited to theoretical propositions that are sociological or social psychological in nature. Certain biological or psychological factors undoubtedly play a role in generating delinquent conduct by some adolescents at some times. However, as general explanations they seem to lack empirical support. (P. 10)

Recent researchers on female delinquency have been at least as negative about biological theories. Campbell (1981) noted that "biological variables have been particularly popular in explanations of female delinquency" (p. 48) but stated that "explanations of human behavior in terms of genetics or biology are always dubious" (p. 47).

Why is biology and crime a taboo topic for sociological criminologists? Part of the reason lies in the association between biology and Lombroso, who is ritually beaten and made fun of in the major textbooks. As Mednick (1977b, p. ix) pointed out, "any theory with biological implications was rapidly associated with the almost poetically evil name of Lombroso and regarded with suspicion." This is despite the fact that "none of the biology of today was available to Lombroso. . . . Lombroso discussed phenotypic traits such as skull size and shape and length of arms, none of which are directly linked to behavior by our current knowledge of the brain" (Jeffery, 1979, p. 9).

Another possible reason has been put forward by Jeffery (1980):

Criminology came to be dominated by Sutherland as a result of this textbook and his other contributions. . . . The text, which is still in existence (Sutherland and Cressey, 1974), rejects psychology and biology. (P. 118)

On the basis of a questionnaire sent to persons heavily cited in the criminological literature, Geis and Meier (1978) also reported that Sutherland's textbook and his other works had been nominated as the most influential books. Textbooks of more recent origin also give little space or emphasis to biological factors. For example, Empey (1978) devoted only 10 pages to biological theories out of over 200 on explanations of delinquency.

There are other reasons for sociological criminologists' dislike of biology. Some dislike not just biology but any scientific approach, because they are unwilling to tolerate any degree of determinism. British sociologists have been greatly influenced by Matza's (1969) arguments in favor of free will. Taylor et al. (1973) have articulated many objections to science in general and biology in particular. The following sentence summarizes many of these objections:

The man who breaks the window of the British Embassy in Dublin might well have a poor autonomic response but both his lack of reflex and violent behavior can only be understood in terms of the meanings he gave to the situation and the social context of the movement for a United Ireland. (P. 60)

Personally, I do not see why this act and others should not be explained by reference to biological, psychological, social–psychological, and social factors.

Some of the distaste for biology is based on misconceptions – for example, that if a characteristic is inherited it is fixed for life. Of course, what is inherited is a range of potentialities, and what actually happens depends crucially on the interaction between the individual and the environment. Another misconception is that, because nearly everyone commits delinquent acts, these acts cannot be explained by reference to biological variables. This misconception often depends on two others, that (a) everyone commits delinquent acts *to the same degree* and (b) biological variables are rare defects. Other beliefs have been identified by Jeffery (1980):

Environmentalism, the idea that the . . . environment controls behavior through nonphysical means and nonphysical processes; *equipotentiality,* the assumption that every individual is capable of the same behaviors – given the same environment – as every other individual; and *dualism,* the belief that the state of nature is bifurcated into mind versus matter, genetics versus environment . . . (Pp. 117–18)

Sociological criminologists' dislike of biological approaches is also fueled by worries about practical implications. As Mednick and Volavka (1980, p. 144) have pointed out, there is the fear that "biological findings could be misused politically as a pretext for not ameliorating the racial, social, and cultural disadvantages associated with high crime rates." Other worries center on the use of drugs to control prisoners (e.g., Fitzgerald & Sim, 1982, p. 117). Whatever the reasons for the objections of criminologists to biological approaches, it would be advisable for biological researchers to give careful consideration to these reasons and prepare full replies to them wherever possible.

An optimistic conclusion

In this chapter I have not attempted to review specific findings regarding biological variables and crime, nor have I attempted to review the biological theories underlying biological variables. I have not even attempted to review the theoretical basis of predictions about pulse rate, the one biological variable (admittedly a rather gross peripheral indicator) studied in some detail. The point has been to emphasize the links between biological and nonbiological variables.

I have argued that biological findings are sufficiently promising for criminologists to include biological variables in their theories and research projects. I have reviewed some of the advantages and problems of biological measurement and pointed out the necessity of trying to establish (a) how biological variables affect nonbiological ones, (b) how nonbiological variables affect biological ones, and (c) how biological and nonbiological variables interact. I recommended a longitudinal survey involving cooperation among researchers from different disciplines and frequent measurement of biological and nonbiological variables in order to study the role of both in the development of delinquency and crime.

In many ways, biology is a taboo topic for many sociological criminologists. However, I do not wish to subscribe to the pessimism of Jeffery (1980, p. 122), who argues that "the academic community is not committed to the pursuit of truth, but rather to the preservation of ideology." I find this version of conflict theory unpalatable, although, as a scientist, I am willing to be convinced of the truth of this statement by empirical research.

I would prefer to test the hypothesis that it is (eventually) possible to convince skeptics of the truth of unpopular theories by empirical research. As a case study, Hirschi and Hindelang (1977) reviewed research on IQ, one of a "class of variables traditionally ignored by sociological students of crime and delinquency [that] will not lose their status as alternative hypotheses simply by being ignored [but] will continue to restrict and even embarrass sociological theory until some effort is made to incorporate them" (p. 585). They concluded that IQ was at least as important a correlate of delinquency as social class or race.

This unfashionable conclusion has influenced criminological textbooks. For example, Hirschi and Hindelang (1977) quoted the first edition of Gibbons's (1970) textbook in connection with their statement that "many textbooks do not even mention IQ" (p. 572). The third edition of this textbook (Gibbons, 1981) contains a paragraph referring to Hirschi and Hindelang's review and states that "the facts seem clear that intelligence is an extremely important variable that differentiates juvenile offenders, particularly officially processed youths, from nondelinquents, in spite of much sociological wisdom to the contrary" (p. 107). Of course, a skeptic could argue that Hirschi and Hindelang's review has entered the mainstream of sociological thought (if that is true) only because they concluded that IQ was related to delinquency through the more important variable of school performance. This conclusion, not threatening to "sociological wisdom," was also reached by West and Farrington (1973, p. 94).

The implication I would draw from Hirschi and Hindelang (1977) is that taboo topics can be studied and that taboo findings can influence the mainstream of criminological thought. I believe that, if Marvin Wolfgang, for example, published an article in a leading sociological or criminological journal demonstrating (by persuasive empirical research) a relation between some biological variable and a measure of crime, this would enter the textbooks and become part of current criminological wisdom. The challenge to biological researchers is to disentangle the links between

biological and nonbiological variables and build up an impressive corpus
of knowledge about biology and crime.

References

Becker, H. S. (1963). *Outsiders*. New York: Free Press.
Buckle, A., & Farrington, D. P. (1982). An observational study of shoplifting. Unpublished
   manuscript, Cambridge University.
Campbell, A. (1981). *Girl delinquents*. Oxford: Blackwell.
Clarke, R. V. G. (1977). Psychology and crime. *Bulletin of the British Psychological Society,
   30*, 280–3.
Cohen, S. (1974). Criminology and the sociology of deviance in Britain. In P. Rock & M.
   McIntosh (Eds.), *Deviance and social control*. London: Tavistock.
Davies, J. G. V., & Maliphant, R. (1971). Autonomic responses of male adolescents exhibit-
   ing refractory behavior in school. *Journal of Child Psychology and Psychiatry, 12*, 115–
   27.
Elliot, D. S., Ageton, S. S., & Canter, R. J. (1979). An integrated theoretical perspective on
   delinquent behavior. *Journal of Research in Crime and Delinquency, 16*, 3–27.
Empey, L. T. (1978). *American delinquency*. Homewood, IL: Dorsey Press.
Farrington, D. P. (1973). Self-reports of deviant behavior: Predictive and stable? *Journal of
   Criminal Law and Criminology, 64*, 99–110.
Farrington, D. P. (1977). The effects of public labelling. *British Journal of Criminology, 17*,
   112–25.
Farrington, D. P. (1978). The family backgrounds of aggressive youths. In L. Hersov, M.
   Berger, & Shaffer, D. (Eds.), *Aggression and antisocial behavior in childhood and
   adolescence*. Oxford: Pergamon.
Farrington, D. P. (1981, November). *Delinquency from 10 to 25*. Paper given at Society for
   Life History Research meeting on antecedents of aggression and antisocial behavior,
   Monterey, CA.
Farrington, D. P. (1982a). Randomized experiments on crime and justice. In N. Morris & M.
   Tonry (Eds.), *Crime and justice* (Vol. 4). University of Chicago Press.
Farrington, D. P. (1982b). *Stepping stones to adult criminal careers*. Paper given at a
   conference on development of antisocial and prosocial behavior, Voss, Norway.
Farrington, D. P., & West, D. J. (1981). The Cambridge Study in Delinquent Development.
   In S. A. Mednick & A. E. Baert (Eds.), *Prospective longitudinal research*. New York:
   Oxford University Press.
Fitzgerald, M., & Sim, J. (1982). *British prisons* (2nd ed.). Oxford: Blackwell.
Geis, G., & Meier, R. F. (1978). Looking backward and forward: Criminologists on crimi-
   nology as a career. *Criminology, 16*, 273–88.
Gibbons, D. C. (1970). *Delinquent behavior*. Englewood Cliffs, NJ: Prentice-Hall.
Gibbons, D. C. (1981). Delinquent behavior (3rd ed.). Englewood Cliffs, NJ: Prentice-Hall.
Gordon, R. A. (1980). Research on IQ, race, and delinquency: Taboo or not taboo? In E.
   Sagarin (Ed.), *Taboos in criminology*. Beverly Hills, CA: Sage.
Hippchen, L. J. (Ed.). (1978). *Ecologic–biochemical approaches to treatment of delin-
   quents and criminals*. New York: Van Nostrand Reinhold.
Hirschi, T. (1969). *Causes of delinquency*. Berkeley: University of California Press.
Hirschi, T. (1980). Labelling theory and juvenile delinquency: An assessment of the evi-
   dence. In W. R. Gove (Ed.), *The labelling of deviance* (2nd ed.). Beverly Hills, CA:
   Sage.

Hirschi, T., & Hindelang, M. J. (1977). Intelligence and delinquency: A revisionist review. *American Sociological Review, 42*, 571–87.

Jeffery, C. R. (1979). Biology and crime: The new neo-Lombrosians. In C. R. Jeffery (Ed.), *Biology and crime*. Beverly Hills, CA: Sage.

Jeffery, C. R. (1980). Sociobiology and criminology: The long lean years of the unthinkable and the unmentionable. In E. Sagarin (Ed.), *Taboos in criminology*. Beverly Hills, CA: Sage.

Johnson, R. E. (1979). *Juvenile delinquency and its origins*. Cambridge University Press.

Kelly, H. E. (1979). Biosociology and crime. In C. R. Jeffery (Ed.), *Biology and crime*. Beverly Hills, CA: Sage.

Lemert, E. M. (1972). *Human deviance, social problems, and social control* (2nd ed.). Englewood Cliffs, NJ: Prentice-Hall.

Magnusson, D., Duner, A., & Zetterblom, G. (1975). *Adjustment*. Stockholm: Almqvist & Wiksell.

Matza, D. (1969). *Becoming deviant*. Englewood Cliffs, NJ: Prentice-Hall.

McCord, W., McCord, J., & Zola, I. K. (1959). *Origins of crime*. New York: Columbia University Press.

Mednick, S. A. (1977a). A biosocial theory of the learning of law-abiding behavior. In S. A. Mednick & K. O. Christiansen (Eds.), *Biosocial bases of criminal behavior*. New York: Gardner Press.

Mednick, S. A. (1977b). Preface. In S. A. Mednick & K. O. Christiansen (Eds.), *Biosocial bases of criminal behavior*. New York: Gardner Press.

Mednick, S. A., & Volavka, J. (1980). Biology and crime. In N. Morris & M. Tonry (Eds.), *Crime and justice* (Vol. 2). University of Chicago Press.

Mednick, S. A., Volavka, J., Gabrielli, W. F., & Itil, T. M. (1981). EEG as a predictor of antisocial behavior. *Criminology, 19*, 219–29.

Moyer, K. (1979). What is the potential for biological violence control? In C. R. Jeffery (Ed.), *Biology and crime*. Beverly Hills, CA: Sage.

Parker, H., & Giller, H. (1981). More and less the same: British delinquency research since the sixties. *British Journal of Criminology, 21*, 230–45.

Sagarin, E. (1980). Taboo subjects and taboo viewpoints in criminology. In E. Sagarin (Ed.), *Taboos in criminology*. Beverly Hills, CA: Sage.

Sechrest, L., White, S. O., & Brown, E. D. (1979). *The rehabilitation of criminal offenders*. Washington, DC: National Academy of Sciences.

Shah, S. A., & Roth, L. H. (1974). Biological and psychophysiological factors in criminality. In D. Glaser (Ed.), *Handbook of criminology*. Chicago: Rand McNally.

Sutherland, E. H., & Cressey, D. R. (1974). *Criminology* (9th ed.). Philadelphia: Lippincott.

Taylor, I., Walton, P., & Young, J. (1973). *The new criminology*. London: Routledge & Kegan Paul.

Trasler, G. B. (1962). *The explanation of criminality*. London: Routledge & Kegan Paul.

Trasler, G. B. (1978). Relations between psychopathy and persistent criminality: Methodological and theoretical issues. In R. D. Hare & D. Schalling (Eds.), *Psychopathic behavior*. New York: Wiley.

Wadsworth, M. E. J. (1976). Delinquency, pulse rates, and early emotional deprivation. *British Journal of Criminology, 16*, 245–56.

Wadsworth, M. E. J. (1979). *Roots of delinquency*. London: Martin Robertson.

West, D. J. (1969). *Present conduct and future delinquency*. London: Heinemann.

West, D. J. (1982). *Delinquency*. London: Heinemann.

West, D. J., & Farrington, D. P. (1973). *Who becomes delinquent?* London: Heinemann.

West, D. J., & Farrington, D. P. (1977). *The delinquent way of life*. London: Heinemann.

Witkin, H. A., Mednick, S. A., Schulsinger, F., Bakkestrom, E., Christiansen, K. O.,

Goodenough, D. R., Hirschorn, K., Lundsteen, C., Owen, D. R., Philip, J., Rubin, D. B., & Stocking, M. (1976). Criminality in XYY and XXY men. *Science, 193,* 547–55.

Wolfgang, M. E., Figlio, R. M., & Sellin, T. (1972). *Delinquency in a birth cohort.* University of Chicago Press.

4 Definitions of antisocial behavior in biosocial research

Preben Wolf

Because this volume is concerned with the interdisciplinary field of biosocial research, it seems appropriate to begin here with a look at the way biologists (including psychiatrists and some psychologists) define certain concepts that may have different meanings in the context of social science, a context with which criminologists are often more familiar.

Definitions are useful to the extent that they provide common understanding on which to base communication and argument. Each of the sciences involved has its own technical terms not always easily understood by outsiders. When scientists from one field (e.g., biology) want to use terms referring to aspects of the subject matter of some other sciences (e.g., sociology), they often seem to be guided in their choice of expression solely by conventional or common-sense definitions of the concept in question. Sometimes they make this choice because they are not sufficiently acquainted with the technical meanings of a term as it is used in the other science and sometimes because the expression has no agreed-on technical meaning or application in the other science. The latter may be the case when the term "antisocial" is concerned.

What does "antisocial" mean?

Conventional definitions

Conventional definitions are acquired fairly unsystematically and unconsciously as people see or hear common terms being used repeatedly and consistently. The term "social" is used commonly enough in several contexts to have acquired a number of conventional definitions, and the prefix "anti" is commonly known to mean something like "opposite" or "against." Even if we accept that both "anti" and "social" are common terms, however, the word "antisocial" may not be sufficiently common to have become conventionally defined. A criterion of the sufficient com-

65

monness and salience of a term or concept may be whether it serves as a head word or an entry in indices and in works of reference such as dictionaries and handbooks of general knowledge. If this criterion is accepted, the term "antisocial" is common enough. It can be found in dictionaries of various languages from the present as well as the previous century. The adjective "antisocial" is usually defined as being against or opposed to society or to the social order. The first edition of Henry Cecil Wyld's *Universal Dictionary of the English Language* (1946) has the following entry: "*Anti-social,* adj. – See *anti* & *social*. Opposed to, incompatible with, the principles and conditions which underlie organized society." The compact desk edition of *Webster's New World Dictionary of the American Language,* College Edition (1963) lists the following definitions: "*Antisocial,* adj. 1. not sociable. 2. against the people's welfare." There must be considerable variation among the conventional definitions of antisocial activities or attitudes, behavior, and so on, if there are three or four different definitions in only two very short dictionary entries.

Another difficulty with dictionary definitions of the term "antisocial" is that these definitions may be confused with definitions of the adjective "asocial." However, the compact edition of *Webster's New World Dictionary of the American Language* does not commit such an error. Its definition of "asocial" is quite different from its definition of "antisocial": "*Asocial* – , adj. not social; avoiding contact with others."

Professional and technical definitions

The main purpose of professional and technical definitions does not differ from that of conventional definitions, which is to facilitate communication, but in this case the concern is with communication among fellow professionals and fellow scientists.

Scientists, researchers, university students, and professional people in general usually find it essential to use symbols with greater precision than is required in everyday communication and to formulate their own more technical definitions of terms. The technical definitions of scientists often violate conventional language usage, not only by creating a new technical vocabulary but also by giving conventional terms more precise meaning.

Technical definitions are mainly formulated by professionals in a particular field, who thus share some of their experience with fellows from the same field. Sometimes scientists and other professionals try to formulate definitions in order to communicate with lay people and/or with colleagues from other branches of science. In the first case terms may be defined with the highest precision possible in a given field. In the second and third cases, the danger of falling between two stools is obvious. This is probably why we sometimes find short definitions of terms in (popular) dictionaries of particular sciences or professional fields to be no more precise than some of the conventional definitions from popular handbooks of general knowledge.

A common and loose form of such a definition consists of a mere enumeration of defined terms. It may qualify as a nominal definition assigning meaning to a term by substituting for it a number of appropriate expressions and may be formulated by an expert, but it can fulfill the purpose of simplifying or speeding up communication at only a fairly low level of knowledge. On the other hand, definition by enumeration may serve as a first approximation across fields in interdisciplinary research communication. Any closer cooperation among fields will demand an increased sharing of conceptions and operationalizations.

Let me illustrate definition by enumeration with an example from a field foreign to my own fields, which are sociology and law. The example is taken from authors whose special field is allergiology, and who have a general background in biology (medicine) and psychology (Campbell, 1970; Moyer, 1979).

In a classification of allergic reactions, antisocial behavior is included and defined as "uncooperative, pugnacious, . . . and perhaps cruel" behavior of patients (Moyer, 1979). This is a nominal definition by enumeration of the term "antisocial behavior," which refers to the subject matter of the social sciences but is used by scientists who are oriented toward studies of the individual. Still, it serves its purpose of making communication easier across fields. It conveys the approximate meaning of a term, as used by allergiologists, to members of other scientific branches.

Nevertheless, definition by enumeration is clearly unsatisfactory if we want to study antisocial behavior empirically. We have to connect the term with observable patterns of activity and interactivity. One device for doing so is the operational definition (Lundberg, 1964), which specifies the procedures of observation necessary to identify the referent of the term to be defined. Crime is one example of what is often nominally defined as antisocial behavior and that may be operationally defined in terms of the strategies employed in a given society to identify law violators and to control them. Registered police contacts, arrests, or court convictions are generally used as operational indices of criminality.

Difficulties of definitions

There are some dangers to avoid in discussions of nominal definitions. For example, one might end up merely arguing semantics. It really does not matter whether a certain behavior is called antisocial, asocial, psychopathic, sociopathic, or *X,* as long as it can be defined in such a way that fellow scientists can understand it.

Another danger lies in the lack of common experience among two or more different scientific branches trying to communicate by means of nominal or other technical definitions. In such cases scientists from separate fields may have to fall back on conventional definitions in order to communicate at a basic level.

If the concept of antisocial behavior has any reasonable correspondence with any common phenomenon studied by both behavioral and social scientists, it should be possible to define this concept nominally as well as operationally in a way that will make it easier for the researchers involved to share each other's experiences and to cooperate in interdisciplinary research teams. It should be possible to extract some common elements from the various definitions of antisocial behavior and to use them in the formulation of a compact nominal definition that might facilitate communication in interdisciplinary research. As I see it, the common element, at least by implication, in all definitions of "antisocial behavior" must be an element of norm violation. It is difficult to see how any behavior can be called antisocial if it does not break any social norms. If it can be accepted that antisocial behavior always implies violation of a social norm, it must at the same time be accepted that nonconforming behavior is not necessarily antisocial. This is a question decided by the tolerance limits of the social system in which the nonconforming or deviant behavior takes place. My contention is that what is here called antisocial behavior can be defined as any behavior that violates one or more social norms beyond the tolerance limits of the social system or systems of which the violent norms are part. It follows that the adjective "antisocial" is used to characterize not just a particular kind of behavior, but also the social conditions under which, in principle, almost any kind of behavior can be called antisocial.

Criminality and delinquency are clear examples of antisocial behavior thus defined, and both these concepts are easily defined in operational terms. Criminal behavior is a generally accepted example of antisocial behavior, because it is always injurious to the normative structure of society, and most often to other structures as well, and perhaps also to various interactional or sociability processes in the social systems in which the antisocial activity takes place or to which the antisocial actor belongs.

It is easy to formulate an operational definition of criminality. Crimes known to the police may be one such operationalization. Self-reported crimes or crimes reported by victims are two other possibilities. These definitions, like most operational definitions, have a much more narrow meaning than nominal definitions. But operational definitions are unavoidable in empirical research, and what they may lack in scope they usually gain in their greater precision.

Some practical meanings of antisocial behavior in biosocial research

Einstein once said that if one wants to understand the scientific method one should not listen to what scientists say, but look at what they do. This is a way of finding out about some of the practical meanings of antisocial behavior that cannot be pursued here in detail. A good approximation may be to look at the program titles of some international conferences on antisocial behavior like the one held on aggression and antisocial behavior in Monterey, California, in November 1981 by the Society for Life History Research. A list of papers and discussions of that conference shows that criminal and delinquent behavior is most often taken as a subject of biosocial and related research on the problem of antisocial behavior.

We can also gain information on this point from a fairly recent selection of international and interdisciplinary studies like the well-known volume edited by Sarnoff A. Mednick and the late Karl O. Christiansen (1977) on the biosocial bases of criminal behavior and other antisocial or asocial behavior such as alcoholism and psychopathic behavior. The book is mainly about crime and delinquency; in only 2 of the 19 chapter titles does the word "antisocial" or "asocial" appear. Five titles use the word "psychopathy," and most of the remaining titles specify the various behaviors as criminality, aggression, or alcoholism either explicitly or by implication.

In all of the chapters of the book, which deal with biosocial research on criminal behavior, the behavior studied has been defined operationally in terms of the acts officially registered as criminal offenses by the appropriate authorities, and, correspondingly, criminals are persons who have been registered for committing such acts. These operational definitions are consistent with the nominal definition of antisocial behavior suggested above as norm-violating behavior beyond the tolerance limits of the social system concerned.

Another question is whether definitions of the acts have sufficient practical meaning for biologists and other scientists interested mainly in the characteristics of the individual actors and their possible predispositions to act in more or less antisocial ways. It is easy enough to define a criminal person as one who has been registered for at least one criminal act. For all we know, he or she may never have been registered before and never will be again. If one is interested in the biological aspects of individual predispositions to act in antisocial ways it will be necessary to study recidivists and recidivistic behavior. This is also a recurring theme in most of the chapters of the volume discussed here (Mednick & Christiansen, 1977). Some of the authors stress the importance of the seriousness of the behavior in question. Some biologists tend to call serious or extremely antisocial acts crime (Hall & Lindzey, 1969), and some criminologists call very serious crime antisocial (e.g., Ferri, 1898). It is not just a question of defining antisocial or criminal behavior as either serious or persistent or both, because most serious crimes are committed by recidivists. It is rather a question of whether it will be possible to find a certain measure of frequency or density of antisocial acts committed by an individual that will classify that individual as a criminal or otherwise antisocial person.

In a discussion of biosocial factors and primary prevention of antisocial behavior Mednick (1979) indicates that, in searching for an "explanation of these cases of antisocial behavior which seem to have no apparent social cause," it might be a good idea to concentrate on offenders who are convicted of having committed more than "one, two, or three relatively minor offenses," since these minor offenses "are doubtless instigated by socioeconomic and situational forces." This suggestion implies that it might be expedient for various purposes to operate with a fairly narrow definition of the antisocial or criminal individual. Instead of defining the criminal as a person who has committed at least one punishable offense against the law, one might define the criminal as a person who has committed so much crime or so many offenses that he or she has acquired criminal status or is enacting a criminal role (Sarbin & Allen, 1969).

The number of offenses necessary for an offender to qualify as a criminal might be arbitrarily fixed at four or more registered offenses, as Mednick's formulation suggests. Some previous research results from Denmark also support the suggestion that there may be a turning point in the careers of male offenders, when they pass the level of three officially registered offenses. Table 4.1 (based on unpublished tables from Wolf and Høgh, 1975) indicates that offenders who have been registered from one to three times are significantly more similar to nonoffenders with regard to

Table 4.1. *Correlations of offenders' social status scores as a function of number of registered offenses*

Number of registered offenses	Number of registered offenses				
	4	3	2	1	0
4	—	r = .85	.88	.85	.75
3		—	.95	.96	.91
2			—	.98	.95
1				—	.97
0					—

Note: Offenders with only one to three registered offenses are more similar to each other and to nonoffenders than they are to offenders with four or more registered offenses with regard to status positions.

various social (particularly social class) variables than they are to offenders who have been registered four times or more. A similar but not as clear picture of a turning point at about three or four registrations has been found among young male offenders in a birth cohort from the Copenhagen area with regard to intelligence (see Table 4.2, based on tables from Project Metropolitan, Copenhagen; Høgh & Wolf, 1981).

The two examples just mentioned support the suggestion that one should not label a person criminal or antisocial in biosocial research until he or she has shown sure recidivistic tendencies. Such a view of the criminal person seems to be in accord with widespread feelings among lay people, as formulated in a Danish saying: "Once done is never done."

Table 4.2. *Correlations of offenders' IQ scores as a function of number of registered offenses*

Number of registered offenses	Number of registered offenses					
	7–28	4–6	3	2	1	0
7–28	—	r = .995	.896	.874	.716	.307
4–6		—	.897	.891	.753	.371
3			—	.858	.938	.698
2				—	.937	.725
1					—	.864
0						—

Note: The important parting line of this matrix is between the coefficients of the categories with less than four registered offenses and the coefficients of the categories with four or more registered offenses.

Source: Unpublished tables from Project Metropolitan; see Høgh & Wolf (1981).

The adage is probably of Greek origin, and it indicates that having done a thing only once is as good as not having done it all (Vogel-Jorgensen, 1975). However that may be, some of the misunderstandings that sometimes arise in discussions of antisociability or criminality are produced because we fail to distinguish clearly between talking about criminal or antisocial behavior and talking about criminal or antisocial persons or personalities.

Summary and conclusion

There seems to be no agreed-on definition of antisocial behavior, so the term, as actually applied, may convey very different meanings. It is rarely applied by sociologists and has no important place in sociological discourse, where the social phenomena the term might conceivably denote are usually referred to by various other terms, such as norm-violating, nonconforming, or deviant behavior.

That a concept is defined and its meaning conveyed effectively is probably more important than how it is defined or whether its communicated meaning is accepted by scientists from other fields. A scientist's uses of a technical term and its appropriate definition will vary with the scientific context in which it is applied. I do not suggest that any one of the definitions of antisocial behavior stated above be considered the only generally acceptable definition. I do suggest that it would facilitate communication in biological criminology if no human behavior were characterized as antisocial unless the following minimum requirements were met:

1. The behavior violates one or more social systems.
2. The behavior exceeds the tolerance limits of one or more social systems.
3. It is specified what norms or standards are violated and what tolerance limits are exceeded.
4. It is specified in the context of which social system or systems the norm violations and transgressions of tolerance limits should be seen.

No person should be characterized as antisocial unless he or she has repeatedly behaved in one or more ways that meet these requirements. The frequency, density, and/or seriousness of the antisocial activities of a person should be shown to have reached or exceeded a specified minimum level as indicated, for example, by the total number of antisocial acts, the number of antisocial acts per unit of time or duration of an established antisocial state, the degree of deviation from a given standard, and the severity of the sanction stipulated or applied as a measure of the degree to which the given tolerance limits have been exceeded.

The important thing is not that all of these, and only these, criteria are applied, but that some criteria are specified as part of the definition of the antisocial individual in such a way that it may be possible for interdisciplinary researchers to recognize and consider the basis for such a classification.

References

Campbell, M. B. (1970). Allergy and behavior: Neurologic and psychic syndromes. In F. Speer (Ed.), *Allergy of the nervous system* (pp. 28–46). Springfield, IL: Thomas.

Ferri, E. (1898). *Criminal sociology.* New York: Appleton.

Hall, C. S., & Lindzey, G. (Eds.). (1969). The relevance of Freudian psychology and related viewpoints for the social sciences. In *Handbook of social psychology* (2nd ed.). *Vol. 1: Historical introduction* (Ch. 4). Reading MA: Addison-Wesley.

Høgh, E., & Wolf, P. (1981). Project Metropolitan: A longitudinal study. In S. A. Mednick & A. E. Baert (Eds.), *Prospective longitudinal research.* New York: Oxford University Press.

Lundberg, G. A. (1964). *Foundations of sociology* (Rev. ed.). New York: David McKay.

Mednick, S. A. (1979). Biosocial factors and primary prevention of antisocial behavior. In S. A. Mednick & S. G. Shoham, (Eds.), *New paths in criminology* (pp. 45–53). Lexington, MA: Lexington Books.

Mednick, S. A., & Christiansen, K. O. (Eds.). (1977). *Biosocial bases of criminal behavior.* New York: Gardner Press.

Moyer, K. (1979). What is the potential for biological violence control? In C. R. Jeffery, (Ed.), *Biology and crime* (pp. 19–46). Beverly Hills, CA: Sage.

Sarbin, T., & Allen, V. L. (1969). Role theory. In G. Lindzey & E. Aronson (Eds.), *Handbook of social psychology* (2nd ed.): *Vol 1: Historical introduction* (Ch. 7). Reading, MA: Addison-Wesley.

Svalastoga, K. (1969). *Sociologisk metodik,* Vol 1. Copenhagen: Københavns Universitets Fond til Laeremidler/Jørgen Paludans Forlag.

Vogel-Jørgensen, T. (Ed.). (1975). *Bevingede ord* [Familiar quotations] (5th ed.). Copenhagen: Gads Forlag.

Wolf, P., & Høgh, E. (1975). *Kriminalitet i Velfaerdssamfundet* (4th ed.). Copenhagen: Jørgen Paludans Forlag.

5   Genetic factors in the etiology of criminal behavior

Sarnoff A. Mednick, William F. Gabrielli, Jr.,
and Barry Hutchings

Human behavior patterns are generally ascribed to an interaction of life experiences and genetic predispositions, but the importance of genetic influences in shaping conduct has often been contested. This debate has been especially intense, and often emotional, in explaining criminal behavior (Sarbin & Miller, 1970). Reluctance to consider genetic factors in crime has had political overtones (Haller, 1968), but it may also reflect the fact that, until recently, the evidence for genetic influences consisted mainly of studies of twins, some of which were methodologically questionable.

Christiansen (1977a) reported on the criminality of a total population of 3,586 twin pairs from a well-defined area of Denmark. He found 52% of the twins concordant for criminal behavior for (male–male) identical twin pairs and 22% concordance for (male–male) fraternal twin pairs. This result suggests that identical twins inherit some biological characteristic (or characteristics) that increases their common risk of being registered for criminal behavior.

It has been pointed out, however, that identical twins are treated more alike than are fraternal twins (Christiansen, 1977b). Thus their greater similarity in criminal behavior may be partly related to their shared experience. This has produced a reluctance to accept in full the genetic implications of twin research. The study of adoptions better separates environmental and genetic effects; if convicted adoptees have a disproportionately high number of convicted biological fathers (given appropriate controls), this would suggest the influence of a genetic factor in criminal behavior. This conclusion is supported by the fact that almost none of the adoptees know their biological parents; adoptees often do not even realize they have been adopted.

Two U.S. adoption studies have produced highly suggestive results. Crowe (1975) found an increased rate of criminality in 37 Iowan adoptees with criminal biological mothers. Cadoret (1978) reported on 246 Iowans

Table 5.1. *Number of adoptions in five-year periods*

Years	Male	Female	Total
1924–8	578	1,051	1,629
1929–33	730	1,056	1,786
1934–8	832	1,092	1,924
1939–43	1,650	1,731	3,381
1944–7	2,890	2,782	5,672
(4 years)			
Year uncertain	20	15	35
Total	6,700	7,727	14,427

adopted at birth. Antisocial behavior in these adoptees was significantly related to antisocial behavior in the biological parents. In a study of Swedish adoptees Bohman, Cloninger, Sigvardsson, and von Knorring (1982) found that criminal behavior in the biological parents was significantly related to criminal behavior in the adoptees. This relationship held only for property crimes.

The study to be described in this chapter was based on a register of all 14,427 nonfamilial adoptions in Denmark in the years 1924–47. This register was established at the Psykologisk Institut in Copenhagen by a group of American and Danish investigators (Kety, Rosenthal, Wender, & Schulsinger, 1968). The register includes information on the adoptee and his or her adoptive and biological parents. We hypothesized that registered criminality in the biological parents would be associated with an increased risk of registered criminal behavior in the offspring.

Procedures

Information on all nonfamilial adoptions in the Kingdom of Denmark between 1924 and 1947 ($N = 14,427$) was obtained from records at the Ministry of Justice. The distribution of adoptions by sex of adoptee for five-year periods appears in Table 5.1. Note the increase in adoptions with increasing population, especially during the war years, and the larger number of females adopted.

Criminality data

Court convictions were used as an index of criminal involvement. Minors (below 15 years of age) cannot receive court convictions. Court convictions information is maintained by the chief of the police district in which an individual is born. The court record (Strafferegister) contains information on the date of the conviction, the paragraphs of the law violated, and the sanction. To obtain access to these records it is necessary to know the place of birth. When subjects' conviction records could not be checked, it was usually because of a lack of information or ambiguity regarding their date and/or place of birth. The court record was obtained for all of the subjects for whom date and place of birth were available ($N = 65,516$).

Information was first recorded from the adoption files of the Ministry of Justice. In these files, birthplace was then available for the biological and adoptive parents but not for the adoptees; birthplace for the adoptees was obtained from the Central Persons Register or the local population registers. The Central Persons Register was established in 1968; adoptees who died or emigrated before 1968 were thus excluded from the study. There were some difficulties in these searches. The criminal records of persons who have died or have reached the age of 80 are *sometimes* removed from the registers and archived in the Central Police Office in Copenhagen. Thus if an individual had a court conviction but had died before our search began, his or her record might have been transferred from the local police district to the Copenhagen Central Police Office. There the record would be maintained in a death register. In view of this, the entire population (adoptees and parents) was checked in the death register. If an adoptee had died or emigrated before the age of 30, the adoptee and parents were dropped from the study since the adoptee had not gone through the entire risk period for criminal conviction. A small section of Denmark in southern Jutland belonged to Germany until 1920. If an individual from this area was registered for criminality before 1920 but not *after* 1920, that individual's record was lost to this study.

For each individual we coded the following information: sex, date of birth, address, occupation, place of birth, and size of the community into which the child was adopted. The subjects' occupations permitted us to code socioeconomic status (Svalastoga, 1959). For the adoptees we also coded marital status in 1976.

Not fully identified cases

It will be recalled that in order to check the court register it was necessary to have name, date, and place of birth. A considerable number of cases were lost to this investigation for the following reasons. (a) There was no record of place and/or date of birth. (b) In Denmark the biological mother is required by law to name the biological father. In some few cases she refused, was unsure, or named more than one possible father. These cases were dropped from the population. (c) Among the adoptive parents,

Table 5.2. *Conviction rates of completely identified members of adoptee families*

Family member	Number identified	Number not identified	Number of criminal law court convictions			
			None	One	Two	More than two
Male adoptee	6,129	571	.841	.088	.029	.040
Female adoptee	7,065	662	.972	.020	.005	.003
Adoptive father	13,918	509	.938	.046	.008	.008
Adoptive mother	14,267	160	.981	.015	.002	.002
Biological father	10,604	3,823	.714	.129	.056	.102
Biological mother	12,300	2,127	.911	.064	.012	.013

397 were single women. This was because either the adoptive father died just before the formal adoption or the child was adopted by a single woman (not common in this era). (d) Because of additional difficulties involved in checking the criminal registers before 1910, individuals who were born before January 1, 1885, were excluded from the study.

In the case of exclusion of an *adoptee* for any of the above reasons the entire adoptive family was dropped. If a parent was excluded, the remaining subjects were retained for analysis. Table 5.2 presents the number of fully identified individuals in each of the subject categories.

Results

The data to be reported consist of convictions for violation of the Danish Criminal Code (Straffeloven). The levels of court convictions for each of the members of the adoption family are given in Table 5.2. The biological-father and male-adoptee conviction rates are considerably higher than the rates for the adoptive father. The rate for adoptive fathers is a bit below that (8%) for men of this age group, in this time period (Hurwitz & Christiansen, 1971). Note also that most of the adoptive-father convictions are attributable to one-time offenders. The male adoptees and the biological fathers are more heavily recidivistic.

The rates of conviction for the women are considerably lower and there is considerably less recidivism than there is for men. The biological mothers and female adoptees have higher levels of court convictions than the adoptive mothers. The adoptive mothers are just below the population average for women of this age range and time period, 2.2%. The individuals who gave up their children for adoption, and their biological offspring, show higher rates of court convictions than the general population and the adoptive parents.

In light of current adoption practices one might be surprised that adoptive parents with court convictions were permitted to adopt. It should be recalled, however, that many of these adoptions took place during the Great Depression and World War II. It was more difficult to find willing adoptive homes in these periods owing partly to the relative unavailability of adoptive parents and to the additional number of adoptees available. Adoptive parents were accepted if they had had a 5-year crime-free period before the adoption.

In most of the analyses that follow, we shall consider the relation between parents' criminal convictions and criminal convictions in the adoptees. If either mother or father (biological and/or adoptive) had received a criminal law conviction, the *parents* of that adoptee will be considered criminal. In view of the low level of convictions among the female adoptees, the analyses will concentrate on the criminal behavior of the male adoptees.

Types of crime

Of the adoptive parents, 5.50% were convicted for property crimes; 1.05% committed violent acts; and 0.54% were convicted for sexual offenses. Of the biological parents, 28.12% were responsible for property crimes; 6.51% committed violent crimes; and 3.81% committed sexual offenses. Individuals could be registered for more than one type of crime.

Cross-fostering analysis

Because of the size of the population it is possible to segregate subgroups of adoptees who have combinations of convicted and nonconvicted biological and adoptive parents. Table 5.3 presents the four groups in a design that is analogous to the cross-fostering paradigm used in behavior genetics. As can be seen in the lower-right-hand cell, if neither the biological nor adoptive parents are convicted, 13.5% of their sons are convicted. If the adoptive parents are convicted and the biological parents are not convicted, this figure rises to only 14.7%. Note that 20.0% of the sons are convicted if the adoptive parents are *not* convicted and the biological parents are convicted. If *both* the biological and adoptive parents are convicted, we observe the highest level of conviction in the sons, 24.5%. The comparison analogous to the cross-fostering paradigm favors a partial genetic etiology. We must caution, however, that simply knowing that an

Table 5.3. *Cross-fostering analysis: percentage of adoptive sons convicted of criminal law offenses*

Have adoptive parents been convicted?	Have biological parents been convicted?	
	Yes	No
Yes	24.5 (of 143)	14.7 (of 204)
No	20.0 (of 1,226)	13.5 (of 2,492)

Note: Numbers in parentheses represent the total number for each cell.

adoptive parent has been convicted of a crime does not tell us how crimi-nogenic the adoptee's environment has been. (Recall the preponderance of one-time offenders in the adoptive parents and the adoption agency's condition that the adoptive parents not have a conviction for the 5 years preceding the adoption.) On the other hand, at conception, the genetic influence of the biological father is already complete. Thus this analysis does not yield a fair comparison between environmental and genetic influences included in Table 5.3. However, this initial analysis does indicate that sons with a convicted biological parent have an elevated probability of being convicted. This suggests that some biological characteristic is transmitted from the criminal biological parent that increases the son's risk of obtaining a court conviction for a criminal law offense.

A log-linear analysis of the data in Table 5.3 is presented in Table 5.4.

Table 5.4. *Log-linear analysis: Influences of adoptive-parent and biological-parent convictions on male-adoptee convictions*

Model	Model χ^2	d.f.	p	Improvement χ^2	d.f.	p
Baseline (S, AB)	32.91	3	.001			
Adoptive parent (SA, AB)	30.71	2	.001	2.20	1	n.s.
Biological parent (SB, AB)	1.76	2	.415	31.15	1	.001
Combined influence (SB, SA, AB)	0.30	1	.585	32.61	2	.001
Biological parent given adoptive parent (SB/SA, AB)	—	—		28.95	1	.001
Adoptive parent given biological parent (SA/SB, AB)	—	—		1.46	1	n.s.

Note: S denotes adoptee-son effect; A, adoptive-parent effect; B, biological-parent effect; n.s., not significant.

Adoptive-parent convictions are not associated with a significant increment in the son's level of convictions. The effect of the biological parents' convictions is marked. The model presented in Table 5.4 reveals that, considering only the *additive* effect of the biological parent and the adoptive parent, the improvement in the chi-square value leaves almost no room for improvement by an interaction effect.

The adoptive parents have a low frequency of court convictions. In order to simplify interpretation of the relations reported below we have excluded cases with adoptive-parent criminality. (Analyses completed that did include adoptive-parent criminality did not alter the nature of the findings to be reported.)

Figure 5.1 presents the relation between convictions in the sons and degree of recidivism in the biological parents. The relation is positive and relatively monotonic (with the scales utilized on the X and Y axes). Note also that the relation is highly significant for property crimes and not statistically significant for violent crimes.

The chronic offender

The chronic offender is rare but commits a markedly disproportionate number of criminal offenses. This extremely high rate of offending suggested that genetic predisposition may play an important role in these cases. We examined the relation between convictions of the chronic adoptee offender and his biological parents.

In an important U.S. birth cohort study (Wolfgang, Figlio, & Sellin, 1972), the chronic offender was defined as one who had been arrested five or more times; these chronic offenders comprised 6% of the males and had committed 52% of the offenses. In our adoption cohort we recorded court convictions rather than arrest data. If we select as chronic offenders those with three or more court convictions, this includes 4.09% of the male adoptees. This small group of recidivists accounts for 69.4% of all the court convictions for all the male adoptees. This is a high concentration of crime in a very small fraction of the cohort.

Table 5.5 shows how the chronic offenders, the other offenders (one or two convictions), and the nonoffenders are distributed as a function of level of crime in the biological parents. As can be seen, the proportion of chronic adoptee offenders increases as a function of level of recidivism in the biological parents.

Another way of expressing this concentration of crime is to point out that the chronic male adoptee offenders with biological parents with three or more offenses number only 37. Although they comprise only 1% of the

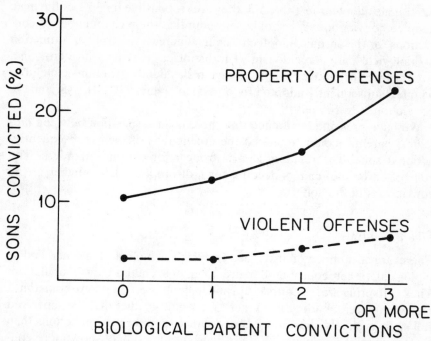

Figure 5.1. Percentage of male adoptee property offenders and violent offenders by biological-parent convictions.

Table 5.5. *Proportion of chronic offenders, other offenders, and nonoffenders among male adoptees as a function of convictions of biological parents*

Number of male-adoptee convictions	Number of biological-parent convictions			
	0	1	2	3 or more
Nonoffenders (no convictions)	.87	.84	.80	.75
Other offenders (1 or 2 convictions)	.10	.12	.15	.17
Chronic offenders (3 or more convictions)	.03	.04	.05	.09
Number of adoptees	2,492	547	233	419

Note: Data do not include cases in which adoptive parents were convicted of criminal law violation.

3,691 male adoptees in Table 5.5, they are responsible for 30% of the male adoptee convictions. We should also note that the mean number of convictions for the chronic adoptee offenders increases sharply as a function of biological parent recidivism. The biological parents with zero, one, two, or three or more convictions have male adoptees (i.e., male children who are subsequently adopted by others) averaging .30, .41, .48, and .70 conviction, respectively.

We have presented evidence that there is an association between biological parents' convictions and the convictions of their (subsequently) adopted sons. The relation seems stronger for chronic offenders. The sons of chronic offenders account for a disproportionate number of the convictions in the cohort.

Sibling analyses

There are a number of instances in which a biological mother and/or biological father contributed more than one child to this population. These offspring are, of course, full and half-siblings; they were sometimes placed in different adoptive homes. We would predict that the separated full siblings should show more concordance for criminal convictions than the separated half-siblings. Both of these groups should show more concordance than two randomly selected, unrelated, separately reared male adoptees.

The probability of any one male adoptee being convicted is .159. The probability of drawing a pair of unrelated, separated male adoptees with at least one having a conviction is .293. The probability that both of the pair will have been convicted is .025. Thus pairwise concordance for unrelated separated male adoptees is 8.5%. This can be seen as a baseline. There were 126 male–male half-sibling pairs placed in separate adoptive homes. Of these, 31 pairs had at least one member of the sibship convicted; of these 31 pairs, 4 pairs were concordant for convictions. This yields a concordance rate for half-siblings of 12.9%. There were 40 male–male full-sibling pairs placed in different adoptive homes. Of these, 15 pairs had at least one member of the sibship convicted; of these 15 pairs, three pairs were concordant for convictions. This yields a concordance rate for full siblings of 20%. These numbers are very small, but the results are in the predicted direction. As the degree of genetic relation increases, the level of concordance increases.

We also considered the level of concordance of the sibling pairs whose biological father was a criminal (had at least one conviction). Of 98 fathers with at least one pair of male–male, separated, adopted-away siblings, 45

Table 5.6. *Concordance for criminal law convictions in male siblings placed in separate adoptive homes*

Degree of genetic relation	Pairwise concordance (%)
Unrelated, raised apart	8.5
Half-siblings, raised apart	12.9
Full siblings, raised apart	20.0
Half-siblings and full siblings, raised apart; criminal father	30.8
Unrelated "siblings" raised together in adoptive home	8.5

had received at least one conviction. [It should be noted that this is a significantly higher rate of convictions (45.9%) than the conviction rate (28.6%) for the total population of biological fathers, $\psi^2(1) = 14.6$, $p < .01$.]

We combined full- and half-sibling pairs (because of the small number and because the siblings shared criminal biological fathers). Of the 45 sibling pairs, 13 had at least one member with a conviction; of these 13, four pairs were concordant for convictions. This yields a concordance rate of 30.8%. Table 5.6 summarizes these sibling analyses. The pairwise concordance rates can be compared with the male–male rates for twins from a population twin study; Christiansen (1977a) reported 36% pairwise concordance for identical twins and a 13% rate for fraternal twins.

Although these numbers are very small, they represent all of the cases, as defined, in a total cohort of adoptions. The results suggest that a number of these separated, adopted siblings inherited some characteristic that predisposed both of them to being convicted for criminal behavior. As would be expected, in those instances in which the biological father was criminal, the effect was enhanced.

Specificity of a genetic relation

Earlier, we mentioned a study of a small sample of adoptees (Crowe, 1975). Crowe reported the impression that there was some similarity in the types of crime committed by the biological mother and the adoptee. This suggests specific genetic predispositions for different types of crime. In order to explore this possibility, we examined the rates of violent crimes in the adoptees as a function of violent crime in the biological parents. We completed similar analyses for property crimes. We also examined more specific types of crime (theft, fraud, assault, etc.) for similarity in the biological parent and the adoptee.

If the genetic predisposition was specific for type of crime, these "specificity" analyses should have resulted in our observing a closer relation between adoptee and biological-parent levels of conviction for each of these types of crime. The best predictor of each type of adoptee crime, however, was number of biological-parent convictions rather than type of biological-parent offense. This suggests that the biological predisposition the adoptee inherits must be of a general nature, partly determining the degree of law abidance shown by the adoptee. It is also possible that the data of this study are too gross for the detection of a specificity relation. This may require careful coding of details of the criminal behavior. This was not possible in our study.

Sex differences

As can be seen in Table 5.2, convictions of females for criminal law violations are very infrequent. It might be speculated that those women who do exhibit a level of criminal behavior that prompts a court conviction must have a severe predisposition for such behavior. Criminal involvement of many men, on the other hand, may tend to be more socially or environmentally inspired. These statements suggest that convictions in the biological mother are more closely related to the adoptee's conviction(s) than criminal behavior in the biological father.

In every analysis we conducted, the relation between biological-mother conviction and adoptee conviction is significantly stronger than the relation between biological-father conviction and adoptee conviction. In comparison with the relation between biological-father and adoptee convictions, convictions of the biological mothers are more closely related to convictions of the daughters. This result is statistically significant, but the relatively low frequency of female convictions forces us to interpret these findings with caution.

Historical period

The period of these adoptions (1924–67) spans some important historical changes in Denmark, including a world war, the Great Depression, and industrialization. It is conceivable that the influence of genetic factors might be affected by these social upheavals. It is also possible that changes in level or type of crime during these years might influence the relations observed. Analyses conducted for the entire population were repeated for each of the 5-year periods. The results were virtually identical for all of the periods and virtually identical to the analyses of the total

Table 5.7. *Percentage of male adoptees with criminal convictions as a function of adoptive and biological parents' socioeconomic status*

Adoptive parents' SES	Biological parents' SES			
	High	Middle	Low	Total
High	9.30	11.52	12.98	11.58
	(441)	(903)	(775)	(2099)
Middle	13.44	15.29	16.86	15.62
	(320)	(870)	(795)	(1985)
Low	13.81	17.25	18.04	17.19
	(210)	(568)	(787)	(1565)
Total	11.64	14.31	16.00	14.55
	(971)	(2341)	(2337)	(5649)

Note: Numbers in parentheses represent total number for each cell.

sample. The social changes during these years did not interact with the relation between biological-parent and adoptee crime.

Controlling genetic influence in examining environmental effects

In many social science investigations genetic characteristics are not considered. In some analyses this may contribute error; sometimes omission may lead to incomplete conclusions. For example, separation from a father is associated with an increased level of delinquency in a son. This has been interpreted as a result of failure of identification or lack of consistent discipline. As we can see from Table 5.2, some fathers who permit themselves to be separated from their child have a relatively high level of criminal convictions. The higher level of delinquency found for separated children might be partially due to a genetic transmission of criminogenic predispositional characteristics from antisocial fathers. If this genetic variance were partially accounted for, the environmental hypotheses could be more precisely tested. We utilized such partial genetic control to study an important criminological variable, social status. We separated the variance ascribable to "genetic" social class and "rearing" social class (Van Dusen, Mednick, Gabrielli, & Hutchings, 1983). We examined adoptee convictions as a joint function of biological parents' social class and adoptive parents' social class. It is clear from inspection of Table 5.7 that male-adoptee convictions vary as a function of both genetic and environmental social class; log-linear analyses reveal that both effects are statistically significant. Although the genetic effect is of interest here, we emphasize that, to our knowledge, this is the first controlled demonstration that *environmental* aspects influence the social class–crime relation. This finding suggests that, regardless of genetic background, improved social conditions are likely to lead to a reduction in criminal behavior.

Table 5.7 is of interest in another regard. Careful inspection reveals a correlation between adoptive-parent socioeconomic status (SES) and biological-parent SES. This represents the attempt by the adoptive agency to match certain characteristics of the two sets of parents in order to increase the likelihood that the adoptee will fit into the adoptive home. In terms of the adoption research design, this correlation is undesirable because it reduces the independence of the genetic rearing and environmental influences on the adoptee. Since social class is not independent of convictions (Table 5.7), it is conceivable that the relation between biological-parent and adoptee convictions is, in part, mediated by social class. Inspection of Table 5.7 reveals, however, that this relation exists at each level of adoptive-parent social class. In addition we have conducted stepwise multiple regression analyses that varied the order of entry of biological-parent convictions and SES and adoptive-parent convictions and SES. These analyses indicate that, independent of SES, biological-parent convictions are significantly related to adoptee convictions.

Methodological issues

Not fully identified subjects

If we are to generalize from the results of this study, it is useful to consider what biases might be introduced by the loss of subjects in specific analyses. Table 5.2 indicates the total number of subjects who could not be fully identified (name, birthday, and birthplace). We should note that we know the name, occupation, birthdate, and other facts concerning most of the lost subjects; in almost all cases a subject could not be checked in the court conviction register because we were not certain of the subject's place of birth.

The information is relatively complete for the adoptive parents. In contrast, 26.5% of the biological fathers and 14.7% of the biological mothers are not fully identified. These differences probably reflect the relative importance of the adoptive and biological parents to the adoption agency. The agency's chief concern was with the placement and welfare of the adoptee. After the adoption, they had less reason to be concerned with the biological parents.

The most general characteristic of those not fully identified is that they tend *slightly* to come from areas outside Copenhagen. Perhaps the urban adoption offices followed more thorough recording procedures than did offices outside the city. The differences are very small. The sons of the biological fathers not fully identified have a rate of 10.3% criminal law convictions; the identified biological fathers' sons have criminal law convictions in 11.4% of cases. In cases in which the biological mother is not fully identified, slightly fewer of the sons have criminal law convictions (9.6%). The adoptees who were not fully identified have biological mothers and biological fathers with slightly higher SES than those who were fully identified. Their rearing (adoptive) homes were of almost identical SES.

Our consideration of the characteristics of those not fully identified does not suggest that their inclusion would have altered the nature of the results presented above. Perhaps the most critical facts in this judgment are that the adopted-away sons of parents not fully identified have levels of criminal law convictions and rearing social status that are approximately the same as for the sons of those parents fully identified. The differences observed are small; it is difficult to formulate any manner in which the lost subjects might have an impact on the relations reported.

Transfer history

Most of these adoptions were the results of pregnancies of unwed women. The adoptive agency had a policy of taking newborns from their biological mothers and either immediately placing them in a previously arranged adoptive home (25.3% of the adoptions) or placing them in an orphanage from which they were available for adoption. Of those placed in an orphanage, 50.6% were placed with an adoptive family in the first year, 12.8% were placed with an adoptive family in the second year, and 11.3% were placed after the age of 2.

Within each of these age-of-transfer groups, analyses were conducted to ascertain whether the biological parents' convictions were related to male-adoptee conviction. Similar significant positive relations were observed at each transfer age. Age of transfer did not interact with genetic influence so as to alter significantly the relations observed with the full population. It should be noted that there was a statistically significant tendency for a high level of adoptee criminality to be associated with more time spent in an orphanage awaiting adoption. This effect was true for males only.

The operational definition of criminal behavior in this study included only court convictions for criminal law offenses. (We completed an analysis of police arrest data using a subsample of this adoption cohort and obtained very similar results; see Hutchings & Mednick, 1977.) Use of the conviction definition has some advantages. We are relatively certain that the individual actually committed the offense recorded. Court convictions imply a high threshold for inclusion; minor offenses are less likely to result in court conviction. There are also disadvantages. The subject's behavior goes through several screening points. Someone must make a complaint to the police, or the police must happen on the scene of the crime. The police must decide that a crime has been committed and apprehend the culprit. The prosecuting attorney must decide that the evidence is sufficient to warrant a court trial. The court must then find the culprit guilty. There are decision points all along the way that may result in the elimination of individuals who have actually committed offenses against the criminal code. Such individuals might then end up among our control subjects (assuming that they do not also commit offenses for which they are convicted). In this case they add error to the analyses. Data comparing self-reports of crimes and official records of crimes suggest, however, that whereas only a fraction of crimes committed by an individual are noted by the police, those who "self-report" more crimes have more crimes recorded in the official registers. Those offenders who are not found in the official registers have typically committed very few and very minor offenses (Christie, Andenaes, & Skerbaekk, 1965).

Labeling of the adoptee

The advantage of the adoption method is the good separation of genetic and rearing contributions to the adoptee's development. But the adoptions were not arranged as controlled experiments. The adoption agency's prime concern was the welfare of the adoptee and the adoptive parents. Prospective adoptive parents were routinely informed about the criminal convictions of the biological parents. This could result in the labeling of the adoptee; this in turn might affect the likelihood that the adoptee would commit criminal acts. Thus the convictions of the biological parents might have had an environmental impact on the adoptee via the reactions of the adoptive parents.

We examined one hypothesis related to this possibility. If the biological parents received a criminal conviction before the adoption, it is likely that the adoptive parents were so informed; if the biological parents' first conviction occurred after the adoption, the adoptive parents could not have been informed. Of the convicted biological parents, 37% had received their first conviction before the adoption took place. In these cases, the adoptive parents were likely to have been informed of this criminal record. In 63% of the cases the first conviction occurred after the adoption; in these cases the conviction information could *not* have been transmitted to the adoptive parents. For all convicted biological parents, the probability of a conviction in their adopted-away son was 15.9%. In cases in which the biological parent was first convicted before adoption, 15.6% of the male adoptees were convicted. In cases in which the biological parent was convicted after the adoption, 16.1% of the male adoptees were convicted. In the case of female adoptees, these figures were 4% and 4%.

These analyses utilized convictions. In a previous analysis with a large subsample of this population a very similar result was obtained by studying the effect of timing of the initial arrest of the biological father (Hutchings & Mednick, 1977). Additional analyses by type or severity of crime revealed no effect of the adoptive parents' having been informed o˚ the convictions of the biological parents. The fact that the adoptive parents had been informed of the biological parents' convictions did not alter the likelihood that the adoptive son would be convicted. This result should not be interpreted as suggesting that labeling (as defined) had no effect on the adoptees' lives. It did not, however, affect the probability that the adoptee would be convicted for a criminal act.

Denmark as a research site

This project was carried out in Denmark; on most crime-related social dimensions, Denmark must rank among the most homogeneous of the Western nations. This fact may have implications for the interpretation of this study. An environment with low variability permits better expression of existing genetic tendencies in individuals living in that environment. This factor probably magnifies the expression of any genetic influence. At the same time, however, the Danish population probably has less genetic variability than some Western nations; this, of course, would minimize the expression of genetic influence in research conducted in Denmark. It is very likely impossible to balance these two considerations quantitatively. We are reassured regarding the generality of our findings by similar results in adoption studies in Sweden and Iowa (Bohman et al., 1982; Crowe, 1975; Cadoret, 1978).

Summary and conclusions

In a total population of adoptions, we noted a relation between biological-parent criminal convictions and criminal convictions in their adopted-away children. The relation is particularly strong for *chronic* adoptee and biological-parent offenders. There was no evidence that the type of biological-parent conviction was related to the type of adoptee conviction. A number of potentially confounding variables were considered; none of these proved sufficient to explain the genetic relation. We conclude that some factor is transmitted by convicted parents that increases the likelihood that their children will be convicted for criminal law offenses. This is especially true of chronic offenders. Because the transmitted factor must be biological, this implies that biological factors are involved in the etiology of at least some criminal behavior.

Biological factors and their interaction with social variables may make useful contributions to our understanding of the causes of criminal behavior.

Acknowledgments

This research was supported by USPHS Grant 31353 from the Center for Studies of Crime and Delinquency. We thank Professor Daniel Glaser, Professor Marvin Wolfgang, and Professor Malcolm Klein for their critical reading of this manuscript.

References

Bohman, M., Cloninger, C., Sigvardsson, S., & von Knorring, A. L. (1982). Predisposition to petty criminality in Swedish adoptees: Genetic and environmental heterogeneity. *Archives of General Psychiatry, 39*(11), 1233–41.

Cadoret, R. J. (1978). Psychopathy in adopted away offspring of biological parents with antisocial behavior. *Archives of General Psychiatry, 35,* 176–84.

Christiansen, K. O. (1977a). A review of studies of criminality among twins. In S. A. Mednick & K. O. Christiansen (Eds.), *Biosocial bases of criminal behavior* (pp. 45–88). New York: Gardner Press.

Christiansen, K. O. (1977b). A preliminary study of criminality among twins. In S. A. Mednick & K. O. Christiansen (Eds.), *Biosocial bases of criminal behavior* (pp. 89–108). New York: Gardner Press.

Christie, N., Andenaes, J., & Skerbaekk, S. (1965). A study of self-reported crime. *Scandinavian Studies in Criminology, 1,* 86–116.

Crowe, R. (1975). Adoptive study of psychopathy: Preliminary results from arrest records and psychiatric hospital records. In R. Fieve, D. Rosenthal, & H. Brill (Eds.), *Genetic research in psychiatry*. Baltimore, MD: Johns Hopkins University Press.

Haller, M. H. (1968). Social science and genetics: A historical perspective. In D. Glass (Ed.), *Genetics*. New York: Rockefeller University Press.

Hurwitz, S., & Christiansen, K. O. (1971). *Kriminologi*. Copenhagen: Glydendal.

Hutchings, B., & Mednick, S. A. (1977). Registered criminality in the adoptive and biological parents of registered male criminal adoptees. In S. A. Mednick & K. O. Christiansen (Eds.), *Biosocial bases of criminal behavior* (pp. 127–42). New York: Gardner Press.

Kety, S. S., Rosenthal, D., Wender, P. H., & Schulsinger, F. (1968). The types and prevalence of mental illness in the biological adoptive families of adopted schizophrenics. In D. Rosenthal & S. S. Kety (Eds.), *The transmission of schizophrenia*. Oxford: Pergamon.

Sarbin, T. R., & Miller, J. E. (1970). Demonism revisited: The XYY chromosomal anomaly. *Issues in Criminology, 5,* 195–207.

Svalastoga, K. (1959). *Prestige, class and mobility*. Copenhagen: Gyldendal.

Van Dusen, K., Mednick, S. A., Gabrielli, W. F., & Hutchings, B. (1983). Social class and crime in an adoption cohort. *Journal of Criminal Law and Criminology, 74*(1), 249–69.

Wolfgang, M. E., Figlio, R. M., & Sellin, T. (1972). *Delinquency in a birth cohort*. University of Chicago Press.

6   Genetic and environmental factors in antisocial behavior disorders

C. R. Cloninger and I. I. Gottesman

Introduction

Recent studies of twins and adoptees have begun to clarify how genetic and environmental factors interact in the development of antisocial behavior. Juvenile delinquency and conduct disorders, adult criminality and antisocial personality disorder, and substance abuse are partly overlapping syndromes, but their genetic relation to one another is uncertain. Antisocial behavior is more common in men than in women, and this sex difference has been helpful to those attempting to understand the transmission and expression of risk for antisocial behavior. In this chapter, we shall review family data from our research programs in St. Louis, Sweden, and Denmark on antisocial behavior and related psychiatric disorders in both men and women with particular attention to recent studies based on general populations of twins and adoptees.

Antisocial personality and related psychiatric disorders

Antisocial personality (ASP) is a disorder manifested by recurrent antisocial and delinquent behavior during adolescence, such as running away from home, fighting, and getting into trouble at school (truancy, suspension, expulsion) as well frequent criminality, poor job performance, and marital instability during adulthood (Guze, 1976; Robins, 1966). Most individuals with uncomplicated ASP commit a small number of petty property offenses during adolescence and early childhood and show little overt criminal behavior after middle age (Bohman, Cloninger, Sigvardsson, & von Knorring, 1982). Those who commit repeated or violent crimes often have alcohol or drug abuse as a complication of their personality disorder. Antisocial personality is about four times more prevalent in men than in women in the United States, and antisocial women have more ill relatives than do antisocial men. This is illustrated in Table 6.1 by data on 277 first-degree relatives of 60 antisocial probands studied in the

Table 6.1. *Antisocial personality in first-degree relatives of antisocial probands*

Sex of ASP probands[a]	Prevalence in general population		Proportion of affected first-degree relatives			
			Men		Women	
	N	%	%	$r \pm$ S.E.	%	$r \pm$ S.E.
Men	329	3.3	16.8 ($N = 119.2$)	.43 ± .07	4.4 ($N = 113.2$)	.33 ± .11
Women	318	0.9	27.7 ($N = 21.7$)	.49 ± .11	10.1 ($N = 19.7$)	.44 ± .16

Note: Overall correlation between relatives is 0.43 ± .05.
[a] ASP, Antisocial personality.

Source: Cloninger et al. (1975, 1978).

United States (Cloninger, Reich, & Guze, 1975; Cloninger, Christiansen, Reich, & Gottesman, 1978). It is possible to estimate the tetrachoric correlation in liability to ASP between relatives from the estimates of the population prevalences and the observed concordance between relatives. Taking sex differences in the population prevalence into account, the four correlations between probands and relatives of either sex did not differ significantly from one another ($r = .43 \pm .05$) despite the fourfold difference in prevalence by sex. This suggests that the familial (genetic plus environmental) factors relevant to the development of ASP are largely the same in men and women. The sex differences in prevalence are due to a higher threshold for expression in women than in men (Cloninger et al, 1975, 1978). In other words, women who develop ASP must have a greater (genetic plus environmental) liability to ASP than men do on average.

What, then, is the clinical counterpart in women of mild ASP in men? What are the clinical characteristics of women whose liability to ASP is greater than the threshold for men but not women? Cloninger (1978) has presented clinical and family data indicating that some cases of Briquet's syndrome or somatization disorder (SD) in women have a common etiology with ASP in men. Clinically, patients with either ASP or SD are described as impulsive and attention seeking, but not necessarily histrionic. High somatic anxiety is characteristic of antisocial men (Robins, 1966), and poor socialization or antisocial behavior is characteristic of somatizer women (Cloninger & Guze, 1973; Guze, Woodruff, & Clayton, 1971). Somatization disorder and ASP aggregate in the same families. There is an excess of ASP and SD in the relatives of probands with either

Table 6.2. *Familial aggregation of antisocial personality and somatization disorder*

Diagnosis and sex of probands	Observed prevalence of illness in general population		Observed prevalence of illness in first-degree relatives					
			Antisocial men		Antisocial women		Somatizer women	
	N	%	N	%	N	%	N	%
Antisocial men	329	3.3	54	25.9	79	6.3	79	9.9
Antisocial women	318	0.9	5	40.0	13	15.4	13	24.0
Somatizer	153	2.4	20	15.0	56	0	56	25.8

Note: Prevalences of somatization disorder and antisocial personality are age-corrected.

Source: Cloninger et al. (1975). Data obtained from interviews with subjects, all subjects were white.

disorder (Table 6.2). Moreover, women with ASP have more relatives with either ASP or SD than do women with SD only. Thus SD appears to be the female counterpart of mild liability to ASP.

Recent results from the Stockholm adoption study support these results about sex differences in the expression of liability to ASP (Bohman, Cloninger, von Knorring, & Sigvardsson, 1984; Cloninger, Sigvardsson, von Knorring, & Bohman, 1984; Sigvardsson, von Knorring, Bohman, & Cloninger, 1984). Four types of families with different clinical features in men and women were found to have distinct genetic and environmental antecedents (Table 6.3). Alcohol abuse was the most prominent clinical characteristic of men in two of these family types (milieu-limited and male-limited alcoholism). Criminal behavior was the most prominent feature of the men in the other two family types.

In one of the latter family types, the men committed property offenses but not crimes against persons. The women also committed property offenses in families with strong genetic loading (usually both biological parents criminal). In families with milder genetic loading, the women had prominent multiple somatic complaints from an early age. These women had a pattern of two or more sick leaves per year for diverse somatic complaints.

In the other family type associated with prominent criminal behavior, the men committed a variety of crimes, including crimes of violence. The women in these families with violent men had a high frequency of back-

Table 6.3. *Family typology of somatization, alcohol abuse, and criminality from the Stockholm adoption study*

Type of family and sex	Characteristic age of onset	Alcohol abuse	Clinical characteristics	
			Criminality	Somatization
Milieu-limited alcoholism				
Women	Adult	Usually mild	None	None
Men	Adult	Usually mild	None	?[a]
Male-limited alcoholism				
Women	Teenage	None	None	Diversiform pattern
Men	Teenage	Most prominent feature, recurrent, often treated	Occasional violence (only after alcohol abuse)	?[a]
Property crime				
Women	Teenage	None	Occasional, in severe cases; property offenses only	Most prominent feature, diversiform pattern
Men	Teenage	None	Property offenses only	?[a]
Violent crime				
Women	Teenage	Occasional	Occasional	Most prominent feature, high frequency
Men	Teenage	Recurrent, seldom treated	Most prominent feature, frequent violence; seldom property offenses	?[a]

[a] Studies of somatization in men are still in progress.

Source: Bohman et al. (1984).

aches, abdominal complaints, and psychiatric disability (Cloninger, in press). These family types were found to be genetically distinct from one another (Bohman, in press). This suggests that different patterns of somatization and of criminal offenses have distinct genetic determination. Twin data concerning this will be examined in the next section.

What about the familial relation between ASP and alcoholism? Is alcoholism also a mild expression of liability to ASP, or is it a consequence of ASP itself? Family data on primary alcoholism and ASP are summarized in Table 6.4 (Cloninger, 1979). Primary alcoholism is familial ($r = .59 \pm .04$), but there is no excess of ASP in the male relatives of nonantisocial alcoholic probands (4%, $r = .03 \pm .06$, not significant). Antisocial personality probands have a slight excess of male relatives with alcohol abuse who do not meet criteria for ASP (15%, $r = .18 \pm .07$), but this is not adjusted for social-class differences from the general population. At least in most cases, primary alcoholism and ASP are genetically independent. This is supported by adoption studies that show no excess of alcoholics among the adopted-away children of antisocial biological parents (Bohman et al., 1982; Cloninger, et al., 1984) and vice versa (Goodwin, Schulsinger, Hermansen, Guze, & Winokur, 1973). Thus alcohol abuse may be a consequence of the behavioral disorder of ASP, but most cases of alcohol abuse in the absence of ASP have a different etiology than does ASP.

Criminality studies involving twins

Many studies of antisocial behavior have been carried out with twins. The results are summarized in Table 6.5 for juvenile delinquency and adult criminality in industrialized societies. These results have markedly different implications for the role of genetic factors in juvenile delinquency and adult criminality. The fact that all the concordance rates are high and about equal regardless of sex or zygosity resembles the result observed when an infectious disease like measles is studied by the twin method. Because there is no difference between monozygotic (MZ) and dizygotic (DZ) rates despite the difference in degree of genetic relatedness, genetic factors appear to be unimportant in most cases of juvenile delinquency. This is consistent with the observation of West and Farrington (1973) that criminality in parents is more strongly associated with delinquency in offspring *after puberty* than before puberty.

Wolfgang (1974) presented data on the risk of crime in a birth cohort up to age 27. The probability of ever having been arrested is .05 at age 12, .35 at age 17, and .43 at age 27. Thus most teenage delinquents were *not*

Table 6.4. *Primary alcoholism and antisocial personality in the general population and first-degree relatives of alcoholic or antisocial probands*

Diagnosis of proband	Prevalence in general population		Proportion of affected first-degree relatives			
			PALC		ASP	
	N	%	%	$r \pm$ S.E.	%	$r \pm$ S.E.
PALC	751	7.6	35.2 ($N = 270$)	$.59 \pm .04^a$	3.7 ($N = 516$)	$.03 \pm .06$
ASP	329	3.3	15.0 ($N = 120$)	$.18 \pm .07^a$	16.7 ($N = 120$)	$.43 \pm .07^a$

Note: PALC denotes primary alcoholism; ASP, antisocial personality. Data are for male probands only.
[a] Correlation between proband and illness in relatives significant ($p < 0.05$).

prepubertal delinquents, but most adult criminals were delinquent as teenagers. The probability of being arrested as an adult (older than age 18 years) is .23 overall; it is .43 among those with any juvenile arrest and .12 among others. Thus samples that begin with juvenile delinquents or with adult criminals represent biased samples that have exaggerated the overlap between juvenile delinquency and adult criminality.

The results on adult criminality have consistently demonstrated substantial differences according to zygosity. The early twin studies were based on highly selected samples, but two more recent studies were based on general populations of twins studied in Norway by Dalgaard and Kringlen (1976) and in Denmark by Christiansen and his associates (Christiansen, 1977; Cloninger et al., 1978; Wolfgang, 1974) in the largest sample in the literature. The probandwise concordances for penal code violations ("narrowly" defined crime) are 26% and 30% in DZ twins and 41% and 51% in MZ twins in the Norwegian and Danish samples, respectively. The differences by zygosity are not significant in the smaller Norwegian sample but highly significant in the Danish sample.

A detailed analysis of preliminary Danish material was presented earlier according to sex and zygosity (Cloninger et al., 1978). A final update of Christiansen's data is presented in Table 6.6 for all twins who were born on the Danish Islands east of the Little Belt from 1881 to 1910 and who survived to age 15. The correlations were .74 for MZ twins and .47 for DZ twins in the Danish sample. Twice the difference between the MZ and DZ correlations provides an estimate of 54% for the heritability of liability to crime. Crime was defined by Christiansen as illegal acts (*egentlig*) that have been sanctioned by some kind of conditional or un-

Table 6.5. *Pairwise twin concordance rates for juvenile delinquency and crime*

Investigator	Sex	Identical twins (MZ)		Fraternal same-sex twins (DZ)	
		No. of pairs	% concordant	No. of pairs	% concordant
Juvenile delinquency					
Rosanoff, Handy, & Plesset (1941)	M	29	100	17	71
Rosanoff et al. (1941)	F	12	92	9	100
Kranz[a] (1937)	M/F	16	69	22	59
Hayashi[b] (1967)	M	15	80	4	75
Sugamata [cited in Hayashi (1967)]	M	6	83	—	—
Shields (1977)	M	5	80	9	78
Adult criminality					
Lange (1931)	—	13	77	17	12
Rosanoff et al. (1941)	M	38	76	23	22
Rosanoff et al. (1941)	F	7	86	4	25
Stumpfl (1936)	M	15	60	17	41
Kranz (1937)	M[c]	31	65	43	54
Yoshimasu (1961)	M	28	61	18	11
Dalgaard & Kringlen (1976)	M[d]	31	26	54	25
Christiansen et al. (1974, 1977)	M[e]	73	34	146	18
Christiansen et al. (1974, 1977)	F[e]	15	20	28	7

[a] Dizygotic (DZ) pairs include 14 opposite-sex pairs.
[b] Includes one new monozygotic (MZ) pair concordant at follow-up (Gottesman, Carey, & Hanson, personal communication, 1980) and excludes one discordant pair of opposite-sex dizygotic.
[c] Two DZ probands are female.
[d] Probandwise, 41% and 26%, respectively.
[e] Update the Christiansen et al. (1977); probandwise, male, 51% and 30%; female, 33% and 13%. This is complete information on all twins born on the Danish Islands (1881–1910).

Source: Gottesman, Carey, and Hanson (1983).

conditional deprivation of liberty after the age of 15 years, the legal age for adult responsibility in Denmark (see Wolf, 1983). In contrast, misdemeanors that were not sanctioned by loss of liberty were shown by Christiansen (1974) to be less heritable.

Dalgaard and Kringlen (1976) suggested that their Norwegian twin data indicated that the greater similarity of MZ twins was caused by greater similarity of environmental experiences. To test this hypothesis they stratified twins according to their degree of psychological closeness to one another. As expected, a slightly greater proportion of MZ twins than of

Table 6.6. *Concordance and correlation for criminality in Christiansen's twins born on the Danish Islands (1881–1910) according to sex and zygosity*

Zygosity	Sex Proband–cotwin	Number of pairs Total	Affected[a]	Con-cordant	Probandwise concordance f/n	%	Corre-lation
MZ	Male–male	365	73	25	50/98	51.0	.74 ± .07
MZ	Female–female	347	15	3	6/18	33.3	.74 ± .12
DZ	Male–male	700	146	26	52/172	30.2	.47 ± .06
DZ	Female–male	2073	30	7	7/30	23.3	.23 ± .10
DZ	Male–female	2073	198	7	7/198	3.5	.23 ± .10
DZ	Female–female	690	28	2	4/30	13.3	.46 ± .11

[a] Number of affected pairs refers to those with at least one criminal proband. There are 483 criminals among 4,997 twin men (9.9%) and 79 criminals among 5,233 twin women (1.5%), including twins of unknown zygosity. This is based on the final update of data November 7, 1980 after exhaustive efforts to determine the zygosity of all criminals.

DZ twins were psychologically close (84% of 31 vs. 74% of 54). Among pairs who were psychologically close, there were no appreciable differences in criminal concordance by zygosity, so the authors argued that environmental influences caused criminality. However, this environmental hypothesis would predict increased criminal concordance among close MZ pairs and decreased concordance among distant MZ pairs. In fact, the opposite was observed! Therefore, a preferable interpretation is that criminality is associated with a lack of psychological attachment or closeness to others. Thus Dalgaard and Kringlen stratified their sample according to a personality variable correlated with criminality, not according to an objective measure of early home environment. Adoption studies have provided a more sensitive test of gene–environment interaction and are discussed later.

Adult criminality is a heterogeneous clinical phenomenon. A diverse set of secular changes in attitudes, historical events (e.g., enemy occupation of a homeland), personality traits, and psychiatric disorders can lead to crime. The two most common psychiatric disorders associated with adult criminality are ASP and alcoholism. The Stockholm adoption study has shown that crime associated with alcohol abuse is often committed against persons, whereas crime in the absence of alcohol abuse is nearly always committed against property only (Bohman et al., 1982). Eysenck and Eysenck (1977) have also shown that criminals who commit different types of crime are distinguishable according to personality traits. Property

Table 6.7. *Concordance and correlation for type of crime in Christiansen's male twins born on the Danish Islands, 1881–1910*

Type of crime in proband	Zygosity	Probandwise concordance for type of crime in cotwins					
		Person			Property only		
		f/n	%	r ± S.E.	f/n	%	r ± S.E.
Against person	MZ	10/24	41.7	.77 ± .11[a]	4/24	16.7	.24 ± 13[b]
	DZ	8/39	20.5	.52 ± .10[a]	9/39	23.1	.35 ± .10[b]
Against property only	MZ	4/70	5.7	.18 ± .13[c]	28/70	40.0	.67 ± .08
	DZ	9/122	7.4	.22 ± .13[c]	20/122	16.4	.29 ± .07

Note: The prevalence of crime against persons in male twins is 139/4997 = 2.8% and of crime against property only is 336/4997 = 6.7%.
[a] $2(r_{MZ} - r_{DZ})$, an estimate of heritability, is .50 for liability to crimes against persons.
[b] $2(r_{MZ} - r_{DZ})$ is .78 for liability to crimes against property.
[c] There is no overlap in genetic liability to crimes against persons and property only ($r_{MZ} = r_{DZ}$).

offenders and violent criminals have both low neuroticism scores and high "psychoticism" scores on their inventory (i.e., they are unreliable and do not form social attachments easily according to Eysenck). Property offenders have low extraversion scores, whereas violent offenders are extraverted and highly impulsive on the Eysenck Personality Questionnaire. The Stockholm adoption study has suggested that petty property criminals have a genetic predisposition distinct from that of criminals who commit violent offenses against persons, as noted in Table 6.3.

The hypothesis that predisposition to committing only property offenses is independent of predisposition to committing crimes against persons can be tested by analysis of Christiansen's twin data. This is summarized in Table 6.7. Heritability of liability to property offenses is 78%, and heritability of liability to crimes against persons is 50%. More remarkable is the finding that there is no significant genetic overlap between the liabilities to crimes against persons and crimes against property only. Future studies of criminality should distinguish criminals according to both number and type of offense as well as those with associated alcohol abuse.

The Danish twin study also provides evidence of the sex specificity of factors in adult criminality. Male and female criminals occurred in the same pair significantly less often than expected if the same familial factors caused criminality in both sexes. Thus the correlation in opposite-sex

DZ pairs ($r = .23 \pm .10$) was lower than in same-sex male pairs ($r = .47 \pm .06$) or same-sex female pairs ($r = .46 \pm .11$). The overlap between familial (genetic and/or environmental) causes of male and female criminality was significantly large but incomplete (50% $\pm$ 19). Further information about these sex differences has been obtained from recent adoption studies.

Adoption studies of antisocial behavior

Adoption studies have been carried out using a variety of measures of antisocial behavior with mixed results. Zur Nieden (1951) in Germany emphasized the good outcomes of most foster-reared children of antisocial parents followed into adulthood. However, she actually found that bad outcome or delinquency occurred in 13% of 15 children of criminal parents and 14% of the 14 children of other antisocial parents compared with only 4% of the total 114 children in the follow-up.

Crowe studied 37 adopted-away children of female felons in Iowa and found an increase in adult criminality and ASP but not alcoholism or any other disorders compared with 37 nonadopted controls (Bohman et al., 1982; Crowe, 1972). The proportion of ill adopted-away children that he observed was the same as the prevalence of 19% observed by Cloninger et al. in nonadopted children of criminal women (see Table 6.1). Crowe found that 19% of the 37 adult adopted-away children of criminal mothers had a criminal conviction: one for two felony property offenses, two for single felony property offenses, four for misdemeanor property offenses, and one for a misdemeanor sexual offense. There were no crimes of violence.

Crowe detected no significant environmental effects in his univariate analysis of case-control data. He partially matched for age at adoptive decree but nevertheless observed that children of criminals with a history of late placement became criminals more often than controls with late placement. This suggested gene–environment interaction, but the difference was not significant ($.05 < p < .10$). More recently, Cadoret, Cain, and Crowe (1983) reanalyzed their data using multivariate methods and confirmed the presence of nonadditive interaction between genetic and environmental factors in adolescent delinquent behavior.

With the benefit of a larger sample size and greater variability without case selection and matching, Hutchings and Mednick detected contributions from criminality in both biological and adoptive parents (Hutchings, 1972; Hutchings & Mednick, 1975). They found that when the adoptive, but not biological, father was criminal 12% of 52 adopted sons were criminals. This risk was not significantly different from risks observed when neither father was criminal (10% of 333 sons) or when only the biological father was criminal (21% of 219 sons). However, more sons were criminal when only the biological father was criminal than when neither father was criminal (21% vs. 10%, $\psi^2 = 11.7$, $p < .001$). More important, when both the biological and adoptive fathers were criminal, the risk in sons was greater than when only the biological father was criminal (36% of 58 vs. 21% of 219, $\psi^2 = 5.8$, $p < .02$). The cross-fostering data of Hutching and Mednick suggest possible gene–environment interaction similar to that demonstrated for alcoholism in the Stockholm adoption study. Unfortunately, classification for both alcohol abuse and criminality was not done by Hutchings and Mednick. Bohman (1978) suggested that the inheritance of a predisposition to criminality could be due primarily to crime as a complication of alcoholism.

However, as noted briefly in an earlier section on ASP and related disorders, recent results of the Stockholm adoption study indicate that predisposition to petty property offenses unassociated with alcohol abuse is heritable independently of any predisposition to alcoholism. The population includes all 862 men and 913 women born out of wedlock in Stockholm, Sweden, from 1930 to 1949 and adopted by nonrelatives at an early age. The sample has been described in detail elsewhere (Bohman et al, 1982; Cloninger, Sigvardsson, Bohman, & von Knorring, 1982; Sigvardsson, Cloninger, Bohman, & von Knorring, 1982). The results regarding crime and alcohol abuse in biological parents and their adopted-away sons are summarized in Tables 6.8 and 6.9. Criminality alone in the biological parents increased the risk of crime but not alcoholism in the adopted-away sons compared with sons of other parents (7.4% vs. 3.5%), whereas the sons of parents with both crime and alcoholism were usually alcohol abusers and not criminal. Further analysis showed that parents with a diagnosis of alcoholism who had crime as a late complication of severe alcohol abuse had an excess of children with alcohol abuse but not crime. When crime occurred as a complication of alcoholism, it was characteristically associated with crimes of violence. In contrast, biological parents with property crimes had an excess of children with property crimes only and no alcohol abuse.

The biological parents of adopted women with penal offenses had also committed an excess of offenses. Such crimes were nearly always property offenses or minor misconduct. In addition, the 16 women who had committed crime alone had at least one parent with one or more criminal convictions more often than the 39 men with crime alone (50% vs. 21%, $\psi^2 = 4.78$, $p < .05$) and more fathers with repeated convictions (31% vs.

Table 6.8. *Prediction of crime and/or alcohol abuse in 862 adopted sons on the basis of crime and/or alcohol abuse in biological parents*

Registration of biological parents					Registration of adopted sons	
Crime only	Alcohol only	Both[a]	Number of adoptees (N)	Type of registration	Observed (row %)	Predicted (row %)
No	No	No	463	Crime	3.5	3.6
				Alcohol	7.1	7.4
				Both	6.5	6.2
Yes	No	No	108	Crime	7.4	6.9
				Alcohol	11.1	10.1
				Both	6.5	6.2
No	Yes	No	141	Crime	5.0	4.8
				Alcohol	12.8	12.2
				Both	9.9	10.1
No	No	Yes	131	Crime	6.1	6.1
				Alcohol	16.8	16.3
				Both	7.6	8.1
Yes	Yes	No	10	Crime	0.0	9.0
				Alcohol	10.0	16.1
				Both	0.0	8.8
Yes	No	Yes	5	Crime	0.0	11.0
				Alcohol	0.0	20.8
				Both	0.0	6.9
No	Yes	Yes	4	Crime	0.0	11.1
				Alcohol	25.0	22.2
				Both	25.0	22.2

Note: The value predicted by the three types of biological-parent registration (crime, alcohol, both) agree well with those observed (residual goodness of fit $\chi^2 = 3.0$, d.f. $= 9$, $p = .96$).
[a] This column indicates that a single individual was reported for both crime and alcohol abuse.

5%, $\psi^2 = 6.97$, $p < .01$). This indicates that genetic predisposition to property criminality must be more severe in order for a woman to become criminal than for a man. This is the same pattern observed for ASP in the United States.

Certain postnatal environmental factors increased the risk of property crime in both sexes, but different factors were important in each sex. Low occupational status of the adoptive father and multiple temporary placements of the adoptee were predictive of criminality in men but not in women. Rural adoptive homes and prolonged institutional care were pre-

Table 6.9. *Parameters of the linear-logistic model predicting crime and/or alcohol abuse in adopted men*

Parental predictor variable	Adoptee response category	Logistic function estimate[a]	χ^2	d.f.	Probability
Intercept	Crime	−2.22	53.2	1	<.01
	Alcohol	−1.43	41.4	1	<.01
	Both	−2.08	58.6	1	<.01
Crime only	Crime	+0.36	3.1	1	.08
	Alcohol	+0.19	1.3	1	.26
	Both	−0.02	0.0	1	.92
Alcohol abuse only	Crime	+0.21	1.0	1	.32
		+0.31	4.5	1	.03
		+0.26	2.6	1	.11
Both crime and alcohol	Crime	+0.35	2.9	1	.09
	Alcohol	+0.48	11.2	1	<.01
	Both	+0.17	0.9	1	.34
Residual	—	—	3.0	9	.96

[a] The model estimated the natural logarithm of the ratio of the number of sons in the designated response category (crime, alcohol, or both) to the number of sons with neither crime nor alcohol abuse.

dictive of criminality in women but not in men. These sex-specific environmental effects may explain the partial independence of liability to crime in men and women that were observed in twins.

Cross-fostering analysis of the Swedish adoptees revealed nonadditive interaction of genetic and environmental risk. In other words, men and women were unlikely to become criminals unless they were at high risk as a consequence of both their biological-parent background and their postnatal environment. This is shown in Figure 6.1 for men and Figure 6.2 for women.

It is important to note that, in the same Swedish population, Bohman found no excess of delinquency before the age of 12 years in adopted-away children of criminal biological parents (Bohman, 1972). Thus the adoption studies appear to confirm the important difference between pre-pubertal "garden-variety" delinquency and later criminal behavior that has also been noted in twins and singletons in relatively intact families.

Discussion

Antisocial behavior has a complex developmental background that is influenced by multiple genetic and environmental factors (Hurwitz &

Christiansen, 1983). The data presented here indicate that the etiologies of prepubertal delinquency, adult property crime, adult crime against persons, and alcoholism are relatively distinct qualitatively from one another in terms of their genetic antecedents.

CLASSIFICATION OF PREDISPOSITION TO PETTY CRIME		OBSERVED MALE ADOPTEES	
CONGENITAL	POSTNATAL	ROW TOTAL (N)	ROW % WITH PETTY CRIME ONLY
Low	Low	666	2.9
Low	High	120	6.7
High	Low	66	12.1
High	High	10	40.0

Figure 6.1. Cross-fostering analysis of petty criminality (without alcohol abuse) in male adoptees. "Congenital" refers to variables about biological parents, whereas "postnatal" refers to variables about rearing experiences and adoptive placement. The classification of predisposition depends on whether the background variables are more like the average characteristics of adoptees with petty crime only (classified as high) than like those of adoptees with no crime and/or alcohol abuse (classified as low).

IS PREDISPOSITION TO PETTY CRIME?		OBSERVED FEMALE ADOPTEES	
CONGENITAL	POSTNATAL	ROW TOTAL (N)	ROW % WITH PETTY CRIME
No	No	566	0.5
No	Yes	209	2.9
Yes	No	93	2.2
Yes	Yes	45	11.1

Figure 6.2. Cross-fostering analysis of petty crime in female adoptees. "Congenital" refers to variables about biological parents, whereas "postnatal" refers to variables about rearing experiences and adoptive placement. The classification of predisposition depends on whether the background variables are more like the average characteristics of adoptees with petty crime only (classified as high) than like those of adoptees with no crime and/or alcohol abuse (classified as low).

There is no evidence that genetic factors are important in prepubertal delinquency as a class. The relevant factors are aspects of home environment and sociocultural factors as shown by the large correlations between sibs reared together regardless of degree of genetic relationship. Thus the only relation between antisocial behavior before and after puberty may be due to indirect associations, such as adult criminals providing deprived childhood environments. Of course, a subset of young offenders who become adult offenders can be identified by follow-back studies (Robins, 1966), and they could be early-onset cases deserving "genetic" explanations. However, past studies of juvenile delinquency are difficult to interpret because attention is seldom paid to the possibility that antisocial behavior at different ages has different antecedents. The prospective adoption study of Bohman (1972) clearly separates the often confounded genetic and environmental antecedents of these behaviors and casts doubt on the notion that childhood conduct disorders as a class are simply the early phase of adult antisocial behavior disorders as suggested by Robins (1966). This does not mean that ASP and adult criminality have no antecedent behavioral manifestations before puberty. For example, attention-deficit disorder (ADD) in childhood may increase the risk of postpubertal delinquency and ASP (Satterfield, Hoppe, & Schell, 1982), and adoption data about ADD suggest genetic overlap with ASP and SD (Morrison & Stewart, 1973). Unfortunately, the relevant studies are difficult to interpret because differences in the age at which antisocial symptoms have occurred have not been related to differences in familial history and environment.

Both twin and adoption studies indicate that genetic factors are important in both crimes against property and crimes against persons, but there is little overlap between genetic predisposition to these two types of criminality when genetic and environmental antecedents are distinguished. The weak familial aggregation of these different patterns of criminal behavior seems to be due to home and/or neighborhood environmental influences. Most cases of antisocial personality coming to the attention of the legal system seem to involve petty property crimes only. Violent crimes may be a complication of alcoholism or of personality traits different from those that predispose individuals to most types of property crime. Careful attention to severity (indexed in various ways, including recidivism and type of crime) and to association with substance abuse is needed in future studies.

Recent adoption data confirm the importance of both genetic and environmental factors in adult criminality, as suggested earlier by twin and family strategies. Sex differences are due to both different genetic thresholds and sex-specific environmental antecedents. The significance of gene–environment interaction has important implications for the prevention and treatment of antisocial behavior. The influence of events that take place in the first year of life on adult outcome (as demonstrated in the Stockholm adoption study) suggest that some form of social assistance to high-risk families soon after birth could be useful. Delay until school age may be appropriate for some forms of prepubertal delinquency, but it is arguable whether the antecedents of prepubertal delinquency and postpubertal antisocial behavior disorders have much in common or will respond to the same interventions. All attempts at intervention with high-risk families must be tempered by our limited ability to predict who will actually develop antisocial behavior and the imperative need to protect individual civil rights. Therefore, we must improve general social circumstances and provide help as early as possible to those who request it.

In addition, the importance of genetic factors indicates that there are biological factors predisposing to a substantial but limited extent toward the development of antisocial behavior. In turn this suggests the potential use of biological treatment to modify as yet unknown physiological substrates, especially because purely behavioral approaches and psychotherapy have had limited benefit. Biological approaches that take into account the heterogeneity of antisocial behavior disorders are described by Cloninger (1983).

The consistency of results from the Stockholm adoption study and the Danish adoption study described by Mednick, Gabrielli, and Hutchings in chapter 5 strongly indicate that both genetic and environmental factors are important in the epigenesis of adult antisocial behavior. Future studies of both the biological and social aspects of antisocial behavior must carefully consider the relation between clinical heterogeneity and etiological heterogeneity demonstrated in the recent twin and adoption studies.

Acknowledgments

This work was supported in part by USPHS Grants MH-31302 and AA-03539 to C. R. Cloninger and I. I. Gottesman, Research Scientist Development Award MH-00048 to C. R. Cloninger, and MH-25311 to S. A. Mednick.

We wish to express our appreciation for the essential contributions of our late colleague, Karl O. Christiansen, and for the advice and technical support of M. Hauge, P. Wolf, B. Hutchings, A. Kongstad, N. Nielsen, J. Goldberg, and Ruth Christiansen.

References

Bohman, M. (1972). A study of adopted children, their background, environment and adjustment. *Acta Pediatrica Scandinavia, 61,* 90–7.

Bohman, M. (1978). Some genetic aspects of alcoholism and criminality: A population of adoptees. *Archives of General Psychiatry, 35,* 269–76.

Bohman, M., Cloninger, C. R., Sigvardsson, S., & von Knorring, A.-L. (1982). Predisposition to petty criminality in Swedish Adoptees: I. Genetic and environmental heterogeneity. *Archives of General Psychiatry, 39,* 1233–41.

Bohman, M., Cloninger, C. R., von Knorring, A.-L., & Sigvardsson, S. (1984). An adoption study of somatoform disorders. III: Crossfostering analysis and genetic relationship to alcoholism and criminality. *Archives of General Psychiatry, 41,* 872–8.

Cadoret, R. J., Cain, C. A., & Crowe, R. R. (1983). Evidence for gene–environment interaction in the development of adolescent antisocial behavior. *Behavior Genetics, 13,* 301–10.

Christiansen, K. O. (1974). Seriousness of criminality and concordance among Danish twins. In R. Hood (Ed.), *Crime, criminology, and public policy.* London: Heinemann.

Christiansen, K. O. (1977). A preliminary study of criminality among twins. In S. Mednick & K. O. Christiansen (Eds.), *Biosocial bases of criminal behavior* (pp. 89–108). New York: Gardner Press.

Cloninger, C. R. (1978). The link between hysteria and sociopathy. In H. S. Akiskal & W. L. Webb (Eds.), *Psychiatric diagnosis: Exploration of biological predictors* (pp. 189–218). New York: Spectrum Press.

Cloninger, C. R. (1983). Drug treatment of antisocial behavior. In D. G. Grahame-Smith, H. Hippius, & G. Winokur (Eds.), *Psychopharmacology* (Vol. 1, pp. 353–70). Amsterdam: Excerpta Media.

Cloninger, C. R., Christiansen, K. O., Reich, T., & Gottesman, I. I. (1978). Implications of sex differences in the prevalences of antisocial personality, alcoholism, and criminality for familial transmission. *Archives of General Psychiatry, 35,* 941–51.

Cloninger, C. R., & Guze, S. B. (1973). Psychiatric illness in the families of female criminals: A study of 288 first-degree relatives. *British Journal of Psychiatry, 122,* 697–703.

Cloninger, C. R., Reich, T., & Guze, S. B. (1975). The multifactorial model of disease transmission: II. Sex differences in the familial transmission of sociopathy (antisocial personality). *British Journal of Psychiatry, 127,* 11–22.

Cloninger, C. R., Reich, T., & Wetzel, R. (1979). In D. Goodwin & C. Erikson (Eds.), *Alcoholism and affective disorders,* (pp. 57–82). New York: Spectrum Press.

Cloninger, C. R., Sigvardsson, S., Bohman, M., & von Knorring, A.-L. (1982). Predisposition to petty criminality in Swedish adoptees: II. Cross-fostering analysis of gene–environment interaction. *Archives of General Psychiatry, 39,* 1242–7.

Cloninger, C. R., Sigvardsson, S., von Knorring, A.-L., & Bohman, M. (1984). An adoption study of somatoform disorders: II. Identification of two discrete somatoform disorders. *Archives of General Psychiatry, 41,* 863–71.

Crowe, R. R. (1972). The adopted offspring of women criminal offenders: A study of their arrest records. *Archives of General Psychiatry, 27,* 600–3.

Dalgaard, O. S., & Kringlen, E. (1976). A Norwegian twin study of criminality. *British Journal of Criminality, 16,* 213–32.

Eysenck, S. B. G., & Eysenck, H. J. (1977). Personality and the classification of adult offenders. *British Journal of Criminology, 17,* 169–79.

Goodwin, D. W., Schulsinger, F., Hermansen, L., Guze, S. B., & Winokur, G. (1973). Alcohol problems in adoptees raised apart from alcoholic biological parents. *Archives of General Psychiatry, 28,* 238–43.

Gottesman, I. I., Carey, G., & Hanson, D. R. (1983). Pearls and perils in epigenetic psychopathology. In S. B. Guze, E. J. Earls, & J. E. Barrett (Eds.), *Childhood psychopathology and development* (pp. 287–300). New York: Raven Press.

Guze, S. B. (1976). *Criminality and psychiatric disorders*. New York: Oxford University Press.

Guze, S. B., Woodruff, R. A., Jr., & Clayton, P. J. (1971). Hysteria and antisocial behavior: Further evidence of an association. *American Journal of Psychiatry, 127,* 957–60.

Hayashi, S. (1967). A study of juvenile delinquency in twins. *Bulletin of the Osaka Medical School, 12,* 373–8.

Hurwitz, S., & Christiansen, K. O. (1983). *Criminology* (Engl. trans. of 3rd ed.). London: Allen & Unwin.

Hutchings, B. (1972). Environmental and genetic factors in psychopathy and criminality. Unpublished thesis, University of London.

Hutchings, B., & Mednick, S. A. (1975). Registered criminality in adoptive and biological parents of registered male criminal adoptees. In R. R. Fieve, D. Rosenthal, & H. Brill (Eds.), *Genetic research in psychiatry* (pp. 105–16). Baltimore, MD: Johns Hopkins University Press.

Kranz, F. (1937). Untersuchungen and Zwillingen in Fursorgeerziehunganstalten. *Zeitschrift Induktive Abstammungs-Vererbungslehre, 73,* 508–12.

Lange, J. (1931). *Crime as destiny* (C. Haldane, Trans.). London: Allen & Unwin.

Morrison, J. R., & Stewart, M. A. (1973). The psychiatric status of the legal families of adopted hyperactive children. *Archives of General Psychiatry, 28,* 888–91.

Robins, L. N. (1966). *Deviant children grown up*. Baltimore, MD: Williams & Wilkins.

Rosanoff, A. J., Handy, I. M., & Plesset, I. R. (1941). The etiology of child behavior difficulties, juvenile delinquency, and adult criminals with special reference to their occurrence in twins. In *Psychiatric Monograph No. 1*. Sacramento, CA: Department of Institutions.

Satterfield, J. H., Hoppe, C. M., & Schell, A. M. (1982). A prospective study of delinquency in 110 attention deficit disorder and 88 normal adolescent boys. *American Journal of Psychiatry, 139,* 795–8.

Shields, J. (1977). *Polygenic influences*. In M. Rutter & L. Hersov (Eds.), *Child psychiatry: Modern approaches* (pp. 22–46). Oxford: Blackwell.

Sigvardsson, S., Cloninger, C. R., Bohman, M., & von Knorring, A.-L. (1982). Predisposition to petty criminality in Swedish adoptees: III. Sex differences and validation of the male typology. *Archives of General Psychiatry, 39,* 1248–53.

Sigvardsson, S., von Knorring, A.-L., Bohman, M., & Cloninger, C. R. (1984). An adoption study of somatoform disorders: I. The relationship of somatization to psychiatric disability. *Archives of General Psychiatry, 41,* 853–9.

Stumpfl, F. (1936). *Die Ursprunge des Verbrechens am Lebenslauf von Zwillingen*. London: Thieme.

West, D. J., & Farrington, D. P. (1973). *Who becomes delinquent?* London: Heinemann.

Wolf, P. (1983). Denmark. In E. H. Johnson (Ed.), *International handbook of contemporary developments in criminology: Europe, Africa, the Middle East, and Asia* (pp. 163–84). Westport, CN: Greenwood Press.

Wolfgang, M. E. (1974). Crime in a birth cohort. In R. Hood (Ed.), *Crime, criminology, and public policy*. London: Heinemann.

Yoshimasu, S. (1961). The criminological significance of the family in the light of the studies of criminal twins. *Acta Criminologiae et Medicinae Legalis Japanica, 27,* 117–41.

Zur Nieden, M. (1951). The influence of constitution and environment upon development of adopted children. *Journal of Psychology, 31,* 91–5.

7 Autonomic nervous system factors in criminal behavior

P. H. Venables

Introduction

Relatively recent reviews of autonomic nervous system factors in criminal behavior (Hare, 1978; Schalling, 1978; Siddle, 1977) have covered many of the important aspects of this subject. It is useful, however, to take stock of the approaches that have been taken and to add, where appropriate, some new data. The study of criminal behavior, particularly when it involves psychophysiological investigation, appears to have developed along a broad front and is by no means exclusively the study of the offender. In consequence, we find studies on the adult criminal and the juvenile delinquent legally defined; the psychopath psychiatrically or psychometrically identified; the (as yet) normal children of criminals or psychopathic parents; the refractory child in a special school; and the child identified in a normal school as being "difficult," aggressive, or unsocialized. The implication is, to some extent, that there is a thread, or at worst a limited number of threads, common to all these approaches.

The potential thread would appear to be socialization (or lack of it) and, underlying that, notions of relative lack of fear responsivity, relative lack of ability to appreciate fear-provoking cues, and relative lack of ability to develop conditioned avoidance responses and to generalize them. Running alongside this thread and not always clearly distinguished from it is the idea that there may be individual differences in aggressivity. In addition, data in certain instances link characteristics of hyperactivity and delinquency. For example, Morrison and Stewart (1971) and Cantwell (1972) provide data suggesting a genetic linkage between hyperactivity and sociopathy, and Offord, Sullivan, Allen, and Abrams (1979) provide data relating early hyperactivity with later antisocial behavior. Many

110

studies rating children's behavior have revealed a close association between hyperactivity and aggression, commonly on the basis of results of factor analyses where items measuring aggression and hyperactivity load on the same factor (see, e.g., Venables, Fletcher, Dalais, Mitchell, Schulsinger, & Mednick, 1982). The necessarily close association between hyperactivity and aggression has been questioned, however, and if it is only the aggressive aspect of the pattern that is responsible for the association with delinquency, this needs to be taken into account. Loney, Langhorne, and Paternite (1978) make the point well: "It is clear that aggressive symptomatology figures more prominently in the hyperkinetic/MBD [minimal brain dysfunction] syndrome than is commonly supposed and that its influence is to a large degree empirically independent of the influence of hyperactive symptomatology. Thus separating the two symptom dimensions is not just useful, it is necessary."

In any investigation of biological factors in criminal behavior it must be axiomatic that an eventual criminal, antisocial, delinquent, and/or aggressive outcome is the result of both biological and environmental or social forces. In many cases the latter may be the stronger, as in the case of the "subcultural" delinquent. It is thus of major importance to attempt to control or assess the contribution of class and social factors in investigations of the role of biological factors. When the variance contributed by biological factors is comparatively small, it may only be within the relative social homogeneity of a favorable social milieu that biological factors become evident.

Finally, probably the most unresearched area is the developmental study of the relation between biological variables and delinquency. It may be that there are entirely different relations between autonomic and behavioral variables at one stage of a child's life and between the same variables at a later stage. It is thus possible that up to a certain developmental stage autonomic variables have no predictive value for later behavior, but when that stage is passed the predictive value of the variable emerges. Inevitably, those examining the development of delinquent behavior from an early age must investigate the precursors of that behavior before it has become fully manifest. This is another reason for the importance of studying children identified as hyperactive or aggressive at an early age.

This chapter is organized to take into account some of the points discussed above as we examine the ways in which particular autonomic variables are related to delinquent behavior. Each commonly studied autonomic variable is taken in turn and its relation to delinquent behavior outlined.

Tonic activity

The rationale for examining the relation between measures of tonic autonomic activity and delinquency stems partly from empirical findings (to be
reviewed) that seem reasonably strong and demand explanation, and
partly from a hypothetical approach that concerns the nature of measurable tonic activity. Implicitly rather than explicitly (in most cases) there is
the notion that levels of tonic activity as measured in a particular subject
are not "basic" but rather reflect the subject's ongoing waking activity,
which may be that of some degree of anxiety or alertness about the world
or more specifically may reflect the subject's tonic reaction to being
placed in an unfamiliar or stressful testing situation. Thus having electrodes attached to one's body and being seated in a quiet, darkened room
and told to wait for noises that will shortly be played through headphones
makes the standard prestimulus minute, during which "resting" measures
are often obtained, a mild stressor eliciting elevated "arousal" levels in
some subjects. Measures of tonic activity under these experimental conditions are probably related to the measurement of "fear responsivity"
mentioned in the introduction as a possible basis for the development and
maintenance of "socialization." It is very evident, however, that tonic
levels of "arousal" are never going to be tidy, unequivocal measures of
fear responsivity, because so much depends on the idiosyncrasies of the
experimental paradigm presentation and the extent of the subject's famil-
iarity with similar situations.

From a different point of view the lack of commonality of different
putative measures of arousal makes it difficult to feel confident that any
one of them is a measure of fear arousal. To illustrate this point, data are
available from an age cross-sectional study carried out in Mauritius (an
island in the Indian Ocean) in which four possible indices of "arousal"
were measured in the minute before the presentation of a standard set of
stimuli. These are heart rate (beats per minute); skin conductance level
(log microsiemens); skin conductance nonspecific responses (number);
and skin potential level (millivolts). There were 640 subjects in the study
consisting of five groups of 128 for each of the age groups, 5, 10, 15, 20,
and 25 years, each group being divided equally by sex, by time of day of
testing (morning vs. afternoon), and by season of testing (hot vs. cool).
Table 7.1 shows the intercorrelation between measures over the total
sample. The data show very clearly that there is no relation between any
of the measures, each of which has at some stage been considered to be a
measure of "arousal."

When the interrelations are examined separately within age groups, the

Table 7.1. *Intercorrelation between autonomic measures to tonic "arousal"*

	SCL	SCR.NS	SPL
SCR.NS	− .02	—	—
SPL	.08	.05	—
HR	.05	− .02	.06

SCR.NS, nonspecific skin conductance response; SPL, skin potential level; HR, heart rate; SCL, skin conductance level.

position is somewhat more in accord with expectations. Among the 5-year-olds (who might be thought of as the most apprehensive about being tested) four of the six correlations are significant, the largest being that between skin conductance level (SCL) and skin conductance responses nonspecific (SCR.NS), which rises to .32. However, in other age groups the significant correlations are small, never accounting for much common variance, and are sporadically distributed. The largest, between heart rate (HR) and SCR.NS in the 25-year-olds, has a value of only .34.

With this background, it is difficult to make statements invoking any higher order concept, such as fear, in regard to the relations between any one measure and delinquency.

Tonic heart rate

An early investigation of the relation of tonic HR levels and refractory behavior was that of Davies and Maliphant (1971). These workers used as their subjects boys at a residential school aged between 12.0 and 16.0 years. The boys were divided into three groups matched for age and educational level on the basis of consensus ratings by their teachers as to the "refractoriness" of their behavior. A mean value for tonic HR level, taken over four periods during the day, showed that the refractory group had a mean tonic HR of 75.6 bpm (beats per minute), which differed significantly from that of the nonrefractory group, which had a mean rate of 84.2 bpm. The "intermediate" group had a mean tonic rate of 78.5 bpm. The two extreme groups were then exposed to two experimental situations involving threat of shock and threat of loss of money for slow response time. Although ceteris paribus the law of initial value would suggest that the group with the lowest HR would show the greatest change in HR on stimulation, in fact in both experimental conditions the refractory group showed a smaller HR increase than the nonrefractory group.

Davies and Maliphant (1971) employed only 30 subjects. In contrast a study by Wadsworth (1976) was based on a sample of 5,362 subjects drawn from a population of 13,687 births in England, Wales, and Scotland, which took place in a week in 1946. Heart rate was measured at a school medical examination when the children in the sample were 11 years of age. This measure was taken after the children had waited while their mothers filled in a questionnaire. It was anticipated that the waiting period would act as a stressor. From the subjects on whom pulse rate data were available a subsample of males was drawn about whom it was possible to find data on delinquency from official records. The period for which these data were potentially available was between ages 8 and 21. Of this sample, 14.8% were delinquent. The mean HR of the controls who were not delinquent was 85.9 bpm, whereas the mean HR of those who were delinquent was 83.9 bpm, which was significantly lower than that of the controls. More impressive differences in HR were found among those 30 subjects who were sexual offenders or who had committed crimes of violence. The HR of these subjects had a mean value of 81.7 bpm.

In this study there were interesting correlations with social variables. The HR for boys who were only children was higher than that for boys from large families; the HR for boys from broken homes was lower than that for boys from intact homes. In interaction with delinquency it was found that, when there had been early emotional deprivation due to a broken home, the rates for delinquents and nondelinquents did not vary. However, when early emotional deprivation had not occurred, the rates of the delinquents were lower than those of the nondelinquents. Thus, as suggested in the introduction, there was a relation of a biological variable to delinquency when the contribution of social factors to the explained variance was minimized, but this was not shown when the social variable appeared to have more importance. A study similar to that of Davies and Maliphant was carried out by Raine and Venables (1981). The subjects in this instance were 101 male school children aged 15 years. Antisocial behavior in the classroom was assessed by each subject's form master using the Quay and Parsons (1970) Unsocialised–Psychopathic Scale of the Behavior Problem Checklist, which measured such behavior as destructiveness, screaming, disobedience, and fighting. A self-report measure of socialization was undertaken using a battery of 18 scales of which 6 were direct measures of undersocialization or delinquent personality and the remainder were personality dimensions that had either theoretically or empirically been related to antisocial behavior. The scores on the scales were factor-analyzed, and the first factor that accounted for 55% of the variance had 5 of the 6 socialization scales loading on it with values between .63 and .79. Scores on this factor were used as measures of socialization. Relations between resting HR and the socialization measures were low in the total sample. The sample, however, was divided into a low- and a high-social-class group on the basis of father's occupation according to the registrar general's classification system.

When this was done, it was found that the relation between teachers' ratings or self-ratings of undersocialization and tonic HR were $-.31$ ($p <$ .025) and $-.36$ ($p < .025$), respectively, in the high-social-class group, whereas the correlations were only $-.03$ and $-.10$ in the low-social-class group. In order to compare this study with that of Davies and Maliphant (1971), which was cited earlier, the total sample, regardless of class, was divided into three equal groups on the basis of rated socialization. The mean HR of the antisocial group was 77.0 bpm and that of the "prosocial" group 82.7. The two groups differed significantly at the $p < .02$ level, thus supporting the finding of Davies and Maliphant, if not with quite the same magnitude of HR differences between the pro- and anti-social groups shown by Davies and Maliphant.

Another means of analyzing the relation between tonic HR and delinquent diathesis is the use of high-risk procedures. In 1972 a study was started in Copenhagen by Mednick, Schulsinger, and Venables. Data were obtained on three groups of subjects: children with a schizophrenic parent, children with a "refractory" (criminal or psychopathic) parent, and controls. At the time of testing the children's mean age was 11 years. Heart rate was recorded along with other psychophysiological indices in a resting period before a set of standard stimuli were presented. Data were available on a total of 245 children. The parents of 130 of these were considered to be psychiatrically normal, and these children formed two groups on the basis of the criminality of their fathers. The mean HR of the 63 children of criminal fathers was 70.5 bpm and that of the 67 children of noncriminal fathers 74.9 bpm. The difference between these two values was significant at the $p < .025$ level. A smaller group of children, in addition to having a father designated criminal or not, also carried a diagnosis for one of the parents of chronic (B1), doubtful (D), or borderline (B3) schizophrenia, following the diagnostic system outlined by Kety, Rosenthal, Wender, Schulsinger, and Jacobsen (1978). [In view of the findings of these authors, that acute schizophrenic reaction (B2) did not appear to be inheritable, subjects whose parents had this diagnosis were omitted from the analysis.] Data were available on a total of 56 subjects. Analyses of variance using criminality of the father and schizophrenia in the father or mother as the factors show a significant interaction ($p < .04$) between these two factors. When the parental diagnosis was schizophrenia in the mother, the father being psychiatrically normal, the mean HR of the 23 children with a criminal father was 70.3 bpm and that of the 12 children with a noncriminal father was 77.7 bpm. This difference approached significance ($p < .08$). These data show that the effect on HR of the father's criminality is apparently the same whether the mother is sick (70.3 bpm) or not (70.5 bpm). However, when the father is not criminal, the effect of the mother's illness becomes apparent, although not at a significant level (77.7 bpm in the mother-sick vs. 74.9 in the mother-not-sick group from the previous analysis). When the father is schizophrenic, the effect of criminality on HR is the reverse of that with a psychiatrically normal father. The mean HR for the 10 children of a schizophrenic criminal father is 76.9 bpm, and that for 11 children of a schizophrenic noncriminal father 71.3 bpm. This difference is not significant, however. The material was also examined on the basis of the father's psychopathy rather than criminality. In a group of children whose mother was rated normal there was no significant effect of the father's psychopathy on the children's tonic HR. A similar nonsignificant effect of the father's psychopathy was evident in a group who had a sick mother and hence a more complicated etiological background.

In summary, these high-risk data appear to show several noteworthy trends. First, when psychiatric complications in the father are eliminated, his legally defined criminality has an effect on his child's HR that is consonant with other studies relating criminality or delinquency with low tonic HR. If the father is diagnosed as psychopathic, his effect on the child's HR is minimal. If, however, he is diagnosed as schizophrenic, the effect of his criminality on his offspring is the reverse of that in the children of psychiatrically normal fathers. It is possible in the case of psychopathic diagnosis that we may be dealing with an unclearly defined diagnostic category, whereas in the case of children of a schizophrenic father criminality might suggest a high degree of "acting out" secondary "psychopathy" and hence a more unfavorable level of schizophrenic pathology leading to a higher HR in the children. Venables (1975) has reviewed data showing a higher tonic HR among schizophrenic than nonschizophrenic subjects.

In view of the link mentioned earlier between childhood hyperactivity and later criminality, it is worthwhile examining some of the data that suggest a link between hyperactivity and HR. The data have been reviewed by Hastings and Barkley (1978) and by Rosenthal and Allen (1978). As far as HR is concerned, the findings are equivocal, some studies reporting a lower HR in hyperactive children than in normal children and some showing no significant difference. It should be noted, however, that one of the most extensive studies reporting no significant difference (Zahn, Abate, Little & Wender, 1975) nevertheless shows that the mean HR of the hyperactive children was 88.1 bpm and that of the normal children 91.2 bpm, the sort of magnitude of difference that in some studies reviewed earlier has distinguished delinquent from nondelinquent populations. One possible confounding factor in these studies is age. Zahn et al.'s population, for instance, was aged 6–12 years. Somewhat circumstantial evidence suggests that this may cover an age range in which the direction of relations may change. B. C. Little (personal communication, 1978), in a study similar to those of Davies and Maliphant and Raine reviewed earlier, found that 9- and 11-year-old children rated antisocial by their teachers had lower HRs than those not so rated. No difference, however, was found in the HRs of children rated pro- or antisocial at age 7 years. A small piece of potentially relevant information is available from the longitudinal study carried out in Mauritius (e.g., Venables et al., 1978). In this study skin conductance, skin potential, and HR were measured on a large sample of 3-year-olds and some relevant aspects of behavior were rated at the same time. Ratings of antisocial behavior were also available for the children at ages 9 and 11. The only rated behavior related to tonic HR when both are measured at age 3 is that of "attention span," which is considered by Laufer and Denhoff (1957) in their classic paper to be one of the elements of the hyperactivity syndrome. However, it was found that distractible boys had a significantly ($p < .001$) *higher* HR than boys with a good attention span. Thus one element of the hyperactive syndrome shows at age 3 a relation that is in the opposite direction to that which might be shown at a later age. The other finding from this study is that in no case was there any relation between HR at age 3 and any measure of antisocial behavior at age 9 or 11 even when the variables of sex and social class were taken into account.

Taking the data on tonic HR as a whole, it would appear that at least from the age of 11 onward there is sufficient evidence to suggest a relation between low HR and aspects of antisocial behavior. On the basis of the rather scanty evidence, it appears that at earlier ages the relation between HR and potential precursors of delinquent behavior are absent or the reverse of that found after the age of 11. However, it is evident that these behavioral precursors are not always clearly differentiated, and it is probably necessary to carry out direct studies on the earliest manifestations of aggressive behavior before we can be certain that they are related to tonic HR.

Tonic skin conductance level

A review by Siddle (1977) on the relation between SCL and psychopathy indicates that "resting" SCL is not consistently lower in psychopaths than in normals when the results from a variety of studies are considered. Hare (1978), however, found that, although the SCL of psychopaths did not always differ significantly from that of nonpsychopaths, the direction of the difference remained consistent. Because of the general uniformity of his selection and laboratory procedures, he considered it to be legitimate to combine data across his studies and, when this was done, showed that there was a highly significant difference between the SCLs of psychopaths and nonpsychopaths, the former showing lower SCLs than the latter. Siddle also reviewed data on SCLs from studies in which the SCLs were measured during periods of stimulation. In these instances the data were reasonably consistent in showing that the SCLs of psychopaths were lower than those of nonpsychopaths, largely because the SCLs of the psychopaths did not increase during stimulation as much as those of the nonpsychopaths. Bearing in mind what has already been said about the extent to which measures of tonic activity, supposedly at rest, reflect different degrees of responsivity to social stimulation, the SCL data are probably on the whole not inconsistent with the data on tonic HR in showing lower levels of tonic activity in psychopaths than in normal subjects. In the study by Raine (1982) no consistent relation was found between SCL and teachers' ratings or self-rating measures of socialization even when social class was taken into account, as was the case with HR data.

In contrast to the finding of a lack of consistent relation between the HRs of 3-year-olds and later measures of delinquency in the longitudinal Mauritian study (Venables et al., 1978), SCL did show some results of predictive interest. Subjects were rated on two occasions, at age 9 and at age 11, on scales incorporating items enabling us to measure delinquent tendencies. The rating at age 9 was made by teachers and was based on the scale of Rutter (1967). The factor structure of the scale in the Mauritian context was examined and two factors extracted, one labeled aggression–hyperactivity and the other worried–fearfulness (Venables et al., 1982). The analysis showed that the factor structure did not make possible a distinction between aggression–delinquency and hyperactivity. Nevertheless, for the purposes of directly examining the relation between psychophysiological variables and delinquency it was considered that the use of a simple measure of delinquency was important, and to that end we devised a scale that included only items related to delinquent behavior.

The rating at age 11 was made by the children's parents and was based on the instrument of Edelbrock and Achenbach (1980). From this scale, measures of hyperactivity, aggression, and delinquency are available.

Only the data for the boys were analyzed. One disturbing feature of the data was a nearly zero correlation between the scores for delinquency at 9 and 11 years of age. Further examination of the data, however, suggested that this could be a function of the way the parents interpreted the questions when rating their children. The correlation between teachers' and parents' ratings of delinquency was −.02 for a low-social-class group and .53 for a high-social-class group. It is likely that teachers and parents of higher social class interpreted the items in the scales in the same way, and that this resulted in related measurement on the two occasions. It could be suggested that the parents of lower social class did not understand items they had to rate (because of relatively less literacy) and the nearly zero correlation between teachers' and low-social-class parents' ratings is due to the unreliability of the latter. However, as reported later, significant relations are found between psychophysiological and delinquency rating measures with low-social-class subjects. The suggestion is thus that the *interpretation* placed on the items is different in low- and high-social-class groups. It is clearly necessary in future studies to assess the different meanings given to aspects of delinquency by different raters. The relation between initial SCL at 3 years of age and *teacher*-rated delinquency in subjects dichotomized by social class showed a significant ($p < .04$) interaction between delinquency and social class. Further analyses showed that the effect of delinquency was not significant in the low-social-class group but was significant ($p < .04$) in the high-social-class subjects. The delinquent subjects had a *higher* SCL than the nondelinquent subjects. The findings are thus not in accord with expectations.

The relation between initial SCL at 3 years of age and *parent*-rated delinquency was examined in the high-social-class group, bearing in mind the possibility of the interpretive differences between classes suggested above. As with the teacher-rated behavior, children rated at age 11 by their parents as exhibiting delinquent behavior had significantly ($p < .003$) *higher* initial SCLs at age 3 than children who were not rated delinquent. Using the low-social-class parents' ratings of delinquency, it was found that in this instance the delinquent subjects at age 11 had significantly ($p < .03$) *lower* SCLs at age 3 than nondelinquents.

This finding is somewhat the reverse of that which might be expected on the basis of the position put forward in the introduction. It was suggested that biological variables would show more clearly in the high-social-class subjects. Hence on the basis of the fact that in general findings on adults show a lower SCL in criminals or delinquents, we might expect the same result in the high-social-class subjects in the Mauritian study. If we can assume that delinquency as rated by teachers and high-social-class parents is the same as that which is understood generally in the literature, then it would appear that the 3-year-old's precursor of delinquency is a high SCL. Whatever it is that the parents of lower social class are rating is evidently different. The fact that teachers' ratings of delinquency in low-social-class children are not related to SCL testifies to this difference but, of course, in this instance is also in line with the notion that delinquency in low-social-class situations may owe more to social than to biological factors.

A high-risk study in Denmark also provides useful material. An off-shoot of the original 1962 study of children at risk for schizophrenia (Mednick & Schulsinger, 1968) is the work reported by Loeb and Mednick (1977). From the original sample in that study, seven subjects had committed crimes leading to at least two convictions by 1972. These seven subjects were carefully matched to seven subjects with no criminal record. Six of the seven criminals had lower initial SCLs measured in 1962 than their noncriminal matches. Because of the small number of subjects involved the mean difference in SCL between these two groups failed to reach significance.

Skin conductance nonspecific response

Nonspecific skin conductance response has been included as a measure of tonic activity because it is treated as such by many authors. For example, Surwillo and Quilter (1965) showed that behavioral indicants of vigilance were related to number of SCR.NSs, and Depue and Fowles (1973), reviewing data on arousal in schizophrenia, suggested that SCR.NS frequency can be used as a measure of "arousal." However, the data presented in Table 7.1 suggest that SCR.NS, SCL, and HR are not related measures of "arousal." In a more dynamic approach Kimmel and Hill (1961) showed that, whereas SCL changed under stress in an expected fashion, SCR.NS did not, and Katkin (1965) concluded after a study in which SCL and SCR.NS frequency were used as "autonomic indicants of stress" that the indices reflected different phenomena. However, in the present context, it is worth noting that Schalling, Lidberg, Levander, and Dahlin (1973) found in a study in which all the subjects were men under arrest that the correlations between SCL and SCR.NS were .41, .48, and .48 during periods of rest, stimulation, and rest, respectively.

Siddle, in his 1977 review of electrodermal activity in psychopathy, states that "there is little evidence to indicate that psychopaths differ from non-psychopaths in terms of frequency of NS.SCRs, at least during resting conditions." However, Schalling (1978) reports a "consistent association between few anticipatory spontaneous fluctuations in skin conductance and high *De* scores (Gough scale)." Hare's (1978) review is more equivocal, suggesting that on the occasions on which few SCR.NSs are found that this is a result of the subject's boredom and that psychopaths tend to become more drowsy and bored in monotonous situations than nonpsychopaths. Hinton, O'Neill, Dishman, and Webster (1979), using 71 maximum-security hospital patients as subjects, divided their sample into "public offenders," who had committed crimes against strangers ranging from sexual assault to murder, and "domestic offenders," whose smaller number of crimes had been committed against a person known to the offender. Hinton et al. suggest that the former group might be labeled primary psychopaths. The numbers of SCR.NSs were very significantly ($p < .001$) fewer in the public-offender than in the domestic-offender group.

In a companion paper, Hinton, O'Neill, Hamilton, and Burke (1980) employed the same measures on 37 maximum-security patients, again divided into public and domestic offenders, who on this occasion were called high- and low-public-risk groups, respectively. The high-public-risk group was again found to have a smaller number of SCR.NSs than the low-risk group. Within Hinton et al.'s population, all the patients in the low-public-risk group were diagnosed as schizophrenic, whereas all but one of the high-public-risk group were labeled personality disorder or psychopath. When age-matched groups of psychopaths and schizophrenics were compared, the former group were found to exhibit significantly fewer SCR.NSs than the latter. Hinton's work thus shows the necessity for careful diagnosis or classification of crime within an offender group in order to ascertain clearly the relations with a psychophysiological variable.

A paper that facilitates the interpretation of the findings on SCR.NS is that of Hare (1982). The subjects in this study were 51 prison inmates divided into three (low, medium, and high) psychopathic groups. The subjects were given a choice of the way they spent their time while waiting for a 120-dB aversive noise. They could either listen to a tone that changed frequency before the aversive noise was transmitted, thus giving warning of its onset, or, alternatively, they could listen to a comedian or to white noise and receive no warning. In one type of trial the aversive noise could be avoided, and in the other the noise was unavoidable. When the noise was unavoidable, most subjects listened to the comedian; that is, they adopted a nonvigilant stance. When, however, the stimulus was unavoidable, 74.5% adopted the nonvigilant attitude. There were no differences among any of the psychophysiological measures, SCL, SCR.NS, and HR, in the nonavoidable trials. However, in the avoidable trials significant differences were shown in numbers of SCR.NSs for the nonvigilant subjects. The nonvigilant subjects in the high-psychopathic group showed a significantly smaller increase over baseline in SCR.NSs than those in the low-psychopathic group. Hare (1982, p. 266) interprets the finding in the following way: "Making use of distraction when an aversive stimulus is avoidable results in less conflict and heightened emotional arousal in psychopaths than in other inmates."

Data from the Mauritian high-risk study were used to examine the extent to which SCR.NSs measured at age 3 were related to teachers' ratings at age 9 and parents' ratings at age 11. The procedure was the same as that with initial SCL examined previously. When *teachers'* ratings at age 9 were used, there was a significant (*p* < .01) difference between the number of SCR.NSs shown by delinquent and nondelinquent subjects. The delinquent subjects, in accord with adult data, showed a lower number of SCR.NSs than nondelinquent subjects. This result is the same in both low- and high-social-class groups. Conversely, when *parents'* ratings at age 11 were used in the high-social-class sample, only a significantly (*p* < .016) *higher* number of SCR.NSs were shown by the delinquent than by the nondelinquent group. This finding is, of course, in line with that from the analysis of the SCL data but is the reverse of that obtained with the teachers' ratings. No significant differences in SCR.NSs were found in the low-social-class group. The numbers of SCRs shown in delinquent and nondelinquent groups are almost identical and hence provide no clue that might or might not suggest any support for the notion of a different concept of delinquency in low and high social classes.

Phasic activity

General considerations

The distinction between tonic and phasic autonomic activity is not always clearly maintained and in some instances is difficult to draw. The need to preserve the distinction may not be immediately apparent but is important in some theoretical approaches to criminality.

In general, the way in which the distinction is usually made is to suggest that phasic responses have an identifiable waveform that is time-locked to the stimulus eliciting the phasic response. In contrast, changes in tonic activity, which can be viewed as responses to continuing changes in stimulation or situation, are generally considered to be longer lasting and not so clearly time-locked to stimulus onset.

The difficulty of maintaining the distinction is seen most markedly with the recovery phase of the response. It is clear, for instance, that a short recovery phase of the SCR is part of an identifiable wave shape. However, when the recovery phase of the SCR is long, it is difficult to decide whether this is a lengthened version of the usual exponential decay or whether there is a maintenance of level of conductivity due to a continuation of tonic activity. The difficulty that arises from this lack of clear distinction is of more than minor interest. It is concerned, for instance, with whether the recovery phenomenon is dependent on relative continuation of innervation of the sweat glands by sympathetic activity or is determined by relatively passive (although centrally controlled) reabsorption of sweat and sweat contents (see Edelberg, 1972; Fowles, 1974; Venables & Christie, 1973). In Mednick's (1977) model of the development of criminality, the rate of recovery of the SCR is a direct index of the rate of recovery of the sympathetic concomitants of fear. A rather different point of view, put forward by Venables (1974) and used by Hare (1978), Schalling (1978), and Levander, Schalling, Lidberg, Bartfai, and Lidberg (1980) as a potential explanation of their results, suggests that short or long SCR recovery may be an index of relative openness or closedness, respectively, of attentional stance akin to that suggested by Lacey (1967), for instance, to be indicated by HR deceleration or acceleration. This view does not necessarily require an identification of long recovery with a maintenance of tonic activity. The view put forward by Venables (1974), which is essentially a modification of that of Edelberg (1970), is at present an agnostic one, the thrust of which is that we do not understand the central control of peripheral *mechanisms* related to recovery. It is still reasonable for heuristic purposes, however, to suggest that on the basis of the work of Bagshaw and Kimble (1972) the limbic system has an important role. A discussion of possible mechanisms at the periphery is given in Venables and Fletcher (1981).

There have been two direct attempts to test the notion that short or long SCR recovery is related, respectively, to openness or closedness to the environment. These have involved the examination of the relation of SCR recovery time to HR deceleration or acceleration.

Lobstein, Webb, and Edholm (1979) showed that long SCR recovery time was significantly negatively related to extent of HR deceleration and positively related to extent of HR acceleration, thus supporting the Venables (1974) position. What was important about their study was that these relations were not shown on initial orienting responses; they were, however, apparent in a late trial in the stimulus series in which the frequency of an orienting tone changed from that used in the series of 15 presented previously. This was clearly an instance of orientation in which there was, to follow Sokolov (1963), a mismatch between the stimulus presented and the "neural model" built up during the preceding stimulation.

The results of the second attempt to examine SCR recovery and HR relations were not as clear. Venables, Gartshore, and O'Riordan (1980) showed in the first orienting response a relation between SCR and HR variables contrary to expectations. However, in a reorientation trial, similar to that in which Lobstein, Webb, and Edholm (1979) obtained their confirmatory result, there were results of importance. The hypothesized relations between SCR *recovery* and HR deceleration or acceleration were not found. However, because SCR rise time and SCR half-recovery time are almost always significantly positively related (see Venables & Christie, 1980, Tables 1.9 and 1.11) the relation of SCR rise time to HR indices was examined. The data showed that long rise time was related to a large extent to cardiac acceleration and hence by extension to a defensive or "closed" stance. If this preliminary finding can be replicated, it points to the value of examining SCR rise time as a potentially important component of the SCR, which does not appear to have been used in studies of delinquency and criminality. It also removes the theoretical discussion from that of recovery to that of initiation of the response.

If Mednick's (1977) position, that long SCR recovery indicates slow recovery from fear (hence leading to poorer avoidance conditioning) is correct, one would expect this slow fear recovery to be seen in other response modalities. The association of long SCR recovery with large HR acceleration would, of course, be in accord with this position, because HR acceleration can be a sympathetically controlled activity. However, data reviewed later suggest that the phase of acceleration on which delinquents differ from normal subjects may be due to a discrimination of vagal tonus. The work of Turpin (1979), which suggests that this original Russian view of the phasic defensive response requires reconsideration, should be noted. He suggests that short-latency (7 sec) HR accelerative responses might have to be classified as startle, and his newly discovered long-latency (30 sec) HR accelerative response has more of the characteristics theoretically required of a defensive response. Such long-latency HR acceleration might provide some of the requirements of Mednick's position, but to date there are no data that are specifically related to such long-latency HR responses in criminal subjects.

This discussion began with the difficulty of distinguishing phasic from tonic activity in the context of long recovery to baseline of autonomic activity. A paper in which this difficulty is particularly apparent is that of Grueninger, Kimble, Grueninger, and Levine (1965), which describes a study in which electrodermal activity was examined in monkeys with frontal ablations. The authors examined the effect of shock on electrodermal response; they reported that, although the frontal and control animals did not differ with regard to amplitudes of GSRs (SCRs), they did differ in the "time for skin resistance to return to pre-shock level." The time taken by the frontal monkeys was markedly longer than that of the controls. However, the recovery times reported in this study are substantially longer than those normally found in the literature on half-recovery times (1,000 sec for frontal monkeys and 550 sec for normal monkeys). Apart from methodological differences between this and more recent studies, Grueninger et al. (1965) exemplify the difficulty of distinguishing tonic and phasic aspects of recovery. Bearing in mind the possibilities of association between cortical frontal disorders and criminality, raised, for instance, by Pontius (1972) and Schalling (1978), the linking finding of long electrodermal recovery in frontal-lesioned monkeys is valuable.

It should be noted, in passing and in relation to the previous discussion of SCR.NSs that Grueninger et al. report fewer nonspecifics in frontal than in normal monkeys, data that might be taken to support the notion of frontal disorder in psychopathic subjects.

Electrodermal activity

Skin conductance response amplitude. The data on the relation of psychopathy to electrodermal orienting are somewhat equivocal. Siddle, Nicol, and Foggitt (1973) reported that among a group of antisocial adolescents those rated most antisocial showed the smallest SCRs to a 75-dB tone. Borkovec (1970) reported similar results with a tone of "moderate" intensity when comparing a psychopathic with a neurotic and subcultural delinquent group. However, Hare (1968), using a clearly defined group of psychopathic inmates, showed no difference between their SCR and that of nonpsychopaths. [It should be noted that when these data were range-corrected (Lykken & Venables, 1971) the psychopaths did in fact show smaller responses than nonpsychopaths.] Hinton et al. (1979, 1980) in their studies of high- and low-public-risk special hospital patients also showed no difference between these groups in SCRs to low-intensity stimuli. High-risk material from Copenhagen (from the same data set as that from which tonic HR differences were reported) showed no difference in SCR orienting response amplitude between the children of criminal fathers and children of noncriminal fathers (Mednick, 1977). However, the same data show that more orienting responses were produced by the children of criminal fathers.

In line with Mednick's (1977) finding Raine, in the unpublished material referred to earlier, showed a significant relation between number of orienting responses and rated socialization among normal 15-year-old schoolboys. The higher the socialization, the greater the number of responses. There was, however, no relation between amplitude of response and socialization. The data from Mauritius show a relation between the first orienting response of a series (but not later responses) in material collected at age 3 and *teacher*-rated delinquency at age 9. The relation, however, is class dependent, as is much other material from this source. Among high-social-class children those rated high on the delinquent scale have *higher* amplitude responses than those rated low, whereas the reverse is the case with low-social-class children. This, as with previous measures reviewed from this source, is somewhat contrary to expectations.

In general, it would appear that with low-intensity stimuli eliciting electrodermal orienting responses, with the exception of the 3-year-old predictive data, there is an inconsistent tendency for the responses in delinquent or delinquent-related groups to be smaller or fewer than in nondelinquent groups.

In the case of responses, possibly classifiable as defensive, to stimuli of intensity greater than 80–85 dB, the position appears to be more unanimous. Hare (1978) reviews studies showing that psychopaths "are electrodermally hypo-responsive to intense or aversive stimuli presented without specific warning." Particularly important are his own data from studies in which stimuli of between 80- and 120-dB intensity were presented to high- and low-psychopathic groups subdivided on the basis of socialization scores of the California Personality Inventory. A significant Psychopathy × Socialization × Intensity interaction was accounted for by the hyporesponsiveness of the low-socialized, high-psychopathic group to high-intensity tones. Although the responses of the subjects in this category to low-intensity tones were not distinguishable from responses of the remainder of the subjects, their responses to tones of 110- and 120-dB intensity were much smaller than the responses of the other subjects. In contrast, there was not a similar finding in Raine's data relating socialization scores in normal schoolboys to amplitude of SCR to intense stimuli.

Raine's results are somewhat surprising in view of the report of Waid (1976) that, in groups of undergraduate students categorized as high-, medium-, and low-socialized on the basis of their socialization scores in the California Personality Inventory, the low- and medium-socialization groups produced significantly smaller SCRs to aversive (98-dB) noise than did the high-socialization group. Of particular importance in Waid's study is the paradigm in which the aversive noise was presented. The aversive noise was preceded at different intervals by a warning tone at 68 dB. The hypothesis being tested was that low-socialization subjects had the ability to use cues of impending noxious events to attenuate their impact. There was, however, no effect of warning interval on size of response to the aversive stimulus, so that it did not appear that warning-signal utilization mediated the amplitude difference of SCR between the groups. This point will be taken up later in relation to HR orientation. The data from Mauritius show no relation between SCR to intense stimuli at age 3 and delinquency rated at age 9 or 11. The only significant finding, which refers to the earlier discussion relating hyperactivity and delinquency, is that the amplitude of the response to the first presentation in a series of an intense (96-dB) noise stimulus is smaller in subjects rated distractible (at age 3) than in those rated attentive. Thus, if the tenuous links between distractibility, hyperactivity, and delinquency are drawn, the data can be put alongside the type of material reviewed by Hare (1978).

Other confirmatory material is derived from the high-risk study of Loeb and Mednick (1977) referred to earlier. They reported that SCR responses in conditioning trials (measured at age 15) were smaller for those later committing crimes than for a matched sample of unconvicted subjects. Although these data were reported as arising from conditioning trials, it should be noted that (a) the conditioned stimulus–unconditioned stimulus (CS–UCS) interval used was only 0.5 sec and, hence, it is difficult to distinguish responses that might be called conditioned from responses to the intense UCS, and (b) the response of the "to-be-delinquent" group was smaller in early trials as well as late trials.

In summary, the data show, with a fair degree of strength, that delinquent or psychopathic subjects are hyporesponsive to intense stimuli in comparison with normal subjects. Hare (1978) has given a comprehensive review of the responsiveness of psychopaths in conditioning and quasiconditioning paradigms, in which the findings again point strongly to their being hyporesponsive electrodermally.

An attempt at direct replication of the "quasi-conditioning temporal gradient of fear" experiment of Hare (1965) was made by Tharp, Maltzman, Syndulko, and Ziskind (1980). The subjects in this instance were "non-institutionalized, compulsive gambler sociopaths" and controls. The paradigm was the same as that used by Hare in which SCR and HR were measured while numbers 1 through 7 were presented and a loud (95-dB) tone was given after the number 7. The sociopaths, like Hare's psychopaths, showed significantly smaller anticipatory responses than the controls and began responding later in the counting sequence than the controls.

Two other papers that have appeared since Hare's review provide confirmation of his position in 1978 but with important additional aspects. Hemming (1981) carried out a conditioning study in the context of an argument that a strong UCS, partial reinforcement, and discrimination learning are experimental parameters that provide the best paradigm for efficient socialization. She also made the point that, because of the social and family factors associated with crime, it is important when examining a possible biological basis for antisocial behavior that the subjects of the study come from relatively high status groups. With this in mind, her study was conducted on subjects whose parents' occupational level placed them in a class not lower than III on the registrar general's scale. The study employed 100-dB white noise as the UCS and five colored lights, of which one was the +ve CS in a discrimination paradigm. The +ve CS was partially reinforced. The analysis involved the examination of conditioned discrimination in extinction. The frequencies of subjects displaying conditional discrimination were compared. It was found that prisoners displayed a smaller number of conditioned responses than normal subjects. Also, during the extinction phase, the magnitude of response to the non-CS lights was smaller among the prisoners than the nonprisoners.

Raine and Venables (1981) also reported a study in which social class was an important variable. This employed 15-year-old normal schoolboys as subjects, rated on scales of socialization. The results obtained in a classical conditioning paradigm employing a 105-dB tone as the UCS and a 65-dB tone as the CS were not strong. However, the authors did demonstrate conditioning in some subjects using responsivity in the post-UCS window in the absence of a UCS as the measure. A significant interaction between socialization and social class showed that among high-social-class subjects the antisocial subjects showed a lower conditioned SCR magnitude than the prosocial subjects. This finding is in accord with that of Hemming (1981). However, the reverse pattern is the case for low-social-class subjects. Raine and Venables interpreted this finding in terms of the notion that "children who are highly conditionable and who have antisocial parents will become 'socialized' into antisocial habits." This argument, of course, demands that there are a larger number of antisocial persons in the lower social classes than in the higher social classes, an argument that is difficult to sustain and probably demands a class-biased interpretation of "socialization."

Skin conductance response recovery. As indicated in the introduction to this section SCR recovery time is subject to different interpretations. At this stage, however, the issue is not one of interpretation but rather one of review of the literature.

Hare (1978) has again provided a comprehensive review of the area. Several points are worthy of reemphasis. One of particular importance for future research is that group differences between psychopaths and non-psychopaths on this index (the recovery times of the psychopaths being longer than those of the nonpsychopaths) are shown only (a) when the intensity of the stimulus evoking the SCR is high; (b) when the SCR is made to a "reorientation" stimulus, that is, one involving a change of stimulus parameter after a series; or (c) when the SCR is measured from the left hand. The last aspect has been noted only recently in studies where bilateral recordings of skin conductance have been made regularly. In contrast, the data reported by Mednick (1977, p. 6) showing that the SCR recovery times of children of criminal fathers are longer than those of children of noncriminal fathers were recorded from the right hand. Skin conductance response half-recovery times were also measured in the pro-spective study by Loeb and Mednick (1977) referred to earlier. A finding of longer recovery times to the intense UCS in subjects who were to become criminal, in comparison with matched controls, was recorded from the left hand.

Studies that have appeared since Hare's (1978) review provide general support for the earlier findings. In Hemming's (1981) study, referred to earlier, recordings were made from "the subject's non-preferred hand." Recovery times reported were those from SCRs to the aversive UCS. The times were 10.60 sec for prisoners and 6.73 sec for normal subjects ($p <$ .01). Levander et al. (1980) reported that, within a group of male crimi-nals, SCR recovery times to a 93-dB tone were longer in those subjects with self-report scores indicating lower socialization than in those with high socialization scores; recordings were from the left hand. Hinton et al. (1979, 1980), using stimuli of "intermediate" (83-dB) intensity, reported that patients in a maximum-security hospital rated as being of "high pub-lic risk" had longer SCR half-recovery time than those of "low public risk." Data from the Mauritius high-risk study again show results con-trary to expectations. Children rated by their parents as aggressive at age

11 had significantly ($p < .006$) *shorter* half-recovery times at age 3 in a reorientation trial than children rated as intermediate or nonaggressive. No differences in recovery time were shown to high-intensity stimuli. Thus, as with other measures, the age 3 material shows inverse relations in the prediction of later delinquent behavior from those relations that appear to be shown after the age of 11.

Other components of SCR. Only one study has reported latency or rise time of SCR as a variable in examining differences between delinquent and nondelinquent groups. In view of the earlier mention of the potential value of measuring SCR rise time, it is interesting that Mednick (1977) reported a significant difference in this variable (designated in his report as "latency to response peak"), showing that children of criminal fathers have a longer rise time than children of noncriminal fathers. Latency (to response onset) does not differentiate the two groups.

Cardiovascular activity

The most extensive review of this field is again that of Hare (1978). The conceptual framework for the work he reported is that of Darrow (1929), Graham and Clifton (1966), and Lacey (1967) suggesting that sensory intake is associated with cardiac deceleration and is an index of the orienting response, whereas cardiac acceleration is associated with sensory rejection and the defensive response.

It is clear from Hare's review that, as far as unsignaled stimuli are concerned, in situations where either orienting or defensive responses might be elicited, the data comparing the responses of psychopaths and nonpsychopaths are equivocal. However, when a conditioning or quasi-conditioning paradigm is used, the data Hare reviews are consistent in suggesting that psychopaths show greater (anticipatory) accelerative responses than normal subjects. The paradigm used by Hare, which clearly shows this result, is the "temporal gradient of fear," in which numbers are counted out and the subject is told that on the count of a particular number he or she will be presented with a loud aversive tone. The psychopathic subjects showed an HR acceleration in the period before the aversive tone that was markedly greater than that shown by nonpsychopathic subjects. Within the psychopathic group of subjects this anticipatory (sensory-rejection) acceleration was shown more strongly by those subjects rated low on socialization. A similar pattern was shown by university students rated low or high on socialization, the former group showing the largest HR preaversive-stimulus acceleration.

Although these studies were replicated (see the subsection on skin conductance response amplitude) in showing smaller electrodermal responses in psychopaths, they were not replicated by Tharp et al. (1980) in the HR modality. In this study no differences were shown between sociopaths and controls. Tharp et al. suggest, however, that the failure to replicate the results may have been due to population differences, their compulsive gambler subjects being noninstitutionalized and different on this account from prison inmates. Nor had they been assessed on a scale of socialization as had Hare's subjects. This author has, in the use of the gradient-of-fear paradigm, shown the importance of dividing his subjects on this measure.

Discussion

Hare's interpretations of the findings of his studies using the gradient-of-fear paradigm are that (1) the greater acceleration shown by the psychopathic or low-socialization subjects indicated their facility for "tuning out" aversive aspects of the environment and (2) the smaller SCRs shown by them in this paradigm are evidence for the effectiveness of this defensive stance.

The tentative interpretation of Hare (1978) and Schalling (1978) of the long recovery time of the SCR shown by psychopathic subjects is that this, too, may indicate a defensive posture and also be in accord with the role ascribed to HR acceleration. Opposing this interpretation is the finding of Waid (1976) that the availability of a warning signal did not modulate the amplitude of SCRs to aversive stimuli shown by psychopathic subjects.

It is necessary to question the functional possibility of the proposed mechanisms. It is obvious that the SCR recovery function cannot modify the amplitude of the SCR that precedes it. It is reasonable, however, that whatever state of the organism that results in a long SCR recovery time may also modify the SCR amplitude.

As far as HR acceleration is concerned the issue in part depends on whether that acceleration is a function of an increase in sympathetic activity or a decrease in vagal tone. Warner and Cox (1962) state that, although the HR response to a step increase in vagal activity may show a time constant of less than 1 sec, sympathetic HR responses are slower with time constants of the general order of 8 sec. Thus, in order that HR acceleration may have a chance of modulating the SCR, which has a latency of between 1 and 3 sec, it must be vagal activity that is involved in the process. The study by Obrist, Wood, and Perez-Reyes (1965) employed a paradigm that is one of "anticipation" of an aversive stimulus in a conditioning experiment. Atropine was used to create a vagal blockade for the purpose of examining the function of vagal activity. Without vagal blockade HR shows a marked acceleration peaking at about 4 or 5 sec postwarning and then showing deceleration up to and continuing beyond the onset of the aversive stimulus, which appears at 7 sec postwarning. With vagal blockade, this later deceleration is eliminated, but the acceleration that is apparent peaks at 7 or 10 sec and is of slow onset and lower amplitude. It would thus appear that only vagally produced acceleration is capable of modulating SCR responsivity.

Examination of the data on the anticipatory HR change presented by Hare, Frazelle, and Cox (1978, Fig. 1) shows that in both nonpsychopathic–high-socialization subjects and psychopathic–low-socialization subjects the initial HR acceleration is of the same latency. However, in the former group there is subsequent deceleration rather like the subjects without vagal blockade of Obrist et al. (1965). In contrast, the psychopathic group shows a larger HR acceleration, which, though it decreases before the onset of the aversive tone, never actually shows a rate lower than the prestimulus rate. The mechanism proposed by Hare thus appears to be functionally feasible and suggests that psychopaths might exemplify an excess of vagal sensitivity or vagal tonus. This, of course, would be concomitant with the findings reported earlier of lower tonic HRs in psychopathic subjects.

The only study that has attempted to examine the possible role of cholinergic mechanisms in SCR recovery is that of Patterson (1976), who related changes in pupil size to SCR recovery time. Unfortunately, his data do not enable one to distinguish the roles of cholinergic and adrenergic mediation.

The data reviewed appear to be in accord with the idea that psychopaths are less capable of experiencing fear – more likely because of an excess of vagal tone than more complex explanations. At this stage, however it is important to continue to acquire good empirical data on which more detailed theories can be erected and to remember that autonomic measures are at best only indirect indices of what psychologists want to measure. We should echo the wisdom of Rescorla and Solomon (1967), who said that "to expect simple heart rate changes . . . to mirror adequately a state such as fear is to over-simplify hopelessly the operation of the cardiovascular system" (p. 168). Exactly the same should be said of the electrodermal system.

In summary, the data from studies on adult subjects or indeed those in their teens, though not entirely unanimous, in general support the notion that criminality, psychopathy, and delinquency are associated with low levels of tonic activity, low levels of electrodermal responsivity, and a pattern of HR acceleration that appears to be vagally influenced.

In contrast, although the data are by no means strong, the results of the Mauritian high-risk study, in which psychophysiological material at age 3 was related to later rated aspects of delinquency, show the reverse of the adult pattern. In other words, delinquent or aggressive patterns of behavior at age 9 or 11 are related to higher levels of activity at age 3. If these data can be considered replicable, it would appear that the early precursor of later delinquent behavior is different from the adult pattern. Bearing in mind that some data suggest that the adult pattern may be seen at age 11, there is presumably some transitional state between age 3 and age 11 that deserves investigation.

The other possibility is, of course, that behavior rated as delinquent or aggressive at age 9 or 11 by teachers or high-social-class parents is not so much delinquent as "active." This, too, may be a function of the Mauritian context in which the data were collected, in which the good child is the passive, quiet one. There is nevertheless a gap in the data that requires an attempt to relate aspects of psychophysiology up to the age of 10 or so with the development of behavior patterns that, if not delinquent in themselves, can be associated with later delinquency.

Acknowledgments

This chapter was prepared while the author was in receipt of a grant from the Leverhulme Trust. The author is grateful to David Mitchell for his analysis of data from the Mauritian high-risk study and to Adrian Raine for permitting the use of some of his unpublished material.

References

Bagshaw, M. H., & Kimble, D. (1972). *Bimodal EDR orienting response characteristics in limbic lesioned monkeys: Correlates with schizophrenic patients.* Paper presented to a meeting of the Society for Psychophysiological Research, Boston, MA.

Borkovec, T. D. (1970). Autonomic reactivity to sensory stimulation in psychopathic, neurotic and normal juvenile delinquents. *Journal of Consulting and Clinical Psychology, 35*, 217–22.

Cantwell, D. P. (1972). Psychiatric illness in the families of hyperactive children. *Archives of General Psychiatry, 27*, 414–17.

Darrow, C. W. (1929). Differences in the physiological reactions to sensory and ideational stimuli. *Psychological Bulletin, 26*, 185–201.

Davies, J. G. V., & Maliphant, R. (1971). Autonomic responses of male adolescents exhibiting refractory behavior in school. *Journal of Child Psychology and Psychiatry, 12*, 115–27.

Depue, R. A., & Fowles, D. C. (1973). Electrodermal activity on an index of arousal in schizophrenics. *Psychological Bulletin, 79*, 233–8.

Edelberg, R. (1970). The information content of the recovery limb of the electrodermal response. *Psychophysiology, 6*, 527–39.

Edelberg, R. (1972). The electrodermal system. In N. S. Greenfield & R. A. Sternbach (Eds.), *Handbook of psychophysiology*. New York: Holt.

Edelbrock, C., & Achenbach, T. M. (1980). A typology of child behavior profile patterns: Distribution and correlates for disturbed children aged 6–16. *Journal of Abnormal Child Psychology, 8*, 441–70.

Fowles, D. C. (1974). Mechanisms of electrodermal activity. In R. F. Thompson & M. M. Patterson (Eds.), *Methods in physiological psychology: Vol. 1. Bioelectric recording techniques: Part C. Receptor–effector processes*. New York: Academic Press.

Graham, F. K., & Clifton, R. K. (1966). Heart rate change as a component of the orienting response. *Psychological Bulletin, 65*, 305–20.

Grueninger, W. E., Kimble, D. P., Grueninger, J., & Levine, S. (1965). GSR and corticosteroid response in monkeys with frontal ablation. *Neuropsychologia, 3*, 205–16.

Hare, R. D. (1965). Temporal gradient of fear arousal in psychopaths. *Journal of Abnormal Psychology, 70*, 442–5.

Hare, R. D. (1968). Psychopathy, autonomic functioning and the orienting response. *Journal of Abnormal Psychology*, Monograph Suppl. *73*, No. 3, Part 2, 1–24.

Hare, R. D. (1978). Electrodermal and cardiovascular correlates of psychopathy. In R. D. Hare & D. Schalling (Eds.), *Psychopathic behavior* (Ch. 7). New York: Wiley.

Hare, R. D. (1982). Psychopathy and physiological activity during anticipation of an aversive stimulus in a distraction paradigm. *Psychophysiology, 19*, 266–71.

Hare, R. D., Frazelle, J., & Cox, D. N. (1978). Psychopathy and physiological responses to threat of an aversive stimulus. *Psychophysiology, 15*, 165–72.

Hastings, J. E., & Barkley, R. A. (1978). A review of psychophysiological research with hyperkinetic children. *Journal of Abnormal Child Psychology, 6*, 413–47.

Hemming, J. H. (1981). Electrodermal indices in a selected prison sample and students. *Personality and Individual Differences, 2*, 37–46.

Hinton, J., O'Neill, N., Dishman, J., & Webster, S. (1979). Electrodermal indices of public offending and recidivision. *Biological Psychology, 9*, 297–309.

Hinton, J., O'Neill, M., Hamilton, S., & Burke, M. (1980). Psychological differentiation between psychopathic and schizophrenic abnormal offenders. *British Journal of Social and Clinical Psychology, 19*, 257–69.

Katkin, E. S. (1965). Relationship between manifest anxiety and two indices of autonomic response to stress. *Journal of Personality and Social Psychology, 2*, 324–33.

Kety, S. S., Rosenthal, D., Wender, P. H., Schulsinger, F., & Jacobsen, B. (1978). The biologic and adoptive families of individuals who became schizophrenic: Prevalence of mental illness and other characteristics. In L. C. Wynne, R. L. Cromwell, & S. Matthysse (Eds.), *The nature of schizophrenia* (Ch. 2). New York: Wiley.

Kimmel, H. D., & Hill, F. A. (1961). A comparison of two electrodermal measures of response to stress. *Journal of Comparative and Physiological Psychology, 54*, 395–7.

Lacey, J. I. (1967). Somatic response patterning and stress: Some revisions of activation theory. In M. H. Appley & R. Trumbull (Eds.), *Psychological stress*. New York: Appleton-Century-Crofts.

Levander, S. E., Schalling, D. S., Lidberg, L., Bartfai, A., & Lidberg, Y. (1980). Skin conductance recovery time and personality in a group of criminals. *Psychophysiology, 17*, 105–11.

Lobstein, T., Webb, B., & Edholm, O. (1979). Orienting response and locus of control. *British Journal of Social and Clinical Psychology, 18*, 13–19.

Loeb, J., & Mednick, S. A. (1977). A prospective study of predictors of criminality: 3.

Electrodermal response patterns. In S. A. Mednick & K. O. Christiansen (Eds.), *Biosocial bases of criminal behavior* (Ch. 17). New York: Gardner Press.

Loney, J., Langhorne, J. E., & Paternite, C. E. (1978). An empirical basis for sub-grouping the hyperkinetic/minimal order dysfunction syndrome. *Journal of Abnormal Psychology, 87,* 431–41.

Lykken, D. T., & Venables, P. H. (1971). Direct measurement of skin conductance: A proposal for standardization. *Psychophysiology, 8,* 656–72.

Mednick, S. A. (1977). A biosocial theory of the learning of law-abiding behavior. In S. A. Mednick & K. O. Christiansen (Eds.), *Biosocial bases of criminal behavior* (Ch. 1). New York: Gardner Press.

Mednick, S. A., & Schulsinger, F. (1968). Some pre-morbid characteristics related to breakdown in children with schizophrenic mothers. In D. Rosenthal & S. S. Kety (Eds.), *The transmission of schizophrenia.* New York: Pergamon.

Morrison, J. R., & Stewart, M. A. (1971). A family study of the hyperactive child syndrome. *Biological Psychiatry, 3,* 189–95.

Obrist, P. A., Wood, D. M., & Perez-Reyes, M. (1965). Heart rate during conditioning in humans: Effects of UCS intensity, vagal blockade and adrenergic block of vasomotor activity. *Journal of Experimental Psychology, 70,* 32–42.

Offord, D. R., Sullivan, K., Allen, N., & Abrams, N. (1979). Delinquency and hyperactivity. *Journal of Nervous and Mental Disease, 167,* 734–41.

Patterson, T. (1976). Skin conductance recovery and pupillometrics in chronic schizophrenia. *Psychophysiology, 13,* 189–95.

Pontius, A. A. (1972). Neurological aspects in some types of delinquency, especially among juveniles: Toward a neurological model of ethical action. *Adolescence, 7,* 289–308.

Quay, H., & Parsons, L. B. (1970). *The differential classification of the juvenile offender.* Washington, DC: Bureau of Prisons.

Raine, A. (1982). Psychophysiology, psychometrics and socialization. Unpublished doctoral dissertation, University of York.

Raine, A., & Venables, P. H. (1981). Classical conditioning and socialization: A biosocial interaction. *Personality and Individual Differences, 2,* 273–83.

Rescorla, R. A., & Solomon, R. L. (1967). Two process learning theory: Relationships between Pavlovian conditioning and instrumental learning. *Psychological Review, 74,* 151–82.

Rosenthal, R. H., & Allen, T. W. (1978). An examination of attention, arousal and learning dysfunctions of hyperkinetic children. *Psychological Bulletin, 85,* 689–715.

Rutter, M. (1967). A children's behavior questionnaire for completion by teachers: Preliminary findings. *Journal of Child Psychology and Psychiatry, 8,* 1–11.

Schalling, D. (1978). Psychopathy-related personality variables and the psychophysiology of socialization. In R. D. Hare & D. Schalling (Eds.), *Psychopathic behavior* (Ch. 6). New York: Wiley.

Schalling, D., Lidberg, L., Levander, S. E., & Dahlin, Y. (1973). Spontaneous autonomic activity as related to psychopathy. *Biological Psychology, 1,* 83–97.

Siddle, D. A. T. (1977). Electrodermal activity and psychopathy. In S. A. Mednick & K. O. Christiansen (Eds.), *Biosocial bases of criminal behavior* (Ch. 12). New York: Gardner Press.

Siddle, D. A. T., Nicol, A. R., & Foggit, R. H. (1973). Habituation and over-extinction of the GSR component of the orienting response in anti-social adolescents. *British Journal of Social and Clinical Psychology, 12,* 303–8.

Sokolov, E. N. (1963). *Perception and the conditioned reflex.* New York: Macmillan.

Surwillo, W. W., & Quilter, R. E. (1965). The relation of frequency of spontaneous skin potential responses to vigilance and age. *Psychophysiology, 1,* 272–6.

Tharp, V. K., Maltzman, I., Syndulko, K., & Ziskind, E. (1980). Autonomic activity during anticipation of an aversive tone in non-institutionalized sociopaths. *Psychophysiology,* *17,* 123–8.

Turpin, G. (1979). A psychobiological approach to the differentiation of orienting and defense responses. In H. D. Kimmel, E. M. Van Olst, & J. F. Orlebeke (Eds.), *The orienting reflex in humans* (Ch. 13). Hillsdale, NJ: Erlbaum.

Venables, P. H. (1974). The recovery limb of the skin conductance response in "high-risk" research. In S. A. Mednick, F. Schulsinger, J. Higgins, & B. Bell (Eds.), *Genetics, environment and psychopathology.* Amsterdam: North Holland.

Venables, P. H. (1975). Psychophysiological studies of schizophrenic pathology. In P. H. Venables & M. J. Christie (Eds.), *Research in Psychophysiology.* (Ch. 12). New York: Wiley.

Venables, P. H., & Christie, M. J. (1973). Mechanisms, instrumentation, recording techniques and quantification of responses. In W. F. Prokasy & D. C. Raskin (Eds.), *Electrodermal activity in psychological research* (Ch. 1). New York: Academic Press.

Venables, P. H., & Christie, M. J. (1980). Electrodermal activity. In I. Martin & P. H. Venables (Eds.), *Techniques in psychophysiology* (Ch. 1). New York: Wiley.

Venables, P. H., & Fletcher, R. P. (1981). The status of skin conductance recovery time: An examination of the Bundy effect. *Psychophysiology, 18,* 10–16.

Venables, P. H., Fletcher, R. P., Dalais, J. C., Mitchell, D. A., Schulsinger, F., & Mednick, S. A. (in press). Factor structure of the Rutter "Children's Behavior Questionnaire" in a primary school population in a developing country. *Journal of Child Psychology and Psychiatry.*

Venables, P. H., Gartshore, S. A., & O'Riordan, P. W. (1980). The function of skin conductance response recovery. *Biological Psychology, 10,* 1–6.

Venables, P. H., Mednick, S. A., Schulsinger, F., Raman, A. C., Bell, B., Dalais, J. C., & Fletcher, R. P. (1978). Screening for risk of mental illness. In G. Serban (Ed.), *Cognitive defects in development of mental illness.* New York: Brunner/Mazel.

Wadsworth, M. E. J. (1976). Delinquency, pulse rates and early emotional deprivation. *British Journal of Criminology, 16,* 245–56.

Waid, W. M. (1976). Skin conductance responses to both signaled and unsignaled noxious stimulation predicts level of socialization. *Journal of Personality and Social Psychology, 5,* 923–9.

Warner, H. R., & Cox, A. (1962). A mathematical model of heart rate control by sympathetic and vagus efferent information. *Journal of Applied Physiology, 17,* 349.

Zahn, T. P., Abate, F., Little, B. C., & Wender, P. H. (1975). Minimal brain dysfunction, stimulant drugs, and autonomic nervous system activity. *Archives of General Psychiatry, 32,* 381–7.

8   Electroencephalogram among criminals

Jan Volavka

The idea that the electroencephalogram (EEG) may contribute to our understanding of criminal behavior is relatively old. Individual case reports of EEG abnormalities in violent criminals have been appearing since the early 1940s (Hill & Sargant, 1943), and the association between violent crime and EEG abnormalities with or without clinical epilepsy has been studied ever since.

Most of these studies were based on visual inspection of EEG tracings (rather than on computerized EEG analyses). The subjects were typically prisoners. One of the best studies of this type (Williams, 1969) used 333 prisoners who had committed violent crimes. The subjects were divided into two groups: repeated violent offenders and those who had committed a single violent act. EEG abnormalities occurred in 64% and 24% of the first and second group, respectively. Subjects with mental retardation, clinical epilepsy, or a history of major head injury were removed from both groups. The distribution of EEG abnormalities then changed to 57% and 12% in the first and second group, respectively. These findings suggest that EEG abnormality was related to violent crime in this prisoner sample even after the author accounted for the effects of gross organic brain disease.

The relation between epilepsy, EEG, and aggression has been debated for several decades. Mark and Ervin (1970) reported that patients with temporal lobe epilepsy are prone to aggression during or immediately after their seizure states. However, Rodin (1973) observed epileptic seizures in 150 patients, 42 of whom had psychomotor automatism during a seizure and 15 of whom had it immediately following a seizure. No aggressive behavior was observed in any of the patients in this study. Lewis, Pincus, Shanok, and Glaser (1982) studied 97 juvenile offenders at a correctional facility. They found a clear relation between the degree of violence and the symptoms of psychomotor epilepsy, including EEG abnormalities.

137

Many other studies relating EEG abnormalities, epilepsy, violence, and crime have been published; a review of that work is available elsewhere (Mednick & Volavka, 1980). Most studies using prisoner samples reveal a relation between violent crime and EEG abnormalities, and they suggest that criminals' EEGs are more frequently classified as abnormal than those of noncriminal control subjects. These issues have not been completely resolved. Several studies reported no differences between the EEGs of criminal and noncriminal populations (Driver, West, & Faulk, 1979; Gibbs, Bagchi, & Bloomberg, 1945). Formidable methodological problems exist in subject sampling and in defining aggressive or violent behavior, EEG abnormality, and epilepsy (Klingman & Goldberg, 1975). These problems account to some extent for the variation in reported results. The definition of EEG characteristics (such as "abnormality") may not be the same for each author, and quantifiable EEG properties such as frequency tend to be more reliably determined. The reliability of the measurements increases if they are performed with electronic instruments (Volavka et al., 1973).

Most studies involving EEG among criminals report some slowing of the EEG frequency. We shall concentrate in this chapter on the slowing within the alpha frequency range (8–13 Hz). Statistically significant slowing of alpha activity was reported in juvenile delinquents (Forssman & Frey, 1953) and also in a series of adult murderers (DeBaudouin, Haumonte, Bessing, & Geissman, 1961). Gibbs et al. (1945) showed that prisoners tend to have a slightly slower alpha activity than controls (the difference was not statistically significant). Many other authors have reported diffuse EEG slowing in criminals without any quantitative data. It seems fair to assume that the slowing of alpha activity is probably a frequent finding among persons exhibiting antisocial behavior. Such slowing is a nonspecific finding that may occur in a wide variety of neuropsychiatric conditions as well as in symptom-free XYY men (Volavka, Mednick, Sergeant, & Rasmussen, 1977a,b). Average alpha frequency increases as a function of age between 5 and 20 years; thus it may be considered an indication of brain maturation, and its slowing may be due to a developmental lag. The idea that physiological brain immaturity may be related to antisocial behavior is at least 40 years old (Hill & Watterson, 1942).

Interpreting the slowing of alpha activity in criminals is very difficult, because we do not know whether the slowing developed before or after the emergence of criminal behavior. If it developed after the emergence of criminal behavior, it may have been a consequence of the criminal activity (e.g., frequent head injuries). If, however, the alpha slowing is an antecedent of antisocial behavior, one might hypothesize that it is a predisposing factor for the development of such behavior.

The only way to establish whether the alpha slowing precedes the development of antisocial behavior is to examine and follow a number of subjects, some of whom will become criminals. In other words, longitudinal prospective studies are needed to answer this question. We have completed two such studies.

Study 1

In 1971–3, we recorded resting EEGs in 129 boys in Copenhagen as part of a prospective study of factors predisposing to delinquency (Mednick, Volavka, Gabrielli, & Itil, 1981). The boys were then 11–13 years old. The EEGs were subjected to computerized period analysis. The records of offenses in the Danish National Police Register served as the measure of delinquency. The subjects were selected for their high risk for delinquency (a large proportion of the children had parents diagnosed as schizophrenic or as having character disorders), and the records reflected this selection: 25 boys (22.5%) had at least one registered theft, and 30 boys (23.3%) at least one traffic infraction. Violent offenses were much less common (3%). Of the 25 thieves, 15 had a record of one offense and 10 had two or more offenses. The relation between EEG and future theft is displayed in Table 8.1. The significance of the differences between the means of EEG activity for nonoffenders, single offenders, and multiple offenders was assessed by analyses of covariance. A separate analysis was performed for each EEG scalp location (derivation) and for each EEG frequency band (a total of 64 analyses). In each analysis, the subject's exact age at the time of the EEG recording was controlled.

The three groups of subjects (no offense, one offense, more than one offense) differed in the relative amount of EEG activity between 8 and 10 Hz. Multiple offenders had significantly more activity in this band than the other subjects in five of the eight EEG derivations (scalp locations). Three of those five derivations were on the right side; two were on the left side. Analogous analyses were performed for traffic offenders; no consistent relations to EEG were found.

This study showed that the relative amount of slow alpha (8–10 Hz) EEG activity in 10- to 13-year-old Danish boys predicted recidivistic thievery. The number of subjects was relatively small, and they were selected to maximize the risk of antisocial behavior. We thought that the results should be replicated in a larger sample; Study 2 was undertaken for that purpose.

Table 8.1. *Mean percent EEG activity in each frequency band for sample males with no theft, one theft, or two or more thefts (for eight EEG derivations)*

EEG deri-vation	Number of thefts	EEG frequency bands (Hz)							
		1.5–3.5	3.5–5.5	5.5–8.0	8.0–10.0	10.0–13.0	13.0–18.0	18.0–26.0	26 & up
T3-P3	0	12	18	25	16	12	7	5	5
	1	11	17	24	17	13	8	5	5
	2	9	13	25	21	15	7	5	5
T4-P4	0	12	17	24	17	13	7	5	4
	1	9	15	23	19	15	8	5	5
	2	10	11	27	24*	15	6*	4	3
C3-A1	0	16	22	24	13	10	7	5	4
	1	13	22	24	13	11	8	5	5
	2	12	19	27	16	11	6	4	4
C4-A2	0	16	22	23	13	10	7	5	4
	1	16	21	24	13	10	7	5	4
	2	13	19	27	15	11	6	4	3
P3-O1	0	11	15	24	22	16	6	3	3
	1	11	14	24	21	16	7	4	3
	2	7	8	24	30*	19	6	3	2
	0	11	14	25	21	15	6	4	3

P4-O2	1	11	13	23	22	18	8	4	3
	2	7	8	26	29*	18	6	3	3
O1-A1	0	12	14	24	22	15	6	3	3
	1	11	13	23	21	16	7	4	3
	2	6	7*	26	32**	18	6	3	2
O2-A2	0	12	14	24	22	15	6	3	3
	1	13	13	23	22	16	7	4	3
	2	8	7	26	30*	18	6	3	2

*p < .05, analyses of variance controlling for age at EEG testing.
**p < .01, analyses of variance controlling for age at EEG testing.
T3-P3: left parietotemporal.
T4-P4: right parietotemporal.
C3-A1: left central–left ear.
C4-A2: right central–right ear.
P3-O1: left parietooccipital.
P4-O2: right parietooccipital.
O1-A1: left occipital–left ear.
O2-A2: right occipital–right ear.

Reprinted with permission from Mednick et al. (1981). *Criminology, 19:223.* © 1981 American Society of Criminology.

Study 2

This study (Petersen, Matousek, Mednick, Volavka, & Pollock, 1982) was conducted in Gothenburg, Sweden. A total of 571 subjects (age range 1–15 years) were selected using very stringent criteria for "normality." Subjects with a history of neuropsychiatric disorder were not included. All subjects received a physical examination; those with abnormal findings were excluded. The principal purpose of this study was to provide an EEG data bank for quantitative EEG developmental standards for the normal population. In 1967–8, the subjects received an EEG examination. The EEGs were subjected to visual assessment as well as to frequency analysis. In 1979 and 1980, information on illegal activities for which these subjects had been apprehended was obtained from the Swedish National Police Register in Stockholm and from the local social welfare offices in Gothenburg. A total of 54 persons in the sample of 571 had committed one or more crimes. Twenty of these 54 offenders had been apprehended for theft. The 517 subjects without any criminal record served as controls.

The hand-measured average alpha frequency in the group of 20 future thieves was significantly lower than in controls. The frequency analysis yielded estimates of EEG power in the slow alpha (7.5–9.5 Hz) and fast alpha (9.5–12.5 Hz) frequency bands. To obtain a measure approximating the alpha frequency, the power in the slow alpha (alpha 1) band was divided by that in the fast alpha (alpha 2) band. The higher the value of this ratio, the slower was the average alpha frequency. The ratio was significantly higher in the persons convicted of theft than in the controls. The results suggest that the slowing of alpha frequency was more pronounced in the (future) multiple offenders than in single offenders (Figure 8.1); this difference between single and multiple offenders was not statistically significant.

In addition to the analyses of alpha frequency, a composite measure reflecting the maturity or developmental level of the EEG ("age ratio") was used to compare the future thieves with the controls. The age ratio was significantly lower in the thieves.

Studies 1 and 2 provide evidence that a specific type of antisocial behavior – thievery – is more likely to develop in persons who have a slowing of alpha frequency than in persons who do not. The studies differed vastly in their criteria for subject selection and (to a smaller extent) in the methods used for recording and analyzing the EEG. The replication of the findings in spite of these methodological differences suggests that the relation between thievery and EEG is relatively robust.

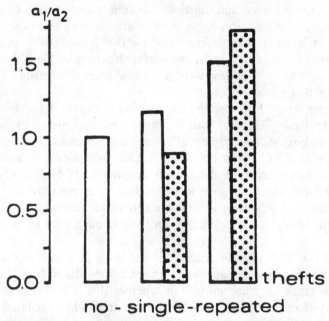

Figure 8.1. Relation between EEG alpha frequency and number of thefts. The alpha frequency is expressed as a ratio of slow to fast alpha activity. The higher the ratio, the slower is the alpha activity. Major thefts (shadowed) and minor thefts (dotted) are displayed separately. Reprinted with permission from Petersen et al. (1982), *Acta Psychiatrica Scandinavica 62*, 331–8. © 1982 Munksgaard International Publishers Ltd., Copenhagen Denmark.

It is possible that the slowing of alpha activity in future thieves reflects a developmental lag. We cannot be sure, because each of these subjects received only one EEG; repeated tests would be needed to study the developmental trajectories. If the slowing were caused by brain injuries, one would not expect to find it in the Swedish sample (Study 2), because subjects with a history of head injury or brain injury were excluded. One could, of course, hypothesize subclinical (perhaps perinatal) brain injuries causing the slowing, but such a hypothesis would be difficult to support or test.

Evidence suggests that genetic factors play a role in petty criminality, including thievery (Bohman, Cloninger, Sigvardsson, & von Knorring, 1982). Certain EEG features are heritable (Vogel, Schalt, Kruger, Propping, & Lehnert, 1979); we are not aware of any study exploring the heritability of the average alpha frequency. It is possible that the slowing represents a biological marker for thievery, but without family EEG studies, we cannot say whether this slowing was genetically transmitted.

One can hypothesize that the alpha slowing reflects a factor or factors that predispose to thievery. A low level of arousal may be associated with difficulty in learning law-abiding behavior (Mednick & Volavka, 1980). Alpha activity normally slows down during drowsiness. Does the slowing of alpha activity in prethieves reflect a low level of arousal? This is a hypothesis that could be tested.

We do not know how specific the relation between alpha slowing and thievery really is. Thievery was by far the most common crime in the Swedish sample; violent crime was so rare that no meaningful analysis of its relation to EEG could be made. Traffic infractions occurred more frequently than thievery in the Danish sample (Study 1), but other types of crimes were again too rare to be studied. It is possible that various types of criminal or antisocial behavior other than thievery are also associated with alpha slowing. We did not have enough data to explore this possibility.

We are not sure whether EEG alpha slowing is a trait that could be detected at any point during adolescence and adulthood (e.g., in the period when crimes are committed) or whether this is a phenomenon that disappears after the subjects reach maturity. It should be pointed out that Studies 1 and 2 were conducted in two of the most egalitarian and ethnically homogeneous societies in the world. In Scandinavia, the differences in income among social classes are much smaller than in the United States and other Western countries. Thus the effects of poverty and racial discrimination on the development of thievery in Scandinavia are very likely to be much weaker than in the United States, and the relative importance of biological factors in the development of antisocial behavior is consequently greater there than in the United States.

We believe that the results of Studies 1 and 2 are sufficiently encouraging to warrant additional research effort in this area. Future studies should include repeated EEG testing in all subjects, long-term follow-ups for antisocial behavior, family studies (including EEG), psychophysiological studies concomitant with EEG to explore the arousal hypothesis further, and subjects at high risk for offenses other than thievery. The results of Studies 1 and 2 should be replicated in societies outside Scandinavia.

References

Bohman, M., Cloninger, C. R., Sigvardsson, S., & von Knorring, A. L. (1982). Predisposition to petty criminality in Swedish adoptees. *Archives of General Psychiatry, 39*, 1233–41.

DeBaudouin, Haumonte, Bessing, & Geissman, P. (1961). Study of a population of 97 confined murderers [in French]. *Annales Medico-Psychologiques, 119* (1), 625–86.

Driver, M. V., West, L. R., & Faulk, M. (1974). Clinical and EEG studies of prisoners charged with murder. *British Journal of Psychiatry 125*, 583–7.

Forssman, H., & Frey, T. S. (1953). Electroencephalograms of boys with behavior disorders. *Acta Psychologica et Neurologica Scandinavica, 28*, 61–73.

Gibbs, F. A., Bagchi, B. K., & Bloomberg, W. (1945). Electroencephalographic study of criminals. *American Journal of Psychiatry, 102*, 294–8.

Hill, D., & Sargant, W. (1943). A Case of matricide. *Lancet, 244*(1), 526–7.

Hill, D., & Watterson, D. (1942). Electro-encephalographic studies of psychopathic personalities. *Journal of Neurology and Psychiatry, 5*(1–2), 47–65.

Klingman, D., & Goldberg, D. A. (1975). Temporal lobe epilepsy and aggression. *Journal of Nervous and Mental Disease, 160*(5), 324–41.

Lewis, D. O., Pincus, J. H., Shanok, S. S., & Glaser, G. H. (1982). Psychomotor epilepsy and violence in a group of incarcerated adolescent boys. *American Journal of Psychiatry, 139*, 882–7.

Mark, V. H., & Ervin, F. R. (1970). *Violence and the brain.* New York: Harper & Row.

Mednick, S. A., & Volavka, J. (1980). Biology and crime. In N. Morris & M. Tonry (Eds.), *Crime and justice: An Annual Review of Research* (Vol. 2, pp. 85–158). University of Chicago Press.

Mednick, S. A., Volavka, J., Gabrielli, W. F., & Itil, T. M. (1981). EEG as a predictor of antisocial behavior, *Criminology, 19*, 219–29.

Petersen, I., Matousek, M., Mednick, S. A., Volavka, J., & Pollock, V. (1982). EEG antecedents of thievery. *Acta Psychiatrica Scandinavica, 62*, 331–8.

Rodin, E. A. (1973). Psychomotor epilepsy and aggressive behavior. *Archives of General Psychiatry, 28*, 210–13.

Vogel, A., Schalt, R., Kruger, J., Propping, P., & Lehnert, K. F. (1979). The electroencephalogram (EEG) as a research tool in human behavior genetics: Psychological examinations in healthy males with various inherited EEG variants: I. Rationale of the study, material, methods, heritability of test parameters. *Human Genetics, 47*, 1–46.

Volavka, J., Matousek, M., Feldstein, S., Roubicek, J., Prior, P., Scott, D. F., Brezinova, V., & Synek, V. (1973). The reliability of EEG assessment. *Zeitschrift für Elektroenzephalographie, Elektromyographie, und verwändte Gebiete, 4*(3), 123–30.

Volavka, J., Mednick, S. A., Sergeant, J., & Rasmussen, L. (1977a). Electroencephalograms of XYY and XXY men. *British Journal of Psychiatry, 130*, 43–7.

Volavka, J., Mednick, S. A., Sergeant, J., & Rasmussen, L. (1977b). EEG spectra in XYY and XXY men. *EEG and Clinical Neurophysiology, 43*, 798–801.

Williams, D. (1969). Neural factors related to habitual aggression: Consideration of differences between those habitual aggressives and others who have committed crimes of violence. *Brain, 92*, 503–20.

9   Childhood diagnostic and neurophysiological predictors of teenage arrest rates: an eight-year prospective study

James H. Satterfield

Introduction

Many disorders of early childhood are transient and are not predictive of psychopathology in later life (Kohlberg, La Cross, & Ricks, 1972). This is clearly not the case for the hyperactive child syndrome. The hyperactive child presents a remarkably immutable syndrome that forecasts an ominous picture of the future. The clinical picture often worsens as the child grows older, with resulting adolescent problems of academic failure and serious antisocial behavior.

Although many follow-up studies of hyperactive children have revealed a substantial subgroup (25%) to be delinquent (Huessy, Metoyer, & Townsend, 1974; Mendelson, Johnson, & Stewart, 1971; Weiss, Minde, Werry, Douglas, & Nemeth, 1971), most studies are flawed by one or more of the following weaknesses: inadequate or missing control group; lack of information as to the nature, frequency, and type of offenses committed; absence of official arrest data; and a substantial number of subjects lost to follow-up. It is generally thought that the teenage delinquency rate among former hyperactive children is higher than that among nonhyperactive control children. However, because of the above-mentioned weaknesses, how much higher the delinquency rate is among the hyperactive group is not known. The amount of predictive information the diagnosis of hyperactive child syndrome conveys regarding teenage delinquency is related to the question of how much higher the rate of teenage delinquency is among former hyperactive children than among nonhyperactive control children. In other words, if the diagnosis adds predictive information, children diagnosed as hyperactive should have an outcome substantially different from those who did not fit the diagnosis. The greater the disparity between the outcome of the two groups, the more information regarding outcome the diagnosis conveys. A major question of interest here is whether the diagnosis of hyperactive child syndrome conveys prognostic information about serious antisocial behavior in later life and, if so, how much information.

Most investigators would agree that the hyperactive child syndrome (minimal brain dysfunction, hyperkinesis, attention-deficit disorder) represents a heterogenic group in terms of etiology and prognosis. The difficulty lies in identifying meaningful subgroups. One approach to this difficult classification problem is to study subjects as children and then later restudy them as adolescents or young adults. At the latter time subgroups can be formed on the basis of different types of outcome. Using this outcome classification, one can then reexamine the childhood measures seeking childhood attributes or events that predict outcome, perhaps even learning something about etiology. We explored such a strategy in a study in which we utilized a broad-based childhood evaluation (behavioral, psychological, psychiatric, social, neurological, and neurophysiological) of subjects and then obtained outcome measures on these same youths 8 years later. As far as is known, this was the first prospective longitudinal study to have an initial data base this broad. A second major focus of the study was the search for neurophysiological predictors of serious antisocial behavior. A third question concerned the long-term benefits, if any, of stimulant drug treatment.

Method

Subject selection

The study to be described here was part of an extensive follow-up of 150 hyperactive and 88 normal control subjects. For reasons described below, we used data only from those subjects known to be living in Los Angeles County at follow-up. This provided us with 110 hyperactive subjects and 75 normal subjects selected in childhood (ages 6–12). All hyperactive children were originally referred between 1970 and 1972 for learning and/or behavioral problems to an outpatient clinic for hyperactive children. Informed consent was obtained from all subjects and from their parents after the experimental procedures were fully explained. To be selected for the hyperactive group, a child had to have the following characteristics: male, attending school, tested normal vision and hearing, IQ at or above 80 on the Wechsler Intelligence Scale for Children (WISC Full Scale), and diagnosed by a child psychiatrist using behavioral criteria that required evidence of a chronic (6 months or longer) symptom pattern of hyperactivity, inattention, and impulsivity as reported by parents and/or teachers. When subjects were selected for this study, the diagnostic category of attention-deficit disorder (ADD) was not in use. Nevertheless, the clinical children in this study were selected by criteria that are similar to DSM-III criteria for ADD with hyperactivity. Normal control children were paid subjects, were selected from public school classes, and were matched to the clinical group for age and sex and, as closely as possible, for race and WISC Full Scale IQ. In order to improve the social-class balance between groups, we added to the control group at follow-up all nonhyperactive brothers (aged 14–20) of our hyperactive subjects who were from low-social-class families living in Los Angeles County. This provided an additional 13 control subjects, for a total of 88 control subjects.

Initial childhood evaluations

All hyperactive subjects were evaluated from several points of view: behavioral, psychological, psychiatric, neurological, and neurophysiological. Control subjects were similarly evaluated, except that they did not receive psychiatric or neurological evaluations. Only childhood behavioral, neurophysiological, and a few psychological measures will be described here.

The Satterfield Teacher and Parent Rating Scales were obtained on most subjects. The teacher rating scale consists of 36 behavioral items rated from 0 to 3: 0, not at all; 1, just a little; 2, pretty much; and 3, very much. A maximum likelihood factor analysis was performed on the individual item scores of this scale, and five orthogonal factors were extracted. An item was retained in a factor only if it loaded 0.5 or greater on that factor. If an item loaded 0.5 or greater on more than one factor, it was retained only in the factor on which it loaded the highest. Factor scores were obtained by averaging the item scores of those items selected for each factor. These five factors were labeled as follows: I, Hyperactive; II, Antisocial; III, Impulsive; IV, Inattentive; V, Withdrawn. Individual items on the Satterfield Teacher Rating Scale have been published previously (Satterfield, Hoppe, & Schell, 1982). The Satterfield Parent Rating Scale is similar to the teacher scale and consists of 45 behavioral items rated from 1 to 3: 1, not at all; 2, sometimes true; and 3, definitely true. Factor scores were computed in a manner similar to that described for the teacher rating scale. The following factors were obtained: I, Hyperactive; II, Inattentive; III, Impulsive; IV, Antisocial; V, Irritable.

Auditory event-related potential (AERP), electroencephalographic (EEG) power spectra, skin resistance level, and eyeblink potential data were obtained on most subjects. Subjects were seated in an easy chair in a soundproof, electrically shielded room. The EEG was recorded using

Grass gold disk electrodes from a double vertex placement. Electrodes were located 2.5 cm from the midline and referred to the ipsilateral earlobe. A ground electrode was placed on the forehead. Eyeblink and eye movement artifacts were monitored from transorbital electrodes, and a running sum of motion and eye movement artifacts was kept and was available at the end of the experiment. Beckman silver/silver chloride electrodes (10 mm diameter) were placed on the first and third fingertips of both hands. Skin resistance was obtained with a direct current of 5 μA (microamperes) and was later converted to skin conductance for analysis.

Subjects were instructed to watch a videotaped cartoon show on a television monitor and to ignore clicks being presented over two loudspeakers, which were placed 45° to the left and right of the subject. Thus the AERPs were being recorded in response to an irrelevant and unattended stimulus. Auditory stimuli were clicks lasting 0.1 msec with an intensity of 90 dB sound pressure level; the television sound was 50 dB sound pressure level throughout the experiment. Stimuli were presented in blocks at two regular rates; a block of 64 stimuli at a slow rate of one stimulus every 2.5 sec alternated with a block of 256 stimuli at a fast rate of two stimuli per second. Only data from the slow stimulus rate were used for analysis.

During the slow stimulus interval, the EEG was sampled at a 2-msec rate for two 500-msec epochs for each stimulus and recorded on digital tape. The first 500-msec epoch (AERP) began 100 msec before the onset of the stimulus, and the second 500-msec epoch began 1 sec after the onset of the stimulus (at which time the evoked potential was over). Data from the first epoch for each stimulus were averaged in order to obtain averaged AERPs. Data from the second epoch were used to obtain EEG power spectral information. Only artifact-free AERP epochs were averaged. The individual artifact-free nonsignal epochs were first transformed by power spectral analysis, and then average power spectral values were computed. The averaged AERP and power spectral data were used for further analysis. The absolute spectral measures (delta = 1.5–3.5 Hz, theta = 3.5–7.5 Hz, alpha = 7.5–12.5 Hz, beta 1 = 12–20 Hz, and beta 2 = 20–30 Hz) were also normalized for analysis as relative power by dividing by total power, excluding power below 1.5 Hz. Skin resistance level was recorded on digital tape every 2 min throughout the experiment, and mean skin conductance level for the experiment was obtained.

Most subjects were tested on a continuous performance task (CPT) in which the subject tracked a moving target with a cursor on an oscilloscope. The subject's score represented his average absolute distance off target. Doing well on this task required the subject's continuous attention.

Clinical EEGs were obtained for many hyperactive subjects. EEG records were classified as normal, "borderline," or abnormal. Details of the method of classification and results have been reported previously (Satterfield, Cantwell, Saul, & Yusin, 1974). Before follow-up, most hyperactive children had received stimulant drug treatment (methyl phenidate) and brief counseling. The mean treatment period was 25.1 months (S.D. = 24.1 months). The socioeconomic status of all families was measured by the Duncan Scale (Duncan, 1961), a six-category scale based on the occupation of the head of the household. This scale was collapsed into three social-class categories (lower, middle, and upper) by combining adjoining categories.

Follow-up measures

At follow-up, several types of outcome measures were obtained on different groups of subjects. Only outcome measures derived from official arrest data are reported. The Los Angeles County Probation Department maintains a central juvenile index of all reported arrests from childhood to 18 years of age for persons living in the county. This information includes type and frequency of offense, whether the youth was institutionalized, and, if so, the type of institution. Although arrests that occur after the age of 18 are not entered into this file, the record is maintained until the subject is more than 21 years old. Because our subjects were 14–20 years old at the time of follow-up, arrests of any of these subjects that occurred between ages 14 and 18 would be found in this file. Once a subject moved out of the county, he would not be at risk for entering the file; therefore, only those subjects still living in Los Angeles County were included in this study. Official arrest information was obtained on all 198 subjects. We classified offenders into two types: serious and nonserious. Nonserious offenders were youths who had been arrested for minor offenses including status crimes, alcohol intoxication, possession of less than an ounce of marijuana, vandalism, and petty theft. Serious offenders were youths who had been arrested for more serious offenses including robbery, burglary, grand theft, grand theft automobile, and assault with a deadly weapon. The majority of subjects (83% of hyperactives and 97% of controls) were white. Separate analyses in each social class of hyperactive offender type by race revealed no difference between blacks and whites; therefore, these groups were combined for purposes of analysis.

Statistical comparisons between the hyperactive and control subjects and between subgroups of hyperactive and control subjects were performed using chi-square or *t* tests, as appropriate.

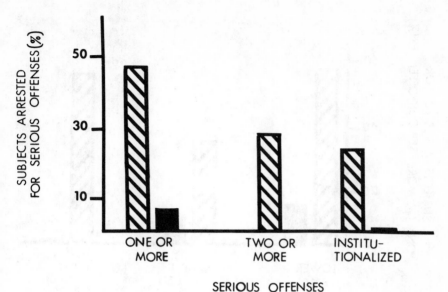

Figure 9.1. Comparison of hyperactive (Striped bars, $n = 110$) and normal (solid bars, $N = 88$) adolescent offender and institutionalization rates.

Results

Diagnosis as a predictor of teenage arrest rates

The overall offender and institutionalization rates for 110 hyperactive and 88 normal youths are shown in Figure 9.1. It can be seen that the hyperactive-offender rates for any serious offense, multiple serious offenses, and institutionalization were, respectively, 6, 28, and 25 times higher than the rates for normal controls. These differences were statistically significant (chi-square = 32.5, 22.7, and 18.7, respectively, with d.f. = 1, $p < .001$). These differences were probably not due to age differences, because the two groups differed by only 4 months in mean age.

However, the two groups were not as well matched in social class. In a previously reported study, we controlled for social-class differences by first stratifying subjects on social class and then comparing delinquency rates for hyperactive and normal groups (Satterfield et al., 1982). We found that the hyperkinetic-offender rates for any serious offense in the lower, middle, and upper social classes were, respectively, 5, 4, and 26 times higher than for control subjects (chi-square = 7.87, $p < .01$; chi-square = 4.48, $p < .05$; and chi-square = 20.2, $p < .001$, respectively, with d.f. = 1; see Figure 9.2). These differences were not due to age,

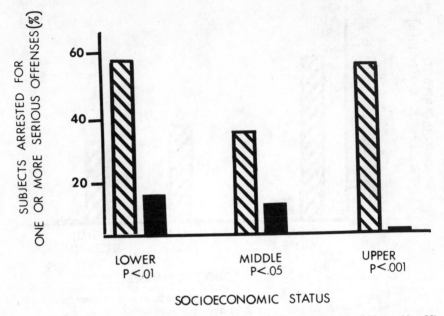

Figure 9.2. Hyperactive (striped bars, $N = 110$) and normal (solid bars, $N = 88$) adolescents stratified on social class and compared on offender rates for one or more arrests for serious offenses.

because the groups compared were not significantly different in age. Lower arrest rates were found for upper-social-class control subjects and for middle-class hyperactive subjects, but these trends were not significant.

For multiple serious offenses, hyperactive-offender rates were seven times greater in the lower social class and more than 25 and 28 times greater in the middle and upper social classes, respectively, than for control subjects (Figure 9.3). These differences were significant for the lower, middle, and upper social classes (chi-square = 6.94, $p < .01$; chi-square = 12.9, $p < .001$; and chi-square = 11.6, $p < .001$, respectively, with d.f. = 1). Finally, as noted in Figure 9.1, the rate of institutionalization for delinquent behavior in the hyperactive group was 25% (27 subjects), whereas in the control group it was 1% (1 subject) (chi-square = 18.7, d.f. = 1, $p < .001$). Hyperactive youths were placed in six types of institution (Table 9.1). Institutionalization patterns varied: Six subjects had been in only one type of institution; 17 subjects in two types, 3 subjects in three types; 1 subject in four types. There was a nonsignificant trend toward lower institutionalization rates in the hyperactive group of

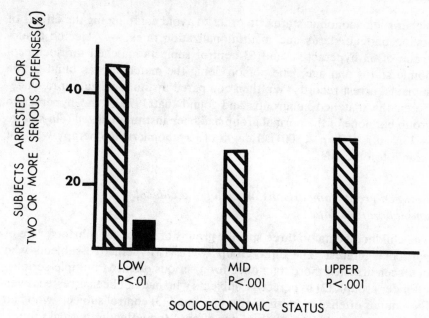

Figure 9.3. Hyperactive (striped bars, $N = 110$) and normal (solid bars, $N = 88$) adolescents stratified on social class and compared on offender rates for two or more arrests for serious offenses.

Table 9.1. *Institutional patterns for 110 hyperactive youths and 88 control boys*

Institution	Hyperactives		Controls	
	N	$\%$	N	$\%$
California Youth Authority	5	5	0	0
Prison or jail	2	2	0	0
County probation	7	6	0	0
Juvenile hall	22	20	1	1
Group residential home	9	8	0	0
Psychiatric hospital	8	7	0	0
Total	27^a	25	1	1

[a] Other numbers total more than 27 because some subjects had been in more than one institution.

higher socioeconomic status. In order to avoid confounding the effects of socioeconomic status and institutionalization rates, we selected a subgroup of 63 hyperactive and 63 control subjects matched for socioeconomic status and age. The person doing the matching was blind to the subjects' arrest records. We then compared institutionalization rates between the matched subgroups and found that 19% of the hyperactive group but none of the normal group had been institutionalized (chi-square = 13.2, d.f. = 1, $p < .001$). Length of psychopharmacotherapy was not related to outcome.

Between-group comparisons on childhood clinical and laboratory data

The childhood data on three specific groups of follow-up subjects were of particular interest. The three groups were (1) hyperactive subjects who had been arrested more than once for a serious offense (multiple-serious-offender group); (2) hyperactive subjects who had not been arrested, even for a minor offense (nonoffender group); and (3) control subjects who had not been arrested, even for a minor offense (nonoffender normal group).

Normal subjects compared with hyperactive subjects. We first compared the normal group with the two hyperactive groups on EEG power spectral measures (Table 9.2). It can be seen that the nonoffender hyperactives were significantly different from the normal group on three absolute power measures having greater than normal power, whereas the offender group did not differ from the normals on any of these measures. When we compared hyperactives with normals on relative (normalized) power, we found both hyperactive groups to be significantly different from the normal group on three measures (Table 9.3). Both hyperactive groups were different in the same direction; that is, both had less relative theta and more relative alpha and beta 2 power. In two of these three measures, the significance level for the nonoffenders was greater than that for the offenders.

When the normal subjects were compared with the two hyperactive groups on AERP measures, we found two amplitude components (P2 and N2) of the nonoffenders to be significantly lower than those of the normal subjects, but *none of the AERP components of the offenders were abnormal* (Table 9.4). AERP component latencies for both groups of hyperactive subjects were not different from those for the normal group. Table 9.5 summarizes the significant EEG and AERP differences between the normal group and the two hyperactive groups. It can be seen that nonoffen-

Table 9.2. *Multiple-serious-offender and nonoffender hyperactives compared with normal nonoffenders on childhood absolute power spectral measures*

Measure	Normals	Hyperactives	
		Offenders	Nonoffenders
N	65	31	45
Mean age (months)	101	101	95.5
EEG Absolute power			
Total	87.4	84.8	102.0*
Delta	28.2	25.8	31.4
Theta	28.9	26.5	30.9
Alpha	18.0	19.9	25.8***
Beta 1	4.9	5.3	5.6
Beta 2	3.2	3.3	4.0**

* $p < .05$.
** $p < .01$.
*** $p < .001$.

der hyperactives differed from normal control subjects on eight measures, whereas offender hyperactives were abnormal on only three measures.

Because the age range of the hyperactive and normal children was 6–12 years, we were able to examine the effects of age on our evoked potential

Table 9.3. *Multiple-serious-offender and nonoffender hyperactives compared with normal nonoffenders on childhood relative power spectral measures*

Measures	Normals	Hyperactives	
		Offenders	Nonoffenders
N	65	31	45
Mean age (months)	101	101	95.5
EEG Relative power			
Delta	32.4	30.5	30
Theta	33.1	31.5*	31.3**
Alpha	20.4	23.2*	24.9***
Beta 1	5.9	6.3	5.5
Beta 2	3.6	3.9*	3.9*

* $p < .05$.
** $p < .01$.
*** $p < .001$.

Table 9.4. *Offender and nonoffender hyperactives compared with nonoffender normals on childhood evoked potential measures*

Measures	Normals	Hyperactives	
		Offenders	Nonoffenders
N	40	26	35
Mean age (months)	102.8	101.8	97.0
AERP Amplitude			
P1	4.5	4.1	4.1
N1	−0.9	−0.9	−0.7
P2	7.7	6.6	6.0*
N2	−6.4	−5.6	−4.3**

* $p < .05$.
** $p < .01$.

Table 9.5. *Hyperactives compared with normals on childhood EEG and AERP measures*

Measure	Hyperactives	
	Nonoffenders	Multiple Serious Offenders
Absolute PSA[a]		
Total power	▲	ns
Alpha	▲▲▲	ns
Beta 2	▲▲	ns
Relative power		
Theta	▼▼	▼
Alpha	▲▲▲	▲
Beta 2	▲	▲
AERP Amplitude		
P2	▼	ns
N2	▼▼	ns

Note: Twenty-one comparisons were made. Arrows indicate direction of group differences; ns denotes not significant.
[a] PSA, power spectrum analysis.
▲, $p < .05$.
▲▲, $p < .01$.
▲▲▲, $p < .001$.

Table 9.6. *AERP correlations with age in hyperactives that are significantly different from normal AERP–Age correlations*

| | | Hyperactives | |
AERP Measure	Normals	Offenders	Nonoffenders
N1 Latency	.26	.12	−.28*
P2 Amplitude	−.18	.21	.52**
N2 Amplitude	−.42	−.06	−.04*

Note: Twenty-four correlations were obtained between age and neuro-physiological measures.
* $p < .05$.
** $p < .01$.

measures in all three groups. Comparisons among normal- and hyperac-tive-group correlations between age and AERP measures revealed three correlations that were significantly different from the normal control group, all three of which were in the nonoffender hyperactive group (Table 9.6).

Two laboratory behavioral measures and one skin conductance mea-sure were available for between-group comparisons (Table 9.7). On the CPT both hyperactive groups did significantly poorer than the normal group. However, the mean score of the nonoffender group was more abnormal than was the mean score of the offender group, though this difference was not significant. Although there were no significant group

Table 9.7. *Multiple-serious-offender and nonoffender hyperactives compared with nonoffender normals on a continuous performance task and conductance level*

| | | Hyperactives | |
Measure	Normals	Offenders	Nonoffenders
N (range)	68–45	31–19	42–29
Age (months)	105	102	95**
CPT[a]	105	146**	171***
SCL[b]	15.0	18.5*	16.4
Eyeblink	401	433	358

[a] Continuous performance task.
[b] Skin conductance level.
* $p < .05$.
** $p < .01$.
*** $p < .001$.

Table 9.8. *Childhood clinical EEG findings in offender and nonoffender hyperactives*

	Hyperactives	
Measure	Nonoffenders	Offenders
N	12	8
Clinical EEG		
Normal	6 (50%)	7 (88%)
Abnormal	6 (50%)	1 (12%)

differences in the number of eyeblinks detected during the experiment, it is of interest that nonoffenders had fewer, and offenders more, eyeblinks than did normal subjects. Although both hyperactive groups had higher skin conductance levels than the normal group, the difference was significant only for the offender hyperactives. This was one of the few instances in which the offender hyperactives were, and the nonoffenders were not, significantly different from normal.

At the time of our initial evaluation we obtained clinical EEGs on a subset of our hyperactive children. We found that the rate of clinical EEG abnormal findings was smaller (12%) in the offender group than in the nonoffender group (50%) (chi-square with d.f. = 1 marginally significant at $p < 0.1$; see Table 9.8).

Nonoffender and offender hyperactives compared on childhood measures. There were a number of measures on which the two hyperactive groups were not found to differ significantly. Some were the WISC Full Scale IQ, WISC Performance IQ, and WISC Verbal IQ; social class; and family type. However, there was a nonsignificant trend for hyperactives from middle-class and from two-biological-parent families to have a lower serious-offender rate.

Comparison of the factor scores from the parent and teacher rating scales revealed that the multiple-offender group had significantly higher scores on the hyperactive and antisocial factors from the parent rating scale and a higher score on the antisocial factor on the teacher rating scale than did the nonoffender group (Table 9.9).

When multiple-serious-offender and nonoffender hyperactives were compared on EEG power spectral and AERP measures, we found that offenders had significantly less absolute power in the theta, alpha, and beta 2 bands and a significantly greater N2 amplitude of the AERP (Table 9.10). Other analyses (unpublished data) revealed an extraordinarily low offender rate for normal children from families with two biological parents. This suggested that environmental and social factors play a minor role in the development of antisocial behavior in these families, and therefore such families might be ideal for the study of biological factors that

Table 9.9. *Childhood parent and teacher behavior rating scale factor scores for multiple-serious-offender and nonoffender hyperactives*

Factor scores	Offenders	Nonoffenders
Parent rating scale		
Hyperactive	2.6*	2.2
Inattentive	2.3	2.1
Impulsive	2.0	1.6
Antisocial	1.1*	0.7
Teacher rating scale		
Hyperactive	2.5	2.3
Inattentive	2.2	2.1
Impulsive	1.6	1.7
Antisocial	1.6*	1.2
Withdrawn	1.5	1.4

* $p < .05$.

Table 9.10. *Multiple-serious-offender and nonoffender hyperactives compared on childhood EEG and AERP measures*

	Hyperactive children	
Measure	Multiple serious offenders	Nonoffenders
N	31–26[a]	45–35
Mean age (months)	101	96
Absolute power		
Total	84.8*	102.0
Theta	26.5*	30.9
Alpha	19.9*	25.8
Beta 2	3.3*	4.0
AEP		
N2 Amplitude	−5.6*	−4.3

Note: Twenty-two comparisons were made.
[a] *N* for AERP is less than that for EEG measures.
* $p < .05$.

Table 9.11. *Multiple serious offenders compared with nonoffender hyperactives from two-parent families*

		Hyperactives	
Measure	Normals	Multiple serious offenders	Nonoffenders
N	30	13–12[a]	27–19
Mean age (months)	103	100	96
AERP			
N2 amplitude	−5.99	−5.78*	−4.08
N2 latency	254	270*	249
EEG Absolute power			
Alpha	17.0	19.7*	28.0
EEG Relative power			
Alpha	19.8	21.3*	26.3
Beta 1	5.9	7.0*	5.7

[a] *N* for AERP is less than *N* for EEG measures.
* $p < .05$.
** $p < .01$.

may underlie antisocial behavior. Following this rationale, we compared all multiple-serious- and nonserious-offender hyperactive children who were living with two biological parents (Table 9.11).

Of interest were the findings of less relative as well as less absolute power in the alpha band, a larger N2 amplitude, and a longer N2 latency in the multiple-serious-offender as compared with the nonserious-offender hyperactives. The findings in the multiple-offender group of a longer N2 latency and lower relative power in the alpha band were not present for the larger sample. The N2 amplitude was the first variable selected when we ran a discriminant function analysis in an attempt to separate these two hyperactive groups. To examine further the predictive power of the N2 amplitude, we rank-ordered the N2 amplitudes (from largest negative value to smallest) and observed the outcome for those subjects from two-biological-parent families. The percentage of the multiple serious offenders falling into the upper quartile of the N2 amplitude (above dashed line in Figure 9.4) was significantly larger (60% vs. 14%) than the percentage of other subjects falling in the same quartile (Fisher's Exact Test, $p < .05$).

The diagnosis of hyperactive child syndrome in two-parent families predicts a poor outcome (multiple arrests for serious offenses) in 29% of

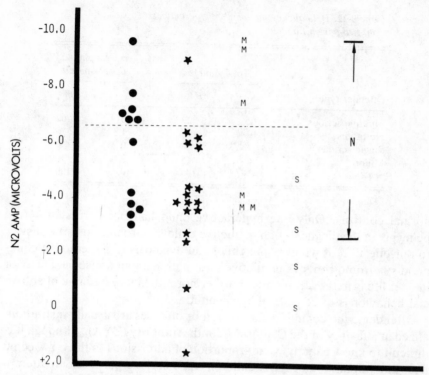

Figure 9.4. Childhood N2 amplitudes as a predictor of poor outcome (multiple arrests for serious offenses). Dashed line indicates upper quartile of N2 amplitude. Sixty percent of subjects above this threshold had a history of repeated arrests for serious offenses. *Key:* ●, multiple serious offender; ★, nonoffender; M, minor offender; S, single serious offender; N, normal nonoffender.

cases (Table 9.12). However, our ability to select children at risk for this type of outcome is considerably enhanced if we add to the diagnostic data information about the subject's AERP N2 amplitude. This enables us to select a subgroup 60% of whom will have a poor outcome (Table 9.12).

Discussion

The data reported here indicate that the rate of teenage antisocial behavior as measured by (a) a single arrest for a serious offense, (b) multiple arrests for serious offenses, or (c) institutionalization for antisocial behavior is many times higher in former hyperactive children than in normal control subjects. This is particularly true for serious types of antisocial behavior, as reflected by multiple-offender and institutionalization rates, which are more than 25 times greater for hyperactive youths than for

Table 9.12. *Delinquency outcome in hyperactives from two-parent families*

Offender type	Total sample		N2 Amplitude, upper quartile	
	N	*%*	*N*	*%*
Multiple serious	12	29	6	60
No offense	19	46	1	10
Single serious	4	10	0	0
Minor	6	15	3	30
Total	41	100	10	100

normal controls. Only one hyperactive child had been arrested before being given the diagnosis of hyperactive child syndrome. Thus the answer to our question of whether the childhood diagnosis of hyperactive childhood syndrome conveys predictive information about antisocial behavior in later life is in the affirmative. Furthermore, the increased risk of antisocial behavior is of considerable magnitude.

Offenders who commit the most serious offenses are usually institutionalized at a facility of the California Youth Authority (CYA). Although it is difficult to know exactly what proportion of admissions to the CYA come from the population of ADD children, for heuristic purposes an attempt should be made to estimate the magnitude of the ADD contribution to this serious type of outcome. Such an estimate can be made if the following parameters are known: (a) the admission rate (number of admissions per 100,000 base population) of all males of a given age to CYA for a 12-month period, (b) the number of ADD boys in the base population of 100,000 males, and (c) the admission rate of these ADD boys to CYA during the same 12-month period.

The 12-month admission rate to CYA facilities in the year 1980 was 192 per 100,000 base population of all males (ADD and normal) aged 12–18 years (G. Howard, California Youth Authority, personal communication, 1982). The number of ADD boys in the base population can be estimated using the prevalence rate reported for ADD boys. The prevalence of ADD among school-age boys is approximately 9% (Miller, Palkes, & Stewart, 1973; Werner et al., 1981). However, the prevalence rate for physician-diagnosed ADD boys is somewhat lower (4.5%) (Bosco & Robin, 1981). Because our ADD population was physician-diagnosed, using this more conservative rate, 4.5%, or 4,500 boys, of the base population of 100,000 are estimated to suffer from the ADD syndrome. The 12-month rate of admission of our ADD boys to CYA facilities in the year 1980 was 3 per

110 youths, or 2.7%. Therefore, of the 4,500 ADD boys, 2.7%, or 122 adolescent ADD boys, would be estimated to have been admitted to CYA in the 12-month period of 1980. As noted above, 192 youths per 100,000 base population were admitted to CYA during this time. Therefore, 122 of the 192 of all males admitted, or 64% of all such admissions, are estimated to have formerly been ADD boys.

The poor outcome for drug treatment alone found here is in agreement with follow-up studies of drug-treated hyperactive children (Riddle & Rapoport, 1976; Weiss, Kruger, Danielson, & Elman, 1975). Despite evidence from these studies that indicates a lack of long-term benefits and despite the absence of any study that demonstrates long-term benefits, stimulant medication alone continues to be one of the most, if not the most, widely used form of treatment of hyperactive children. Such treatment may result in more harm than benefit for the child and family, because it may convince the parents that the child is receiving adequate treatment and divert attention from the need for treatment aimed at other problems such as antisocial behavior. However, stimulant medication is probably still an important aspect of a multimodality treatment approach (Satterfield, Cantwell, & Satterfield, 1979). Multimodality treatment has been demonstrated to result in less antisocial behavior, enhanced academic performance, and better social adjustment, when evaluated after 1, 2, and 3 years of treatment (Satterfield, Cantwell, & Satterfield, 1980; Satterfield et al., 1979; Satterfield, Satterfield, & Cantwell, 1981). Whether it also prevents teenage delinquency must be decided after further follow-up.

Our finding that hyperactive children who later become multiple offenders are rated more antisocial by both parents and teachers than are hyperactive children who do not later become offenders is consistent with a follow-up study of children seen in a child guidance outpatient clinic (Robins & Ratcliff, 1978).

The finding that a large childhood N2 amplitude exists in hyperactive children who become multiple offenders has both clinical and theoretical implications. From a clinical point of view, the selection of subgroups of hyperactive children, most of whom can be predicted to have a poor outcome, is useful for delinquency prevention, because it is more economical to treat only those children who one can be reasonably sure will have a bad outcome without treatment. The theoretical implications of this finding are discussed below.

Comparison of hyperactives who do and do not develop serious antisocial behavior with normal controls revealed that it is the hyperactive child who does *not* develop antisocial behavior who is the most abnormal on a number of brain function and laboratory measures (EEG power spectra and AERP data, Table 9.5; maturation effects on AERP, Table 9.6). In fact, the multiple-offender hyperactives were abnormal on only three of the 45 comparisons ($p < .05$), which is only slightly more than would be expected by chance. The finding of fewer childhood clinical EEG abnormalities in multiple-offender hyperactives as compared with nonoffender hyperactives is consistent with the EEG and AERP data reported above. The latter finding suggests that clinical EEG abnormalities (which we found in 18% of our hyperactive children) may be of value in predicting an *absence* of antisocial behavior in later life among hyperactive children. Although it may be surprising that hyperactive children with EEG abnormalities have the best long-term prognosis, we have previously reported that hyperactive children with abnormal EEGs have a greater likelihood of responding to a 6-week trial of stimulant drug treatment (Satterfield, 1973).

AERP, EEG power spectral, and clinical EEG findings suggest that there may be two distinct subgroups of hyperactive children. The poor-outcome group is characterized by *normal* EEG power spectral and AERP measures, normal age effects on these two measures, normal clinical EEG findings, and higher scores on antisocial and hyperactive factors in childhood and multiple arrests for serious offenses in their teens. The good-outcome subgroup of hyperactive children is characterized by abnormal EEG power spectral values, abnormal AERPs, abnormal EEG and AERP changes with age, abnormal clinical EEGs, lower scores on antisocial and hyperactive factors, and absence of teenage antisocial behavior. It is interesting to conjecture that the childhood disorder of good-outcome hyperactive children with *abnormal* EEG and AERP findings is secondary to an underlying brain dysfunction, whereas the childhood disorder of the poor-outcome with *normal* EEG and AERP findings is secondary to social–environmental factors. If so, then underlying social–environmental factors as a cause of this childhood disorder suggest a poorer prognosis than the same disorder secondary to brain dysfunction. This viewpoint is the opposite of the prevailing one, that abnormal behavior originating in the brain suggests a poorer prognosis than does abnormal behavior with a social–environmental etiology.

Our data clearly indicate that the traditional medical interpretation of EEG and AERP abnormalities does not apply to the hyperactive child. The usual interpretation of a brain function measure that deviates from *normal control data* as indicative of a poor prognosis is not supported by our data. In fact, the data suggest just the opposite; that is, normal EEG and AERP findings indicate a poor prognosis. We shall develop below the idea that these "normal" EEG and AERP findings in hyperactive children are in fact indicative of a brain dysfunction. This alternative interpretation is apparently contradictory to the one suggested above.

Because the concept of an abnormal CNS arousal and inhibitory state has been proposed both for hyperactive children (Satterfield & Cantwell, 1975) and for adults with antisocial personality disorder (Hare, 1978), N2 amplitude, which is thought to be an indicator of CNS arousal (and we believe inhibitory) states, is of particular interest. The amplitude of the N2 component of the AERP has been found to increase markedly with decreasing levels of arousal, such as when subjects are allowed to drowse and fall off to sleep or during a prolonged vigilance task (Fruhstorfer & Bergstrom, 1969; Picton & Hillyard, 1974; Tueting, 1968; Weitzman & Kremen, 1965; Wilkinson, Morlock, & Williams, 1966; Williams, Tepas, & Morlock, 1962), and to decrease with heightened attention and with increased alertness produced by shock or by stimulation of the mesencephalic reticular formation in one human subject (Guerrero-Figueroa & Heath, 1964; Tecce, 1976; Teuting, 1969). In summary, although N2 appears to be insensitive to selective attention, it does appear to reflect the state of general alertness or arousal.

N2 amplitudes for multiple-offender hyperactives were not different from normal but were significantly larger than N2 amplitudes for nonoffender hyperactives (Tables 9.4 and 9.10). This suggests that multiple-offender hyperactives have low cortical arousal and inhibitory levels as compared with nonoffender hyperactives, but normal arousal-inhibitory levels compared with normals. It is interesting to conjecture that the optimal arousal-inhibitory level for hyperactives is different from that for normal subjects. A given arousal-inhibitory level, as reflected by N2 amplitude, may at the same time be indicative of a *normal* level for a normal child and an *abnormal* arousal level for a hyperactive child.

Three other findings are consistent with the concept of a low arousal-inhibitory level in multiple offenders, as compared with nonoffender hyperactives. The long latency of the N2 component of the AERP found for multiple offenders (Table 9.11) is consistent with slower recovery time and a lower arousal-inhibitory level. Multiple offenders also had a greater number of eyeblinks (but not significantly greater) than did nonoffender hyperactives, a finding consistent with a low arousal-inhibitory state.

The lower relative alpha power found in the multiple-offender hyperactives compared with the nonoffender hyperactives is also consistent with a lower arousal-inhibitory state. Craggs reported a fall in the relative EEG alpha power and an increase in reaction time during a prolonged reaction time task with hyperactive children (Craggs, Wright, & Werry, 1980).

Methyl phenidate reduced reaction time while increasing EEG relative alpha power. Shetty (1971) also reported an increase in power in the alpha range after intravenous d-amphetamine administration in "good responder" hyperactive children. It is of interest that an increase in alpha power in our multiple-offender hyperactive subjects with their low arousal-inhibitory states would result in this measure moving farther away from, rather than closer to, values for normal controls. However, response to stimulant medication in hyperactive children results in more normal behavior (as measured both by decreased reaction time and by behavioral rating scales). This shift away from values for normal controls may actually be a shift toward a value that is closer to a more optimal arousal-inhibitory level for hyperactive subjects.

It should be noted that, in several important respects, this is the first study of its kind. Although the findings if valid are of considerable theoretical and clinical importance, replication is necessary to determine their validity. We hope to validate these findings by a follow-up study of 100 hyperactive subjects (Satterfield et al., 1981) who are now the correct age for a cross-validation study.

Acknowledgment

This work was supported, in part, by NIMH Grants MH35498 and MH35497.

References

Bosco, J. J., & Robin, S. S. (1981). Hyperkineses: How common is it and how is it treated? In J. J. Bosco & S. S. Robin (Eds.), *Hyperactive children: The social ecology of identification and treatment*. Academic Press, New York.

Craggs, M. D., Wright, J. J., & Werry, J. S. (1980). A pilot study of the effects of methylphenidate on the vigilance-related EEG in hyperactivity. *Electroencephalography and Clinical Neurophysiology, 48,* 34–42.

Duncan, O. D. (1961). A socioeconomic index for all occupations. In A. J. Reiss (Ed.), *Occupations and social status*. New York: Free Press.

Fruhstorfer, H., & Bergstrom, R. (1969). Human vigilance and auditory evoked responses. *Electroencephalography and Clinical Neurophysiology, 27,* 346–55.

Guerrero-Figueroa, R., & Heath, R. G. (1964). Evoked responses and changes during attentive factors in man. *Archives of Neurology, 10,* 74–84.

Hare, R. D. (1978). Electrodermal and cardiovascular correlates of psychopathy. In R. D. Hare & D. Schalling (Eds.), *Psychopathic behaviors: Approaches to research* (pp. 107–93). New York: Wiley.

Hussey, H., Metoyer, M., & Townsend, M. (1974). Eight- to ten-year follow-up of 84 children treated for behavioral disorder in rural Vermont. *Acta Paedopsychiatry, 10,* 230–5.

Kohlberg, L., La Cross, J., & Ricks, D. (1972). The predictability of adult mental health from childhood behavior. In B. Wolman (Ed.), *Manual of child psychopathology*. New York: McGraw-Hill.

Mendelson, W., Johnson, J., & Stewart, M. (1971). Hyperactive children as teenagers: A follow-up study. *Journal of Nervous and Mental Disorders, 151,* 273–9.

Miller, R., Palkes, H., & Stewart, M. (1973). Hyperactive children in suburban elementary schools. *Child Psychiatry and Human Development, 4,* 121–7.

Picton, T. W., & Hillyard, S. A. (1974). Human auditory evoked potentials: II. Effects of attention. *Electroencephalography and Clinical Neurophysiology, 36,* 191–9.

Riddle, K. D., & Rapoport, J. L. (1976). A two year follow-up of 72 hyperactive boys. *Journal of Nervous and Mental Diseases, 162,* 126–34.

Robins, L. N., & Ratcliff, K. S. (1978). Risk factors in the continuation of childhood antisocial behavior into adulthood. In J. Gersen & M. Susser (Eds.), *International Journal of Mental Health* [special issue].

Satterfield, J. (1973). EEG issues in children with minimal brain dysfunction. *Seminars in Psychiatry, 5,* 35–46.

Satterfield, J. H., & Cantwell, D. P. (1975). Psychopharmacology in the prevention of antisocial and delinquent behavior. *International Journal of Mental Health, 4,* 227–37.

Satterfield, J. H., Cantwell, D. P., & Satterfield, B. T. (1979). Multimodality treatment: A one-year follow-up of 84 hyperactive boys. *Archives of General Psychiatry, 36,* 965–74.

Satterfield, J. H., Cantwell, D. P., & Satterfield, B. T. (1980). Multimodality treatment: A two-year study of 61 hyperactive boys. *Archives of General Psychiatry, 37,* 915–19.

Satterfield, J. H., Cantwell, D. P., Saul, R. E., & Yusin, A. (1974). Intelligence, academic achievement, and EEG abnormalities in hyperactive children. *American Journal of Psychiatry, 131,* 391–5.

Satterfield, J. H., Hoppe, C. M., & Schell, A. M. (1982). A prospective study of delinquency in 110 adolescent boys with attention deficit disorder and 88 normal adolescent boys. *American Journal of Psychiatry, 139,* 795–8.

Satterfield, J. H., Satterfield, B. T., & Cantwell, D. P. (1981). Three-year-multimodality treatment study of 110 hyperactive boys. *Journal of Pediatrics, 98,* 650–5.

Shetty, T. (1971). Alpha rhythms in the hyperkinetic child. *Nature, 234,* 476.

Tecce, J. (1976). *Contemporary theory and analysis.* New York: Appleton-Century-Crofts.

Tueting, P. (1968). Uncertainty and average evoked responses in a guessing situation. Unpublished doctoral dissertation, Columbia University, New York. (University Microfilms No. 69-3097.)

Weiss, G., Kruger, E., Danielson, U., & Elman, M. (1975). Effect of long term treatment of hyperactive children with methylphenidate. *Canadian Medical Association Journal, 112,* 159–65.

Weiss, G., Minde, K., Werry, J., Douglas, V., & Nemeth, E. (1971). Studies on the hyperactive child: VIII. Five year follow-up. *Archives of General Psychiatry, 24,* 409–14.

Weitzman, E. D., & Kremen, H. (1965). Auditory evoked responses during difficult stages of sleep in man. *Electroencephalography and Clinical Neurophysiology, 18,* 65–70.

Werner, E., Bierman, J. M., French, F., Fimonian, P. K., Connor, A., Smith, R. S., & Campbell, M. (1968). Reproductive and environmental causalities: A report on the 10-year follow-up of the children of Kauai Pregnancy Study. *Pediatrics, 42,* 112–27.

Wilkinson, R. T., Morlock, H. C., & Williams, H. L. (1966). Evoked cortical response during vigilance. *Psychonomic Science, 4,* 221–2.

Williams, H. L., Tepas, D. I., & Morlock, H. C. (1962). Evoked responses to clicks and electroencephalogram stages of sleep in man. *Science, 183,* 685–6.

10   Cerebral dysfunctions and persistent juvenile delinquency

W. Buikhuisen

Introduction

One of the advantages of reviewing the neuropsychological literature about criminal behavior is the absence of a long-standing history in this field. The first studies in this area started in the early 1970s (Fitzhugh, 1973; Hurwitz, Bibace, Wolff, & Rowbotham, 1972). These early studies dealt not so much with crime as a dependent variable as with the presence of mediating factors (such as learning disabilities) that might predispose to crime – for example, impaired intellect, which may reduce one's opportunities to succeed in school, in turn increasing the probability of becoming involved in crime (Fitzhugh, 1973). It took some years before the focus of neuropsychological research changed, the objective becoming more and more to understand crime. Special credit for this change should be given to Berman and Siegal (1976) and Yeudall (1977) and his co-workers, whose comprehensive research program was carried out in the Department of Neuropsychology of the Alberta Hospital in Edmonton, Canada.

Neuropsychology and behavior

What is the neuropsychological approach or, more specifically, what is neuropsychology? In general it can be said that in neuropsychology brain–behavior relations are studied. According to Luria (1970) this study has two objectives: pinpointing the brain lesions responsible for specific behavior disorders and collecting data that will lead to a better understanding of the components of complex psychological functions, such as learning, problem solving, and memory, for which the different parts (systems) of the brain are responsible. The relevance of neuropsychology to behavior is also reflected in the fact that this discipline deals with the psychological functions that allow for information processing, the starting point for all behavior. Therefore, to understand criminal behavior, we should pay attention to the quality of the cognitive functions of the criminals who are our subjects. As will be shown, combining neuropsychological and criminological data certainly may help us to explain crime.

Related areas of research

Crime can be studied from any perspective, but why take a neuropsychological approach? Is there reason to believe that such a line of research might help us to understand crime? There certainly is. In areas closely related to neuropsychology, relationships with criminality have frequently been found. One such related area is the domain of intelligence. In a review of the pertinent literature Hirschi and Hindelang (1979) concluded that the assertion that delinquents have lower IQs than nondelinquents is firmly established. Further analyses have led to the conclusion that verbal IQ especially seems to be affected. Studies of delinquents have generally revealed a higher performance (P) IQ than verbal (V) IQ (Andrew, 1974; Hays, Solway, & Schreiner, 1978; Solway, Hays, Roberts & Cody, 1975; Yeudall, Fromm-Auch, & Davies, 1982). As is almost inevitable in social sciences, studies can be enumerated that failed to find this P > V discrepancy. Haynes and Bensch (1981) have hypothesized that such inconsistencies reflect the heterogeneity of delinquents, an often neglected issue in criminology. Given the relation between intelligence and crime, it should not come as a surprise that connections have also been found between crime and learning disabilities[1] (Unger, 1978; Poremba, 1975; Zinkus & Gottlieb, 1978) or, more particularly, reading disabilities (Ross, 1977). Among delinquents a high incidence of these learning problems has been observed. This observation should not tempt us to conclude that learning disabilities are "the root of all evil." Delinquents are characterized by a variety of factors, and each of them alone or, more likely, in combination with others may contribute to the origins of crime. The observation does not mean that learning disabilities *are* a cause of crime, let alone that juvenile delinquency could be prevented by greater participation of delinquents in remedial teaching programs. Learning disabilities might, like other characteristics of chronic juvenile delinquents such as low self-esteem and disturbed parent–child interactions, be caused partly by unidentified cognitive dysfunctions (Buikhuisen, 1982). If this is the case these characteristics are sequelae of a disturbed developmental process. Therefore, they should be regarded as symptoms. It should be obvious that treating only one of these symptoms (e.g., learning problems) cannot be expected to be an effective cure for juvenile delinquency. It is this psychodynamic effect that Coons (1982) is overlooking in his otherwise valuable observations about learning disabilities and criminality. It is comforting that Coons, too, observes that more learning-disabled boys than normal boys are officially identified as delinquent, although he prefers to explain this as (another) token of selective treatment by the justice system.

Neuropsychological research: methodological considerations

The studies to be reviewed in this chapter have been carried out from many different perspectives. Perhaps their most common feature is that they originated outside the context of traditional criminology. This fact is especially reflected in the lack of attempts to integrate the recent results of neuropsychological research into existing criminological theories. The interest in carrying out neuropsychological examinations of criminal subjects has developed primarily in a clinical setting. This origin has not been without consequences for the composition of the samples of offenders studied (predominantly hospitalized subjects). Clinical origins may also have had an impact on the level of sophistication of the research. There are exceptions, of course, but too many of them could be labeled as (numerically) extended case studies. A good example of this is the paper of Gilbert and Gravier (1982), a case study of the relation between cerebral dysfunction, homicide, and psychosis. It presents a thorough description of the life and individual traits (including neuropsychological ones) of a hospitalized psychotic patient convicted of homicide. It also presents evidence that confirms prevailing (neuro)psychological theories, but unfortunately it leaves the interested reader with all kinds of questions. Why was this case selected for publication? Do comparable cases have a similar history and individual makeup? More important, of what kind of population is this patient representative?

The latter question of *sample representativeness* often puzzles the reader of research in the field of neuropsychology. To illustrate this point a selection of samples that have been studied is described below:

1. Hurwitz et al. (1972, p. 389): "Delinquent boys adjudicated by the courts as juvenile delinquents and detained at a reception center under the jurisdiction of the Commonwealth of Massachusetts"
2. Andrew (1982, p. 376): "Probationed juvenile offenders"
3. Pontius and Ruttiger (1976, p. 511): "Delinquent subjects, known to have committed indictable acts"
4. Pontius and Yudowitz (1980, p. 113): "Physically healthy men convicted of criminal acts for which they were serving a prison sentence not longer than 2 years"

5. Slavin (1978, p. 80): "Subjects . . . under the jurisdiction of the juvenile court between February 1, 1975 and June 30, 1975"

The *number of subjects* involved in the studies to be discussed has not always been satisfactory. Sample sizes of the index group vary from 1 to about 100. Unfortunately, too many samples are quite small, especially when we look at the subsamples involved. In some cases the number of variables examined even exceeds or parallels the number of subjects in the index group (Hurwitz et al., 1972; Krynicki, 1978).

It is obvious that the small size of the samples involved in neuropsychological research with delinquents limits the level of sophistication of the statistical methods available for data analysis. Efforts to control for potential intervening variables are almost completely lacking. In the majority of the research reported, univariate statistics are applied in designs that unfortunately do not always meet the required methodological standards. This problem is also pertinent to those few studies where multivariate analyses were applied. Almost without exception, the researchers failed to match index group and control group in such a way that differences found between the groups could be safely attributed to the selected independent variables, whatever cognitive dysfunction they might represent. For instance, in the study of Yeudall et al. (1982) (which certainly can be considered one of the best) the subjects in fact were similar only in age, sex, and handedness. They were not matched on important factors like social class or level of education. Both groups differed significantly with regard to the Wechsler Intelligence Scale for Children (WISC) IQ score. (For the WISC the average score for delinquents and nondelinquents was, respectively, 95.0 and 119.8!) Efforts to control for this difference in the IQ of the two groups were only partly successful; hence we are still faced with doubts about the extent to which the neuropsychological differences between the two groups can be attributed to this difference in intelligence.

A positive aspect of the methodology of neuropsychological research with delinquents is the *validity of the tests* used. In this respect criminologically oriented researchers may profit from the work carried out by clinical (neuro)psychologists. Internationally accepted neuropsychological tests have been developed that allow for cross-cultural comparisons. Examples of such tests are the Halstead Reitan Neuropsychological Test Battery and Luria's Neuropsychological Test Battery, which are broadband spectrum tests, and the Benton Visual Retention Test and the Stroop Color Word Test, which tap more specific psychological functions.

Format for presenting the results

As mentioned above the neuropsychological approach in criminology is rather new. The number of studies carried out to date is limited. Discussing the results is not always easy, because the tests administered and the populations studied may differ considerably, a situation that does not particularly facilitate interstudy comparison.

This problem was solved as follows. Starting from the psychological functions they are said to measure, the tests were grouped according to the parts of the brain where these functions are supposed to be located. Of course, this is a rather crude way of presenting the data. Our scheme certainly does not represent a reliable topography of the brain. It is not meant to do so. Because our approach is a pragmatic one – structuring data that otherwise would be very difficult to handle – we feel this ad hoc presentation is justified.

As can be seen from Table 10.1 we selected the following headings: general, (pre)motoric, frontal, temporal, parietal, and parietopostcentral. Under each heading are listed the tests assigned to that category. Next, for each study reviewed we indicated which tests were administered and whether these tests successfully discriminated between the groups studied. To express the direction of the results, we used the following symbols. An equals sign (=) indicates that no difference could be established between the index group (delinquents) and the contrast group (control group or groups displaying deviant behavior other than delinquency). A plus (+) or minus (−) sign indicates that the tests differentiate significantly between index group and contrast group. The minus sign means that on the average the members of the delinquent group had a poorer score on these tests, and a plus sign denotes a study in which the delinquents scored better than the contrast group.

Results

In Table 10.1 we have presented the results of our analysis of the neuropsychological research in which delinquents were examined. The most striking outcome is the consistency of the results. Almost without exception, delinquents do not perform as well as control subjects. This observation is in accord with Yeudall's conclusion. Summarizing his work, he concludes, "The findings of our research over a six-year period, involving over 500 criminals referred to our department for assessment, has consistently indicated a high incidence of abnormal neuropsychological profiles in the persistent criminal offender" (Yeudall, 1978, p. 20). Another outcome, the relatively poorer performance of the delinquent groups on the Wechsler Adult Intelligence Scale (WAIS), confirms Hirschi and Hindelang's (1979) observation that the assertion that delinquents have lower IQs than nondelinquents can no longer be ignored. The P > V sign is also confirmed by our survey of the literature. An interesting question concerns where in the brain these observed neuropsychological dysfunctions are "located."[2] According to Table 10.1 three brain regions are suggested: the (pre)frontal and temporal lobes and the parietal cortex.

Looking in more detail at Table 10.1, we conclude the following:

1. Delinquents as a group show deficits in their ability to comprehend, manipulate, and utilize conceptual material (Berman & Siegal, 1976; Yeudall et al., 1982).
2. Delinquents as a group show poor performance on tasks relying on sequencing skills or perceptual organization (Berman & Siegal, 1976; Hurwitz et al., 1972; Pontius & Yudowitz, 1980; Yeudall et al., 1982).
3. Delinquents as a group are characterized by impaired vision and impaired visual information processing (Slavin, 1978).
4. Delinquents as a group consistently perform more poorly on tasks requiring sustained levels of concentration and attention than do controls (Voorhees, 1981; Yeudall et al., 1982). Their ability to recall is significantly reduced when interference tasks are implemented (Voorhees, 1981).

Interpretation of the results

We have seen that the assertion that delinquents have a higher incidence of abnormal neuropsychological profiles is supported by 11 studies. Now the crucial question is how this observation can help us to understand crime. What is, for instance, the significance of the fact that the observed neuropsychological dysfunctions are to a great extent associated with the frontal and temporal lobes (see note 2)? To address this question we must describe the general functions of these lobes. The frontal lobe, for instance, plays an important role in the regulation and inhibition of behavior. According to Luria (1973) the frontal regions of the brain play a decisive role in the formation of plans and intentions and in the regulation and verification of complex behavior. Planning action, assessing its outcomes, and changing the course of action if necessary are typical frontal lobe functions. According to Yeudall (1978), damage in this region may result in a mosaic of the following symptoms:

An impairment in formation of plans and intention; reduction in the ability to evaluate the consequences of one's actions; reduction in higher cognitive intellectual functioning involving abstract reasoning and concept formation; reduction in the ability to sustain attention, concentration or motivation; reduction in the effectiveness of language to regulate future behavior; increases in distractibility,

Table 10.1. *Results of neuropsychological research with offenders*

Localization and tests	1	2	3	4	5	6	7	8	9	10	11
General											
Verbal IQ < performance IQ	Yes	Yes						Yes		Yes	
WAIS, performance IQ	–	–	–			=[a]					
WAIS, block design	–		–				–				
WAIS, picture completion	–										
Knox cubes										–	
WAIS, verbal IQ	–	–	–			=[b]					
WAIS, vocabulary	–		–				–				
Token test		–									
WAIS, information	–						–				
WAIS, comprehension	–						–				
Word fluency		–									
Impressive–expressive speech (Lurai)						–					
(Pre)motoric											
Finger tapping (HRNTB)[a]	=							=			
Dynamometer (HRNTB)[a]		+									
Rhythm test	=										
Purdue Pegboard Test		=									
Frontal											
Porteus mazes				–							
WAIS, picture arrangement	–										
Stroop Color Word Test					–						
Trail making											
A	–	–									
B	–	–									
Tapping test			–	–							
Meander test			–		–						
Category test	–		–								
Tactile performance test		=							–		–
Sequencing and tapping (Lurai)					–						
Knox cubes										–	
Narratives								–			
Raven Progressive Matrices	–		=								

Table 10.1. *(Continued)*

Localization and tests	1	2	3	4	5	6	7	8	9	10	11
Temporal											
Digit repetition			−								
Seashore test		−									
Benton Visual Retention Test			−								
William Clinical Memory		−									
Verbal memory						−					
Speech sound	−	−									
Perception test (HRNTB)							−				
WAIS, similarities	−		−								
Oral word fluency		−									
Naming repeated objects				−							
Parietal											
Bender Gestalt Test				−	−						
Benton Visual Retention Test			−								
Memory for design test			−		=						
WAIS, block design	−		−				−				
WAIS, picture completion	−						−				
WISC, verbal IQ; WISC, digit span											−
Porteus mazes			−								
Embedded figures			−	=							
Visual motor integration				=							
Visual functions					−						
Optometric examination									−		
WAIS, arithmetic	−						−				
Arithmetic skills (Luria)				−							
Parietopostcentral											
Fingertip number writing			−								

a HRNTB, Halstead–Reitan Neuropsychological Test Battery.
a IW 76.
b IW 78.
Key to sources of data: 1, Berman and Siegal (1976); 2, Yeudall et al. (1982); 3, Spellacy (1978); 4, Hurwitz et al. (1972); 5, Voorhees (1981); 6, Krynicki (1978); 7, Fitzhugh (1973); 8, Pontius (1972); 9, Slavin (1982); 10, Gilbert and Garvier (1982); 11, Andrew (1982).

impulsivity and disinhibition. Damage confined to the orbital limbic region of the frontal lobes results in the following symptoms: lack of self-control; emotional outbursts; dramatic changes in personality; lack of, or indifference to, emotional feelings or conflicts (loss of normal guilt, shame, remorse, etc.); increases in impulsivity; a decrease in inhibition in sexual and aggressive behavior; and increased sensitivity to alcohol. (P. 34)

Criminologists have shown that many of these symptoms are related to criminal behavior.

These proposals of Luria (1973) and Yeudall (1978) implicating the frontal lobe in the planning and regulation of behavior suggest a hypothesis: Frontal lobe deficits should be specific to certain types of criminal acts. For example, they should be found more often among subjects guilty of impulsive and poorly planned illegal behaviors than among professional criminals or "white-collar" criminals, whose illegal acts are often complex and well planned.

Starting from Luria's (1966) and Teuber's (1966) observations about the functions of the frontal lobe, Pontius (1972) has developed a neuropsychological theory of crime. Frontal lobe dysfunctions due to a developmental lag (and/or neuropathological deficit), she argues, are the basis for some forms of juvenile delinquency. Because of these frontal lobe impairments, delinquents are not able to shift the principle of actions of an ongoing activity, although they know what they do is wrong (dissociation between knowing and doing).

Berman and Siegal (1976) emphasize another frontal lobe function. According to them poor performance on the category test (which measures a typical frontal lobe function) clearly reflects the inability of delinquents to profit cognitively from experience. Thus frontal lobe dysfunction could explain the high incidence of recidivism among some categories of offenders.

Temporal lobe dysfunctions are related to a different set of symptoms, those involving the subjective consciousness of the individual. According to Williams (1969), the temporal lobes "are much more closely indentified with the subject himself; they involve his emotional life, his instinctive feelings and activities and his visceral responses to environmental change." Here, too, it would not be difficult to present criminological data to support the hypothesis of temporal lobe dysfunctions among some categories of criminals (see note 2). With regard to the emotional and visceral responses see, for instance, Hare and Schalling (1978) and Mednick and Christiansen (1977).

Another feature of the central nervous system (CNS) that might help us to understand crime is lateralization. Yeudall et al. (1982) found in their study of persistent juvenile offenders a higher incidence of dysfunction of the nondominant (usually right) hemisphere. Recent studies suggest that both hemispheres contribute differently to the experience and perception of emotion. In his review Wexler (1980) concludes that, whereas the right hemisphere plays a larger role in the perception of and reaction to negatively emotionally charged stimuli (such as fear), the left hemisphere is more active in response to positively emotionally charged stimuli (such as joy). These observations bring us to the hypothesis that because of the observed right-hemisphere dysfunctions the delinquents concerned are not able to experience the fear and negative emotions necessary for sensitivity to the threat of sanctions. Fear triggers the release of hormones or neuropeptides of the pituitary gland (e.g., vasopressin and endorphins) and increases the responsiveness of the autonomic nervous system (ANS). Both factors have a positive effect on avoidance learning (De Wied, Bohus, Gispen, Urban, & Wimersma Greidanus, 1976; Schmauck, 1970). Because avoidance learning is fear-motivated behavior (Mowrer, 1947), these processes explain why it is likely that subjects who do not experience fear are more prone to becoming criminal. This hypothesis might also explain why psychopaths are able to learn avoidance-behavior if positive sanctions, for example, money, are applied (Schachter & Latané, 1964). Experience of these sanctions is related to the *left* hemisphere.

Multidisciplinary approaches

So far, in trying to explain crime, a univariate approach has been pursued. The prevalence of neuropsychological dysfunctions among delinquents having been established, direct relations have been inferred between such deficits and crime. Behavior, however, is a function of individual *and* situational factors. The interaction between individuals and their environment eventually determines the way behavior develops. In these complex interactions neuropsychological factors may play a role. This does not imply that neuropsychological factors never have a direct effect on crime. Lack of self-control resulting from prefrontal lesions certainly may further aggressive behavior. However, more often neuropsychological impairment will have an *indirect* effect on behavior. This indirect model is reflected in the work of Slavin (1978), who emphasizes the importance of information-processing defects for the etiology of crime but more particularly in the way Berman and Siegal (1976) and Yeudall (1979) view the relation between cognitive dysfunctions and crime. To Berman and Siegal (1976) a path can be drawn from neuropsychological deficits to adaptive disabilities to learning disabilities and school dropout behavior. Parallel with this development, changes in personality (lack of self-esteem) take place, which also may predispose to crime. This process is vividly pictured by Berman and Siegal:

The type of boy who is sent to a training school is typically one who has difficulty in conceptualizing or making sense out of the world that surrounds him. He usually lacks the verbal skills that are necessary to function effectively with the people with whom he interacts and in situations in which he finds himself (i.e., multiproblem families, ghetto life, and unsatisfactory teacher–student relationships in school). As a consequence of this conceptual and verbal deficit he has difficulty in making the complex interpersonal compromises and solutions that enable the more gifted individual to control his world and function more effectively in it. By virtue of these things, and in spite of a mild degree of clumsiness or incoordination, the delinquent boy's motor capabilities represent his most adaptive tool. The pattern which then emerges is that of an individual who, with poor judgment, acts swiftly and without thinking about the reasons for, effectiveness of, or consequences of his actions.
   Along similar lines, the boy's intellectual impoverishment, immaturity, and lack of coordination have kept him from enjoying success in academic, vocational, athletic, and social endeavors. These are the kinds of achievement valued by our culture from which the nondelinquent boy derives satisfaction. The boy seen typically in training schools instead has been forced by virtue of his own ineptness to seek out deviant ways to bolster his damaged self-esteem and to find his place in life. The frustration of his unsuccessful attempts serve to generate anger and aggressive behavior which only exacerbate his difficulties legally and interpersonally. (P. 252)

Cerebral dysfunctions and delinquent behavior: a theory

It goes without saying that good information-processing capacities are essential, not to say a conditio sine qua non, for an adequate adaptation to the environment. When growing up, children are confronted with a social world that expects them to behave in a certain way. What exactly is expected may vary from (sub)culture to (sub)culture, but whatever the expectations, children have to learn to live up to them. During infancy and early childhood, the primary caretakers (usually the parents) are responsible for the transmission of the norms and values of the surrounding culture. Of course, the outcome of this process depends on whether the values transmitted are in accordance with those of the dominant culture and the way in which they are transmitted. Inconsistent child-rearing practices certainly have an adverse effect and may lead to antisocial behavior (Glueck & Glueck, 1950; Hewitt & Jenkins, 1946).

   However, the outcome of the socialization process does not depend solely on the child's social environment. Another condition to be fulfilled is the child's fitness to learn. In infancy and early childhood this social learning process is predominantly reduced to avoidance learning. It has been demonstrated that avoidance learning is correlated with factors like extraversion (Eysenck & Eysenck, 1970), impulsivity (Gray, 1976), and ANS functioning, especially galvanic skin response (Lykken, 1957; Schmauck, 1970). As a learning process, avoidance learning also has a cognitive component. Here the neuropsychology comes in. Children have to discover the relation between their behavior and the reaction of the environment (Buikhuisen, 1982). This reaction from the environment, which in avoidance learning has aversive emotional loading, should be able to deter a child. Whether this condition will be fulfilled depends on two factors. First, the child should be able to recognize the (emotional) contents of a message received. This message may be "delivered" in a very subtle way, for instance, by the parents using facial expressions to transmit disapproval of the child's behavior. These abstract signs have to be detected by the child, a process that presupposes adequate visual capacities, including many visual functions, like being able to see "gestalts" or, the opposite, parts in a whole. Second, the child must be able to experience negative emotions, which is typically thought to be a right-hemisphere function (Wexler, 1980). Table 10.1 demonstrates that many persistent delinquents suffer from those neuropsychological deficits that may seriously impair their capacities for avoidance learning. Delinquents show deficits in their ability to comprehend and recall, they suffer from various cognitive dysfunctions that affect their capacity for information processing, they are characterized by impaired vision, and, as a group, perform consistently poorly on tasks requiring sustained levels of concentration and attention.

From here it is only one step to a failing socialization process. Unfortunately, the consequences of this failure are not confined to an impaired ability to internalize the norms and values of the social environment. The fact that the child repeatedly fails to obey the rules of his parental home will have a great impact on the parent–child interaction. In the socialization process pressure is not limited to the child. The parents, too, are under pressure. They are responsible for transmitting to their child the norms and values of the society. If the child does not behave according to these rules, the parents will be blamed. They know this. Therefore, the pressure they feel in this respect will be passed onto the child. Because it appears that the child does not want to obey, the parents will look for other ways to make the child listen. If they are still unsuccessful, the situation can easily escalate; the parents will resort more and more to physical punishment, predisposing the family to child abuse.[3] Gradually, it will become more and more difficult for the parents to love their child. The child will be aware of this change in attitude. He or she will feel rejected and emotionally deprived but will lack the adaptive and cognitive skills to solve the problem. Indeed, as Berman and Siegal (1976) have pointed out this parental rejection will negatively affect the child's feelings of self-esteem and personality development.

To cope with continuous stress, the child looks for adequate defense mechanisms. On a psychological level he or she may show indifference, which unfortunately will further the process of emotional drifting apart of parents and child. It is tempting to speculate that the child may resort to a kind of physiological defense mechanism, engaging in behavior such as "avoidance" that reduces the autonomic arousal level, which in turn will make it possible for the child to avoid having to experience things emotionally. Another possibility is that depressed ANS responsiveness is another symptom of the same CNS damage that results in the neuropsychological deficits mentioned above. These hypothesized mechanisms could explain why persistent delinquency is accompanied by low ANS reactivity (Siddle, 1977). Unfortunately, the price the child must pay for this defense mechanism is high and has serious consequences for future development. A general flattening of emotionality means that the child will give up the basis for emotional attachment with significant others in the environment (family, school, peers, neighborhood, etc.). This attachment, as Hirschi (1969) has pointed out, is a conditio sine qua non for accepting and internalizing the norms and values of the culture in which we participate.

So far we have discussed the emotional consequences of the disturbed parent–child relationship as sequelae of a failing socialization process. It should be obvious that the cerebral dysfunctions mentioned above that seriously impair children's capacity to learn the norms and values of their culture may also influence their performance at school. Unfortunately, by the time these children are in elementary school they will have interpersonal problems at home. In the meantime they will have built up an image of uncooperativeness and incorrigibility. The almost inevitable problems at school will be interpreted in the context of previous (mis)behavior, which makes it the more likely that the cognitive impairments of these children will remain unrecognized. These undetected deficiencies, resulting in failure to live up to school standards, will again make the children targets of criticism, which, of course, will further lower their self-esteem. At school they will become more and more difficult to handle. Having to go to school may become a constant frustration, stimulating truancy, again having a detrimental effect on school performance (Buikhuisen & Meijs, 1981). Since at that age parents and the school are their most important role models, these children may look for other models among peers who live under similar adverse conditions. Differential association theory (Cressey, 1964) teaches us that this new environment will drive these children farther from their parents, the school, and the values of the dominant culture. Lack of attachment to these systems will lower the remaining barriers for nonconforming behavior and open the doors to deviancy. What form this deviant behavior will eventually take is determined by the principle of differential opportunity (Cloward & Ohlin, 1960) in a comprehensive sense. In this sense the concept of opportunity refers not only to what the environment is offering these children, but also to their individual makeup. Here too deviant behavior will be the result of the interaction between individual and situational factors. The outcome of this interaction process is difficult to predict. One thing is certain, however: Coming from underprivileged areas, lacking an adequate education, growing up under unfavorable economic conditions, and lacking any attachment to a prosocial system will not make it very likely that these adolescents will look for legitimate means to achieve their goals. Therefore, many of these youngsters will finally choose the delinquent solution. In this process behavioral tendencies caused by cerebral dysfunctions – acting impulsively, not being able to foresee the consequences of their choices, inability to change the course of action, and others – might again play a role. More important, however, is the fact that in early childhood these neuropsychological dysfunctions constituted the basis for an impaired socialization process that almost inevitably leads to deviancy.

Acknowledgments

The author wishes to thank Dr. R. Hijman for his constructive comments on this chapter and Mr. R. Bouter and Mrs. E. M. Zielstra for assisting in collecting the pertinent literature.

Notes

1 For more controversial results see Spreen (1981).
2 Because these lobes have many connections with the limbic structures, it is impossible to say where exactly the dysfunctions are located.
3 So far we have related the failing socialization process to cognitive dysfunctions in the child. Of course, it is also possible that the parents are also suffering from cognitive deficits similar to those of their child. These deficits may influence their fitness to train the child and as such the outcome of the socialization process. For instance, if a parent has cognitive verbal deficits he or she may be more likely to resort to physical punishment than to instruction and reasoning in order to train the child.

References

Andrew, J. M. (1974). Delinquents, the Wechsler P–V sign and the I-level system. *Journal of Clinical Psychology, 301,* 331–5.

Andrew, J. M. (1982). Memory and violent crime among delinquents. *Criminal Justice and Behavior, 9*(3), 364–71.

Berman, A., & Siegal, A. (1976). A neuropsychological approach to the etiology, prevention and treatment of juvenile delinquency. In A. Davids (Ed.), *Child personality and psychopathology: Current topics.* New York: Wiley.

Buikhuisen, W. (1982). Aggressive behavior and cognitive disorders. *International Journal of Law and Psychiatry, 5,* 205–17.

Buikhuisen, W., & Meijs, B. W. G. P. (1981, November). *A psychosocial approach to recidivism: An application of a latent variable causal modeling technique.* Paper presented at the Life History Research meeting, Monterey, CA.

Cloward, R. A., & Ohlin, L. E. (1960). *Delinquency and opportunity: A theory of delinquent gangs.* New York: Free Press.

Coons, W. H. (1982). Learning disabilities and criminality. *Canadian Journal of Criminology,* July.

Cressey, D. R. (1964). *Delinquency, crime and differential association.* The Hague: Martinus Nijhoff.

De Wied, D., Bohus, B., Gispen, W. H., Urban, I., & Wimersma Greidanus, T. B. (1976). Hormonal influences on motivational, learning, and memory processes. In E. J. Sachar (Ed.), *Hormones, behavior and psychopathology.* New York: Raven Press.

Eysenck, H. J., & Eysenck, S. B. G. (1970). Crime and personality: An empirical study of the three-factor theory. *British Journal of Criminology, 10.*

Fitzhugh, K. B. (1973). Some neuropsychological features of delinquent subjects. *Perceptual and Motor Skills, 36,* 494.

Gilbert, M., & Gravier, B. (1982). *Cerebral dysfunction, homicide and psychosis: Case study.* Montreal: Institut Philippe-Pinel.

Glueck, S., & Glueck, E. (1950). *Unraveling juvenile delinquency.* New York: Commonwealth Fund.

Gray, J. A. (1976). The behavioral inhibition system: A possible substrate for anxiety. In M. P. Feldman & A. Broadhurst (eds.), *Theoretical and experimental bases of the behavior therapies.* New York: Wiley.

Hare, R. D., & Schalling, D. (1978). *Psychopathic behaviour: Approaches to research.* New York: Wiley.

Haynes, J. P., & Bensch, M. (1981). The $P > V$ sign on the WISC-R and recidivism in delinquents. *Journal of Consulting and Clinical Psychology, 49,*(3), 480–1.

Hays, J. R., Solway, J. S., & Schreiner, D. (1978). Intellectual characteristics of juvenile murderers versus status offenders. *Psychological Reports, 43,* 80–2.

Hewitt, L. E., & Jenkins, R. L. (1946). *Fundamental patterns of maladjustment.* Detroit, MI: Green.

Hirschi, T. (1969). *Causes of delinquency.* Berkeley & Los Angeles: University of California Press.

Hirschi, T., & Hindelang, M. J. (1979). Intelligence and delinquency: A revisionist review. In S. L. Messinger, & E. Bittner (Eds.), *Criminology review yearbook* (Vol. 2). Beverly Hills, CA: Sage.

Hurwitz, I., Bibace, R., Wolff, P., & Rowbotham, B. (1972). Neurological function of normal boys, delinquent boys, and boys with learning problems. *Perceptual and Motor Skills, 35,* 387–94.

Krynicki, V. E. (1978). Cerebral dysfunction in repetitively assaultive offenders. *Journal of Nervous and Mental Disease, 166,* 59–67.

Luria, A. R. (1966). *Higher cortical functions in man.* New York: Basic Books.

Luria, A. R. (1970). The functional organization of the brain. *Scientific American, 222,* 66–78.

Luria, A. R. (1973). The frontal lobes and the regulation of behavior. In K. H. Pribram & A. R. Luria (Eds.), *Psychophysiology of the frontal lobes.* New York: Academic Press.

Lykken, D. T. (1957). A study of anxiety in the sociopathic personality. *Journal of Abnormal and Social Psychology, 55,* 6–10.

Mednick, S. A., & Christiansen, K. O. (1977). *Biosocial bases of criminal behavior.* New York: Gardner Press.

Mowrer, O. H. (1947). On the dual nature of learning: A reinterpretation of "conditioning" and "problem-solving." *Harvard Education Review, 17,* 102–48.

Pontius, A. A. (1972). Neurological aspects in some types of delinquency, especially among juveniles: Toward a neurological model of ethical action. *Adolescence, 7,*(27), 289–308.

Pontius, A. A., & Ruttiger, K. F. (1976). Frontal lobe system maturational lag in juvenile delinquents shown in narratives test. *Adolescence, 11,* 509–18.

Pontius, A. A., & Yudowitz, B. S. (1980). Frontal lobe system dysfunction in some criminal actions as shown in the narratives test. *Journal of Nervous and Mental Disease, 168*(2), 111–17.

Poremba, C. D. (1975). Learning disabilities, youth and delinquency: Programs for intervention. In H. Myklebust (Ed.), *Progress in learning disabilities* (Vol. 3). New York: Grune & Stratton.

Ross, R. R. (1977). *Reading disability and crime – link and remediation: An annotated bibliography.* University of Ottawa, Department of Criminology.

Schachter, S., & Latané, B. (1964). Crime cognition and the autonomic nervous system. *Nebraska Symposium on Motivation, 12.*

Schmauck, F. J. (1970). Punishment, arousal and avoidance learning in sociopaths. *Journal of Abnormal Psychology, 76*(3), 325–35.

Siddle, D. A. T. (1977). Electrodermal activity and psychopathy. In S. A. Mednick & K. O. Christiansen (Eds.), *Biosocial bases of criminal behavior* (pp. 199–213). New York: Gardner Press.

Slavin, S. H. (1978). Information processing defects in delinquents. In *Ecologic–biochemical approaches to treatment of delinquents and criminals* (pp. 75–104). New York: Van Nostrand Reinhold.

Solway, J. S., Hays, J. R., Roberts, T. K., & Cody, J. A. (1975). Comparison of WISC profiles of alleged juvenile delinquents living at home versus those incarcerated. *Psychological Reports, 37,* 403–7.

Spellacy, F. (1978). Neuropsychological discrimination between violent and nonviolent men. *Journal of Clinical Psychology, 34,* 49–52.

Spreen, O. (1981). The relationship between learning disability, neurological impairment, and delinquency. *Journal of Nervous and Mental Disease, 169*(12).

Teuber, H. L. (1966). Some behavioral consequences of frontal lobe lesions in rodents, carnivores and primates. *Proceedings of the 18th International Congress of Psychologists, 18,* (95).

Unger, K. V. (1978). Learning disabilities and juvenile delinquency. *Journal of Juvenile & Family Courts,* February.

Voorhees, J. (1981). Neuropsychological differences between juvenile delinquents and functional adolescents: A preliminary study. *Adolescence, 16*(61), 57–66.

Wexler, B. E. (1980). Cerebral laterality and psychiatry: A review of the literature. *American Journal of Psychiatry, 137*(3), 279–91.

Williams, D. (1969). Temporal lobe syndromes. In P. J. Vinken & G. W. Bruyn (Eds.), *Handbook of clinical neurology: Localization in clinical neurology.* Amsterdam: North Holland.

Yeudall, L. T. (1977). Neuropsychological assessment of forensic disorders. *Canadian Mental Health, 25,* 7–16.

Yeudall, L. T. (1978). *The neuropsychology of aggression,* Clarence M. Hincks Memorial Lectures, Edmonton, Alberta, Canada.

Yeudall, L. T. (1979, September). A neuropsychosocial perspective of persistent juvenile delinquency and criminal behavior. Discussion paper at a meeting of the New York Academy of Sciences.

Yeudall, L. T., Fromm-Auch, D., & Davies, P. (1982). Neuropsychological impairment of persistent delinquency. *Journal of Nervous and Mental Disease, 170*(5), 257–65.

Zinkus, P. W., & Gottlieb, M. I. (1978). Learning disabilities and juvenile delinquency. *Clinical Pediatrics, 17*(10).

11 Violent behavior and cerebral hemisphere function

Israel Nachshon and Deborah Denno

Introduction

A distinct feature of the positive school of criminology is its concern with the individual criminal rather than with the phenomenon of crime. The focal issue is why, under similar environmental conditions, one person becomes a criminal, whereas the other does not. To confront this issue, research on criminal behavior must be directed toward the study of the personal characteristics of individual criminals rather than toward the analysis of criminal acts. Since personal characteristics are based partly on biological processes, these processes must be taken into consideration if criminal behavior is to be understood.

With this notion in mind, Lombroso (1874), the founder of the positive school of criminology, devoted much effort to the study of what he thought was the criminal's inadequacy and degeneracy as manifested by physical characteristics, or stigmata. Among the numerous stigmata that Lombroso investigated, two indicated lateral asymmetries, namely, abnormal asymmetry of the face and imbalance of the cerebral hemispheres. Subsequently, Talbot (1898) reported three lateral abnormalities among criminals: atypical asymmetries of the bulk and gyral development of the cerebral hemispheres and defective development of the great interhemispheric commissures. Finally, cranial asymmetries in violent criminals were reported by Lydston (1904).

Because, according to phrenological theory, structure determined function and the exterior of the skull conformed to the interior and to the shape of the brain (Vold, 1958/1979; pp. 51, 53), it was thought that cranial asymmetry might represent hemispheric asymmetry. Therefore, criminals who showed atypical cranial asymmetry presumably suffered from hemisphere dysfunction. However, successive failures to substantiate its theories with sound empirical verification brought about the fall of phrenology as a scientific discipline (Fink, 1915/1962, p. 19; Vold, 1958/1979, p. 55). Consequently, hypotheses concerning brain–behavior relations were gen-

185

erally abandoned. However, as Nachshon (1983) has noted, the revival of biosocial approaches in criminology facilitated, among other events, a renewal of interest in assumptions associating pathological and deviant behavior with unilateral hemisphere dysfunction (e.g., Flor-Henry & Yeudall, 1973).

These assumptions are the subject of this chapter. In the following sections, theories and data concerning the association between delinquent behavior and hemisphere function will be presented, and their contribution to the understanding of the etiology of delinquency will be evaluated.

Hemispheric asymmetry

In order to appreciate the possible association between hemisphere function or dysfunction and behavior, the concept of hemispheric asymmetry must be clarified. This concept implies that there is a division of labor between the two cerebral hemispheres of the brain. For most individuals the left cerebral hemisphere specializes in an analytic, sequential mode of information processing, whereas the right hemisphere specializes in a holistic, parallel mode of processing (see Bradshaw & Nettleton, 1981).

As a consequence of the differential hemispheric preferences for sequential and parallel modes of information processing, input that is normally processed sequentially (e.g., verbal stimuli) is usually mediated by the left hemisphere, whereas input that is normally processed in a parallel way (e.g., spatial stimuli) is usually mediated by the right hemisphere (Atkinson & Egeth, 1973; Bryden, 1976; Carmon, 1978; Carmon & Nachshon, 1971; Halperin, Nachshon, & Carmon, 1973; Moskovitch, 1979; Nachshon, 1973; Nachshon & Carmon, 1975).

This pattern of hemispheric asymmetry is more pronounced in right-handers (who prefer the use of the right over the left hand in performing manual tasks) than in left-handers (who do not show right-hand preference), because left-handers have relatively more heterogeneous modes of hemispheric specialization. For example, about 40% of left-handers appear to show right-hemispheric or bilateral language representation, in contrast to nearly all right-handers, who show left-hemispheric language representation (for reviews, see Herron, 1980).

Right-handers constitute about 90% of the entire population (Nachshon, Denno, & Aurand, 1983; Porac, Coren, & Duncan, 1980). Therefore, an association can be established between hand preference and hemispheric asymmetry whereby in most people the preferred hand is contralateral to the hemisphere that specializes in an analytic, sequential mode of information processing. Similar associations with hemispheric asymmetry can be established for other lateral preferences, such as foot and (to a lesser extent) eye preferences, which also show right-sided distribution in the entire population (Nachshon et al., 1983; Porac et al., 1980).

Behavioral manifestations of hemispheric asymmetry might be linked to unilateral hemisphere dysfunctions. For example, unusual patterns of lateral preferences and impaired performance on verbal or spatial tasks may indicate differential effects of specific, unilateral hemisphere dysfunctions. In general, impaired performance on a task that normally taps processes mediated by a given hemisphere might indicate a dysfunction of that hemisphere. Hence an impaired performance on verbal tasks may be associated with a left-hemisphere dysfunction, whereas an impaired performance on spatial tasks may be associated with a right-hemisphere dysfunction.

Hemisphere function and intelligence test scores

The association between reduced verbal and spatial test scores by subjects with left- and right-hemisphere dysfunction, respectively, has been used as an interpretation of unusual patterns of intellectual functioning by subjects with behavior disorders. Intelligence scales, such as the Wechsler Adult Intelligence Scale (WAIS), Wechsler Intelligence Scale for Children (WISC), and the Wechsler–Bellevue Scale, include two subscales: the verbal subscale, which taps verbal skills (e.g., vocabulary and verbal comprehension) and the performance subscale, which taps spatial skills (e.g., picture completion and block design). In line with their respective stimulus properties, verbal skills are usually mediated by the left hemisphere, and spatial skills are usually mediated by the right hemisphere. Normal subjects achieve similar scores on both subscales, indicating balanced functioning of the two hemispheres. However, it has been shown that subjects with behavior disorders (such as delinquents, psychopaths, acting-out juveniles, and recidivist criminals) score poorly on the verbal subscale but normally on the performance subscale (Altus and Clark 1949; Andrew, 1974a,b; 1978b; Blank, 1958; Clark & Moore, 1950; Corotto, 1961; Diller, 1952; Manne, Kandel, & Rosenthal, 1962; Wechsler, 1958; Wiens, Matarazzo, & Gver, 1959; Yeudall & Wardell, 1978). This pattern suggests an imbalanced functioning of the two hemispheres. (Different findings were reported, however, by Field, 1960; Foster, 1959; and Kahn, 1968; for details, see Nachshon, 1983.)

Reviewing the pertinent literature, Nachshon (1983) concluded that this unusual pattern of performance on intelligence scales can be attributed to a left-hemisphere dysfunction rather than to psychosocial factors, such as learning difficulties. For example, one of the studies (Yeudall & Wardell, 1978) showed that, regardless of learning difficulties, recidivist criminals scored poorly on neuropsychological and electrophysiological tests of left-hemisphere function and on the verbal WAIS tests; however, they scored normally on comparable tests of right-hemisphere function. Gabrielli and Mednick (1981) reported that an association between a neurological index of left-hemisphere dysfunction (pathological left-handedness) and delinquency was not mediated by verbal IQ.

Hemisphere function and behavior disorders: clinical evidence

Clinical evidence of the relation between hemisphere function and disorderly behavior first appeared more than a decade ago, when Flor-Henry (1973) and Flor-Henry and Yeudall (1973) advanced the hypothesis that psychopathy is associated with left-hemisphere dysfunction. Their hypothesis was based on Serafetinides's (1965) finding of overt physical aggressiveness in 36 of 100 consecutive temporal lobe epileptics, most of whom had a left temporal lobe focus. These findings were corroborated by Falconer & Taylor (1970), Lishman (1966), and Taylor (1969, 1972).

Subsequently, Yeudall and Fromm-Auch (1979) showed that predominantly left-hemisphere dysfunction was evident among psychopaths, alcoholics with personality disorders, male adolescents with severe conduct disturbances, and male violent criminals. In a similar study on violent and nonviolent criminals, Yeudall (1979) found that, among subjects with neuropsychological impairments, 72% of the violent criminals had left-hemisphere dysfunction, whereas 79% of the nonviolent criminals had right-hemisphere dysfunction. Right-hemisphere dysfunction was also found in subjects with affective personality disorders and in alcoholics with affective disorders (Yeudall & Fromm-Auch, 1979).

As Nachshon (1983) pointed out, these studies appear to show that violent behavior is associated with left-hemisphere dysfunction, whereas affective disorders are associated with right-hemisphere dysfunction. This conclusion is supported by Yeudall and Wardell's (1978) electrophysiological data, which demonstrated that, during the processing of verbal stimuli, violent subjects failed to show the normal activation pattern, particularly in the left hemisphere. Overall, 91% of the violent criminals had significant signs of neurological impairments; among them, 73% had greater deficits in the left than in the right hemisphere.

Yeudall's studies were criticized, however, by Hare (1979), who argued that the evaluation of their results was difficult, because "little information was given on the procedures used to select subjects and on the specific methods used to arrive at a diagnosis of a cerebral dysfunction. Further, it appears that the forensic population from which the subjects were obtained is a somewhat special one, consisting of persistent offenders charged with serious crimes (mostly of violence) and who exhibit a high incidence of salient neurological disorders'' (p. 605). Hare noted that test performance with criminals may be more an indication of motivational or attentional difficulties than an indication of cerebral dysfunction.

In light of such conflicting interpretations among investigators, it is clear that clinical data on cerebral functioning in criminals cannot be used as supportive evidence for any particular hypothesis.

Psychopathy and visual-field differences

Experimental support for the hypothesis that violent behavior is associated with left-hemisphere dysfunction is scarce. Hare (1979) was the first to use field differences in tachistoscopic recognition as a measure of hemispheric functioning in psychopaths. Under this procedure the subject identifies visual stimuli exposed for very short durations by means of a tachistoscope. Different visual stimuli are projected randomly either to the left or to the right visual field. If the subject's gaze is fixated at a centrally located point, the stimuli are transmitted, via the two eyes, from each of the two visual fields to the contralateral hemisphere. That is, stimuli projected to the left visual field are directly transmitted to the right hemisphere, whereas stimuli projected to the right visual field are directly transmitted to the left hemisphere. Cross-hemisphere transmission of information is carried out by the corpus callosum, which connects the two cerebral hemispheres. Under these conditions, stimuli are identified more accurately from the visual field contralateral to the hemisphere that mediates the processing of those stimuli. Therefore, verbal stimuli, which are usually processed in the left hemisphere, are more accurately identified from the right visual field, whereas spatial stimuli, which are usually processed in the right hemisphere, are more accurately identified from the left visual field. Deviation from this pattern may indicate hemisphere dysfunction.

In Hare's study (1979) psychopaths and controls were presented with three-letter words projected either to the left or to the right visual field. No group differences in right-visual-field superiority for stimulus identification were found. However, when in a subsequent study (Hare & Frazelle, 1981) more complex stimuli were projected, psychopaths failed to show the visual-field superiority effect. The authors interpreted this finding as indicating a possible lack of hemispheric asymmetry in psychopaths. However, it could be argued that the failure to show visual-field differences was due to a decrease in the right-visual-field superiority as a result of a left-hemisphere dysfunction.

Lateral preferences and behavior disorders

Support for the association between criminal behavior and left-hemisphere dysfunction can be found in a study on the differential distributions of lateral preferences among members of various offender groups. An examination of this association, however, requires some preliminary discussion of the research on the etiology of lateral preferences in order for the development of behavioral disorder to be more fully understood.

Normal and pathological lateral preferences. As mentioned previously, a minority of the population shows left-side preferences of limbs and sense organs. Left-sidedness, like right-sidedness, is considered normal and is probably genetically determined (Annet, 1972; Levy & Nagylaki, 1972). In addition to normal left-sided individuals, however, there are individuals whose left-sidedness is pathological, because it might be related to stressful prenatal and perinatal events. Specifically, it has been proposed (Ashton, 1982; Bakan, 1971, 1977, 1978; Bakan, Dibb, & Reid, 1973; Levy & Gur, 1980; Liederman & Coryell, 1982; Porac & Coren, 1976; Satz, 1972, 1973, 1979; Silva & Satz, 1979) that, because each hemisphere controls the contralateral side of the body, early stress in a given hemisphere, from oxygen deprivation (hypoxia), for example, can result in an impaired performance on the contralateral side of the body. If the impairment affects the preferred side, a pathological shift in lateral preferences of bodily paired parts might result.

This hypothesis of pathological lateral preferences has been tested by a number of investigators, with conflicting results. Some authors (Annett & Ockwell, 1980; Schwartz, 1977; Searleman, Tsao, & Balzer, 1980; Tan & Nettleton, 1980) reported no relation between hand preference and birth stress. Hicks, Dusek, Larsen, Williams, and Pellegrini (1980) did find a relation between hand preference and self-reported birth complications, but they considered the magnitude of the right–left shift too small to account for left-handedness. Coren and Porac (1980) found a relatively low incidence of right-hand preference in a group of male subjects who had sustained birth stress, according to maternal reports. However, the other lateral indices (eye, foot, and ear) were not related to birth stress; in females, all indices were unrelated.

In the largest study yet conducted on the relation between hand and eye preference and birth stress, Ehrlichman (1982) reported no association with hand preference and numerous birth events collected in the Boston area as part of the NIH Collaborative Perinatal Project. However, in a sample of nearly 6,000 girls and boys, left-eye preference was found to be significantly related to birth stress among boys.

Data inconsistencies seem to limit conclusions regarding the relation between left-sidedness and birth stress. According to Coren, Searleman, & Porac (1982), however, "methodological limitations, rather than an absence of a relationship between birth stress and lateral preferences, may be responsible for the predominantly negative findings reported in the published literature" (p. 479).

In a methodologically sound study, Coren et al. (1982) examined the relation between 8 indices of birth stress and 13 indices of hand, foot, eye, and ear preferences. Their data indicated "a shift toward left-sidedness, or at least away from right-sidedness in birth stressed individuals, with the largest effects found for males" (p. 485).

In conclusion, it appears that, although the evidence for the relation between early stress and lateral preferences is not conclusive, recent findings suggest that pathological left-sidedness may be associated with prenatal and perinatal trauma.

Pathological left-sidedness and associated disorders. If, indeed, pathological left-sidedness is associated with early stress to the left hemisphere, an increased incidence of left-sidedness in a given population may be associated with left-hemisphere dysfunction. In fact, pathological conditions – such as schizophrenia, epilepsy, mental retardation, and dyslexia – which are associated with left-hemisphere dysfunction, have also been linked to left-side preferences (Boklage, 1977; Colby & Parkinson, 1977; Dvirskii, 1976; Flor-Henry, 1979; Gur, 1977; Hécaen & Ajuriaguerra, 1964; Lishman & McMeekan, 1976; Luchins, Pollin, & Wyatt 1980; Oddy & Lobstein, 1972; Piran, Bigler, & Cohen, 1982; Satz, 1972, 1973, 1979; Walker & Birch, 1970; Wold, 1968).

Studies examining the association between left-side preference and delinquency, however, show conflicting results. For example, Palmer (1963) reported that undifferentiated handedness was associated with maladjustment. More recently, Fitzhugh (1973) detected that nearly one-third of a group of juvenile delinquents was left-handed. Using writing as a criterion for hand preference, Andrew (1978a) found that about 19% of a sample of male offenders preferred the left over the right hand. Because writing is frequently subject to social pressure, however, it is the worst criterion of hand preference, especially when used alone. Moreover, in a subsequent study (Andrew, 1980), left-handed offenders appeared to be less violent than right-handed offenders. Similarly, in Wardell and Yeudall's (1980) study of psychopaths with left-hemisphere dysfunction established by neuropsychological and psychophysiological indices, 14% were left-handers – a proportion that may be within the normal range.

Considering lateral eye and foot preferences as well as hand preference, Krynicki (1978) reported that assaultive patients who had signs of left-hemisphere dysfunction showed a decreased incidence of right-sidedness in all three preferences. This distribution was similar to distributions established for psychiatric patients (Lishman & McMeekan, 1976; Walker & Birch, 1970). However, Hare (1979) did not detect differences between psychopaths and nonpsychopaths in handedness and in an overall index of lateral preference (hand, eye, and foot).

In an attempt to relate measurements of lateral preferences (taken in 1972) to delinquent behavior (ascertained in 1978), Gabrielli and Mednick (1980) found that delinquents showed significant left preferences of hand and foot, but not of eye. For example, considering hand preference, 64.7% of the left-handers, but only 29.5% of the right-handers, were arrested at least once. Furthermore, among offenders with multiple arrests, 33% were left-handers; among offenders with a single crime, 11% were left-handers; and among nonoffenders only 7% were left-handers. Lateral preferences explained a higher proportion of the variance in delinquency than the social factors examined. In line with Gur's (1977) interpretation of similar patterns of lateral preferences in schizophrenics (overrepresentation of left-handedness and left-footedness but not of left-eyedness), Gabrielli and Mednick (1980) suggested that their findings indicated an association between left-hemisphere dysfunction and delinquency. Specifically, delinquency was associated with left-hand and left-foot preferences, but not with left-eye preference; it was assumed that anatomical considerations precluded a relation between eye preference and hemisphere function. (For more information on eye–hemisphere connections, see Porac & Coren, 1976.)

The present study

A review of the pertinent literature indicates that the association between left-hemisphere dysfunction and delinquency is supported by three sources: cognitive, clinical, and experimental data. The most consistent support comes from the differential performance of delinquents on the verbal and spatial subscales of intelligence tests. Despite some contradictory data and suggestions of alternative interpretations, most studies suggest that delinquents tend to achieve lower scores on verbal, relative to spatial, tests and that this response pattern may be associated with left-hemisphere dysfunction. However, because intelligence tests were not specifically valid measures of neuropsychological deficits, the results should be considered suggestive rather than conclusive.

Neuropsychological and electrophysiological evidence for an association between left-hemisphere dysfunction and delinquency was provided by Yeudall and his associates. Because of the select nature of their clinical populations, however, and other methodological difficulties, their findings may not be generalizable to other subjects.

When the left-hemisphere-dysfunction hypothesis was tested experimentally, no strong, unequivocal support was obtained. Similarly, the relations between lateral preferences and delinquency were not consistently apparent.

The lack of consistent support for an association between delinquent behavior and left-hemisphere dysfunction suggests further exploration of this topic. The main purpose of the study to be described here was to test the hypothesis that delinquent subjects evidence a higher incidence of left-sidedness than do control subjects, as measured by hand, eye, and foot preferences. An additional aim was to ascertain whether left-side preference was more prevalent among specific types of delinquents, particularly violent offenders.

Method

Subjects. The subjects in this study were selected from a sample of 2,958 black children whose mothers had participated in the Philadelphia Collaborative Perinatal Project (CPP) at Pennsylvania Hospital between 1959 and 1962. Pennsylvania Hospital was one of 12 medical centers selected by the National Institute of Neurological Diseases and Stroke in a nationwide study of genetic, biological, and environmental influences on child development. Thus the sample reflects, in part, the characteristics of children born to a self-selected group of women who were interested in receiving inexpensive maternity care provided by a public clinic. A description of the CPP study can be found in Broman, Nichols, and Kennedy (1975) and Niswander and Gordon (1972).

Only male subjects with complete laterality data taken at age 7 years ± 6 months and who resided in Philadelphia until their 18th birthday were included in the analyses. Females were excluded because of their relatively low level of police contacts. Subjects who resided outside Philadelphia were excluded so that their undetected delinquency involvement would not bias the analyses. Extensive comparisons between included and excluded CPP subjects, based on these criteria, revealed no significant differences between groups on key socioeconomic variables and other pertinent factors (Denno, 1982). Thus it can be assumed that the final sample of 1,066 black males examined in the present study is representative, in terms of selection criteria, of the total sample of black CPP subjects.

Delinquency measures. Delinquency measures were based on official police record data collected in the city of Philadelphia for all subjects between the ages of 10 and 18 years. Data collection techniques for police records and categories of delinquency are similar to those used by Wolfgang, Figlio, and Sellin, (1972) and in current analyses of delinquency data at the Center for Studies in Criminology and Criminal Law at the University of Pennsylvania. A detailed description of the arrest data collection and coding procedure, the intercoding reliability check, major variables, and offender categories can be found elsewhere (Center for Studies in Criminology and Criminal Law, 1981).

The advantages of using official arrest records for specifying delinquency involvement relative to other points of contact in the juvenile justice system, such as a court trial, have been discussed by Wolfgang et al. (1972). Most important is the relatively less biased nature of the police contact, the first in a chain of events in the juvenile justice process. In addition, demographic and socioeconomic distributions of offenders designated by police contacts are similar to distributions of offense data gathered from other sources, such as victimization surveys or self-report questionnaires (e.g., see Elliot & Ageton, 1980; Hindelang, 1978; Hindelang, Hirschi, & Weiss, 1979). These advantages of using arrest data offset, to a considerable extent, the disadvantages of using arrest data, which have been described extensively (Hood & Sparks, 1970; Wolfgang, 1963).

Altogether, subjects were divided into six hierarchical offense categories based on the most serious type of police contact. A police contact included both arrest and remedial status offenses. Remedial offenses are those that come to the attention of the police but do not result in arrest. Very violent and violent offenders were those individuals who had had a police contact for at least one injury offense at any time during their juvenile career (during the ages of 10 to 18 years). Damage offenders had had a police contact for at least one property damage offense and possibly theft or nonindex offenses but no injury offenses. Theft offenders had had a police contact for at least one theft offense but no injury or damage offenses. Nonindex offenders had had a police contact for the nonindex-type offenses only.

Laterality measures. Scoring criteria for measuring lateral preferences in hand, eye, and foot when subjects were 7 years ± 6 months have been described in detail (see U.S. Department of Health, Education, and Welfare, 1966, pp. 22–3). Tests were administered by experienced psychologists when subjects attended a variety of pediatric and neurological examinations at the hospital of the University of Pennsylvania. Criteria for scoring and lateral preference categories used for this study are briefly described as follows:

1. *Hand preference.* Hand preference was treated as a dichotomous variable. Predominantly left-handed individuals constituted one group; predominantly right-handed individuals constituted the other group. The few remaining individuals with variable or ambidextrous handedness were excluded from analysis. Hand preference in the CPP was determined by placing three pencils, each of a different color, directly in front of the child, who was then asked to make an "X" on a piece of paper with each pencil. If the same hand was not used with each of the three pencils, the test was repeated two more times. Any preference that occurred fewer than four out of five times was coded "variable."

2. *Eye preference.* Eye preference was treated as a dichotomous variable. Left-eyed individuals constituted one group; right-eyed individuals constituted the other group. Individuals with variable preference were excluded from analysis. Eye preference in the CPP was determined by asking a child to look through a kaleidoscope after picking it up with both hands. The test was repeated three times with both hands on the kaleidoscope. Any preference less than perfect was coded "variable."

3. *Foot preference.* Foot preference was treated both as a dichotomous and a trichotomous variable. Predominantly left-footed individuals constituted one group; predominantly right-footed individuals constituted the other group when a dichotomous variable was used. Left-, right-, and variable-footed individuals constituted the first, second, and third groups, respectively, when a trichotomous variable was used. Foot preference in the CPP was determined by asking a child to stand with both feet together and kick a 3- to 4-inch Wiffle ball, which was placed 1 foot directly in front of the child. A consistent foot preference was then noted by the experimenter during three trials. If two right and one left (or vice versa) responses were observed, two more trials were performed and any preference that occurred fewer than four out of five times was coded "variable."

Table 11.1. *Distribution of offender categories*

Offender category	Offense type	N	Percentage of total sample	Percentage of offenders only
Very violent	Murder, rape or attempted rape, assault with intent to kill, aggravated assault	57	5.4	18.2
Violent	Personal injury offenses excluding those in the very violent category	45	4.2	14.4
Damage	Property damage, without personal injury	34	3.2	10.9
Theft	Theft, without personal injury or property damage	43	4.0	13.7
Nonindex	Minor offenses, not included in the above categories	134	12.6	42.8
Nonoffender	Nonoffender controls	753	70.6	—
Total sample		1066	100.0	—
Offenders only		313	—	100.0

Results

Delinquency. Distributions of offender categories are presented in Table 11.1. Altogether, 313 (29.3%) of the 1,066 males selected for study had had some form of police contact that had resulted in a remedial disposition or an arrest. Of the total sample of subjects, nearly 10% had experienced a police contact for an offense involving some kind of personal injury; these offenders were divided nearly equally between those considered to be very violent and those considered to be relatively less violent. Offenders whose most serious offense had involved damage or theft had a somewhat lower representation in the sample. As expected, a disproportionate number of offenders had as their most serious contact a nonindex offense, such as a runaway or truancy.

Among the total sample of offenders only, nearly one-third had experienced a police contact that involved some form of personal injury; this proportion comprised the 18.2% of very violent offenders and the 14.3% of violent offenders. The proportions of damage and theft offenders in the offender sample ranged between 10% and 14%. Nonindex offenders dominated the offender categories.

Lateral preferences and delinquency status. Distributions of hand, eye, and foot preferences by delinquency status are shown in Table 11.2. In

Table 11.2. *Distribution of hand, eye, and foot preferences by offender status*

Lateral preference	Offender status						
	Offender		Nonoffender		Total		
	N	%	N	%	N	%	
Hand							
Left	27	8.6	97	12.9	124	11.6	
Right	286	91.4	656	87.1	942	88.4	
Eye							
Left	131	41.9	301	40.0	432	40.5	
Right	182	58.1	452	60.0	634	59.5	
Foot							
Left	24	7.7	81	10.8	105	9.8	
Right	251	80.2	594	78.9	845	79.3	
Variable	38	12.1	78	10.3	116	10.9	
Total for each lateral preference	313	100.0	753	100.0	1066	100.0	

general, distributions of lateral preferences for the total sample were similar to those reported elsewhere (e.g., Porac, Coren, & Duncan, 1980). As expected, most subjects showed right-hand preference, and more subjects showed right-eye preference than left-eye preference. More than three-quarters of the subjects showed right-foot preference, and nearly equivalent percentages showed left- and variable-foot preference.

Significant differences were found between nonoffenders and offenders in hand preference only. Significantly, more nonoffenders showed left-hand preference than offenders [$\psi^2(1) = 3.90$, $p < .05$]. No significant differences appeared in eye preference [$\psi^2(1) = 0.32$, $p > .05$] or in distributions of foot preference [$\psi^2(2) = 2.84$, $p > .05$].

Lateral preferences and offender categories. Distributions of lateral preference by offender categories are shown in Table 11.3. Concerning hand preference, distributions of right-hand preference ranged from 87.1% for nonoffenders to 93.3% for theft offenders. However, log-linear analyses showed no overall significant differences among groups when examined simultaneously.

Similar trends appeared for distributions of foot preference given a left–right dichotomy. Distributions of right-foot preference ranged from 88.0%

Table 11.3. *Lateral preferences of hand, eye, and foot by offender category*

Lateral preference	Offender category											
	Very violent		Violent		Damage		Theft		Nonindex		Nonoffender	
	N	%	N	%	N	%	N	%	N	%	N	%
Hand												
Left	6	10.5	3	6.7	4	11.7	3	7.0	11	8.2	97	12.9
Right	51	89.5	42	93.3	30	88.3	40	93.0	123	91.8	656	87.1
Eye												
Left	34	59.7	21	46.7	8	23.5	20	46.5	48	34.8	301	40.0
Right	23	40.3	24	53.3	26	76.5	23	53.5	86	64.2	452	60.0
Foot												
Left	5	8.8	3	6.7	3	8.8	4	9.3	9	6.7	81	10.8
Right	43	75.4	38	84.4	24	70.6	32	74.4	114	85.1	594	78.9
Variable	9	15.8	4	8.9	7	20.6	7	16.3	11	8.2	78	10.3
Total for each lateral preference	57	100.0	45	100.0	34	100.0	43	100.0	134	100.0	753	100.0

for nonoffenders to 92.6% for violent and nonindex offenders. Log-linear analyses, however, showed no significant differences among groups. Similarly, no significant between-group differences appeared when distributions of variable-foot preference were added as a separate group. With the additional group, distributions of right-foot preference ranged from 70.6% for the damage offenders to 85.1% for the nonindex offenders.

For eye preference, however, there were significant between-group differences, particularly for violent offenders. Overall, 60% of the nonoffenders and about 64% of the nonindex offenders showed right-eye preference, as compared with about 53% of the violent offenders and theft offenders. In contrast, considerably fewer (40%) of the very violent offenders and relatively more (76%) of the damage offenders showed right-eye preference. The overall group differences in eye preference were highly significant [$\psi^2(5) = 15.39, p < .008$].

Further analyses showed that very violent offenders differed significantly from nonoffenders [$\psi^2(1) = 6.54, p < .02$], from the nonindex offenders [$\psi^2(1) = 11.48, p < .001$], and from the damage offenders [$\psi^2(1) = 26.94, p < .001$]. Damage offenders differed significantly from all other groups [theft offenders: $\psi^2(1) = 11.60, p < .001$; nonoffenders: $\psi^2(1) = 6.36, p < .02$; violent offenders: $\psi^2(1) = 11.80, p < .001$; nonindex offenders: $\psi^2(1) = 4.60; p < .05$]. Other group differences were not statistically significant.

Cross-preferences and offender categories. Distributions of cross-preferences appear in Table 11.4. Overall, two preference combinations account for about three-quarters (74.5%) of the population: 47.3% of the subjects who showed consistent right-side preferences on all three lateral indices and 27.2% of the subjects who showed right-hand and right-foot preference but left-eye preference. Only 3.8% of the subjects showed consistent left-side preferences on all three lateral indices.

Most right-handers showed right-eye (61.7%) and right-foot (84.2%) preferences; only 5.2% showed left-foot preference. However, most left-handers showed left-eye (58.0%) but no predominant type of foot preference (45.1%); only 41.1% showed right-foot preference. Differences between right- and left-handers were significant for both eye preference [$\psi^2(1) = 17.88, p < .001$] and foot preference [$\psi^2(2) = 27.64, p < .001$].

A higher proportion of subjects with right-eye preference showed right-foot preference, relative to left-eyed subjects. Overall, 6.7% of the right-eyed subjects showed left-foot preference, relative to 14.3% of the left-eyed subjects. Differences between the two eyedness groups in foot preference were highly significant [$\psi^2(2) = 20.10, p < .001$].

Table 11.4. Cross-preferences of hand, eye, and foot

Lateral index[a]			Offense											
			Very violent		Violent		Damage		Theft		Nonindex		No offense		Total	
Hand	Eye	Foot	N	%	N	%	N	%	N	%	N	%	N	%	N	%
Lateral preferences																
R	R	R	17	29.8	18	40.1	21	61.8	22	51.1	72	53.7	354	47.0	504	47.3
R	R	V	4	7.0	2	4.4	4	11.8	1	2.3	6	4.5	34	4.5	51	5.8
R	R	L	0	0	1	2.2	1	2.9	0	0	5	3.7	20	2.6	27	2.5
R	L	R	24	42.1	18	40.1	1	2.9	10	23.3	34	25.4	203	26.9	290	27.2
R	L	V	5	8.8	2	4.4	3	8.8	6	14.0	4	3.0	28	3.7	48	4.5
R	L	L	1	1.8	1	2.2	0	0	1	2.3	2	1.5	17	2.3	22	2.0
L	R	R	2	3.5	2	4.4	0	0	0	0	3	2.2	18	2.4	25	2.4
L	R	V	0	0	0	0	0	0	0	0	0	0	11	1.5	11	1.0
L	R	L	0	0	1	2.2	0	0	0	0	0	0	15	2.0	16	1.5
L	L	R	0	0	0	0	2	5.9	0	0	5	3.7	19	2.5	26	2.4
L	L	V	0	0	0	0	0	0	0	0	1	0.8	5	0.7	6	0.6
L	L	L	4	7.0	0	0	2	5.9	3	7.0	2	1.5	29	3.9	40	3.8
Total			57	100.0	45	100.0	34	100.0	43	100.0	134	100.0	753	100.0	1066	100.0
Cross-preferences																
All cross-preferences combined			36	63.2	27	59.9	11	32.3	18	41.9	60	44.8	370	49.1	522	48.9

[a] R, Right; L, left; V, variable.

Group differences in the frequencies of cross-lateral preferences (i.e., all patterns of preference except for RRR and LLL)* were also evident. As Table 11.4 shows, the highest percentages of cross-preferences appeared among the violent subjects; 63.2% of the very violent offenders and 59.9% of the violent offenders had cross-preferences, relative to 47.6% for all other groups. These differences were further analyzed by comparing the frequencies of cross-preferences with the frequencies of unidirectional preferences (RRR + LLL) through a series of chi-square tests. Altogether, the frequencies for very violent subjects were different from those for damage offenders [$\psi^2(1) = 7.10$, $p < .01$], theft offenders [$\psi^2(1) = 4.45$, $p < .05$], nonindex offenders [$\psi^2(1) = 4.80$, $p < .05$], and nonoffenders [$\psi^2(1) = 3.19$, $p < .10$]. However, the frequencies were not different from those for the violent offenders [$\psi^2(1) = 0.1$, $p > .10$], suggesting a similarity among subjects with a history of injury, as determined by police contacts. Frequencies for damage offenders were significantly different from those for violent offenders [$\psi^2(1) = 5.68$, $p < .02$] and for nonoffenders [$\psi^2(1) = 4.38$, $p < .05$], but not for other groups. All other group differences were not statistically significant.

As Table 11.4 further shows, aside from the very violent and the violent offenders, the RRR preference pattern occurred with the highest frequency for all groups. For the very violent offenders the RLR pattern occurred the most frequently; for the violent offenders the RLR pattern occurred with a frequency equal to that of the RRR pattern. The second most frequently occurring pattern was the RLR, which appeared for the theft and nonindex offenders and the nonoffenders. The last major pattern of cross-preferences, RRV, was shown among damage offenders, who had the highest frequency of the RRR pattern compared with all other groups.

In summary, for the very violent offenders, frequencies for the RRR and RLR patterns were in a reverse direction of occurrence from those for the other groups. The most frequent pattern was RLR, followed by RRR. For the violent offenders, the percentages of these patterns were equal. The number of subjects in the remaining cross-preference groups was too small for meaningful analysis.

It is important to note that, considering the large number of chi-square tests that have been conducted, a number of results in the analyses could have occurred by chance. However, in light of the consistencies and trends in the data, particularly for very violent and violent offenders, this

---

* The letters L, R, and V stand for left-, right-, or variable-hand, -eye, and -foot preference, in that order.

possibility is diminished. The results may therefore be considered sufficiently meaningful to be discussed.

Discussion

Validity of lateral preference measurements. Before the findings of the present study are discussed, the adequacy of the lateral preference measurements ought to be assessed. As Nachshon et al. (1983) pointed out, the lateral preference measures used for the CPP could be criticized for inadequacy and variability across the three lateral indices. Despite these drawbacks, however, the distributions of the lateral preferences obtained by these measures on the entire CPP sample (Nachshon et al., 1983), as well as on the sample examined in the present study, very much resembled those reported by Porac, Coren, and Duncan (1980) with a comparable sample and with a validated questionnaire. It can be assumed, therefore, that the measures in the present study serve as valid indices of lateral preferences.

Lateral preferences among different offenders. Nonoffenders showed a significantly higher incidence of left-handedness than offenders, although no significant differences appeared in the distributions of eye and foot preferences. This finding contradicts results reported previously (Andrew, 1978a; Fitzhugh, 1973; Gabrielli & Mednick, 1980) showing a relatively higher incidence of left-handedness among offenders; however, the finding is congruent with other results (Andrew, 1980; Wardell & Yeudall, 1980), which failed to show an association between offensive behavior and left-handedness. As will be shown below, differential sample characteristics might account for the differences in the results of the various studies.

Considering the six different categories of offender groups, no significant differences in distributions of right-side preferences for hand and foot were found. However, significant differences appeared for eye preference. Except for the very violent offenders, the majority of subjects in each group showed right-eye preference, particularly the damage offenders. The greater incidence of right-eye preference among damage offenders relative to all other groups may be considered normal, however, because the incidence is comparable to frequencies of right-eye preference reported in previous research (Porac, Coren, & Duncan, 1980).

In contrast, very violent offenders showed a reverse pattern of lateral preference; most (60%) had left- rather than right-eye preference. As discussed in the introduction to this chapter, an increased incidence of left-side preference in a given population may be related to left-hemisphere dysfunction (Gur & Gur, 1980; Porac & Coren, 1976; Satz, 1972, 1973, 1979; Silva & Satz, 1979). Consequently, the significantly higher incidence of left-eye preference among very violent offenders might serve as an indication of left-hemisphere dysfunction. Yeudall's (1979) report of a left-hemisphere dysfunction among violent, as opposed to nonviolent, criminals provides support for this conclusion.

Relating eye preference to hemisphere function may seem unwarranted, however. Because the projections of each eye to the two hemispheres are bilateral, Porac and Coren (1976) concluded that there is no anatomical basis for a hemisphere–eye association. Yet new electrophysiological data showing hemispheric control of the contralateral eye suggest that a hemisphere–eye association may exist. Recording visual evoked potentials from the two eyes, Seyal and his associates (Seyal, Sato, White, & Porter, 1981) found higher amplitudes from the dominant than from the nondominant eye. This tendency was stronger among right- than left-eye-dominant subjects. The authors interpreted these findings as providing electrophysiological evidence for eye asymmetry in the nervous system, because asymmetry in visual evoked potentials, produced by stimulating the dominant or the nondominant eye, may imply "the presence of a morphological or physiological substrate in the visual cortex that generates the asymmetric response" (Seyal et al., 1981, p. 424). In light of previous findings (Gur, 1977; Nachshon et al., 1983; Porac, Coren, Steiger, & Duncan, 1980), it is reasonable to assume that eye preference in the present study may be related, at least partially, to hemispheric asymmetry. If, indeed, eye preference, like hand and foot preferences, is associated with hemispheric asymmetry, the three lateral preferences should be interrelated. In line with previous findings (Nachshon et al., 1983), the data of the present study may indeed indicate such an interrelationship. However, hand preference is more closely associated with foot preference than with eye preference (see Nachshon et al., 1983).

The finding of a partial rather than full correspondence among the three indices of lateral preferences may be attributed to environmental influences and their possible differential association with preference development. Consider, for example, possible effects of brain trauma at birth. In line with an extension of Satz's model of pathological lateral preferences (Porac and Coren, 1976; Satz, 1972, 1973, 1979; Silva & Satz, 1979), Levy and Gur (1980) hypothesized that, in cases of birth trauma affecting left-hemisphere function, lateral preferences may shift from right to left. It can be further hypothesized that, if the various lateral preferences are not equally vulnerable to the effects of birth trauma, discrepancies in lateral preferences may appear. As shown by the CPP data (Ehrlichman, 1982), for males left-eye preference, but not left-hand preference, was related to birth stress. Presumably, eye preference may be more vulnerable to birth trauma than hand (and foot) preferences and consequently may be the first to shift from right to left (Levy, 1980; Nachshon et al., 1983). A pattern of right-hand and right-foot preferences accompanied by a left-eye preference might then appear.

In the present study this pattern appeared among the violent offenders. As Table 11.4 shows, the most frequent pattern of cross-preferences among the violent subjects was RLR: 42.1% and 40.1% for the very violent and the violent offenders, respectively. The pattern occurred among only 25.7% of all other groups. Furthermore, the violent offenders showed a clear overall tendency for left-side preferences, because preference of the RRR pattern was the least frequent among the very violent (29.8%) and the violent offenders (40.1%); the pattern occurred among 48.6% of all other groups. Distributions of the LLL pattern were not analyzed because of the small number of subjects preferring this pattern.

Patterns of cross-preferences. In light of suggestions (Gur & Gur, 1974) that an unusual proportion of cross-preferences may be related to cerebral dysfunction and perhaps to birth trauma, distributions of cross-preferences in the various offender groups were examined. As the data in Table 11.4 show, frequencies of cross-preferences, as compared with frequencies of unidirectional preferences, were highest among violent offenders, particularly the very violent. The relation between violent offender status and cross-preference patterns suggests that birth trauma may be an important etiological factor to examine in future analyses, in terms of both hemisphere function and behavior.

The possible importance of early environmental factors relative to lateral preference and interpersonal behavior may explain, in part, the difference between the results of this study and the findings reported by Gabrielli and Mednick (1980). The two studies differ on a number of important variables. First, subjects' demographic and environmental conditions varied considerably. The subjects in Gabrielli and Mednick's study were white Danes, whereas in the present study the subjects were black Americans. Because blacks and whites may have somewhat different patterns of hemispheric organization (Denno, Meijs, Nachshon, & Aurand, 1982; TenHoughton, 1980; Thompson, Bogen, & March, 1979), which are, at least partially, reflected in patterns of lateral preferences (Nachshon et al., 1983), differential patterns of lateral preferences between blacks and whites could be expected. Second, the subjects in Gabrielli and Mednick's study had primarily traffic and theft offenses and very few violent offenses. Offense status was recorded initially at age 15. In contrast, a sizable number of subjects in the present study had serious police contacts, and offense status was initially recorded at age 10, with a peak of reported offense behavior at age 14 (see Denno, 1982).

Although Gabrielli and Mednick (1980) analyzed offense frequency rather than offense category (the variable analyzed in the present study), the relation between seriousness of offense category and number of police contacts experienced has been clearly established in other analyses of the CPP data (Denno, 1982). Thus it may be assumed that this differential focus in analyses does not have a large influence on results.

Overall, it is difficult to compare the two studies or to relate their different results to particular variables. Taken together, however, the results indicate a possible association between delinquency status and left-hemisphere dysfunction, as indicated by specific patterns of lateral preferences. Because of the paucity of supporting experimental data and in view of the differential results obtained in the two studies where lateral preferences were examined, the findings of the present study should be interpreted with caution. More research is certainly needed to delineate the association among patterns of lateral preferences, cerebral structure and function, and their behavioral correlates.

Unilateral hemisphere dysfunction and violent behavior. Although an association between hemisphere dysfunction and behavior disorders does not imply that the former causes the latter, one may speculate about possible relations between the two.

According to Yeudall (1980), a right-hemisphere dysfunction may disrupt the control of emotionality, which is normally controlled by the right hemisphere, and thus facilitate impulsive outbursts of violence. In contrast, a left-hemisphere dysfunction may disrupt the regulatory role of language in controlling violent impulses and the development of foresight and anticipation of the negative consequences of violent behavior, both of which are normally mediated by the left hemisphere. Consequently, a left-hemisphere dysfunction might facilitate violent behavior.

An alternative hypothesis might refer to the differential strategies of information processing employed by the two cerebral hemispheres. As Semmes (1968) pointed out, information is processed more diffusely in the right hemisphere and more focally in the left hemisphere. A similar differentiation in terms of modes of orienting responses was proposed by Myslobodsky and Rattok (1977). They suggested that the right hemisphere reacts to impeding stimulation in an undifferentiated, diffuse mode and is therefore suitable for mediating the emotion-laden "fight or flight" behavior. In contrast, the left hemisphere reacts to stimulation in a differentiated stimulus-specific mode, which, under normal conditions, initiates proper behavioral responses. Under threatening conditions, however, a malfunctioning left hemisphere might respond inappropriately, for example, by facilitating aggressive responses. This inappropriate goal-directed response mode is distinguishable from impulsive emotional outbursts, which are associated with a malfunctioning right hemisphere.

Relation of biological and social factors to criminal behavior. Possible associations between hemisphere dysfunction and behavior disorders do not exclude relations with other biological and social factors. As has been repeatedly pointed out (Addad, 1980; Bach-y-Rita, 1975; Benton, 1981; Bohman, Cloninger, Sigvardsson, & von Knorring, 1982; Buikhuisen, 1979; Christiansen, 1977; Cloninger, Sigvardsson, Bohman, & Knorring, 1982; Fishman, 1981; Jeffrey, 1978; Moyer, 1976; Nachshon, 1982; Rubin, Reinisch, & Haskett, 1981; Sigvardsson, Cloninger, Bohman, & Knorring, 1982; Yeudall, 1977; Yeudall, Fedora, Fedora, & Wardell, 1981; Yeudall, Fromm-Auch, & Davies, 1982), no biological factor, normal or abnormal, predetermines behavior, because behavior is a product of interacting biological and environmental events. Even Lombroso eventually modified his theory and methodology to include socioeconomic and environmental data (see Vold, 1979/1958, p. 39). The significance of biological factors is a controversial issue, however.

An environmental approach can be represented by Wolfgang's (1975) argument that humans cannot be innately criminal because the concept of crime is socially defined and varies with time and place. Also, most criminals obey most laws. According to Wolfgang, "everything we know about criminal behavior indicates that it is learned" (Wolfgang, 1975, p. 462). Therefore, although not formally ignored, biological and psychological variables can be "suspended, postponed, or dismissed after consideration" (Wolfgang, 1978, p. 4).

An opposite, biological approach can be represented by Flor-Henry's (1978) argument that male aggression is rooted in biologically determined, lateralized, neuroendocrinological organization and therefore cannot be attributed to sociological factors and to child-rearing practices. Hemispheric organization is, in turn, a result of either genetic–constitutional interaction or of acquired hemisphere dysfunction.

The biosocial approach maintains, however, that neither sociological nor biological factors alone can account for the complexity of human behavior (Nachshon, 1982). Biological factors, such as hemisphere dysfunction, are associated with behavior only through the mediation of non-biological factors. However, there are behavioral manifestations where individual differences in psychological or biological factors cannot be ignored if behavior is to be fully understood.

It is noticeable that, although Wolfgang was opposed to criminal predeterminism, (1975) he seemed receptive to the idea that "behaving capacities" are genetically determined. Wolfgang did not elaborate on the nature of those "behaving capacities," but Jeffrey (1978) explicitly proposed that individuals are endowed with capacities to interact with the environment. For example, he explained that "sociopathy and alcoholism are not inherited, but a biochemical preparedness for such behavior is present in the brain, which, if given a certain type of environment, will produce sociopathy or alcoholism" (p. 162).

Evidence that biochemical processes in the brain may predispose some persons to react negatively to facilitating environmental events suggests that behavior is a function of both predisposing and facilitatory factors. Predisposing factors influence the overall probability of a certain behavior, whereas facilitatory factors influence its time and place. However, predisposition is not necessarily biological, and facilitation is not necessarily environmental. The reverse may also occur. An observed correlation between variables A and B may indicate that A affects B, or that B affects A, or that both A and B are affected by a third variable C. For example, when a person is exposed to a frightening stimulation, two correlated processes, a cognitive awareness (a sense of fear) and a physiological activation (increased sensitivity of the sympathetic nervous system) are evident. This observed correlation has been interpreted in three ways: Cognition affects autonomous functions (the "common-sense" theory); autonomous reactions affect cognition (James-Lange's theory); or both cognitive and physiological changes are brought about by a thalamic mediation (Cannon-Bard's theory) (see Strongman, 1973).

Regarding violence, a positive correlation has been found in rhesus monkeys among the level of the male sex hormone, plasma testosterone, and aggressive behavior. As Rose, Gordon, and Bernstein (1972) and Rose, Bernstein, Gordon, and Catlin (1974) have shown, however, once the social status of a monkey in its colony is established, changes in the level of testosterone in the body do *not* affect the social status of the monkey, whereas changes in the social status do affect the level of testosterone. When male monkeys were placed among weaker monkeys, their testosterone level increased; when they were placed among stronger monkeys, their testosterone level decreased. Similarly, in Dixson and Herbert's (1977) study, castrated Talapoin monkeys showed an increase in aggressive behavior following an implantation of a pellot of testosterone, which was directed toward subordinate males only. This pattern of behavior suggests that predisposing (environmental) past experiences influenced the facilitatory (biological) hormonal effects. A similar conclusion has been reached by Horney (1978) concerning the relation between menstrual cycles and antisocial behavior in women. It is quite possible, she said, "that the antisocial behaviors and concomitant events produce hormonal changes, rather than vice versa" (p. 32). Biological association, therefore, does not imply biological causation.

The relative contribution of biological and social factors to criminal behavior perhaps becomes clearest in examinations of serious repetitive offenders. Some authors have referred to the finding by Wolfgang and his associates (Wolfgang, 1975; Wolfgang et al., 1972) that, within a given birth cohort of males, 6.3% were responsible for 52% of all delinquencies recorded. Evidence that a small minority in a population is associated with more than half of the offenses suggests that biological and psychological factors may be relatively more important contributors to recidivist behavior than social factors.

Indeed, in discussing genetic and neurological etiologies of aggressive behavior, Mednick (1980) and Monroe et al., (1977) explicitly stated that their populations probably consisted of recidivist offenders similar to those identified by Wolfgang (1975). Wolfgang's finding is also strikingly similar to Mark and Ervin's (1970) observation that "an appreciable percentage of the relatively few individuals guilty of repeated personal violence are to be found in the five to ten percent of the population, whose brains do not function in a perfectly normal way" (p. 5). From these observations it follows that a disproportionate percentage of violent, repetitive offenders may evidence some sort of brain dysfunction. This conclusion does not suggest, however, that brain dysfunction is the sole correlate of violent behavior, to the exclusion of social and environmental factors. Rather, brain dysfunction may be only one of many important factors associated with a specific subgroup of persistent offenders (Yeudall et al., 1982). In fact, it can safely be assumed that most violence is *not* linked to brain dysfunction (Bach-y-Rita, 1975).

Moreover, even if an association between brain dysfunction and violent behavior were found, it would more likely be indirect than direct. For example, brain dysfunction may adversely affect one's perception of the world and adaptive ability to cope with frustrating events, as Yeudall (1980) and Yeudall and Wardell (1978) have suggested; or dysfunction may disrupt the effects of the orienting responses, which normally regulate responsivity, as suggested above. Despite their differences, both hy-

potheses concerning brain–behavior relations imply that associations between hemisphere dysfunction and behavior are mediated by psychological processes that provide the link between neurological and social processes. (For further discussion of the relation between brain dysfunction
and behavior disorder, see Shuman, 1977.)

Another viewpoint concerning the nature of the biosocial association
with criminal behavior focuses on the relation between dysfunction of
the nervous system and socioeconomic status. Christiansen (1977) and
Mednick and his associates (Mednick, 1979, 1980; Mednick, Pollock,
Volavka, & Gabrielli, 1982) postulated that in lower classes, where
resistance to crime is weak, criminals tend to be relatively more psychologically and neurologically normal than in the higher classes, where resistance to crime is strong, and criminals tend to be relatively more psychologically and neurologically deviant. For example, Mednick (1977)
found that slow electrodermal responses, which indicate a dysfunction in
the autonomic nervous system, were related to criminality, especially in
higher socioeconomic classes.

Another hypothesis concerning the association between psychophysiological and social variables was put forward by Yeudall and his associates (Yeudall, 1977; Yeudall et al., 1981). Noting that brain dysfunction is
more prevalent in lower than in higher socioeconomic classes (Montague,
1972), Yeudall and his associates postulated that individuals belonging to
the lower classes are relatively less likely to receive proper medical treatment when necessary, especially in their earliest years. Consequently,
they are relatively more likely to encounter difficulties in school and to
react to social frustrations in a criminal manner. Hence lower class individuals have a higher probability of having brain dysfunction and consequently deviant or criminal behavior than higher class individuals.

These hypotheses do not address the possible influences of differential
police behavior toward lower class individuals or other, similar types of
intervening factors that would be unrelated to an offender's biological
capacities. Thus a biosocial approach to the study of criminal behavior
requires a multivariate design that includes many important biological,
psychological, and social variables, so that their relative influences can be
weighed simultaneously.

On a practical level, the notion of a biosocial etiology of violent behavior implies that behavior modification can be achieved not only by altering
the individual's environment, but also by altering what Moyer (1976, p.
284) calls "the internal milieu." That means that control of violent behavior, *where violence is associated with biological dysfunction,* can be
achieved by medical means (see Monroe et al., 1977). Hence "instrumen-

tal aggression,'' which is purely learned and is not correlated with specific physiological processes (Moyer, 1980), cannot be treated medically.

The scope and limits of the medical model in behavior modification can be further delineated by an example taken from the field of psychopathology. Among schizophrenics is a given subgroup whose primary problem may be related to brain damage, particularly in the left frontal lobe. These patients do not respond adequately to treatment that is useful for other patients. Consequently, it was advised (Golden et al., 1981) that special methods of medical treatment that are specifically suited for this subgroup be determined.

The application of medical treatment in those limited cases where it is useful does not imply that social methods of behavior modification are ineffective. Indeed, because human behavior is mostly learned and because biological factors are related to behavior only through an interaction with social and environmental events, it is clear that social factors play a major role in the etiology and modification of deviant behavior. Despite arguments to the contrary (Moran, 1978), Lombrosian concepts of criminal predeterminism have long been discarded (see Fink, 1962, p. 8), and they do not underly current research on the biosocial bases of violent and criminal behavior (see Wolfgang, 1977). In fact, it is possible that the "remarkable historical resiliency of the biomedical approach to crime" (Nassi & Abramowitz, 1976, p. 605), which has been noticed by proponents and opponents alike, is due to the awareness, on the part of contemporary biosocial researchers, of both the promises and limitations of that approach.

Acknowledgments

This study was partially supported by Grant 78-NI-AX-0125 from the Law Enforcement Assistance Administration, National Institute of Justice, given to Dr. Marvin E. Wolfgang, Director, Center for Studies in Criminology and Criminal Law, University of Pennsylvania. The points of view are those of the authors and do not necessarily represent the views of the U.S. Department of Justice. The authors thank Dr. Wolfgang for his support, comments, and encouragement and Mr. Steven Aurand for his help in data analysis. The analyses were conducted while the first author was a visitor at the Center for Studies in Criminology and Criminal Law, University of Pennsylvania.

References

Addad, M. (1980). Violence from an integrative point of view. *Crime and Social Deviance, 8*, 5–24 [Hebrew].

Altus, W. D., & Clark, J. H. (1949). Subtest variation of the Wechsler–Bellevue for two institutionalized behavior problem groups. *Journal of Consulting Psychology, 13*, 444–7.

Andrew, J. M. (1974a). Delinquency, the Wechsler P > V sign, and the I-level system. *Journal of Clinical Psychology, 30,* 331–5.

Andrew, J. M. (1974b). Immaturity, delinquency, and the Wechsler P > V sign. *Journal of Abnormal Child Psychology, 2,* 245–51.

Andrew, J. M. (1978a). Laterality on the tapping test among legal offenders. *Journal of Clinical Child Psychology, 7,* 149–50.

Andrew, J. M. (1978b). The classic Wechsler P > V sign and violent crime. *Crime and Justice, 6,* 246–8.

Andrew, J. M. (1980). Are left handers less violent? *Journal of Youth and Adolescence, 9,* 1–10.

Annett, M. (1972). The distribution of manual asymmetry. *British Journal of Psychology, 63,* 343–58.

Annett, M., & Ockwell, A. (1980). Birth order, birth stress and handedness. *Cortex, 16,* 181–8.

Ashton, G. C. (1982). Handedness: An alternative hypothesis. *Behavior Genetics, 12,* 125–47.

Atkinson, J., & Egeth, H. (1973). Right hemisphere superiority in visual orientation matching. *Canadian Journal of Psychology, 27,* 152–8.

Bach-y-Rita, G. (1975). Biological basis of aggressive behavior: Clinical aspects. In H. J. Widroe (Ed.), *Human behavior and brain function.* Springfield, IL: Thomas.

Bakan, P. (1971). Handedness and birth order. *Nature, 229,* 195.

Bakan, P. (1977). Left-handedness and birth order revisited. *Neuropsychologia, 15,* 837–9.

Bakan, P. (1978). Why left handedness? *Behavioral and Brain Sciences, 2,* 279–80.

Bakan, P., Dibb, G., & Reid, P. (1973). Handedness and birth stress. *Neuropsychologia, 11,* 363–6.

Benton, D. (1981). The extrapolation from animals to man: The example of testosterone and aggression. In P. F. Brain & D. Benton (Eds.), *Multidisciplinary approaches to aggression research.* Amsterdam: Elsevier/North Holland Biomedical Press.

Blank, L. (1958). The intellectual functioning of delinquents. *Journal of Social Psychology, 47,* 9–14.

Bohman, M., Cloninger, R., Sigvardsson, S., & von Knorring, A.-L. (1982). Predisposition to petty criminality in Swedish adoptees: I. Genetic and environmental heterogeneity. *Archives of General Psychiatry, 39,* 1233–41.

Boklage, C. E. (1977). Schizophrenia, brain asymmetry development, and twinning: Cellular relationship with etiological and possible prognostic implications. *Biological Psychiatry, 12,* 19–35.

Bradshaw, J. L., & Nettleton, N. C. (1981). The nature of hemispheric specialization in man. *Behavioral and Brain Sciences, 4,* 51–91.

Broman, S. H., Nichols, P. L., & Kennedy, W. A. (1975). *Preschool IQ: Prenatal and early developmental correlates.* Hillsdale, NJ: Erlbaum.

Bryden, M. P. (1976). Response bias and hemispheric differences in dot localization. *Perception and Psychophysics, 19,* 23–8.

Buikhausen, W. (1979). An alternative approach to the etiology of crime. In S. A. Mednick & S. G. Shoham (Eds.), *New paths in criminology* (pp. 27–44). Lexington, MA: Lexington Books.

Carmon, A. (1978). Spatial and temporal factors in visual perception of patients with unilateral cerebral lesions. In M. Kinsbourne (Ed.), *Asymemtrical function of the brain.* Cambridge University Press.

Carmon, A., & Nachshon, I. (1971). Effect of unilateral brain damage on perception of temporal order. *Cortex, 7,* 410–18.

Center for Studies in Criminology and Criminal Law. (1981). Collection and coding of offense data for the biosocial project. Unpublished manuscript, University of Pennsylvania, Philadelphia.

Christiansen, K. O. (1977). A review of studies of criminality among twins. In S. A. Mednick & K. O. Christiansen (Eds.), *Biosocial bases of criminal behavior* (pp. 45–88). New York: Gardner Press.

Clark, J. H., & Moore, J. H. (1950). The relationship of Wechsler–Bellevue patterns to psychiatric diagnosis of army and air force prisoners. *Journal of Consulting Psychology, 14,* 493–5.

Cloninger, R., Sigvardsson, S., Bohman, M., & Knorring, A.-L. (1982). Predisposition to petty criminality in Swedish adoptees: II. Cross-fostering analysis of gene–environment interaction. *Archives of General Psychiatry, 39,* 1242–7.

Colby, K. M., & Parkinson, C. (1977). Handedness in autistic children. *Journal of Autism and Childhood Schizophrenia, 7,* 3–9.

Coren, S., & Porac, C. (1980). Birth factors and laterality: Effects of birth order, parental age, and birth stress on four indices of lateral preference. *Behavior Genetics, 10,* 123–38.

Coren, S., Searleman, A., & Porac, C. (1982). The effects of specific birth stress on four indices of lateral preference. *Canadian Journal of Psychology, 36,* 478–87.

Corotto, L. V. (1961). The relation of performance to verbal IQ in acting-out juveniles. *Journal of Psychological Studies, 12,* 162–6.

Denno, D. (1982). Sex differences in cognition and crime: Early developmental, biological and sociological correlates. Unpublished doctoral dissertation, University of Pennsylvania, Philadelphia.

Denno, D., Meijs, B., Nachshon, I., & Aurand, S. (1982). Early cognitive function: Sex and race differences. *International Journal of Neuroscience, 16,* 159–72.

Diller, L. (1952). A comparison of the test performance of delinquent and nondelinquent girls. *Journal of Genetic Psychology, 81,* 167–83.

Dixson, A. F., & Herbert, J. (1977). Testosterone, aggressive behavior and dominance rank in captive adult male Talapoin monkeys. *Physiology and Behavior, 18,* 539–43.

Dvirskii, A. E. (1976). Functional asymmetry of the cerebral hemispheres in clinical types of schizophrenia. *Neuroscience and Behavioral Physiology, 7,* 236–9.

Ehrlichman, H. (1982). Perinatal factors in hand and eye preference: Data from the Collaborative Perinatal Project. *International Journal of Neuroscience, 17,* 17–22.

Elliot, D. S., & Ageton, S. S. (1980). Reconciling race and class differences in self-reported and official estimates of delinquency. *American Sociological Review, 45,* 95–110.

Falconer, M. A., & Taylor, D. C. (1970). Temporal lobe epilepsy: Clinical features, pathology diagnosis and treatment. In J. H. Price (Ed.), *Modern trends in psychological medicine.* London: Butterworths.

Field, J. G. (1960). The performance–verbal IQ discrepancy in a group of sociopaths. *Journal of Clinical Psychology, 16,* 321–2.

Fink, A. E. (1962). *Causes of crime: Biological theories in the United States 1800–1915.* New York: Barnes. (Originally published 1938.)

Fishman, G. (1981). Positivism and neo-Lombrosianism. In I. L. Barak-Glantz & C. R. Huff (Eds.), *The mad, the bad, and the different.* Lexington, MA: Lexington Books.

Fitzhugh, K. B. (1973). Some neuropsychological features of delinquent subjects. *Perceptual and Motor Skills, 36,* 494.

Flor-Henry, P. (1973). Psychiatric syndromes considered as manifestations of lateralized temporal–limbic dysfunction. In L. V. Latiner & K. E. Livingston (Eds.), *Surgical approaches in psychiatry.* Lancaster, Engl.: Medical and Technical Publishing.

Flor-Henry, P. (1978). Gender, hemispheric specialization and psychopathology. *Social Sciences and Medicine, 12b,* 155–62.

Flor-Henry, P. (1979). On certain aspects of the localization of the cerebral systems regulating and determining emotion. *Biological Psychiatry, 14,* 677–98.

Flor-Henry, P., & Yeudall, L. T. (1973). Lateralized cerebral dysfunction in depression and in aggressive criminal psychopathy: Further observations. *International Research Communications System,* July, p. 31.

Foster, A. L. (1959). A note concerning the intelligence of delinquents. *Journal of Clinical Psychology, 15,* 78–9.

Gabrielli, W. F., & Mednick, S. A. (1980). Sinistrality and delinquency. *Journal of Abnormal Psychology, 89,* 654–61.

Golden, C. J., Graber, B., Coffman, J., Berg, R. A., Newlin, D. B., & Bloch, S. (1981). Structural brain deficits in schizophrenia. *Archives of General Psychiatry, 38,* 1014–17.

Gur, R. C., & Gur, R. E. (1974). Handedness, sex, and eyedness as moderating variables in the relation between hypnotic susceptibility and functional brain asymmetry. *Journal of Abnormal Psychology, 83,* 635–43.

Gur, R. C., & Gur, R. E. (1980). Handedness and individual differences in hemispheric activation. In J. Herron (Ed.), *Neuropsychology of left-handedness..* New York: Academic Press.

Gur, R. E. (1977). Motoric laterality imbalance in schizophrenia: A possible concomitant of left hemisphere dysfunction. *Archives of General Psychiatry, 34,* 33–7.

Halperin, Y., Nachshon, I., & Carmon, A. (1973). Shift of ear superiority in dichotic listening to temporally patterned nonverbal stimuli. *Journal of the Acoustical Society of America, 53,* 46–50.

Hare, R. D. (1979). Psychopathy and laterality of cerebral function. *Journal of Abnormal Psychology, 88,* 605–10.

Hare, R. D., & Frazelle, J. (1981, November). *Psychobiological correlates of criminal psychopathy.* Paper presented at a symposium on biosocial correlates of crime and delinquency, annual meeting of the American Society of Criminology, Washington, D.C.

Hécaen, H., & Ajuriaguerra, J. (1964). *Left handedness.* New York: Grune & Stratton.

Herron, J. (Ed.). (1980). *Neuropsychology of left handedness.* New York: Academic Press.

Hicks, R. A., Dusek, C., Larsen, F., Williams, S., & Pellegrini, R. J. (1980). Birth complications and the distribution of handedness. *Cortex, 16,* 483–6.

Hindelang, M. J. (1978). Race and involvement in common law personal crimes. *American Sociological Review, 43,* 93–109.

Hindelang, M. J., Hirschi, T., & Weis, J. G. (1979). Correlates of delinquency: The illusion of discrepancy between self-report and official measures. *American Sociological Review, 44,* 995–1014.

Hood, R., & Sparks, R. (1970). *Key issues in criminology.* New York: McGraw-Hill.

Horney, J. (1978). Menstrual cycles and criminal responsibility. *Law and Human Behavior, 2,* 25–36.

Jeffrey, C. R. (1978). Criminology as an interdisciplinary behavioral science. *Criminology, 16,* 149–69.

Kahn, M. W. (1968). Superior performance IQ of murderers as a function of overt act or diagnosis. *Journal of Social Psychology, 76,* 113–16.

Krynicki, V. E. (1978). Cerebral dysfunction in repetitively assaultive adolescents. *Journal of Nervous and Mental Disease, 166,* 59–67.

Levy, J. (1980). Cerebral asymmetry and the psychology of man. In M. C. Wittrock (Ed.), *The brain and psychology.* New York: Academic Press.

Levy, J., & Gur, R. C. (1980). Individual differences in psychoneurological organization. In J. Herron (Ed.), *Neuropsychology of left-handedness.* New York: Academic Press.

Levy, J., & Nagylaki, T. (1972). A model for the genetics of handedness. *Genetics, 72,* 117–28.

Liederman, J., & Coryell, J. (1982). The origin of left hand preference: Pathological and non-pathological influences. *Neuropsychologia, 20,* 721–5.

Lishman, W. A. (1966). Brain damage in relation to psychiatric disability after head injury. *British Journal of Psychiatry, 114,* 373–410.

Lishman, W. A., & McMeekan, E. R. L. (1976). Hand preference patterns in psychiatric patients. *British Journal of Psychiatry, 129,* 158–66.

Lombroso, C. (1874). *L'uomo delinquente.* Torino, Italy: Bocca.

Luchins, D., Pollin, W., & Wyatt, R. J. (1980). Laterality in monozygotic schizophrenic twins: An alternative hypothesis. *Biological Psychiatry, 15,* 87–93.

Lydston, G. F. (1904). *The diseases of society.* Philadelphia: Lippincott.

Manne, S. H., Kandel, A., & Rosenthal, D. (1962). Differences between performance IQ and verbal IQ in a severely sociopathic population. *Journal of Clinical Psychology, 18,* 73–7.

Mark, V. H., & Ervin, F. R. (1970). *Violence and the brain.* New York: Harper & Row.

Mednick, S. A. (1977). A biosocial theory of the learning of law-abiding behavior. In S. A. Mednick & K. O. Christiansen (Eds.), *Biosocial bases of criminal behavior* (pp. 1–8). New York: Gardner Press.

Mednick, S. A. (1979). Biosocial factors and primary prevention of antisocial behavior. In S. A. Mednick & S. G. Shoham (Eds.), *New paths in criminology.* Lexington, MA: Lexington Books.

Mednick, S. A. (1980). Human nature, crime, and society: Keynote address. In F. Wright, C. Bahn, & R. W. Rieber (Eds.), *Forensic psychology and psychiatry* (Annals of the New York Academy of Sciences, Vol. 347). New York: New York Academy of Sciences.

Mednick, S. A., Pollock, V., Volavka, J., & Gabrielli, W. F. (1982). Biology and violence. In M. E. Wolfgang & N. A. Weiner (Eds.), *Criminal violence.* Beverly Hills, CA: Sage.

Monroe, R. R., Hulfish, B., Balis, G., Lion, J., Rubin, J., McDonald, M., & Barick, J. D. (1977). Neurologic findings in recidivist aggressors. In C. Shagess, S. Gershon, & A. J. Friedhoff (Eds.), *Psychopathology and brain dysfunction.* New York: Raven Press.

Montague, L. (1972). Sociogenic brain damage. *American Anthropologist, 74,* 1045–61.

Moran, R. (1978). Biomedical research and the politics of crime control: An historical perspective. *Contemporary Crises, 2,* 335–7.

Moskovitch, M. (1979). Information processing and the cerebral hemispheres. In M. S. Gazzaniga (Ed.), *Handbook of behavioral neurobiology: Vol. 2: Neuropsychology.* New York: Plenum Press.

Moyer, K. E. (1976). *The psychobiology of aggression.* New York: Harper & Row.

Moyer, K. E. (1980). Brain mechanisms and crime. In C. H. Faust & D. R. Webster (Eds.), *Anatomy of criminal justice.* Lexington, MA: Lexington Books.

Myslobodsky, M., & Rattok, J. (1977). Bilateral electrodermal activity in waking man. *Acta Psychologica, 41,* 273–82.

Nachshon, I. (1973). Effects of cerebral dominance and attention on dichotic listening. *Journal of Life Sciences, 3,* 107–14.

Nachshon, I. (1982). Toward biosocial approaches in criminology. *Journal of Social and Biological Structures, 5,* 1–9.

Nachshon, I. (1983). Hemisphere dysfunction in psychopathy and behavior disorders. In M. Myslobodsky (Ed.), *Hemisyndromes: Psychobiology, neurology, psychiatry.* New York: Academic Press.

Nachshon, I., & Carmon, A. (1975). Hand preference in sequential and spatial discrimination tasks. *Cortex, 11,* 123–31.

Nachshon, I., Denno, D., & Aurand, S. (1983). Lateral preferences of hand, eye and foot: Relation to cerebral dominance. *International Journal of Neuroscience, 18,* 1–10.

Nassi, A. J., & Abramowitz, S. I. (1976). From phrenology to psychosurgery and back again: Biological studies of criminality. *American Journal of Orthopsychiatry, 46,* 591–607.

Niswander, K., & Gordon, M. (1972). *The women and their pregnancies.* Washington, DC: Department of Health, Education, and Welfare.

Oddy, H. C., & Lobstein, T. J. (1972). Hand and eye dominance in schizophrenia. *British Journal of Psychiatry, 120,* 331–2.

Palmer, R. D. (1963). Hand differentiation and psychological functioning. *Journal of Personality, 31,* 445–61.

Piran, N., Bigler, E. D., & Cohen, D. (1982). Monotonic laterality and eye dominance suggest unique pattern of cerebral organization in schzophrenia. *Archives of General Psychiatry, 39,* 1008–10.

Porac, C., & Coren, S. (1976). The dominant eye. *Psychological Bulletin, 83,* 880–97.

Porac, C., Coren, S., & Duncan, P. (1980). Life-span age trends in laterality. *Journal of Gerontology, 35,* 715–21.

Porac, C., Coren, S., Steiger, J. H., & Duncan, P. (1980). Human laterality: A multidimensional approach. *Canadian Journal of Psychology, 34,* 91–6.

Rose, R. M., Bernstein, I. S., Gordon, T. P., & Catlin, S. F. (1974). Androgens and aggression: A review and recent findings in primates. In R. L. Holloway (Ed.), *Primate aggression: Territoriality and xenophobia.* New York: Academic Press.

Rose, R. M., Gordon, T. P., & Bernstein, I. S. (1972). Plasma testosterone levels in the male rhesus: Influence of sexual and social stimuli. *Science, 178,* 643–5.

Rubin, R. T., Reinisch, J. M., & Haskett, R. F. (1981). Postnatal gonadal stereoid effects on human behavior. *Science, 211,* 1318–24.

Satz, P. (1972). Pathological left handedness: An explanatory model. *Cortex, 8,* 121–35.

Satz, P. (1973). Left handedness and early brain insult: An explanation. *Neuropsychologia, 11,* 115–17.

Satz, P. (1979). Pathological left-handedness: Cross-cultural tests of a model. *Neuropsychologia, 17,* 77–81.

Schwartz, M. (1977). Left-handedness and high-risk pregnancy. *Neuropsychologia, 15,* 341–4.

Searleman, A., Tsao, Y.-C., & Balzer, W. (1980). A reexamination of the relationship between birth stress and handedness. *Clinical Neuropsychology, 2,* 124–8.

Semmes, J. (1968). Hemispheric specialization: A possible clue to mechanism. *Neuropsychology, 6,* 11–27.

Serafetinides, E. A. (1965). Aggressiveness in temporal lobe epileptics and its relation to cerebral dysfunction and environmental factors. *Epilepsia, 6,* 33–42.

Seyal, M., Sato, S., White, B. G., & Porter, R. J. (1981). Visual evoked potentials and eye dominance. *Electroencephalography and Clinical Neurophysiology, 52,* 424–8.

Shuman, S. I. (1977). *Psychosurgery and the medical control of violence: Autonomy and deviance.* Detroit: Wayne State University Press.

Sigvardsson, S., Cloninger, R., Bohman, M., & Knorring, A.-L. (1982). Predisposition to petty criminality in Swedish adoptees: IV. Sex differences and validation of male typology. *Archives of General Psychiatry, 39,* 1248–53.

Silvia, D. A., & Satz, P. (1979). Pathological left handedness: Evaluation of a model. *Brain and Language, 7,* 8–16.

Strongman, K. T. (1973). *The psychology of emotion.* New York: Wiley.

Talbot, E. S. (1898). A study of the stigmata of degeneracy among the American criminal youth. *Journal of the American Medical Association, 30,* 849–56.

Tan, L. E., & Nettleton, N. C. (1980). Left handedness, birth order and birth stress. *Cortex, 16*, 363–74.

Taylor, D. C. (1969). Aggression and epilepsy. *Journal of Psychosomatic Research, 13*, 229–36.

Taylor, D. C. (1972). Mental state and temporal lobe epilepsy: A correlative account of 100 patients treated surgically. *Epilepsia, 13*, 727–65.

TenHouten, W. D. (1980). Social dominance and cerebral hemisphericity: Discriminating race, socioeconomic status, and sex groups by performance on two lateralized tests. *International Journal of Neuroscience, 10*, 223–32.

Thompson, A. L., Bogen, J. E., & March, J. F., Jr. (1979). Cultural hemisphericity: Evidence from cognitive tests. *International Journal of Neuroscience, 9*, 37–43.

U.S. Department of Health, Education, and Welfare. (1966). *Collaborative study on cerebral palsy, mental retardation, and other neurological and sensory disorders of infancy and childhood: Part 111-B. Manuals: Pediatric–Neurology.* Bethesda, MD: National Institute of Health.

Vold, G. B. (1979). *Theoretical Criminology* (2nd ed., prepared by T. J. Bernard). New York: Oxford University Press. (Originally published 1958.)

Walker, H. A., & Birch, H. G. (1970). Lateral preference and right–left awareness in schizophrenic children. *Journal of Nervous and Mental Disease, 151*, 341–51.

Wardell, D., & Yeudall, L. T. (1980). A multidimensional approach to criminal disorders: The assessment of impulsivity and its relation to crime. *Advanced Behavior Research and Therapy, 2*, 159–77.

Wechsler, D. (1958). *The measurement and appraisal of adult intelligence* (4th ed.). Baltimore, MD: Williams & Wilkins.

Wiens, A. N., Matarazzo, J. D., & Gver, R. D. (1959). Performance and verbal IQ in a group of sociopaths. *Journal of Clinical Psychology, 15*, 191–3.

Wold, R. M. (1968). Dominance – fact or fantasy: Its significance in learning disabilities. *Journal of the American Optometric Association, 39*, 908–16.

Wolfgang, M. E. (1963). Uniform crime report: A critical appraisal. *University of Pennsylvania Law Review, 3*, 708–38.

Wolfgang, M. E. (1975). Delinquency and violence from the viewpoint of criminology. In W. S. Field & W. A. Sweet (Eds.), *Neural bases of violence and aggression.* St. Louis, MO: Green.

Wolfgang, M. E. (1977). Foreword. In S. A. Mednick & K. O. Christiansen (Eds.), *Biosocial bases of criminal behavior.* New York: Gardner Press.

Wolfgang, M. E. (1978). The sociology of aggression: Crime and violence. *Australian Journal of Forensic Sciences, 11*, 3–30.

Wolfgang, M. E., Figlio, R. M., & Sellin, T. (1972). *Delinquency in a birth cohort.* University of Chicago Press.

Yeudall, L. T. (1977). Neuropsychological assessment of forensic disorders. *Canada's Mental Health, 25*, 7–16.

Yeudall, L. T. (1979, February). *Neuropsychological concomitants of persistent criminal behavior.* Paper presented at the annual meeting of the Ontario Psychological Association, Toronto.

Yeudall, L. T. (1980). A neuropsychological perspective of persistent juvenile delinquency and criminal behavior: Discussion. In F. Wright, C. Bahn, & R. W. Rieber (Eds.), *Forensic psychology and psychiatry* (Annals of the New York Academy of Sciences, Vol. 347). New York: New York Academy of Sciences.

Yeudall, L. T., Fedora, P., Fedora, S., & Wardell, D. (1981). Neurosocial perspective on the assessment and etiology of persistent criminality. *Australian Journal of Forensic Science, 13*, 131–59; *14*, 20–44.

Yeudall, L. T., & Fromm-Auch, D. (1979). Neuropsychological impairments in various psychopathological populations. In J. Gruzelier & P. Flor-Henry (Eds.), *Hemisphere asymmetries of function in psychopathology*. Amsterdam: Elsevier/North Holland Biomedical Press.

Yeudall, L. T., Fromm-Auch, D., & Davies, P. (1982). Neuropsychological impairment in persistent delinquency. *Journal of Nervous and Mental Disease, 170,* 257–65.

Yeudall, L. T., & Wardell, D. M. (1978). Neuropsychological correlates of criminal psychopathy: Part 2. Discrimination and prediction of dangerous and recidivistic offenders. In L. Beliveau, G. Canepa, & D. Szabo (Eds.), *Human aggression and its dangerousness*. Montreal: Pinel Institute.

12 Perceptual asymmetries and information processing in psychopaths

Robert D. Hare and John F. Connolly

Introduction

There have been several attempts to explain psychopathy in terms of brain damage or dysfunction. Most of these attempts have relied heavily on evidence obtained from routine electroencephalographic (EEG) examinations, neuropsychological tests, and behavioral comparisons between psychopaths and patients with brain damage (e.g., Elliott, 1978; Flor-Henry, 1976; Gorenstein, 1982; Hare, 1979; Syndulko, 1978; see also Chapter 11). In general, however, gross brain damage interpretations of psychopathy have not been very convincing, partly because much of the supporting evidence comes from clinical reports and research studies with a variety of methodological problems and limitations, including the use of vague, inconsistent, and unreliable diagnostic procedures, a tendency to focus on special forensic populations for which neurological impairment is suspected (e.g., court referrals involving violent and inexplicable crimes), and a failure to exert adequate experimental control (e.g., see Hare, 1984b; Syndulko, 1978). Although it is possible that firm evidence of palpable organicity will be found in psychopaths, we believe that it might be more fruitful to investigate the ways in which psychopaths may differ from others in the functional organization of cerebral processes and in their use of cognitive, attentional, and motivational strategies.

In line with this approach we present some exploratory data on the cerebral organization of language functions in criminal psychopaths. There are several reasons for our interest in the language processes of psychopaths. For example, the actual behavior of psychopaths is often strikingly inconsistent with their verbalized thoughts, feelings, and intentions. We agree with Cleckley (1976) that this discrepancy between what psychopaths say and what they do involves something more than simple lying, dissimulation, or hypocrisy. Cleckley has suggested that the speech of psychopaths is in fact a mechanically correct artifact that masks a profound, deep-seated semantic disorder in which the formal, semantic,

218

and affective components of language have somehow become dissociated from one another. We know little or nothing about the neuropsychological nature of this "disorder" or, for that matter, whether or not it "exists." However, we do know that there is something odd about the way in which psychopaths use language. There are, of course, many ways of investigating language processes in normal and pathological populations. Particularly useful are procedures that permit inferences to be made about the cerebral organization of language function. These include *dichotic listening* and *divided visual field* (DVF) techniques, both of which were used in the series of investigations discussed in this chapter. Before describing the results of these studies we shall provide (a) a description of the procedures we use for the assessment of psychopathy and (b) a brief overview of the rationale for using dichotic listening and DVF techniques to investigate cerebral asymmetry in psychopaths.

Assessment of psychopathy

Although there is good agreement on the major clinical and behavioral characteristics of the psychopath (see Cleckley, 1976; Hare & Cox, 1978; McCord, 1982; Millon, 1981; Reid, 1978), the use of a wide variety of diagnostic procedures means that meaningful comparisons among studies are often difficult or impossible to make. The problem is particularly severe when attempts are made to compare studies based on clinical–behavioral assessments with those based on self-report inventories (see Hare, 1984a).

The assessment procedures used in our research are closely tied to the clinical conception of psychopathy provided by Cleckley (1976). Until recently the principal assessment procedure involved global ratings (7-point scale) of the extent to which an inmate's behavior over a long period of time was consistent with Cleckley's (1976) conception of psychopathy. These ratings have proved to be reliable (interrater correlations around .90) and valid (see Hare & Cox, 1978). However, highly experienced personnel are required to make the ratings, and the subjective nature of the procedure makes it difficult for other investigators to know exactly how a given rating was obtained. For these reasons, we now use a 22-item checklist (Hare, 1980; Hare & Frazelle, 1980) for the assessment of psychopathy; like the 7-point ratings, the checklist is based on the clinical profile of the psychopath provided by Cleckely. The checklist items are listed in Table 12.1. Each item is scored on a 3-point scale (0, 1, 2) according to the extent to which it applies to the subject; total scores can thus range from 0 to 44. In our prison research two investigators generally

Table 12.1. *Checklist items for the assessment of psychopathy*

*1.	Glibness/superficial charm
2.	Previous diagnosis as psychopath (or similar)
*3.	Egocentricity/grandiose sense of self-worth
4.	Proneness to boredom/low frustration tolerance
*5.	Pathological lying and deception
*6.	Conning/lack of sincerity
*7.	Lack of remorse or guilt
*8.	Lack of affect and emotional depth
*9.	Callous/lack of empathy
10.	Parasitic life-style
*11.	Short-tempered/poor behavioral controls
*12.	Promiscuous sexual relations
*13.	Early behavior problems
*14.	Lack of realistic long-term plans
15.	Impulsivity
16.	Irresponsible behavior as parent
*17.	Frequent marital relationships
18.	Juvenile delinquency
*19.	Poor probation or parole risk
*20.	Failure to accept responsibility for own actions
*21.	Many types of offense
22.	Drug/alcohol abuse not direct cause of antisocial behavior

Note: Asterisks mark items used in the shortened version; see text.

Source: Hare (1980).

complete a checklist for each inmate, using interview and case history data. A psychometric analysis of the checklist (Schroeder, Schroeder, & Hare, 1983) yielded classical test theory indices of reliability (inter- and intrarater correlations, alpha coefficients) of .82 to .93 for five separate studies and an overall alpha coefficient of .90 ($N = 301$). Data on the validity of the checklist as a measure of psychopathy are presented by Hare (1980, 1983, 1984a) and by Schroeder et al. (1983). The mean checklist score (averaged across two raters) for a sample of 274 male inmates (Hare, 1984a) was 27.4 (S.D. = 8.3).

Some of the checklist items require information that may not be readily available to other investigators, and several other items have distributions that are not very satisfactory from a psychometric point of view. For these reasons a shortened version of the checklist can be used; it consists of the 15 items marked with an asterisk in Table 12.1. The mean score (averaged across two raters) for the sample of 274 inmates referred to above was 18.9 (S.D. = 5.9); coefficient alpha was .88.

In addition to the checklist, we routinely have two clinicians indepen-

Table 12.2. *Correlations (above diagonal) and kappa coefficients of agreement (below diagonal) among three procedures for the assessment of psychopathy*

Procedure	1	2	3
Checklist	—	.80	.67
Rating	.93	—	.57
DSM-III	.79	.71	—

Source: Based on data presented in Hare (1984).

dently make diagnoses of antisocial personality disorder (APD) according to the criteria listed in the third edition of the American Psychiatric Association's (1980) *Diagnostic and Statistical Manual of Mental Disorders* (DSM-III). These diagnoses of APD are very reliable; for example, the kappa coefficient of agreement (Fleiss, 1981) for the 274 inmates described above was .79, indicating that 79% of the joint diagnoses were in agreement, with chance excluded. The extent to which global ratings, checklist scores, and DSM-III diagnoses of APD are related to one another is summarized in Table 12.2; complete details are available in Hare (1984). Values above the diagonal are correlation coefficients, and values below the diagonal are kappa coefficients of diagnostic agreement. In computing correlations, a DSM-III diagnosis of APD was treated as either presence (a diagnosis from two clinicians) or absence (a diagnosis from neither clinician) of APD; correlations involving DSM-III were therefore point biserial. The kappa coefficients were based on comparisons between high- and low-psychopathy groups (upper and lower thirds of the distribution in the case of checklist scores and ratings, and 2 and 0 diagnoses of APD in the case of DSM-III).

Cerebral asymmetry

The concept of different functions being associated with one or other of the cerebral hemispheres has a long history. In the nineteenth century Broca and Dax proposed that language functions were situated in the left hemisphere, and Jackson proposed that visuospatial functions were concentrated in the right hemisphere. Hemispheric lateralization and its relation to psychological processes inspired some interest in the 100 years following Broca and Dax (e.g., Zangwill, 1960). However, since the early 1960s there has been a surge of interest in the area (e.g., Beaumont, 1982; Bryden, 1982; Hellige, 1983; Kinsbourne, 1978) instigated by technological advances in neuropsychological techniques allowing sophisticated analysis of brain *function* as well as structure. In addition, the possibility of elucidating the mechanisms of psychiatric disorders, such as the schizophrenias, using brain lateralization models has generated much research.

It has become clear that the anatomy of the cerebral hemispheres is asymmetric (e.g., Rubens, 1977; Witelson, 1980), as are neurotransmitter pathways and distributions (e.g., Glick, Jerussi, & Zimmerberg, 1977; Oke, Keller, Melford, & Adams, 1978); these *structural* asymmetries have also been linked to observed functional asymmetries (e.g., Glick et al., 1977; Witelson, 1980). However, the major research effort in this field has been directed at lateralization of psychological functions. Much of the evidence for the lateralization of psychological processes has come from experiments using DVF techniques and dichotic listening.

The DVF technique enables one to present stimuli directly to either hemisphere by making use of the neurophysiology of the primary optic pathway. The optic nerves from each nasal hemiretina project contralaterally, whereas those from the temporal hemiretinae project ipsilaterally. Presentation of a stimulus to the left or right of a fixation point impinges on the nasal hemiretina of one eye and the temporal hemiretina of another. For example, a stimulus presented in the right visual field (RVF) will project onto the nasal hemiretina of the right eye and the temporal hemiretina of the left eye, the former projecting contralaterally to the left hemisphere and the latter ipsilaterally to the left hemisphere. By means of this technique inferences can be drawn concerning hemispheric asymmetries in the psychological processing of specific types of stimuli.

The neurophysiology of the auditory pathways is not as well defined as that of the optic pathways. For this reason, the mechanisms underlying the dichotic listening technique are inferred. Nevertheless, Kimura's (1967) model of the dominance of the contralateral projections combined with the active occlusion of the flow of information along ipsilateral pathways has served as a good model for many of the effects observed in the dichotic listening experiment.

The dichotic listening method involves the presentation of stimuli simultaneously to both ears. The nature of the stimuli and tasks can vary substantially. One common procedure involves the presentation of different word strings to each ear; in turn, the subject is required to identify in some way the words actually heard. As with the DVF procedure, results from dichotic listening experiments are typically used to infer hemisphere functions and specialization.

The experiments to be described in this chapter concentrated on language-based stimuli and tasks and thus, theoretically, left-hemisphere functioning. Therefore, a brief review of DVF and dichotic effects with left-hemisphere tasks in normal subjects will be given.

Divided visual field research using language-based tasks and stimuli has provided a body of research that generally is impressively consistent. Both identification of and reaction time to these stimuli have been found to be superior or faster when the stimuli are presented in the RVF and thus directed to the left hemisphere (see, e.g., Beaumont, 1982; Bryden, 1982, for reviews). One can delineate these effects by looking at "stage" of verbal processing or the nature of the language task or stimuli used. For example, an RVF advantage is typically found using language-based stimuli (e.g., words, letters, digits). However, a more complicated situation is found when the nature of the word stimuli is varied in terms of manageability, abstractness, and concreteness. Paivio (1969) has hypothesized that stimuli can be coded in both visual and verbal memory, the key factor being the imageability of the stimulus. Working within this framework it has been hypothesized that abstract and concrete words should be processed differently by the hemispheres. Concrete words are more easily imagined and as a result would be processed verbally (left hemisphere) or visually (right hemisphere). Results compatible with this formulation have been found and tend to "outweight" negative reports (see Beaumont, 1982b). Because concrete words can be processed readily by either hemisphere, they have been associated with weak laterality effects, whereas abstract words have evoked strong RVF–left-hemisphere effects (Day, 1977; Ellis & Shepherd, 1974; Elman, Takahashi, & Tohsaku, 1981; Hatta, 1977; Hines, 1976, 1977; Sasanuma, Itoh, Mori, & Kobayashi, 1977).

Moving on to the dichotic listening methodology, we again find a fairly consistent pattern in the literature. Generally speaking, a right-ear advantage (REA) (reflecting left-hemisphere functioning in most theoretical formulations) is found for the identification of stimuli in language-related tasks (e.g., Kimura, 1961a,b; see also Bryden, 1982).

There are a number of factors not directly related to lateralized hemisphere functioning that, in theory, could produce the REA. For example, the original reports of Kimura used the free-recall method for subjects to identify what they had just heard. It has been suggested that, because most subjects choose to report stimuli heard in the right ear first, the REA is attributable to memory factors associated with the starting-ear bias (Inglis, 1962, 1968). However, this issue has been carefully examined (Bryden, 1982; Satz, Achenbach, Pattishall, & Fennell, 1965; Zurif & Bryden, 1969) and the weight of the evidence indicates that, although starting-ear bias can affect the magnitude of the REA it cannot account for it.

Another factor suggested as an extraneous variable that could account for the REA is attention. The dichotic listening procedure requires subjects to divide their attention between both ears, and their ability to do so could be variable or systematically biased in such a way as to influence the final-ear advantage. However, using six pairs of words and a procedure in which the subject attended to one ear at a time, Schwartz (1970) found a strong REA. Similar results have been demonstrated using the monitoring techniques with single pairs of words (e.g., Geffen & Caudrey, 1981).

Thus research that has controlled for attention has still demonstrated the REA. Nonetheless, it would be ill-advised to ignore the fact that variables unrelated to cerebral functional lateralization can have effects on the REA. In fact, it has even been argued that, owing to considerable individual differences in auditory pathway dominance, the dichotic listening procedure is of limited value in assessing functional asymmetries (Teng, 1981). This point as well as the issue of whether asymmetries are attributable to structural or dynamic processes (e.g., Cohen, 1982) or arousal asymmetries (Levy, Heller, Banich, & Burton, 1983; Tucker, 1981) will be dealt with in the discussion of the results with psychopathic prisoners.

Dichotic listening

Complete details of this study can be found in Hare and McPherson (1984). The subjects were 146 white male prison inmates divided into three groups on the basis of checklist scores and DSM-III diagnoses of APD. Psychopaths (Group P) consisted of 45 inmates with a mean checklist score of greater than 33 and a diagnosis of APD. Nonpsychopaths (Group NP) consisted of 43 inmates with a checklist score below 24 and failure to satisfy the criteria for a diagnosis of APD. The 58 inmates who did not meet the criteria for either Group P or Group NP constituted a "middle" group (Group M). Although the data from all three groups were analyzed, we were interested primarily in comparisons between Groups P and NP, that is, between groups in which symptom overlap was minimized. We might note that the cutoff scores for the checklist were similar to those used in previous research; they define approximately the upper and lower thirds of the distribution of checklist scores. The use of multiple criteria rests on the assumption that both the checklist and diagnoses of APD are imperfect measures of the same construct, psychopathy.

None of the dichotic listening results to be presented were related to age, education, IQ, or handedness. Mean age, years of formal education, and IQ were 29.5 (S.D. = 6.2), 10.8 (S.D. = 2.4), and 102.2 (S.D. = 12.0), respectively. Handedness was assessed with a lateral preference questionnaire (Porac & Coren, 1981); 69.2% of the inmates were consistently right-handed. For comparison purposes, dichotic listening data were also obtained from 159 male noncriminals (Group NC); mean age and years of formal education were 27.5 (S.D. = 7.7) and 13.8 (S.D. = 3.1), respectively. Handedness scores were available for 147 of these subjects, 72.8% of whom were right-handed.

The dichotic listening task (Hayden & Spellacy, 1969) consisted of 22 sets of one-syllable words recorded on tape and delivered through stereophonic headphones. Each set was made up of three pairs of words. The members of each pair (one presented in each ear) began simultaneously, had the same initial letter, and were matched for acoustic length. The interval between successive pairs was 1 sec, and 10 sec elapsed between the end of one set and the start of the next. The subject was told that after each trial (set of words) he was to report aloud all the words he could recall from that trial, without regard for the order of presentation or the ear in which the words were heard.

The basic data consisted of the number of words correctly recalled in each ear, to a maximum of 66. A laterality coefficient was also computed for each subject, using the formula $(R_c - L_c)/(L_c + R_c)$ if overall accuracy (sum of left- and right-ear scores over the complete test) was less than 50%, and the formula $(R_c - L_c)/(L_e + R_e)$ if accuracy was greater than 50%, where c and e stand for correct responses and errors, respectively (Marshall, Kaplan, & Holmes, 1975). The resulting laterality coefficients can range from -1 (left-ear superiority) to $+1$ (right-ear superiority) and are typically independent of accuracy.

The mean left- and right-ear scores obtained by the total sample of 146 criminals (C) and the 159 noncriminals (NC) are plotted in Figure 12.1. The overall level of performance (accuracy) of the noncriminals was significantly greater than that of the criminals ($p < .001$). The noncriminals had a mean laterality coefficient of .20 (S.D. = 29), a value that was not significantly different from the laterality coefficient of .17 (S.D. = 26) obtained by the criminals. Similarly, the difference between criminals and noncriminals in the percentage of subjects with an REA (defined as a laterality coefficient of at least .05) was not significant; 70.4% of the noncriminals and 65.8% of the criminals had an REA. Thus the overall performance of the noncriminals was better than that of the criminals, but the two groups did not differ in the extent to which performance favored

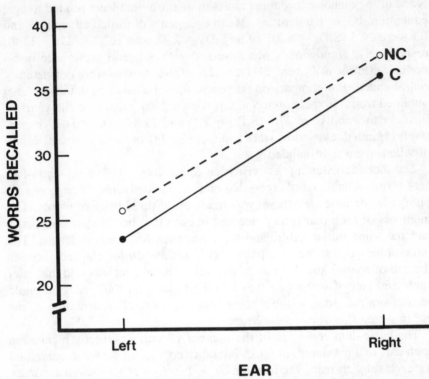

Figure 12.1. Mean number of words presented in the left and right ear that were correctly recalled by criminals (C) and noncriminals (NC). Adapted from Hare and McPherson (1984) by permission of the publisher; © 1984 by the American Psychological Association.

the right ear, that is, in the size of the REA. The most reasonable explanation for these results is that the criminals simply were less interested in the task or less motivated to perform well. It is also possible that the criminals had less "attentional capacity" at their command than did the noncriminals.

Although these differences between criminals and noncriminals are interesting, our primary concern was with the relation between psychopathy and dichotic listening performance. The left- and right-ear scores of the two criminal subgroups of most interest to us (P and NP) are plotted in Figure 12.2. It is clear that Group P recalled fewer words presented to the right ear but more words presented to the left ear than did Group NP. The mean laterality coefficients obtained by Groups P and NP were, respectively, .10 (S.D. = .25) and .28 (S.D. = .23), a significant difference ($p <$

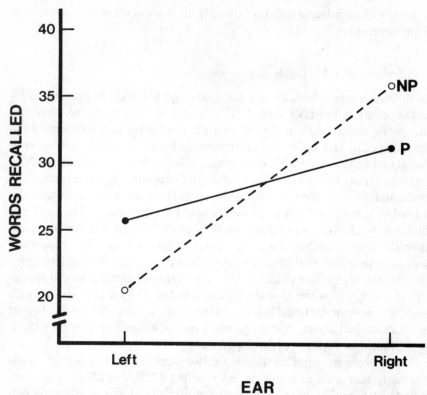

Figure 12.2. Mean number of words presented in the left and right ear that were correctly recalled by psychopathic (P) and nonpsychopathic (NP) criminals. Adapted from Hare & McPherson (1984) by permission of the publisher; © 1984 by the American Psychological Association.

.005). In addition, 83.7% of the inmates in Group NP, but only 55.6% of those in Group P, exhibited an REA according to the criterion described above. Moreover, Group P had a smaller mean laterality coefficient ($p <$ .05) and a smaller percentage of subjects with an REA ($p < .05$) than did the noncriminal group. That is, compared with noncriminals and criminals, psychopaths exhibited a reduced REA.

These results were obtained with a divided-attention procedure in which the subject was instructed to report words heard in both ears. However, essentially the same results were obtained when the subject was instructed to attend to a specific ear and to report only words heard in that ear. Even with this focused-attention procedure, the performance of psychopaths was significantly less lateralized than that of the other criminals.

Before attempting to interpret these results, we shall present some data from several DVF studies.

Divided visual field studies

In the first study (Hare, 1979) a tachistoscope was used to present three-letter words in the LVF and RVF. The words were arranged vertically and were located 1.5° to the left or right (unilateral presentation) of the fixation point. The subject was instructed to fixate on a dot in the center of the visual field of the tachistoscope and to indicate when he was ready to begin the trial. The trial consisted of a brief exposure (80 msec for half the trials and 40 msec for the rest) of the stimulus word; coincident with the stimulus, a number from 1 to 9 replaced the fixation point. The subject's task was to identify the number that had appeared at the fixation point and then the word that had appeared lateral to the number. This procedure was used in order to discourage the subject from attempting to anticipate (by shifting his fixation point) which visual field the stimulus would appear in. The subjects were 55 male prison inmates divided into groups with high (P), medium (M), and low (NP) ratings of psychopathy on the 7-point scale described above. Mean age and years of education were 28.4 (S.D. = 5.8) and 9.8 (S.D. = 2.1), respectively.

There were no significant group differences in the number of words correctly identified in either the RVF or the LVF. For all inmates combined, RVF performance (81.8% correct responses) was significantly better ($p < .001$) than LVF performance (73.7% correct responses). That is, psychopaths and other criminals showed the same sort of RVF superiority on the verbal task that is frequently found with normal, noncriminal individuals. However, the task involved only simple identification of common words, and it was suggested that group differences might emerge if tasks requiring a greater degree of semantic processing were used.

Two studies were carried out with Jeffrey Jutai to test this proposition. Because the manuscript describing these studies is still in preparation, only some preliminary results are presented here. The basic procedure of both studies was similar to that used in the DVF study described above. Briefly, a series of four-letter words (vertical arrangement) was presented for 80 msec 1.5° to the left or right of a central fixation point. The words were exemplars of the following four categories: WEAPON, BIRD, VE-HICLE, 4-FOOTED ANIMAL. As in the previous study, a trial consisted of the simultaneous presentation of a digit (1–9) at the fixation point and the stimulus word lateral to the digit. Three different types of trial or conditions were used. In the simple recognition (SR) condition the subject was first shown a cue card and was then required to indicate whether the stimulus word presented tachistoscopically matched the word printed on the cue card. In the lower order (more concrete) categorization (LC) condition the cue card contained the name of one of the four-word categories (WEAPON, BIRD, VEHICLE, 4-FOOTED ANIMAL) followed by a question mark. The subject's task was to indicate whether the stimulus word was a member of the class printed on the cue card. In the higher order (more abstract) categorization (HC) condition, the words "LIVING THING?" were printed on the cue card, and the subject had to determine whether the stimulus word was a member of this superordinate class. Regardless of the condition involved, the subject was required to do the following: (1) respond to the stimulus word as quickly as possible by pressing one of two microswitches (one for yes and the other for no) and (2) report the number that had appeared at the fixation point and then the stimulus word that had appeared lateral to the number. The order in which the three conditions were presented was counterbalanced across subjects. There were 32 trials for each condition, that is, 16 stimulus presentations in the LVF and 16 in the RVF. Half of the responses were made with the right hand and half with the left hand, in counterbalanced order. The subjects were 27 male prison inmates, each consistently right-handed according to the Porac and Coren (1981) laterality questionnaire. Mean age and education were 28.6 (S.D. = 6.1) and 9.6 (S.D. = 2.2), respectively.

The mean reaction time (msec) to words presented in each visual field and under each condition is shown for all 27 subjects in Figure 12.3. As might be expected, reaction times were considerably shorter in the SR condition than in the two conditions (LC, HC) requiring a greater degree of semantic processing. According to a model of semantic memory proposed by Collins and Quillian (1970),[1] latencies in the HC condition should have been longer than those in the LC condition, but only the RVF data showed a trend consistent with this prediction. Perhaps the most interesting finding was that the direction of perceptual asymmetry depended on the type of condition involved. In the LC condition reaction times to words presented in the RVF (i.e., left hemisphere) were significantly shorter than those to words in the LVF (right hemisphere). However, just the opposite occurred in the HC condition, with response latencies to words in the RVF being significantly *longer* than to words in the LVF. That is, the LC condition produced the left-hemisphere superiority that one would normally expect from a semantic task of this sort. When the subjects were required to make judgments about a larger (superordinate) semantic category, however, superiority shifted to the right hemi-

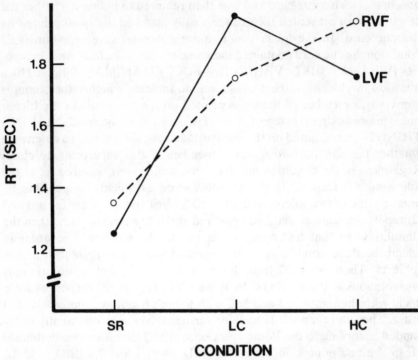

Figure 12.3. Mean reaction times (RT) obtained by criminals in response to words presented in the left visual field (LVF) and in the right visual field (RVF). SR, simple recognition; LC, lower order categorization; HC, higher order categorization.

sphere! This visual field × condition interaction tended to be greater for inmates with high ratings of psychopathy (7-point scale) than for those with low ratings; however, the effect was not significant. Additional analyses indicated that significantly fewer errors were made in the SR condition than in either the LC or the HC condition. However, the visual-field effects observed with the reaction time data were not duplicated with the error rate data.

The results of this study were puzzling, because they seemed to indicate that criminals, particularly psychopathic ones, show a relative right-hemisphere advantage on a task that should be more easily handled by the left hemisphere. We therefore conducted another study using a larger sample of prison inmates and a noncriminal control group. The basic procedure remained the same, except that the number of trials in each of the three conditions was increased from 32 to 128 so as to improve the reliability of the response measures. The subjects were 39 male prison

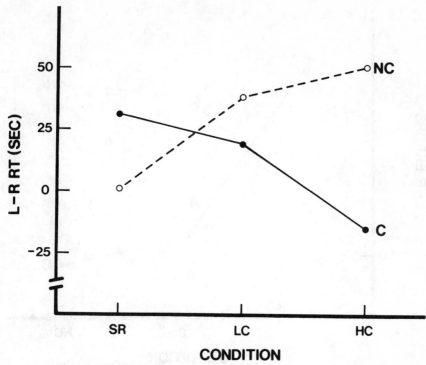

Figure 12.4. Mean reaction time differences between visual fields (LVF − RVF) obtained by criminals (C) and noncriminals (NC) as a function of level of semantic processing. Scores above 0 indicate left-hemisphere superiority. SR, simple recognition; LC, lower order categorization; HC, higher order categorization.

inmates divided into high- (P), medium- (M), and low-psychopathy (NP) groups (N = 13 for each group) on the basis of the 22-item checklist. A group of 25 male noncriminals were recruited from local unemployment centers. All subjects were consistently right-handed. The data have not yet been analyzed completely, and only some preliminary findings can be presented here. Reaction times and error rates were calculated for each visual field and condition. Simple difference scores (LVF − RVF) were then computed.[2] The results for the criminals (C) and noncriminals (NC) are plotted in Figures 12.4 and 12.5; in each case, scores above 0 indicate relative left-hemisphere superiority (i.e., faster reaction times and fewer errors in the RVF), and scores below 0 indicate right-hemisphere superiority (i.e., faster reaction times and fewer errors in the LVF). The performance of the criminals was consistent with the results of the previous study: the degree of perceptual asymmetry in favor of the RVF *decreased* across the SR, LC, and HC conditions. That is, the left-hemisphere supe-

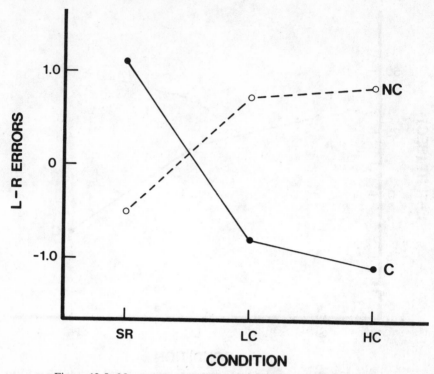

Figure 12.5. Mean error rate differences between visual fields (LVF − RVF) obtained by criminals (C) and noncriminals (NC) as a function of level of semantic processing. Scores above 0 indicate left hemisphere superiority. SR, simple recognition; LC, lower order categorization; HC, higher order categorization.

riority during simple recognition of verbal stimuli gave way to right-hemisphere superiority when a greater degree of semantic processing was required. In contrast, the degree of perceptual asymmetry in favor of the RVF shown by the noncriminals increased across the SR, LC, and HC conditions. Although there was no hemisphere advantage during simple recognition, the superiority of the left hemisphere (relative to the right) increased as the semantic processing requirements increased. If the performance of the noncriminals is considered to be normal, that is, what one would expect on a verbal categorization task, then the performance of the criminals would be considered unusual, to say the least. However, additional analyses clearly indicated that the difference between criminals and noncriminals was due almost entirely to the performance of a particular subgroup of criminals, namely, the psychopaths (P). In fact, the pattern of perceptual asymmetries of the nonpsychopaths (NP) was not much differ-

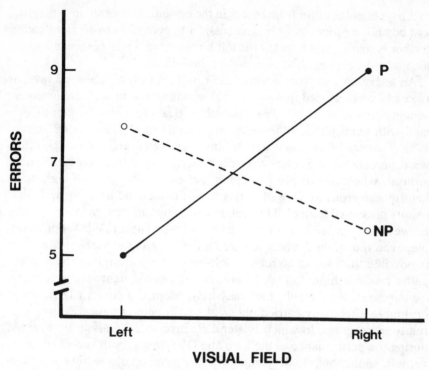

Figure 12.6. Mean number of errors in each visual field obtained by psychopaths (P) and nonpsychopaths (NP) in the higher order categorization (HC) condition.

ent from that of the noncriminals. The most dramatic difference between the psychopaths and the other criminals occurred in the HC condition, with error rate as the dependent variable. The mean number of errors made by Groups P and NP in the LVF and RVF is plotted in Figure 12.6. Group P exhibited right-hemisphere superiority (more errors in the RVF), and Group NP exhibited left-hemisphere superiority (more errors in the LVF).

Conclusions

Lateralized information-processing tasks have been used by many investigators to make inferences about cerebral function and organization. There are, of course, many difficulties in doing so, because perceptual asymmetries can be produced by factors that have little or nothing to do with cerebral organization and specialization. Nevertheless, the consistency of the results described in this chapter at least raises the possibility that psychopaths differ from others in the organization of some perceptual and cognitive processes.[3] In particular, a hypothesis worth investigating further is that in psychopaths the left hemisphere is not as specialized for linguistic processing as it is in normal individuals.

An alternative interpretation of the results is possible. Several investigators have suggested that perceptual asymmetries, as well as some personality characteristics and psychopathological processes, may be associated with hemispheric differences in arousal (e.g., Hellige, 1983; Levy, 1983; Tucker, 1981). According to this asymmetric arousal model, rightward perceptual biases are the result of relatively high left-hemisphere arousal, whereas leftward perceptual biases are the result of high right-hemisphere arousal. Viewed in this way, the dichotic listening and DVF results presented here could be related to group differences in the balance between left- and right-hemisphere arousal (see Tucker, 1981). For example, even though both tasks required the processing of verbal material, it is possible that, for some reason, left-hemisphere arousal in the psychopaths was not high enough to produce the usual rightward perceptual asymmetries. As a result, they may have adopted a strategy (e.g., imagery) more effectively carried out by the right hemisphere. Research currently in progress, in which bilateral electrocortical activity is recorded during the performance of dichotic and DVF tasks (both verbal and nonverbal), should help to determine whether psychopaths exhibit an abnormal or unusual balance between left and right cerebral arousal. Meanwhile, we should note that an asymmetric arousal hypothesis is not necessarily incompatible with the hypothesis that language is weakly lateralized in psychopaths.

Whatever the merits of these two hypotheses, it is clear that we still know very little about language processes in psychopaths. We know even less about how perceptual and cerebral asymmetries of the sort postulated here can help to explain the behavior of psychopaths (see Hare & McPherson, 1984). We might speculate, however, that if psychopaths are not strongly lateralized for language or if their dominant hemisphere characteristically is underaroused, they may tend to use cognitive strategies and overt behaviors that rely little on verbal, logical, and sequential operations (see Tucker, 1981). Similarly, language would be expected to play a relatively ineffective role in the regulation of their behavior (see Luria, 1974; Schalling, 1978). Both possibilities, though highly speculative, may have some bearing on Cleckley's (1976) suggestion that psychopaths have a deep-seated semantic disorder in which the normal connections between semantic and affective components of language are missing or dysfunctional.

Acknowledgments

The preparation of this chapter and the research reported were supported by Grant MT-4511 from the Medical Research Council of Canada. The contributions of Leslie McPherson, Jeffrey Jutai, and Adelle Forth and the cooperation of the staff and inmates of Mission Medium Security Institution are gratefully acknowledged.

Notes

1 The model assumes that a decision about whether a word is part of a larger category (e.g., living things) requires that decisions be made about inclusion in lower order categories (e.g., animal).
2 Laterality coefficients were also computed using the procedure described by Marshall, Kaplan, and Holmes (1975). The results were similar to those obtained with simple difference scores.
3 For reasons presented elsewhere (Hare & McPherson, 1984; see also Bruder, 1983; Connolly, 1985; Connolly, Gruzelier, & Manchanda, 1983; Marin & Tucker, 1981), we do not consider the results to be consistent with the assertion (Flor-Henry, 1976) that psychopathy, like schizophrenia, is associated with left cerebral damage or dysfunction.

References

American Psychiatric Association. (1980). *Diagnostic and statistical manual of mental disorders* (3rd ed.). Washington, DC: Author.

Beaumont, J. G. (Ed.). (1982). *Divided visual field studies in cerebral organization.* New York: Academic Press.

Bruder, G. E. (1983). Cerebral laterality and psychopathology: A review of dichotic listening studies. *Schizophrenia Bulletin, 9,* 134–51.

Bryden, M. P. (1982). *Laterality: Functional asymmetry in the intact brain.* New York: Academic Press.

Cleckley, H. (1976). *The mask of sanity* (5th ed.). St. Louis, MO: Mosby.

Cohen, G. (1982). Theoretical interpretations of lateral asymmetries. In J. G. Beaumont (Ed.), *Divided visual field studies of cerebral organization* (pp. 87–111). New York: Academic Press.

Collins, A. M., & Quillian, M. R. (1970). Does category size affect categorization time? *Journal of Verbal Learning and Verbal Behavior, 9,* 432–8.

Connolly, J. F. (1985). Stability of path-way hemispheric differences in the auditory event-related potential (ERP) to monaural stimulation. *Psychophysiology, 22,* 87–95.

Connolly, J. F., Gruzelier, J., & Manchanda, R. (1983). Electrocortical and perceptual asymmetries in schizophrenia. In P. Flor-Henry & J. Gruzelier (Eds.), *Laterality and psychopathology.* Amsterdam: Elsevier/North Holland Biomedical Press.

Day, J. (1977). Right hemisphere language processing in normal right handers. *Journal of Experimental Psychology: Human Perception and Performance, 3,* 518–28.

Elliott, F. (1978). Neurological aspects of antisocial behavior. In W. H. Reid (Ed.), *The psychopath: A comprehensive study of antisocial disorders and behaviors.* New York: Brunner/Mazel.

Ellis, H. D., & Shepherd, J. W. (1974). Recognition of abstract and concrete words presented in left and right visual fields. *Journal of Experimental Psychology, 103,* 1035–6.

Elman, J. L., Takahashi, K., & Tohsaku, Y. H. (1981). Lateral asymmetries for the identification of concrete and abstract Kanji. *Neuropsychologia, 19,* 407–12.

Fleiss, J. L. (1981). *Statistical methods for rates and proportions.* New York: Wiley.

Flor-Henry, P. (1976). Lateralized temporal–limbic dysfunction and psychopathology. *Annals of the New York Academy of Sciences, 280,* 777–97.

Geffen, G., & Caudrey, D. (1981). Reliability and validity of the dichotic monitoring test for language laterality. *Neuropsychologia, 19,* 413–24.

Glick, S. D., Jerussi, T. P., & Zimmerberg, B. (1977). Behavioral and neuropharmacological correlates of nigrostriatal asymmetry in rats. In S. Harnard, R. W. Doty, L. Goldstein, J. J. Jaynes, & G. Krauthamer (Eds.), *Lateralization in the nervous system* (pp. 213–49). New York: Academic Press.

Gorenstein, E. E. (1982). Frontal lobe functions in psychopaths. *Journal of Abnormal Psychology, 91,* 368–79.

Hare, R. D. (1979). Psychopathy and laterality of cerebral function. *Journal of Abnormal Psychology, 88,* 605–10.

Hare, R. D. (1980). A research scale for the assessment of psychopathy in criminal populations. *Personality and Individual Differences, 1,* 111–17.

Hare, R. D. (1983). Diagnosis of antisocial personality disorder in two prison populations. *American Journal of Psychiatry, 140,* 887–90.

Hare, R. D. (1984a). A comparison of procedures for the assessment of psychopathy. Manuscript submitted for publication.

Hare, R. D. (1984b). Performance of psychopaths on cognitive tasks related to frontal lobe function. *Journal of Abnormal Psychology, 93.*

Hare, R. D., & Cox, D. N. (1978). Clinical and empirical conceptions of psychopathy. In R. D. Hare & D. Schalling (Eds.), *Psychopathic behavior: Approaches to research.* New York: Wiley.

Hare, R. D., & Frazelle, J. (1980). Some preliminary notes on the use of a research scale for the assessment of psychopathy in criminal populations. Unpublished manuscript, University of British Columbia, Department of Psychology, Vancouver, Canada.

Hare, R. D., & McPherson, L. M. (1984). Psychopathy and perceptual asymmetry during verbal dichotic listening. *Journal of Abnormal Psychology, 93,* 141–9.

Hatta, T. (1977). Recognition of Japanese Kanji in the left and right visual fields. *Neuropsychologia, 15,* 685–8.

Hayden, S., & Spellacy, F. (Speakers) (1969). *Dichotic triads tape* (Cassette). Victoria, Canada: University of Victoria, Department of Psychology.

Hellige, J. B. (1983). Hemisphere × task interaction and the study of laterality. In J. B. Hellige (Ed.), *Cerebral hemisphere asymmetry: Method, theory, and application.* New York: Praeger.

Hines, D. (1976). Recognition of verbs, abstract nouns, and concrete nouns from the left and right visual fields. *Neuropsychologia, 14,* 211–16.

Hines, D. (1977). Differences in tachistoscopic recognition between abstract and concrete words as a function of visual field and frequency. *Cortex, 13,* 66–73.

Inglis, J. (1962). Dichotic stimulation, temporal lobe damage, and the perception and storage of auditory stimuli: A note on Kimura's findings. *Canadian Journal of Psychology, 16,* 11–17.

Inglis, J. (1968). Dichotic listening and performance. *British Journal of Psychology, 59,* 415–22.

Kimura, D. (1961a). Some effects of temporal lobe damage on auditory perception. *Canadian Journal of Psychology, 15,* 156–65.

Kimura, D. (1961b). Cerebral dominance and the perception of verbal stimuli. *Canadian Journal of Psychology, 15,* 166–71.

Kimura, D. (1967). Functional asymmetry of the brain in dichotic listening. *Cortex, 3,* 163–78.

Kinsbourne, M. (Ed.). (1978). *Asymmetrical function of the brain.*Cambridge University Press.

Levy, J. (1983). Individual differences in cerebral hemisphere asymmetry: Theoretical issues and experimental conditions. In J. B. Hellige (Ed.), *Cerebral hemisphere asymmetry: Method, theory, and application.* New York: Praeger.

Levy, J., Heller, W., Banick, M. T., & Burton, L. A. (1983). Are variations among right-handed individuals in perceptual asymmetries caused by characteristic arousal differences between hemispheres? *Journal of Experimental Psychology: Human Perception and Performance, 9,* 329–59.

Luria, A. R. (1974). *The working brain.* New York: Penguin Books.

Marin, R. S., & Tucker, G. J. (1981). Psychopathology and hemisphere dysfunction: A review. *Journal of Nervous and Mental Disease, 169,* 546–57.

Marshall, J. C., Kaplan, D., & Holmes, J. M. (1975). The measurement of laterality. *Neuropsychologia, 13,* 315–22.

McCord, W. M. (1982). *The psychopath and milieu therapy.* New York: Academic Press.

Millon, T. (1981). *Disorders of personality; DSM-III: Axis II.* New York: Wiley.

Oke, A., Keller, R., Melford, I., & Adams, R. (1978). Lateralization of norepinephrine in human thalamus. *Science, 200,* 1411–13.

Paivio, A. (1969). Mental imagery in associative learning and thought. *Psychological Review, 7,* 241–63.

Porac, C., & Coren, S. (1981). *Lateral preferences and human behavior.* New York: Springer-Verlag.

Reid, W. H. (Ed.). (1978). *The psychopath: A comprehensive study of antisocial disorders and behaviors.* New York: Brunner/Mazel.

Rubens, A. B. (1977). Anatomical asymmetries of human cerebral cortex. In S. Harnad, R. W. Doty, L. Goldstein, J. Jaynes, & G. Krauthamer (Eds.), *Lateralization in the nervous system.* New York: Academic Press.

Sasanuma, S., Itoh, M., Mori, K., & Kobayashi, V. (1977). Tachistoscopic recognition of Kana and Kanji words. *Neuropsychologia, 15,* 547–53.

Satz, P., Achenbach, K., Pattishall, E., & Fennell, E. (1965). Order of report, ear asymmetry, and handedness in dichotic listening. *Cortex, 1,* 377–96.

Schalling, D. (1978). Psychopathy-related personality variables and the psychophysiology of socialization. In R. D. Hare & D. Schalling (Eds.), *Psychopathic behavior: Approaches to research.* New York: Wiley.

Schroeder, M. L., Schroeder, K. G., & Hare, R. D. (1983). Generalizability of a checklist for assessment of psychopathy. *Journal of Consulting and Clinical Psychology, 51,* 511–16.

Schwartz, M. (1970). Competition in dichotic listening. Unpublished doctoral dissertation, University of Waterloo, Ontario.

Syndulko, K. (1978). Electrocortical investigations of sociopathy. In R. D. Hare & D. Schalling (Eds.), *Psychopathic behavior: Approaches to research.* New York: John Wiley.

Teng, E. L. (1981). Dichotic ear difference is a poor index for the functional asymmetry between the cerebral hemispheres. *Neuropsychologia, 19,* 235–40.

Tucker, D. M. (1981). Lateral brain function, emotion, and conceptualization. *Psychological Bulletin, 89,* 19–46.

Witelson, S. F. (1980). Neuroanatomical asymmetry in left handers: A review and implications for functional asymmetry. In J. Herron (Ed.), *Neuropsychology of left handedness*. New York: Academic Press.

Zangwill, D. (1960). *Cerebral dominance and its relation to psychological function*. Edinburgh: Oliver & Boyd.

Zurif, E. B., & Bryden, M. P. (1969). Familial handedness and left-right differences in auditory and visual perception. *Neuropsychologia, 7,* 179–87.

13   The neuroendocrinology and neurochemistry of antisocial behavior

Robert T. Rubin

"Antisocial behavior" is a very broad term encompassing acts ranging in severity from misdemeanors such as petty theft to murder. Thus a specific role for neurochemical or neuroendocrine factors certainly cannot be postulated or elucidated to explain such behavior in its entirety. Even when the term "antisocial" is used in other than a legal or criminological sense – for example, when it is applied in psychiatric diagnostics in an attempt to define and understand individual human behavior more fully – it remains overinclusive. From a clinical standpoint, the term "antisocial" most often signifies antisocial personality disorder (American Psychiatric Association, 1952, 1968, 1980), which in the third edition of the American Psychiatric Association's *Diagnostic and Statistical Manual of Mental Disorders* (DSM-III) is considered an "axis II" personality disorder, which may or may not coexist with certain "axis I" clinical syndromes or other conditions. Simply stated, this means that, according to current diagnostic nomenclature, an antisocial personality disorder theoretically could coexist with an organic mental disorder, substance use disorder, paranoid disorder, depressive disorder, psychosexual disorder, and so on.

For the diagnosis of antisocial personality disorder, the individual must be at least 18 years old and have a history, before the age of 15, of three or more symptoms that include truancy, expulsion or suspension from school, delinquency, running away, lying, substance abuse, thefts, vandalism, fights, and so on. Then, after age 18, the individual must show four or more behaviors that include inconsistent work patterns, inability to function as a responsible parent, unlawful activities, inability to maintain an enduring attachment to a sexual partner, irritability and aggressiveness, failure to honor financial obligations, impulsivity or failure to plan ahead, repeated lying, and recklessness with a motor vehicle. In particular, the pattern of antisocial behavior must be continuous, with no

239

intervening period of at least 5 years without such behavior between the age of 15 and the present, unless the individual was bedridden or incarcerated. Finally, such behavior cannot be due to severe mental retardation, schizophrenia, or manic episodes (American Psychiatric Association, 1980).

Dimensions of antisocial behavior also appear in several other diagnostic categories, including conduct disorder, which consists of the typical childhood signs of antisocial personality disorder, and adult antisocial behavior, a condition not attributable to a mental disorder in which criminal or other aggressive or antisocial behavior occurs among individuals who do not meet all the criteria for antisocial personality disorder or the criteria for any other axis I mental disorder. Thus, even within psychiatric diagnostics, the term "antisocial" denotes, inter alia, pathological childhood behavioral traits, a persistent and pervasive adult personality disorder, and adult behavior that is subsumed under the legal or criminological definition of antisocial.

Because of the apparently irreconcilable semantic differences surrounding the term "antisocial," many investigators involved in physiological studies of antisocial behavior, including those performing neuroendocrine and neurochemical studies, have chosen to focus on a particular component that intuitively might have a physiological basis or correlate. In this regard, interpersonal violence, including rape, assault, and murder, has been a behavior of interest. Still, semantic problems remain – for example, the interchangeability of the terms "aggression" and "violence" in many writings. When these terms are used synonymously, they become overgeneralizations. In the following discussion, therefore, aggression is defined as any vigorous adaptive behavior, in a nonjudgmental sense, or as more explicitly delineated by Valzelli (1981, p. 64) "that component of normal behavior which, under different stimulus-bound and goal-directed forms, is released for satisfying vital needs and for removing or overcoming any threat to the physical and/or psychological integrity subserving the self- and species-preservation of a living organism." Aggressive behavior thus implies an active encounter with one's environment for the purpose of coping with environmental stressors – the "fight" component of Cannon's "fight or flight" dichotomy (Cannon, 1932). To facilitate the understanding of observed patterns of aggressive behavior in experimental situations, Moyer (1968) delineated several categories of aggression: predatory, intermale, fear-induced, irritable, territorial, maternal, and instrumental. The neurophysiological, neuroendocrine, and neurochemical substrates of these categories appear to be different; for example, testosterone plays an important role in intermale aggression in animals, but it has relatively little influence on predatory aggression (Moyer, 1974). Similarly, different types of aggressive behavior may be facilitated or inhibited by brain stimulation, lesioning, or ablation, particularly in the amygdaloid complex, hypothalamus, and other limbic system areas (Klüver & Bucy, 1939; Moyer, 1968).

Violence, in the following discussion, is defined as destructive behavior directed against members of the same species (one's fellow humans) in situations and circumstances in which alternative forms of adaptive behavior are possible or, as described by Valzelli (1981, p. 153), "the degeneration of aggression . . . released either as a consequence of pathological disruption of brain control mechanisms or by an intentional oriented education that enhances ideological intolerance." Thus violence, in contrast to aggression, has a pejorative connotation. This is not an easy distinction to make, for the pejoration depends on the perceptions of both the persons involved and the observers. Lief (1963) made a useful distinction among three types of violence: the type driven by rage (e.g., "crimes of passion"), a detached type in which the significant aspect is the violent act (e.g., adolescent gang attacks), and a detached type in which the significant component is the destruction of the object of attack (e.g., warfare). These types of violence might contain, as components, more than one of Moyer's (1968) categories of aggression. For example, rageful violence might contain elements of fear-induced, irritable, and maternal aggression, whereas detached violence in which the significant aspect is the violent act might contain components of intermale, territorial, and instrumental aggression. Detached violence in which the significant component is the destruction of the object of attack might be described as pure instrumental aggression. It should be evident, then, that the neuroendocrine and neurochemical substrates of these three kinds of violence would not be discerned easily, particularly with reference to rageful violence and detached violence in which the significant aspect is the violent act. Furthermore, violent behavior can be a dimension of most major mental illnesses (Berger & Gulevich, 1981). Thus a complex interaction of biological (genetic, neuroendocrine, neurochemical, neurophysiological), psychological (learned behavior, role modeling, etc.), and sociocultural factors undoubtedly underlies most identifiable forms of violence. Elucidating these multiple factors and determining the strength of their interactions has been an almost insurmountable task. Nevertheless, a great deal of research has been undertaken, and many data, often conflicting, are available from human studies as well as animal studies. In this chapter the human neuroendocrine and neurochemical data will be reviewed, with animal studies being adduced as necessary.

Neuroendocrine correlates of aggression and violence

It is important to recognize that neuroendocrine and neurochemical influences on behavior, including aggression and violence, begin during the time of intrauterine development of the central nervous system (CNS). Of course, undernutrition can result in global deficits in CNS function, including increased aggressivity, (Dodge, Prensky, & Feigin, 1975; Smart, 1981). In different mammalian species, prenatal and/or early postnatal exposure to gonadal sex steroid hormones exerts an organizing effect on the CNS and also alters CNS responsiveness to subsequent hormone stimulation (Baker, 1980; Gorski, 1971, 1980; Goy, 1968; Harlan, Gordon & Gorski, 1979; Money, 1973, 1977; Phoenix, Goy, & Young, 1967; Reinisch, 1976; Reinisch & Karow, 1977). For some sexually dimorphic behaviors (behaviors that are different between the sexes), the exposure of the developing brain to gonadal steroids is all that appears to be of consequence; that is, these hormones are *behaviorally organizing*. For example, the treatment of female rhesus monkeys with gonadal steroids prenatally can result in increased malelike play behavior in these animals as juveniles and increased aggressive behavior in adulthood (Goy, 1968; Goy, Wolf, & Eisele, 1977; Phoenix et al, 1967). The administration of gonadal steroids in postnatal life can also be *behaviorally activating;* for example, the expression of malelike sexual behavior in adult female rhesus monkeys requires not only prenatal exposure to testosterone but also concurrent androgenic stimulation in adulthood (Eaton, Goy, & Phoenix, 1973). In addition, gonadal steroid activation of other behaviors appears not to require a specific early hormonal exposure for its effect; for example, long-term testosterone treatment of ovariectomized adult female rhesus monkeys results in malelike yawning, sex exploration, and sex display, even though the animals were not exposed to testosterone before or immediately after birth (Eaton et al., 1973).

Not only the hormonal milieu but also early environmental experience appears to influence the postnatal development of the CNS. Brain–environment interactions in the human occur at least as early as the first minutes after birth (Condon & Sander, 1974). The actual morphological development of the brain depends on environmental stimulation. This is true not only for gross sensory deficits, such as the disturbed brain maturation following the blinding of experimental animals, but also for more subtle influences, such as the thickness of dendritic branching. Certainly at a finer biochemical level (e.g., the laying down of memory traces in ribonucleic acid), the environment influences the CNS for as long as the organism remains receptive. It is a truism that the nature–nurture interaction occurs throughout the life span of the individual.

The main androgenic hormone, testosterone, is believed to have both organizing and activating effects on human aggressive behavior. Its action on the CNS appears to contribute to the heightened self-assertiveness and other-directed activity of boys and men compared with girls and women. However, one key question is whether, among men themselves, interindividual differences in the amount of testosterone reaching the brain and interacting with receptors in an ongoing manner play some role in determining interindividual differences in aggressive and hostile feelings and behavior. Studies attempting to answer this question have included the correlation of circulating testosterone concentrations in blood with both subjectively felt hostility and overtly aggressive behavior in normal men and violent and nonviolent criminals; the examination of men with genetic differences in testosterone production for differences in hostility, aggression, and violence; and the determination of the behavioral effects of testosterone administered to hypogonadal men and antiandrogenic agents administered to men convicted of sex crimes (Benton, 1981; Brown, 1980; Kling, 1975; Moyer, 1974; Nieschlag, 1979; Rose, 1972, 1975, 1978; Rubin, Reinisch, & Haskett, 1981; Sheard, 1979; Simon, 1981).

The studies that have related measures of hostility, aggressive behavior, and social dominance to measures of testosterone secretion can be divided into two groups: those that used psychological rating scales and observer ratings to quantify levels of hostility in otherwise normal subjects and those that used indices of overt aggressive and violent acts in antisocial individuals, mainly prisoners (Table 13.1). In the studies done on normal volunteers, the results have been quite variable. Persky, Smith, and Basu (1971) found the production of testosterone in 18 healthy young men to be highly correlated with a measure of aggression derived from the Buss–Durkee Hostility Inventory; four psychological measures of aggression and hostility accounted for 82% of the variance in testosterone production rate. However, in the same study, age was the principal correlate of testosterone production in 15 healthy older men; there was no relation between testosterone and measures of hostility.

Additional rating scale studies have followed that of Persky et al. (1971). Meyer-Bahlburg, Boon, Sharma, and Edwards (1974) identified five low-aggression and six high-aggression undergraduate college students by screening with the Buss–Durkee Hostility Inventory. In contrast to the subjects of Persky et al. (1971), the two groups of students did not show any significant differences in plasma level or production rate of testosterone. Doering et al. (1975) administered the Multiple Affect Ad-

Table 13.1. *Testosterone–aggression/violence studies in men*

Subjects	Measure of hostility	Correlation	Reference
Normal subjects			
18 healthy young men	Buss–Durkee Hostility Scale	Strongly positive	Persky et al. (1971)
15 healthy older men	Buss–Durkee Hostility Scale	None	Persky et al. (1971)
11 college men	Buss–Durkee Hostility Scale	None	Meyer-Bahlburg et al. (1974)
20 healthy young men	MAACL	Weakly positive	Doering et al. (1975)
101 healthy young men	Buss–Durkee Hostility Scale	Weakly positive	Monti et al. (1977)
40 adult male alcoholics	Buss–Durkee, MAACL	None	Persky et al. (1977)
14 male college hockey players	Coaches' ratings	Weakly positive	Scaramella and Brown (1978)
58 normal adolescent boys	Various inventories	Moderately positive	Olweus et al. (1980)
15 male wrestlers	Winning/losing	Positive with winning	Elias (1981)
Violent prisoners			
21 young inmates	Buss–Durkee Hostility Scale	None	Kreuz and Rose (1972)
21 young inmates	History of violence in ado-lescence	Moderately positive	Kreuz and Rose (1972)
36 adult inmates	Buss–Durkee Hostility Scale	Moderately positive	Ehrenkranz et al. (1974)
36 adult inmates	History of chronic violence	Moderately positive	Ehrenkranz et al. (1974)
52 rapists, 12 child molesters	Buss–Durkee Hostility Scale	None	Rada et al. (1976)
52 rapists, 12 child molesters	Amount of violence in attack	Weakly positive	Rada et al. (1976)
11 violent, 11 nonviolent		None	Matthews (1979)
22 adult inmates		Weakly positive	Mattson et al. (1980)
80 adolescents	40 recidivistic delinquent, 40 normal		
57 inmates	History of chronic violence	Moderately positive	Rubin et al. (personal com-munication, UCLA).

jective Checklist and measured plasma testosterone levels every other day for 2 months in 20 healthy young adult men. Intrasubject correlations of the affects of hostility, anxiety, and depression with testosterone were both positive and negative, whereas intersubject correlations among these three affects and testosterone were all positive but statistically nonsignificant. Similarly, Monti, Brown, and Corriveau (1977), using questionnaires for anxiety, hostility, sexual interest, and so on and measuring serum testosterone, studied 101 healthy young adult men on two separate days. Some of the psychological measures correlated significantly with testosterone, but only because of the large sample size; all correlations were quite low. Aggression as measured by the Buss–Durkee Hostility Inventory did not correlate with testosterone at all. Persky et al. (1977) found no significant correlation between hostility, as measured by the Buss–Durkee Hostility Inventory and the Multiple Affect Adjective Checklist, and plasma testosterone in 40 male alcoholics who averaged 36 years of age and who had been drinking heavily for 2 to 35 years.

In contrast, Scaramella and Brown (1978) reported a significant correlation between aggressive behavior, as rated by coaches, and serum testosterone in 14 male college hockey players, but again the correlation was low. Olweus, Mattson, Schalling, and Löw (1980) administered a number of personality inventories and rating scales to 58 normal adolescent boys, aged 16, and determined plasma testosterone on two occasions about a month apart. The correlation between plasma testosterone and self-reports of physical and verbal aggression, reflecting responsivity to provocation and threat, and lack of frustration tolerance were significantly positive, the shared variance being about 40%. Although pubertal stage was also positively related to testosterone levels, this factor did not account for the relation between testosterone and the psychological measures. Elias (1981) studied 15 male wrestlers during competitive matches and found greater increases in both serum cortisol and testosterone in the winners than in the losers. These data were interpreted to suggest that humans, like other social mammals, may undergo hormone changes in response to victory (dominance) or defeat (submission).

Taken together, these data in normal subjects indicate that there is no consistent correlation between various measures of hostility, aggression, and similar behavior, as determined both by rating scales and by observed behavior, and circulating testosterone levels (Table 13.1). Most normal subjects usually do not show overtly violent behavior, so that reliance must be placed on self-report measures, such as the Buss–Durkee Hostility Inventory (Buss & Durkee, 1957). These rating scales may reflect the immediate state of the individual rather than any long-term behavior pattern and thus would be an inappropriate correlate for a hormone that has a putative long-term activating effect on aggression and hostility. Similarly, sports competitions such as hockey and wrestling are contrived circumstances in which most participants show aggression but generally in a sportsman-like manner; hockey may be an exception in that outbursts of rage among the players is not uncommon during a game.

In contrast, studies of testosterone levels in aggressive, assaultive, and violent male prisoners have been somewhat more consistent in demonstrating a relation between such behaviors and increased circulating testosterone (Table 13.1). Kreuz and Rose (1972) measured plasma testosterone and indices of fighting and verbal aggression in 21 young prison inmates. Although plasma testosterone levels did not differ between fighting and nonfighting individuals and did not correlate with psychological test scores, including the Buss–Durkee Hostility Inventory, 10 prisoners with histories of more violent crimes in adolescence did have a significantly higher mean level of testosterone than the 11 prisoners without such a history. From these data, Kreuz and Rose (1972) hypothesized that, in a population predisposed by social factors to develop antisocial behavior, testosterone may be an important additional factor placing some individuals at risk for committing more violent crimes during adolescence, when testosterone levels are increasing. This is a cogent hypothesis in that it takes account of a likely interaction between social triggers or sanctions for antisocial behavior at a time in the individual's life when his CNS is exposed to major increases in androgenic hormones.

Ehrenkranz, Bliss, and Sheard (1974) measured plasma testosterone in 36 male prisoners – 12 with chronic violent behavior, 12 who were socially dominant without physical violence, and 12 who were neither physically violent nor socially dominant. The violent group scored significantly higher on total hostility, as measured by the Buss–Durkee Hostility Inventory, than did either of the other two groups, and this group also had a significantly higher mean plasma testosterone level than the other groups. Also, the socially dominant group had a significantly higher mean level of testosterone than the nondominant group. Rada, Laws, and Kellner (1976) classified 52 rapists and 12 child molesters according to the degree of violence expressed during the attack. The five most violent rapists had a higher mean morning plasma testosterone concentration than the other rapists, the child molesters, or normal control subjects. The mean Buss–Durkee Hostility Inventory score for all the rapists was significantly higher than the mean for the normal control subjects, but individual hostility scores did not correlate with plasma testosterone. Mattson, Schalling, Olweus, Löw, and Swenson (1980) found a slightly but significantly higher mean plasma testosterone level in 40 male recidivistic delinquent adolescents compared with a group of normal adolescents of the same age and pubertal stages. Those delinquents who had committed armed robbery had a somewhat higher mean testosterone level than the less violent offenders, but this difference was nonsignificant. In contrast, Matthews (1979) found no difference in mean plasma testosterone levels between 11 male prisoners with a history of violent crimes and 11 other prisoners pair-matched for age, height, weight, and time spent in prison but who were convicted for nonviolent crimes and who had no history of aggressive tendencies.

These studies of circulating plasma testosterone levels in antisocial individuals with objectively identifiable violent behavior are relatively few, but they have been somewhat consistent in their findings of increased testosterone in those subjects with histories of particularly violent behaviors, for example, rapist-murderers (Table 13.1). These individuals often have a long and vivid history of such behavior. Although they have high hostility scores on the Buss–Durkee Hostility Inventory and other psychological measures of aggression, across individuals these hostility measures do not correlate with plasma testosterone, suggesting, as mentioned earlier, a relative weakness of these tests in detecting long-term personality and behavioral traits.

In the testosterone–aggression studies reviewed above, testosterone values were consistently within the normal range, both in the normal subjects and in the violent criminals. There is a clearer relation between testosterone and behavior in individuals with pathological alterations of testosterone levels, including those secondary to genetic anomalies, and in individuals with induced alterations in hormone levels. A large reduction in circulating testosterone diminishes a number of behavioral characteristics in men, including aggressiveness and sexual appetite. The behavioral effects are considerably more pronounced if this reduction occurs before puberty than if it occurs after puberty. Certain chromosomal abnormalities can produce prepubertal hypogonadism, notably 47,XXY (Klinefelter's syndrome) and its variants (Becker, 1972; Lev-Ran, 1977; Zuppinger, Engel, Forbes, Mantooth, & Claffey, 1967). In this syndrome a dysgenesis of the testes beginning in late fetal development and continuing throughout childhood and puberty reduces the endocrine function of the testes to various degrees. These patients often respond both physically and behaviorally to testosterone replacement therapy, developing a masculine body build and increased sexual interest, including heterosexual fantasies, penile erections, and overt sexual behavior. Exogenously administered testosterone frequently has the same effects in hypogonadal men, irrespective of the cause of their hypogonadism (Bancroft & Skakkebaek, 1979; Davidson, Camargo, & Smith, 1979). However, exogenous testosterone administration has not been noted to predispose men receiving such treatment to violent or otherwise antisocial behaviors.

Just as the administration of testosterone has been used to normalize sexual drive and sexual activity in hypogonadal men, the administration of antiandrogenic agents has been used to reduce aberrant sexual behaviors in men with these antisocial tendencies (Blumer & Migeon, 1975; Cooper, 1981; Cooper, Ismail, Phanjoo, & Love, 1972; Davies, 1974; Meyer et al., 1977; Money, Wiedeking, Walker, Migeon, Meyer, & Borgaonkar, 1975; Van Moffaert, 1976). The administration of antiandrogens has replaced surgical castration as a way of lowering circulating testosterone levels. The two drugs most often used are cyproterone acetate and medroxyprogesterone acetate, both of which have antigonadotropic and progestogenic as well as antiandrogenic properties, lowering both circulating gonadotropin and testosterone levels. Individuals treated with these agents usually have had normal basal circulating testosterone levels, which were reduced during treatment by 30% to 75%, generally to within the hypogonadal range.

Individuals with compulsive sexual thoughts, often of a paraphilic nature, and with impulsive and violent overt behaviors have been treated successfully. The behavioral effects of antiandrogens appear to be specific for disordered sexual thoughts and behaviors; these drugs are less effective in reducing nonsexual violent outbursts. The paraphilias that have responded to treatment with these compounds include pedophilia, masochism, incest, transvestism, and exhibitionism (Money et al., 1975). Not only were actual erotic practices reduced by 50% to 100%, but erotic mental imagery was also reduced. The insistent and compulsive mental imagery of illegal erotic practices was especially disturbing to the subjects, who experienced the reduction of this imagery upon treatment as a relief (Money et al., 1975). For such individuals, the most effective treatment program has been pharmacotherapy with antiandrogens combined with a well-designed, strong program of counseling and psychotherapy.

As is evident from the studies cited above, there remains a definite controversy concerning the role of androgenic hormones in human aggressive and violent behaviors, particularly with reference to postnatal testosterone influences in individuals who have no genetic or other metabolic defect of testosterone production or metabolism and who do not have pharmacological alterations of their circulating hormone levels. Some aspects of the controversy may arise from differences in methodology, and other aspects may arise from differences among investigators in their constructs of aggression and violence. With respect to the former, serious questions can be raised about the methods used to assess aggression and violence potential. Does the Buss–Durkee Hostility Inventory measure trait hostility or state hostility? Which is more likely to be related to the influence of testosterone in the CNS? If testosterone indeed is behaviorally activating as well as organizing, how long does that activation take? Is the activation a threshold phenomenon, that is, a certain minimal amount of hormone being necessary (Simon, 1981), or are testosterone levels related to aggression and violence in a graded manner?

Even though overt violence is a state phenomenon, there may be trait substrates to violent outbursts – for example, the omnipresent, preoccupying sexual fantasies of men who commit sex offenses only periodically. Olweus (1979) concluded from a review of 16 studies that there is a substantial intraindividual stability to aggressive behavior and reaction patterns across time, similar to the stability of scores on intelligence tests. With reference to the physiology of testosterone itself, it is known that testosterone exhibits a circadian rhythm in blood, with higher levels occurring at night during sleep. In normal adult men the circadian component accounts for about 20% of the total variability of plasma levels (de Lacerda, Kowarski, Johanson, Athanasiou, & Migeon, 1973), but in pubertal adolescent boys the nocturnal phase of testosterone secretion is very high compared with the diurnal phase (i.e., the circadian amplitude is much greater, even though average levels are not as high as in the fully adult male) (Judd, Parker, Siler, & Yen, 1974). Thus in order to assess profiles of circulating testosterone fully, venous catheterization studies with frequent blood sampling must be accomplished over periods of at least 24 hours; these have not yet been done with aggressive or violent subjects. Even for an accurate level of circulating testosterone to be measured at any time of the day or night, at least three blood samples, 10–20 min apart, must be taken and averaged, because testosterone, like most hormones, is secreted episodically (Goldzieher, Dozier, Smith, & Steinberger, 1976). None of the aforementioned studies of testosterone in either normal men or violent criminals have used a full 24-hour sampling schedule, and only a few have assessed testosterone in more than a single blood sample. Thus the hormone measurement error inherent in these studies is great.

Two other aspects of testosterone physiology deserve mention. First, testosterone, as well as the other gonadal and adrenal steroid hormones, circulates mainly bound to steroid-binding globulin proteins. Only a small percentage of hormone is free in blood, and it is believed that it is the free hormone component that is available for attachment to receptors and thus is physiologically active. All studies to date have reported total (both free and bound) testosterone concentrations, which may have masked interindividual differences in free hormone concentrations. Second, nothing is known about interindividual variation in cellular testosterone receptor sensitivity in subjects who do not have an obvious receptor defect. In the rat CNS, androgen receptors are present in the anterior pituitary, hypothalamus, preoptic area, and cerebral cortex; these receptors clearly are different from the estrogen receptors in the same brain structures (McEwen, 1980; Naess, Attramdal, & Hansson, 1977). Genetically determined androgen resistance, due to defective hormone receptors, is an identified clinical syndrome in human males (Bardin & Wright, 1980), but the possibility of more subtle differences in receptor sensitivity, without resultant physical anomalies, remains unexplored. Until (a) agreement is reached on the type of violent antisocial behavior being studied, (b) appropriate measurement techniques for that behavior are validated, and (c) methodological refinements in the measurement of testosterone and the determination of its physiological influence at the cellular receptor level are effected, the present controversy surrounding the putative activating effect of testosterone on aggression and violence appears doomed to remain unresolved.

Neurochemical correlates of aggression and violence

As outlined above, the data on the neuroendocrine correlates of aggression and violence, with particular reference to the most thoroughly studied relation, that of testosterone in men, are sparse and conflicting. Whereas even fewer studies have been conducted on the neurochemical correlates of aggression and violence in human subjects, the experimental animal literature is replete with neurochemical studies using several different experimental paradigms to elicit some kind of aggression response (Eichelman, 1979; Eichelman, Elliott, & Barchas, 1981; Karczmar, Richardson, & Kindel, 1978; Rodgers, 1981; Valzelli, 1981). The paradigms have included isolation-induced fighting in mice, shock-induced fighting and predatory attack in rats, the development of dominance or submission hierarchies among males in rat colonies, and fighting behavior in rats generated by extinction of a food-reinforced response (Rodgers, 1981). The latter two techniques are preferred over the former three, because they do not rely on artificial stimulation to provoke fighting among the animals, which may be defensive as well as aggressive. Although (a) only a narrow range of animal species has been studied, (b) the conditions in which the animals have been housed for observation and the stimuli used to elicit the aggressive responses have sometimes been inappropriate, and (c) the recording and analysis of behavior have not been fully standardized (Huntingford, 1980), a plethora of studies have been performed, and some general conclusions can be formulated.

With reference to the biogenic amine neurotransmitters, norepinephrine, dopamine, and serotonin, evidence to date suggests that all three play a role in the regulation of aggressive behaviors in animals. Central nervous system levels and turnover rates of all three of these neurotransmitters, as well as others such as acetylcholine, have been altered experimentally by various pharmacological manipulations. Central nervous system serotonin has been increased by increasing its precursor amino acid, tryptophan, and by blocking its metabolic degradation by inhibition of the enzyme monoamine oxidase. Central nervous system serotonin has been reduced by enhancing the metabolism of its substrate, tryptophan, by induction through other metabolic pathways, and by blockade of the rate-limiting enzyme involved in serotonin synthesis, tryptophan hydroxylase, by compounds such as parachlorophenylalanine. Similar pharmacological manipulative strategies have been used for several other neurotransmitters.

Many studies have suggested that increased norepinephrine activity in the CNS correlates with, and may even be the trigger for, affective (intermale, irritable, territorial, and maternal) aggression, whereas it appears to inhibit predatory aggression. Dopamine is similar to norepinephrine in its activity profile, augmenting affective aggression and inhibiting predatory aggression. Activation of the cholinergic system appears to augment both affective and predatory aggression, whereas activation of the serotoninergic system is inhibitory for both types of aggression.

From just this brief summary of the neurochemical correlates of animal aggression, the complexity of this field is apparent. Different experimental paradigms may yield different results, and the dimension of aggression in the behaviors of the animals in these paradigms is primarily one of interpretation by the observers. As indicated, the possible interactions of only four neurotransmitters in influencing aggressive behavior are many, and these four compounds represent only a small number of the identified neuroregulators in the CNS. For example, the inhibitory neurotransmitters γ-aminobutyric acid and glycine represent the major portion of chemical neurotransmission in the brain. There are also other classes of neuroregulators, including the pituitary hormone-releasing and -inhibiting factors, some of the pituitary hormones themselves, and the opioid peptides (endorphins and enkephalins) (Barchas, Akil, Elliott, Holman, & Watson, 1978; Eichelman et al., 1981).

Not only is the neurochemistry of aggression and violence in animals complex, but comparative data from human subjects are sparse and tentative. Domino and Krause (1974) measured plasma concentrations of tryptophan, the amino acid precursor of serotonin, before and after an oral tryptophan loading dose in 28 adult male chronic schizophrenics, 5 acute schizophrenics, 24 male volunteer prisoners, and a group of young adult male control subjects. The subjects in all four groups had been drug free for at least 1 month before the study. Fasting morning and evening plasma tryptophan levels were within the normal range for all groups, but the acute schizophrenics and prison volunteers had significantly lower mean plasma tryptophan levels than the normal controls and chronic schizophrenics. After tryptophan loading, the tryptophan tolerance curve of the prisoner volunteers was markedly different from that of both the normal controls and the chronic schizophrenics, the prisoners having a lower peak tryptophan concentration and a more prolonged decline of tryptophan to baseline. Although this study might suggest that prisoners could have reduced CNS serotonin, because their circulating levels of the serotonin precursor, tryptophan, were lower than those among other groups of subjects, the prisoners were not assessed along the dimension of aggressive and violent behaviors. Therefore, the implications of this study for human aggression are very weak.

Bioulac, Benezech, Renaud, Roche, and Noël (1978) studied cerebrospinal fluid (CSF) biogenic amine metabolites in six 47,XYY male patients, all of whom were institutionalized for antisocial behavior (arson, death threats, burglary, animal torture, assaults, fights, and robbery). Sleep recordings on these subjects indicated that sleep staging was normal, except for a slight decrease in total sleep time. Metabolism of dopamine, as estimated by CSF homovanillic acid turnover, was normal, whereas serotonin metabolism, as indicated by a dramatic decrease in CSF 5-hydroxyindoleacetic acid turnover, was reduced. These data are somewhat supportive of the hypothesis that reduced CNS serotonin may be a neurochemical substrate for increased violence, but the lack of an institutionalized nonviolent control group and the general observation that XYY men are not particularly violence prone (Rubin et al., 1981) make the findings of this study tenuous as well.

Sandler, Ruthven, Goodwin, Field, and Matthews (1979) studied 10 male violent prisoners and 10 nonviolent prisoners pair-matched for age, height, weight, and time spent in prison, but with no history of aggressive tendencies, by measuring plasma concentrations of free and conjugated phenylacetic acid, the major metabolite of phenylethylamine (an endogenous compound closely related to amphetamine). The violent prisoners had significantly higher circulating levels of both free and conjugated phenylacetic acid than the nonviolent, pair-matched controls. Sandler et al. (1979) pointed out that amphetamine and other psychostimulant drugs have a calming effect on hyperactive children with minimal brain dysfunction and suggested that the phenylethylamine overproduction detected in their violent prisoners represented "a compensatory response by the body in its attempt to curb aggressive tendencies present by virtue of some as-yet unknown functional derangement." However, the investigators did point out that the extent to which plasma phenylacetic acid levels reflect CNS phenylethylamine concentrations remains unknown.

Brown, Goodwin, Ballenger, Goyer, and Major (1979) and Brown, Ballenger, Minichiello, and Goodwin (1979) studied CSF concentrations of 5-hydroxyindoleacetic acid, homovanillic acid, and methoxyhydroxyphenylglycol, representing the major CNS metabolites of serotonin, dopamine, and norepinephrine, respectively, in 26 young adult military men with no history of major psychiatric illness but with various personality disorders and difficulties adjusting to the military environment. The subjects had no history of medical disorders and no drug use or abuse within 10 days of the study. Information on aggressive and violent behaviors was collected through 4 to 6 weeks of inpatient observation, full psychiatric and medical history, physical examination, and military job performance assessment. Emphasis was given to a lifetime history of aggressive behavior, particularly in response to authority figures. Across the subjects, a history of aggressive behavior showed no correlation with the dopamine metabolite, a significantly positive correlation ($+.64$) with the norepinephrine metabolite, and a signficantly negative correlation ($-.78$) with the serotonin metabolite. Brown et al. (1982) also studied CSF concentrations of the aforementioned metabolites of serotonin, dopamine, and norepinephrine in 12 young adult military men hospitalized for borderline personality disorder, some of whom had secondary diagnoses of brief reactive psychosis or schizoid personality disorder. These subjects were sicker than the subjects of their earlier study (Brown, Goodwin, Goyer, & Major, 1979; Brown, Ballenger, Minichiello, & Goodwin, 1979). The subjects had no history of medical disorders and no drug use or abuse within 10 days of the study. Information on aggressive and violent behaviors was collected as in the earlier study. The results were similar to those of the earlier study, in that a history of aggressive behavior showed no correlation with the dopamine metabolite but a significantly negative correlation ($-.53$) with the serotonin metabolite. However, in this study there was no correlation between a history of aggressive behavior and the norepinephrine metabolite.

Although there were several methodological limitations to these two studies, not the least of which is the variable extent to which lumbar CSF metabolites reflect brain, as opposed to spinal cord, biogenic amine metabolism, the results nevertheless are in accord with the animal data, summarized earlier, indicating that CNS norepinephrine neurotransmission may augment aggression and serotonin neurotransmission may decrease it.

Hinton (1981) performed a small pilot study on eight prisoners with multiple convictions for larceny and assaults, assessing their case records for the degree of physical violence in their antisocial acts and measuring norepinephrine to epinephrine ratios in their urine. There was a highly significant correlation (+.72) between violence ranking and these ratios, the changes being primarily in norepinephrine component. Here, too, only tenuous inferences can be made about CNS neurotransmitter activity in human aggression and violence, because the major fraction of urine norepinephrine comes from the peripheral sympathetic nervous system and not from the CNS.

There is greater evidence for the role of external biochemical factors in human violence. Specifically, abuse of alcohol and other substances (e.g. phencyclidine) is clearly related to human violent behavior. Because of its widespread abuse, alcohol may be the most important compound in this regard; alcohol intoxication has been associated with incidents along the entire spectrum of violence, from reckless driving to murder. The relation between alcohol and violence appears to be most clearly defined in persons whose underlying antisocial personality disorder predisposes them both to drinking and to violent behavior (Coid, 1982). Phencyclidine abuse has been of epidemic proportions in some parts of the United States since the early 1970s, and many intoxicated individuals have committed crazed, extremely violent acts, including murder and suicide (Noguchi & Nakamura, 1978). The pharmacological actions of these drugs are responsible for the increased antisocial behavior of abusers, and many of these actions are on the aforementioned CNS neurotransmitter systems. Different propensities to react with violence to alcohol and other substances of abuse exist among individuals, but these differences have not yet been related experimentally to functional differences in human CNS neurotransmitter systems.

Conclusions

The foregoing presentation of neuroendocrine and neurochemical studies of human aggression and violence highlights the complexity of the interaction between hormones, neuroregulators, and antisocial behavior. As is evident from the studies reviewed, the state of knowledge in the neuroendocrine and neurochemical areas is different. With reference to testosterone and aggression in men, measures of aggressive and violent behavior have been used to characterize groups of particularly violent individuals, but these measures have not been consistently related to increased plasma testosterone levels. Testosterone is not the only gonadal steroid hormone to have been studied in this regard; other examples are the estrogens and progesterone and their relation to dimensions of mood during the menstrual cycle, especially in women who have the so-called premenstrual tension syndrome, with outbursts of violent behavior surrounding the time of menses (Dalton, 1980; Rubin et al., 1981). In this area of research there has been a careful elucidation of hormone profiles both in women with normal menstrual cycles and in those with premenstrual tension syndrome, but the behavioral disturbances of premenstrual tension are just beginning to be codified. Furthermore, there has not been a consistent correlation between altered hormone profiles and disturbances of mood in women with this syndrome.

In contrast to the neuroendocrine studies, most of the neurochemical studies of aggression have been conducted in experimental laboratory animals. There have been additional areas of animal research that were not presented; for example, there are differing CNS neurochemistries in genetically inbred strains of mice that have different innate propensities for fighting behavior (Eichelman et al., 1981). These animal models are interesting in and of themselves, but they are far removed from the heterogeneous genetic makeup of most violent persons.

Though this review has focused on some of the biological correlates of human aggression and violence, it should not be construed as implying that these biological dimensions are preeminent substrates for these behaviors. Present-day knowledge indicates that there is a complex interaction between neuroendocrine and neurochemical influences on brain function and psychosocial and environmental forces that results in the expression of human aggression and violence. Thus the concept of a "nature versus nurture" dichotomy is anachronistic; the goal of future research must be to delineate the relative contributions of both sets of influences on these dimensions of antisocial behavior.

Continued research in these areas has practical implications, the most important of which are related to the kinds of treatment that are useful for violent individuals. Some sex offenders have responded to androgen antagonists, as mentioned earlier; some women with severe premenstrual mood disturbances have responded to particular hormone therapies; and other types of violent individuals, those, for example, with intermittent explosive disorders, have responded to psychotropic drugs such as lithium or, if there have been associated EEG abnormalities, to more traditional anticonvulsive agents such as diphenylhydantoin (Itil, 1981; Itil & Mukhopadhyay, 1978; Lena, 1979; Leventhal & Brodie, 1981; Sheard, 1978). Indeed, pharmacological approaches to the alleviation of violent behaviors have been among the most successful. Virtually all the classes of drugs used in neuropsychiatry – antipsychotics, antimanic agents, antianxiety agents, antidepressants, anticonvulsants, and sedatives – have been used effectively in certain individuals, once the psychopathological process underlying the violent behavior has been diagnosed (Cloninger, 1983; Madden & Lion, 1981). The success of diverse treatments in a variety of individuals with violent antisocial behaviors has been possible only because of adherence to the principle of neuroendocrine – and neurochemical – environment interaction and recognition that the various contributions of neuroendocrine, neurochemical, and psychosocial factors in different individuals dictate that approaches to treatment be individualized. As future research makes it possible to discern more accurately the relative contributions of each of these factors to human aggressive and violent behavior in specific individuals, effective and humane treatment approaches can be applied with even greater confidence.

Summary

Most research on the neuroendocrine and neurochemical correlates of antisocial behavior has focused on violent interpersonal behaviors such as assault, rape, and murder. The propensity of certain individuals toward violent antisocial behavior most likely develops over time, perhaps even having its origins during fetal development. The exposure of the fetal human brain to differing concentrations of androgenic hormones is the probable determinant of male versus female hypothalamic function and reproductive physiology. Long-term sexually dimorphic behavioral patterns, as well, may be set by this early hormonal milieu of the CNS.

Men evidence higher levels of most types of violence than women, and they perpetrate the majority of egregiously antisocial acts. Because circulating concentrations of testosterone, the primary androgenic hormone, are considerably higher in men than in women, the influence of this hormone may be one biological substrate of violent behavior. Correlations between circulating testosterone levels and violence have been sought in a number of studies, which have employed different groups of subjects and different methods for quantifying levels of aggression and violence.

These studies have ranged from the analysis of hostility questionnaires administered to normal male college students to the collection of histories of violent acts in male prisoners. Most have shown no relation between circulating testosterone and the behavioral measures, although a few intriguing studies have revealed higher testosterone levels in groups of especially violent persons, such as incarcerated rapist-murderers.

Endogenous biochemical substances other than testosterone have been investigated, but most studies have involved laboratory animals, with few and tenuous data being available from human studies. There is greater evidence for the role of external biochemical factors in violence; specifically, alcohol and drug (e.g., phencyclidine) abuse. Alcohol ingestion appears to be the most important in this regard; its relation to violence is clear. The pharmacological actions of these drugs are responsible for the increased antisocial behavior of abusers, although individuals differ in their propensities to react to these drugs.

Pharmacological approaches to the alleviation of violent behaviors have been among the most successful. Virtually all the classes of drugs used in neuropsychiatry have been used effectively with certain violent individuals. The heterogeneity of useful drugs bespeaks the heterogeneity of etiology – schizophrenia, manic depression, dementia, hyperirritability syndromes, and epilepsy, inter alia. Nevertheless, violent antisocial acts do occur in the absence of any discernible exogenous or endogenous biochemical or neuroendocrine disturbance, and they may not respond to drug or other somatic therapies, suggesting that such behavior can also be learned or conditioned. Thus elucidating the biosocial basis of human antisocial behavior remains difficult, because both the biological and the psychosocial contributions, and especially their interactions, must be quantified.

Acknowledgments

Supported by Office of Naval Research Contract NOOO14-81-K-0561 and National Institute of Mental Health Research Scientist Award MH 47363. Debra Hanaya provided expert secretarial assistance.

References

American Psychiatric Association (1952). *Diagnostic and statistical manual of mental disorders*. Washington, DC: Author.

American Psychiatric Association (1968). *Diagnostic and statistical manual of mental disorders* (2nd ed.). Washington, DC: Author.

American Psychiatric Association (1980). *Diagnostic and statistical manual of mental disorders* (3rd ed.). Washington, DC: Author.

Baker, S. W. (1980). Psychosexual differentiation in the human. *Biological Reproduction*, 22, 61–72.

Bancroft, J., & Skakkebaek, N. E. (1979). Androgens and human sexual behavior. In *Sex, hormones and behaviour* (Ciba Foundation Symposium 62). Amsterdam: Excerpta Medica.

Barchas, J. D., Akil, H., Elliott, G. R., Holman, R. B., & Watson, S. J. (1978). Behavioral neurochemistry: Neuroregulators and behavioral states. *Science, 200*, 964–73.

Bardin, C. W., & Wright, W. (1980). Androgen receptor deficiency: Testicular feminization, its variants, and differential diagnosis. *Annals of Clinical Research, 12*, 236–42.

Becker, K. L. (1972). Clinical and therapeutic experiences with Klinefelter's syndrome. *Fertility and Sterility, 23*, 568–78.

Benton, D. (1981). The extrapolation from animals to man: The example of testosterone and aggression. In: P. F. Brain & D. Benton (Eds.), *Multidisciplinary approaches to aggression research*, (pp. 401–18). Amsterdam: Elsevier/North Holland.

Berger, P. A., & Gulevich, G. D. (1981). Violence and mental illness. In D. A. Hamburg & M. B. Trudeau (Eds.), *Biobehavioral aspects of aggression* (pp. 141–68). New York: Alan R. Liss.

Bioulac, B., Benezech, M., Renaud, B., Roche, D., & Noël, B. (1978). Biogenic amines in 47,XYY syndrome. *Neuropsychobiology, 4*, 366–70.

Blumer, D., & Migeon, C. (1975). Hormone and hormonal agents in the treatment of aggression. *Journal of Nervous and Mental Disorders, 160*, 127–37.

Brown, G. L., Ballenger, J. C., Minichiello, M. D., & Goodwin, F. K. (1979). Human aggression and its relationship to cerebrospinal fluid, 5-hydroxyindoleacetic acid, 3-methoxy-4-hydroxyphenylglycol, and homovanillic acid. In M. Sandler (Ed.), *Psychopharmacology of aggression* (pp. 131–48). New York: Raven Press.

Brown, G. L., Ebert, M. H., Goyer, P. F., Jimerson, D. C., Klein, W. J., Bunney, W. E., & Goodwin, F. K. (1982). Aggression, suicide and serotonin: Relationships to CSF amine metabolites. *American Journal of Psychiatry, 139*, 741–6.

Brown, G. L., Goodwin, F. K., Ballenger, J. C., Goyer, P. F., & Major, L. F. (1979). Aggression in human correlates with cerebrospinal fluid amine metabolites. *Psychiatric Research, 1*, 131–9.

Brown, W. A. (1980). Testosterone and human behavior. *International Journal of Mental Health, 9*(3–4), 45–66.

Buss, A. H., & Durkee, A. (1957). An inventory for assessing different kinds of hostility. *Journal of Consulting Psychology, 21*, 343–9.

Cannon, W. B. (1932). *The wisdom of the body*. New York: Norton.

Cloninger, C. R. (1983). Drug treatment of antisocial behavior. In D. Graham-Smith, H. Hippius, & G. Winokur (Eds.), *Clinical psychopharmacology* (Vol. 2, pp. 353–70). Amsterdam: Excerpta Medica.

Coid, J. (1982). Alcoholism and violence. *Drug and Alcohol Dependence, 9*, 1–14.

Condon, W. S., & Sander, I. W. (1974). Neonate movement is synchronized with adult speech: Interactional participation and language acquisition. *Science, 181*, 99–101.

Cooper, A. G. (1981). A placebo-controlled trial of the antiandrogen cyproterone acetate in deviant hypersexuality. *Comprehensive Psychiatry, 22*, 458–65.

Cooper, A. J., Ismail, A. A. A., Phanjoo, A. L., & Love, D. L. (1972). Antiandrogen (cyproterone acetate) therapy in deviant hypersexuality. *British Journal of Psychiatry, 120*, 59–63.

Dalton, K. (1980). Cyclical criminal acts in premenstrual syndrome. *Lancet, ii*, 1070–1.

Davidson, J. M., Camargo, C. A., & Smith, E. R. (1979). Effects of androgen on sexual behavior in hypogonadal men. *Journal of Clinical Endocrinology and Metabolism, 48*, 955–8.

Davies, T. S. (1974). Cyproterone acetate for male hypersexuality. *Journal of International Medical Research, 2,* 159–63.

de Lacerda, L., Kowarski, A., Johanson, A. J., Athanasiou, R., & Migeon, C. (1973). Integrated concentration and circadian variation of plasma testosterone in normal men. *Journal of Clinical Endocrinology and Metabolism, 37,* 366–71.

Dodge, P. R., Prensky, A. L., & Feigin, R. D. (1975). *Nutrition and the developing nervous system.* St. Louis, MO: Mosby.

Doering, C. H., Brodie, H. K. H., Kraemer, H. C., Moos, R. H., Becker, H. B., & Hamburg, D. A. (1975). Negative affect and plasma testosterone: A longitudinal human study. *Psychosomatic Medicine, 37,* 484–91.

Domino, E. F., & Krause, R. R. (1974). Plasma tryptophan tolerance curves in drug free normal controls, schizophrenic patients and prisoner volunteers. *Journal of Psychiatric Research, 10,* 247–61.

Eaton, G. G., Goy, R. W., & Phoenix, C. H. (1973). Effects of testosterone treatment in adulthood on sexual behaviour of female pseudohermaphrodite rhesus monkeys. *Nature, New Biology, 242,* 119–20.

Ehrenkranz, J., Bliss, E., & Sheard, M. H. (1974). Plasma testosterone: Correlation with aggressive behavior and social dominance in man. *Psychosomatic Medicine, 36,* 469–75.

Eichelman, B. (1979). The role of biogenic amines in aggressive behavior. In M. Sandler (Ed.), *Psychopharmacology of aggression* (pp. 61–93). New York: Raven Press.

Eichelman, B., Elliott, G. R., & Barchas, J. D. (1981). Biochemical, pharmacological, and genetic aspects of aggression. In D. A. Hamburg & M. B. Trudeau (Eds.), *Biobehavioral aspects of aggression* (pp. 51–84). New York: Liss.

Elias, M. (1981). Serum cortisol, testosterone, and testosterone-binding globulin responses to competitive fighting in human males. *Aggressive Behavior, 7,* 215–24.

Goldzieher, J. W., Dozier, T. S., Smith, K. D., & Steinberger, E. (1976). Improving the diagnostic reliability of rapidly fluctuating plasma hormone levels by optimized multiple-sampling techniques. *Journal of Clinical Endocrinology and Metabolism, 43,* 824–30.

Gorski, R. A. (1971). Gonadal hormones and the perinatal development of neuroendocrine function. In L. Martini & W. F. Ganong (Eds.), *Frontiers in neuroendocrinology 1971* (pp. 237–90). New York: Oxford University Press.

Gorski, R. A. (1980). Sexual differentiation of the brain. In D. T. Krieger & J. C. Hughes (Eds.), *Neuroendocrinology* (pp. 215–22). Sunderland, MA: Sinauer Associates.

Goy, R. W. (1968). Organizing effects of androgen on the behaviour of rhesus monkeys. In R. P. Michael (Ed.), *Endocrinology and human behaviour* (pp. 12–31). London: Oxford University Press.

Goy, R. W., Wolf, J. E., & Eisele, S. G. (1977). Experimental female hermaphroditism in rhesus monkeys: Anatomical and psychological characteristics. In J. Money & H. Musaph (Eds.), *Handbook of sexology* (pp. 139–56). Amsterdam: Elsevier/North Holland Biomedical Press.

Harlan, R. E., Gordon, J. H., & Gorski, R. A. (1979). Sexual differentiation of the brain: Implications for neuroscience. In D. M. Schneider (Ed.), *Reviews of neuroscience* (Vol. 4, pp. 31–71). New York: Raven Press.

Hinton, J. W. (1981). Biological approaches to criminality. In P. F. Brain & D. Benton (Eds.), *Multidisciplinary approaches to aggression research* (pp. 447–61). Amsterdam: Elsevier/North Holland.

Huntingford, F. A. (1980). A review of the methods used to describe and measure aggressive behavior in physiological studies. *Aggressive Behavior, 6,* 205–15.

Itil, T. M. (1981). Drug therapy in the management of aggression. In P. F. Brain & D. Benton

(Eds.), *Multidisciplinary approaches to aggression research* (pp. 489–502). Amsterdam: Elsevier/North Holland.

Itil, T. M., & Mukhopadhyay, S. (1978). Pharmacological management of human violence. *Modern Problems in Pharmacopsychology, 13,* 139–58.

Judd, H. L., Parker, D. C., Siler, T. M., & Yen, S. S. C. (1974). The nocturnal rise of plasma testosterone in pubertal boys. *Journal of Clinical Endocrinology and Metabolism, 38,* 710–13.

Karczmar, A. G., Richardson, D. L., & Kindel, G. (1978). Neuropharmacological and related aspects of animal aggression. *Progress in Neuro-Psychopharmacology, 2,* 611–31.

Kling, A. (1975). Testosterone and aggressive behavior in man and non-human primates. In B. E. Eleftheriou & R. L. Sprott (Eds.), *Hormonal correlates of behavior: Vol 1. A lifespan view* (pp. 305–23). New York: Plenum Press.

Klüver, H., & Bucy, P. C. (1939). Preliminary analysis of functions of temporal lobes in monkeys. *Archives of Neurological Psychiatry, 42,* 979–1000.

Kreuz, L. E., & Rose, R. M. (1972). Assessment of aggressive behavior and plasma testosterone in a young criminal population. *Psychosomatic Medicine, 34,* 321–32.

Lena, B. (1979). Lithium therapy in hyperaggressive behavior in adolescence. In M. Sandler (Ed.), *Psychopharmacology of aggression* (pp. 197–203). New York: Raven Press.

Leventhal, B. L., & Brodie, H. K. H. (1981). The pharmacology of violence. In D. A. Hamburg & M. B. Trudeau (Eds.), *Biobehavioral aspects of aggression* (pp. 85–106). New York: Liss.

Lev-Ran, A. (1977). Sex reversal as related to clinical syndromes in human beings. In J. Money & H. Musaph (Eds.), *Handbook of sexology,* (pp. 157–73). Amsterdam: Elsevier/North-Holland.

Lief, H. I. (1963). Contemporary forms of violence. In J. H. Masserman (Ed.), *Violence and war: With clinical studies, science and psychoanalysis VI* (pp. 55–68). New York: Grune & Stratton.

Madden, D. J., & Lion, J. R. (1981). Clinical management of aggression. In P. F. Brain & D. Benton (Eds.), *Multidisciplinary approaches to aggression research* (pp. 477–88). Amsterdam: Elsevier/North Holland.

Matthews, R. (1979). Testosterone levels in aggressive offenders. In M. Sandler (Ed.), *Psychopharmacology of aggression* (pp. 123–30). New York: Raven Press.

Mattson, Å., Schalling, D., Olweus, D., Löw, H., & Swenson, J. (1980). Plasma testosterone, aggressive behavior, and personality dimensions in young male delinquents. *Journal of the American Academy of Child Psychiatry, 19,* 476–90.

McEwen, B. S. (1980). The brain as a target organ of endocrine hormones. In D. T. Krieger & J. C. Hughes (Eds.), *Neuroendocrinology* (pp. 33–42). Sunderland, MA: Sinauer.

Meyer, W. J., Walker, P. A., Wiederking, C., Money, J., Kowarski, A. A., Migeon, C., & Borgaonkar, D. S. (1977). Pituitary function in adult males receiving medroxyprogesterone acetate. *Fertility and Sterility, 28,* 1072–6.

Meyer-Bahlburg, H. F. L., Boon, D. A., Sharma, M., & Edwards, J. A. (1974). Aggressiveness and testosterone measures in man. *Psychosomatic Medicine, 36,* 269–74.

Money, J. (1973). Effects of prenatal androgenization and deandrogenization on behavior in human beings. In W. F. Ganong & L. Martini (Eds.), *Frontiers in neuroendocrinology 1973* (pp. 249–66). New York: Oxford University Press.

Money, J., Wiedeking, C., Walker, P., Migeon, C., Meyer, W., & Borgaonkar, D. (1975). 47,XYY and 46,XY males with antisocial and/or sex-offending behavior: Antiandrogen therapy plus counseling. *Psychoneuroendocrinology, 1,* 165–78.

Monti, P. M., Brown, W. A., & Corriveau, D. P. (1977). Testosterone and components of aggressive and sexual behavior in man. *American Journal of Psychiatry, 134,* 692–4.

Moyer, K. E. (1968). Kinds of aggression and their physiological basis. *Communications and Behavioral Biology, Part A, 22,* 65–87.

Moyer, K. E. (1974). Sex differences in aggression. In R. C. Friedman, R. M. Richart, & R. L. van de Wiele (Eds.), *Sex differences in behavior* (pp. 335–72). New York: Wiley.

Naess, O., Attramdal, A., & Hansson, V. (1977). Receptors for testosterone and 5α-dihydrotestosterone in the anterior pituitary and various areas of the brain. In P. Troen & H. R. Nankin (Eds.), *The testis in normal and infertile men* (pp. 227–41). New York: Raven.

Nieschlag, E. (1979). The endocrine function of the human testis in regard to sexuality. In *Sex, hormones, and behaviour* (Ciba Foundation Symposium 62). Amsterdam: Excerpta Medica.

Noguchi, T. T., & Nakamura, G. R. (1978). Phencyclidine-related deaths in Los Angeles County, 1976. *Journal of Forensic Science, 23,* 503–7.

Olweus, D. (1979). Stability of aggressive reaction patterns in males: A review. *Psychological Bulletin, 86,* 852–75.

Olweus, D., Mattson, Å., Schalling, D., & Löw, H. (1980). Testosterone, aggression, physical, and personality dimensions in normal adolescent males. *Psychosomatic Medicine, 42,* 253–69.

Persky, H., O'Brien, C. P., Fine, E., Howard, W. J., Khan, M. A., & Beck, R. W. (1977). The effect of alcohol and smoking on testosterone function and aggression in chronic alcoholics. *American Journal of Psychiatry, 134,* 621–5.

Persky, H., Smith, K. D., & Basu, G. K. (1971). Relation of psychologic measures of aggression and hostility to testosterone production in man. *Psychosomatic Medicine, 33,* 265–77.

Phoenix, C. H., Goy, R. W., & Young, W. C. (1967). Sexual behavior: General aspects. In L. Martini & W. F. Ganong (Eds.), *Neuroendocrinology* (Vol 2, pp. 163–96). New York: Academic Press.

Rada, R. T., Laws, D. R., & Kellner, R. (1976). Plasma testosterone levels in the rapist. *Psychosomatic Medicine, 38,* 257–68.

Reinisch, J. M. (1976). Effects of prenatal hormone exposure on physical and psychological development in humans and animals: With a note on the state of the field. In E. J. Sachar (Ed.), *Hormones, behavior, and psychopathology* (pp. 69–94). New York: Raven Press.

Reinisch, J. M., & Karow, W. G. (1977). Prenatal exposure to synthetic progestins and estrogens: Effects on human development. *Archives of Sexual Behavior, 6,* 257–88.

Rodgers, R. J. (1981). Drugs, aggression and behavioral methods. In P. F. Brain & D. Benton (Eds.), *Multidisciplinary approaches to aggression research* (pp. 325–40). Amsterdam: Elsevier/North Holland.

Rose, R. M. (1972). The psychological effects of androgens and estrogens: A review. In R. I. Shader (Ed.), *Psychiatric complications of medical drugs* (pp. 251–93). New York: Raven Press.

Rose, R. M. (1975). Testosterone, aggression, and homosexuality: A review of the literature and implications for future research. In E. J. Sachar (Ed.), *Topics in psychoendocrinology* (pp. 83–103). New York: Grune & Stratton.

Rose, R. M. (1978). Neuroendocrine correlates of sexual and aggressive behavior in humans. In M. A. Lipton, A. Di Mascio, & K. F. Killam (Eds.), *Psychopharmacology: A generation of progress* (pp. 541–52). New York: Raven Press.

Rubin, R. T., Reinisch, J. M., & Haskett, R. F. (1981). Postnatal gonadal steroid effects on human behavior. *Science, 211,* 1318–24.

Sandler, M., Ruthven, C. R. J., Goodwin, B. L., Field, H., & Matthews, R. (1979). Phenylethylamine in human aggressive behavior. In M. Sandler (Ed.), *Psychopharmacology of aggression* (pp. 149–58). New York: Raven Press.

Scaramella, T. J., & Brown, W. A. (1978). Serum testosterone and aggressiveness in hockey players. *Psychosomatic Medicine, 40,* 262–5.

Sheard, M. H. (1978). The effect of lithium and other ions on aggressive behavior. *Modern Problems in Pharmacopsychology, 13,* 53–68.

Sheard, M. H. (1979). Testosterone and aggression. In M. Sandler (Ed.), *Psychopharmacology of aggression* (pp. 111–21). New York: Raven Press.

Simon, N. G. (1981). Hormones and human aggression: A comparative perspective. *International Journal of Mental Health, 10*(2–3), 60–74.

Smart, J. L. (1981). Undernutrition and aggression. In P. F. Brain & D. Benton (Eds.), *Multidisciplinary approaches to aggression research* (pp. 179–91). Amsterdam: Elsevier/North Holland.

Valzelli, L. (1981). *Psychobiology of aggression and violence.* New York: Raven Press.

Van Moffaert, M. (1976). Social reintegration of sexual delinquents by a combination of psychotherapy and anti-androgen treatment. *Acta Psychiatrica Scandinavica, 53,* 29–34.

Zuppinger, K., Engel, E., Forbes, A. P., Mantooth, L., & Claffey, J. (1967). Klinefelter's syndrome, a clinical and cytogenetic study in twenty-four cases. *Acta Endocrinologica, 54*(Suppl. 113), 5–48.

14   Testosterone and adrenaline: aggressive antisocial behavior in normal adolescent males

Dan Olweus

This chapter consists of two relatively independent parts. One concerns the relation between aggressive antisocial behavior and testosterone, the other the relation between the same or related behavior patterns and adrenaline. In many ways these relations are quite different, but there is a common denominator in that both parts refer to an association of hormonal factors with aggressive antisocial behavior. In addition, the empirical results presented are based on the same sample of healthy male adolescent subjects. The study of the adrenaline – behavior relation has not been reported before. Basic information on the testosterone study can be found in other publications (e.g., Olweus, in 1983; Olweus, Mattsson, Schalling, & Löw, 1980). In this chapter, some new analyses of testosterone – behavior relations will be presented in a causal analytic framework.

Testosterone

Relatively recent studies of the relation between plasma testosterone levels and aggressive antisocial behavior in the human male have yielded somewhat conflicting results (for references, see Olweus et al., 1980). However, when combined with findings of animal studies (e.g., Moyer, 1976; Rose, 1975), the empirical results on human males suggest that there may be a positive relation between plasma testosterone levels and one or more aspects of aggressive, impulsive, and antisocial behavior patterns. For animals, the findings also indicate that testosterone may have a causal influence on some forms of aggressive behavior. This, of course, does not preclude the possibility that an individual's testosterone level is affected by environmental and experiential factors (including the individual's own behavior).

263

If a positive relation is found between testosterone level and a particular aggressive or antisocial characteristic (and this relation can be given a causal interpretation), it is essential to find out what the mechanisms mediating that relation are. It is also of great interest to get an idea of the relative importance of the possible influence of testosterone on behavior. To highlight this issue, it is essential to have data on individual differences in the relevant behavioral characteristics before production of testosterone (in sizable quantities) is initiated as well as after it has been going on for some time. Such information was available in the project to be described here.

The issue of possible mechanisms in the testosterone–behavior relation has been discussed in a previous publication (Olweus, 1983). However, that discussion was couched in general terms, and in this context the analyses will be elaborated in a path analytic framework. For such analyses to be reasonably complete and nonspurious, it is essential to include information on other, causally prior variables that may affect the individual's level of testosterone as well as his behavior patterns. A good deal of such data were also available in the present study.

Procedure

The subjects were 58 healthy boys, 15–17 years old, with a median age of 16. They were selected from the public school districts of Solna, a suburb in the Stockholm metropolitan area in Sweden, to provide a roughly random sample of the total male student population of grade 9 (275 boys). The boys provided two sets of blood samples (separated by 1 month) for plasma testosterone assays. The test–retest reliability or the stability of the individual differences, as expressed in the correlation between the two sets of measurements, was .63. The reliability of the individual average testosterone levels was .77 (Spearman–Brown corrected). The mean testosterone value for the whole group was 544 ± 141 ng/100 ml (range 197–901 ng/100 ml).

Of the 58 boys, 3 were in Tanner Pubertal Stage 3, 9 in Stage 4, and 43 in Stage 5 (adult) according to pubic hair development. The correlation between pubertal stage and testosterone level was .44.

Approximately 1 month before the blood samples were drawn, the subjects completed a number of personality inventories (see Olweus et al., 1980). In addition, highly reliable peer ratings of habitual aggressive behavior and physical strength were available. Data on such physical variables as height, weight, chest circumference, and pubertal stage were collected during a physical examination.

Table 14.1. *Correlation between testosterone levels and individual items from the verbal and physical aggression scales* (N = 58)

Item	Correlation coefficient (r)
Verbal aggression	
1. When an adult is unfair to me, I get angry and protest.	.18
2. When an adult tries to take my place in a line, I firmly tell him it is my place.	.24
3. When a teacher criticizes me, I tend to answer back and protest.	.33
4. When a teacher has promised that we will have some fun but then changes his (her) mind, I protest.	.19
5. When an adult tries to boss me around, I resist strongly.	.33
Physical aggression	
6. When a boy starts fighting with me, I fight back.	.33
7. When a boy is nasty with me, I try to get even with him.	.37
8. When a boy teases me, I try to give him a good beating.	.15
9. I fight with other boys at school.[a]	.05
10. I really admire the fighters among the boys.[a]	.11

[a] These items do not contain a clear element of provocation.

Testosterone and aggression

The basic finding of the study was a substantial correlation of testosterone level with each of two scales of the Olweus Aggression Inventory: verbal aggression ($r = .38$) and physical aggression ($r = .36$). The simple composite of these two scales correlated .44 with testosterone level.

Closer analysis of the individual items of the verbal and physical aggression scales revealed an interesting pattern: It was primarily items involving a response to provocation, including threat or unfair treatment, that showed a clear correlation with testosterone levels (Table 14.1). The first eight items of Table 14.1 all contain an element of provocation, by adults or peers. The correlations with testosterone were quite high for several of these items, considering the fact that the reliability of individual items is generally rather low. Conversely, the correlations for the last two items, which do not imply provocation, were negligible. In addition, the only peer rating scale containing an element of provocation, verbal protest, showed the highest correlation ($r = .24$) with testosterone level. The wording of this rating dimension was as follows: "When a teacher criticizes him, he tends to answer back and protest." The correlation of testosterone with the composite of the three peer rating dimensions – starts fights, verbal protest, and verbal hurt – was .21. This composite has been used in several of my studies as a broad measure of aggressive, destructive behavior (e.g., Olweus, 1984).

In summarizing these findings, it was concluded that dimensions reflecting intensity and/or frequency of aggressive responses to provocation and threat were most clearly and directly related to testosterone. Other dimensions measuring aggressive attitude or impulses and unprovoked physical or verbal aggression also showed positive, but weaker correlations with testosterone.

Testosterone and frustration tolerance

Another result of interest was the positive correlation ($r = .28$) between testosterone levels and a self-report scale called lack of frustration tolerance. This scale contained only three items, all of them focusing on the individual's habitual level of impatience and irritability ("I become easily impatient and irritable if I have to wait"; "Others say that I easily lose patience"; "I become easily impatient if I have to keep on with the same thing for a long time"). The internal consistency (α) reliability of this short scale was .59. The above results suggested that adolescent boys with higher levels of testosterone tended to be habitually more impatient and irritable than boys with lower testosterone levels.

Causal interpretations

A few comments on methodology. The main findings of the present study were positive associations of testosterone level with the self-report scales of verbal and physical aggression, mainly reflecting responsiveness to provocation and threat and lack of frustration tolerance. In addition, lower positive correlations were obtained with peer ratings of aggressive behavior and a self-report scale of antisocial behavior (covering such behaviors as petty theft, truancy, and destruction of others' property; $r = .17$).

Theoretical considerations and preliminary statistical analyses of the available data suggested that testosterone in adolescent boys might have two chief effects on behavior: One was mainly a direct influence on what can be called provoked aggressive behavior as measured by the self-report scales of verbal and physical aggression. The other was a more indirect effect on unprovoked (or destructive) aggression, reflected in the peer rating composite, and generally antisocial behavior (measured by the self-report scale of antisocial behavior) via the mediating variable (relative) lack of frustration tolerance (called low frustration tolerance in the following). These and other possibilities will now be explored using the technique of path analysis.

The above statements are based on the assumption that testosterone influences aggressive behavior. Such an assumption is not unreasonable in view of the findings from many experimental studies on animals. In addition, because data for the aggression and frustration tolerance variables were also available at an earlier time, at grade 6 (median age, 13 years), this permitted testing of the possibility that an individual's level of testosterone was basically "determined" by these same variables measured 3 years earlier. If such effects were found, this would very likely imply that what appeared to be a causal effect of testosterone on aggressive behavior was, completely or partly, spurious. Similarly, the inclusion of child-rearing variables (derived from parent interviews), which in previous analyses (Olweus, 1980) had been found to be important in the development of aggressive behavior (chiefly unprovoked aggressive behavior), provided additional possibilities of detecting spuriousness in the testosterone-aggression relation.

Details about path analysis and some relevant references to the literature on this topic can be found in Olweus (1980). Because the present sample was of limited size, the choice was made to retain path coefficients of variables that, in a stepwise regression, accounted for at least 1% of the variance in the relevant dependent variable. The same procedure was followed in Olweus (1980).

Finally, it should be emphasized that the findings and interpretations presented here should be regarded as suggestive rather than conclusive. The results should be replicated with other samples before our interpretation can be considered reasonably tenable.

Testosterone and provoked aggressive behavior. The main results from the path analysis are presented in Figure 14.1. In this context, primary attention will be directed to the right side of the figure. The substantial coefficient ($\beta = .34$) for the path leading from testosterone to provoked aggressive behavior at grade 9 confirms the preliminary impression that testosterone has a direct causal influence on this aggression variable, reflecting responsiveness to provocation and threat. The original correlation of .44 was moderately reduced only when other, causally prior variables were controlled for. Given the causal ordering implied in the model, this result indicates that a higher level of testosterone leads to an increased readiness to respond vigorously and assertively to provocations and threats.

The figure also shows that testosterone resulted in a reduction in frus-

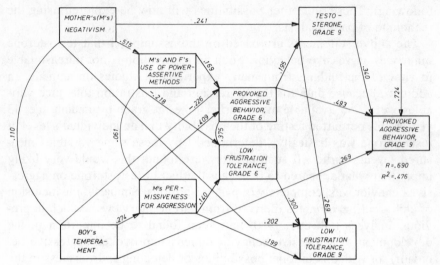

Figure 14.1. Path diagram of variables determining provoked aggressive behavior at grade 9 (N = 58).

tration tolerance at grade 9 (β = .269). It should be noted, however, that low frustration tolerance at grade 9 had no effect on the provoked aggression variable. This is in contrast with the results to be discussed below.

As could be expected, the largest path coefficient leading to provoked aggressive behavior at grade 9 (β = .493) came from the variable itself measured 3 years earlier. This indicates a moderate degree of stability over time (r = .539) in this variable (see Olweus, 1979). However, the relative stability of the variable did not prevent testosterone from having a substantial effect on grade 9 behavior, as discussed above.

Testosterone and unprovoked aggressive behavior. The pattern of findings is shown in Figure 14.2. Here it should be noted that testosterone had no direct effect on the ultimate dependent variable, unprovoked aggressive behavior at grade 9. There was, however, a clear indirect effect (.269 × .337 = .091), with low frustration tolerance at grade 9 as a mediating variable. The stability of the ultimate dependent variable was somewhat higher in this case (β = .582; r = .623) than in Figure 14.1.

Two additional aspects of the study deserve mention. First, there were no paths from unprovoked aggressive behavior at grade 6 or low frustration tolerance at grade 6 to the testosterone variable. Thus the boys' levels of testosterone were not "determined" by these causally prior variables. Second, there was only a weak correlation between unpro-

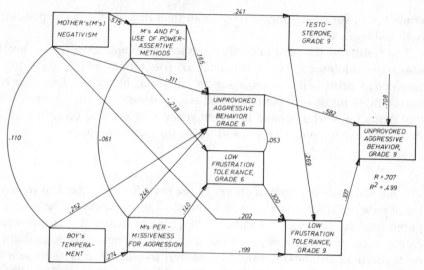

Figure 14.2. Path diagram of variables determining unprovoked aggressive behavior grade 9 ($N = 58$).

voked aggressive behavior and low frustration tolerance at grade 6 ($r = .053$), whereas the correlation between them was considerably higher at grade 9 ($r = .408$). Thus an association had emerged in the period from grade 6 to 9, and according to the path analytic results, testosterone was the major variable accounting for the association. This pattern of findings clearly supports the assumption that testosterone may act as a causal variable and influence some forms of aggressive behavior in humans.

In summary, the path analytic results indicate that a high level of testosterone in puberty makes a boy more impatient and irritable, which increases his readiness to engage in aggressive behavior of the unprovoked and destructive kind (starting fights and saying nasty things without provocation). In contrast with the findings for provoked aggressive behavior, the effects of testosterone were indirect in the present case.

Testosterone and antisocial behavior. The relation of testosterone level to the self-report scale of antisocial behavior (grade 9) was positive but fairly weak ($r = .17$). A path analysis with the scale of antisocial behavior as the ultimate dependent variable (not shown here) gave results that very much paralleled those for unprovoked aggressive behavior at grade 9. As would be expected, the correlation of these two variables was substantial ($r = .610$). Thus testosterone had only an indirect effect on antisocial behavior at grade 9 mediated by low frustration tolerance. The coefficient for the path from low frustration tolerance at grade 9 to antisocial behavior at grade 9 was somewhat larger (β = .460) than that for the corresponding path in Figure 14.2.

The results of the path analysis suggest that a high testosterone level lowers an adolescent boy's tolerance of frustration, which leads to a heightened probability of engaging in antisocial behavior. This line of reasoning is intuitively plausible and is consistent with the observation that many boys who behave in an antisocial way seem to do so out of a desire for excitement, change, and thrills (to avoid boredom).

The possible role of pubertal stage. In the present study, the best indicator of pubertal stage was a classification into Tanner stages on the basis of pubic hair development. If pubertal stage were included as a possible causal variable in the analyses (which may seem somewhat superfluous on theoretical grounds) it would be natural to place it after the grade 6 variables but before testosterone and the other grade 9 variables. When the three path analyses were repeated with pubertal stage included, the path coefficients relevant to our discussion were practically unchanged. The effects of pubertal stage were totally indirect and mediated by the testosterone variable, as would be expected on theoretical grounds.

Strength of relations and conclusion

To gain perspective on the preceding discussion, it is essential to consider the relative importance of testosterone in determining aggressive antisocial behavior. With regard to provoked aggressive behavior at grade 9, the analyses indicated that the role of testosterone may be relatively marked. It may be added that the child-rearing factors found to be important in the development of unprovoked aggressive behavior had weaker effects on the provoked aggressive behavior variable.

Considering the boys' readiness to engage in aggressive, destructive, and antisocial behavior, it is obvious that testosterone was only one of many possible causal factors, and one with indirect and fairly weak effects. At the same time, it should be made clear that the reported coefficients, based on fallible variables, were underestimates of the true relations. All in all, it can be concluded that the role of testosterone in the development of aggressive antisocial behavior patterns certainly merits further study.

Adrenaline

Procedure

In the same study reported in the preceding sections, my colleagues (D. Schalling, A. Mattsson, and L. Levi) and I collected data on catecholamine excretion in the urine. On each of two mornings, separated by approximately 1 month, the subjects ($N = 59$) provided two samples of urine. The interval between the two sample collections in a day was about 2 hours. The first of the examination days can generally be considered to have been more stressful than the second one, because it involved a venipuncture (for the determination of testosterone level) and the majority of the boys (62%) had never experienced this procedure before. In addition, the investigation took place in hospital localities unknown to the boys. On the second day, no blood samples were drawn and the boys delivered their two urine collections in a relatively familiar environment, the school nurse's office.

The urine samples were analyzed for free adrenaline and noradrenaline by a fluorimetric technique (Andersson, Hovmöller, Karlsson & Svensson, 1974; von Euler & Lishajko, 1961). To take weight differences into account, the catecholamine variables were expressed in units of picomole divided by body weight. However, the results would not have been much different if the analyses had been made on weight-uncorrected values.

Because the relations noted were weaker and less consistent with noradrenaline and with ratios of noradrenaline to adrenaline, only findings with the adrenaline dimension will be discussed here. The average correlation of the four adrenaline samples was .45. If the average of the four measurements is used as a composite measure of adrenaline level, the reliability of this composite can be estimated to be .762 (by the Spearman–Brown formula). The correlation of the first and the second sets of measurements was .48 (uncorrected for measurement errors), indicating moderate stability over approximately 1 month.

These analyses of measurement characteristics suggest that the use of a single adrenaline sample in a study may be of limited value, unless the relations or effects investigated are quite strong.

Some results

From the perspective of this volume, the most interesting finding was a clear negative correlation of $-.44$ between adrenaline level and the peer rating composite of unprovoked aggressive, destructive behavior (start fights, verbal protest, and verbal hurt; see the section on testosterone and aggression). If corrected for unreliability of measurement, this coefficient becomes $-.55$. Thus the more aggressive boys had lower levels of adrenaline excretion in these situations.

Similarly, a group of 14 highly aggressive bullies (see Olweus, 1978) chosen by teacher nominations (four of the bullies were included in the random sample of "normal" adolescents) had clearly lower levels of adrenaline than the remaining boys. I shall return in a later section to this finding of a negative relation between adrenaline level and unprovoked aggressive behavior, but first it is important to consider a few other results.

Adrenaline level correlated negatively ($r = -.48$) with the extraversion–introversion scale from the Eysenck Personality Questionnaire (Eysenck & Eysenck, 1975) and positively with, in particular, the psychic anxiety scale ($r = .42$) from the Multi-Component Anxiety Inventory (Schalling, Cronholm, & Åsberg, 1975) and the Situation-Oriented Questionnaire ($r = .39$). The latter measure (situational anxiety) was developed to assess the subjects' degree of state anxiety and worry in relation to the venipuncture and the investigative situation (see Olweus et al., 1980, for a brief description of this scale). The psychic anxiety scale, however, was designed to reflect more habitual anxiety reasons (trait anxiety). Their intercorrelation was .56, whereas the correlation of unprovoked aggressive behavior with the extraversion scale was .46.

The peer rating dimension of unprovoked aggressive behavior was largely independent of the two anxiety scales ($r = -.18$ with psychic anxiety and $r = -.13$ with situational anxiety), whereas the extraversion scale showed higher correlations with them ($r = -.41$ and $-.38$, respectively).

Results along these lines, though somewhat weaker, were also obtained with other self-report scales: negative relations of adrenaline level with scales measuring aggressive, impulsive, acting-out behavior and positive associations with measures of different aspects of anxiety, apprehension, and feelings of inadequacy.

Determination of an individual's adrenaline level

These findings lead to the question: What factors determine an individual's level of adrenaline excretion? Of course, this question cannot be fully dealt with here. I shall focus on only a few central factors, of relevance from the present psychoendocrinological perspective.

It has been shown in extensive research programs (e.g., Frankenhaeuser, 1971, 1979; Levi, 1972) that situations characterized by novelty, uncertainty, change, effort, vigilance, and achievement demands tend to increase adrenaline excretion. It has also been found that emotionally stressful and threatening situations result in a higher adrenaline output. Sometimes the diffuse word "stress" has been used as a blanket term for situations that increase the individual's level of adrenaline excretion.

In an attempt to provide a possible integration of the somewhat disparate findings in the literature, a model of factors and processes involved in the determination of an individual's adrenaline output will be presented. It should be noted, however, that only some of the main ideas can be outlined here and that the formulation is tentative; one or more aspects may need revision.

Going back to the empirical findings, the boys' adrenaline levels seemed to be related primarily to two partly independent behavioral dimensions. One reflected aggressive, outgoing, acting-out behavior and its opposite, well-controlled socialized, introverted, nonaggressive behavior. This dimension is represented in the present study by the composite of unprovoked aggressive behavior and extraversion (given equal weight). The other was anxious, insecure versus nonanxious, emotionally stable reaction patterns, here defined by the composite of psychic anxiety and situational anxiety (given equal weight).

The correlations of these composites with adrenaline level were $-.526$ and $.465$, respectively. When the two composites were combined in a multiple regression equation with adrenaline level as the dependent variable, R was $.601$. Addition of the interaction between the two composites $(X_1 \times X_2)$ increased the multiple regression to $.641$ ($p < .05$ for addition of the interaction term.) The interpretation of this interaction is that the negative relation between aggressive, acting-out behavior and adrenaline level becomes increasingly strong for higher levels of anxiety. Conversely, the positive relation between anxiety and adrenaline becomes more marked the more well-controlled and socialized the boy is.

If corrected for attenuation, this multiple regression will be well above $.70$, which means that approximately 50% of the variance in average adrenaline levels can be accounted for by these two dimensions, measured without error.

A tentative model

A diagram of the proposed model is shown in Figure 14.3. In agreement with the representational system of structural modeling, rectangles designate manifest, measured variables, whereas ellipses portray latent, unob-

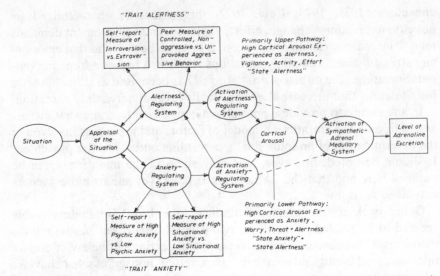

Figure 14.3. Tentative model of variables and processes involved in the determination of adrenaline excretion.

served variables. The arrows show the direction of influence. Though the basic elements of the model are somewhat different and certain additions have been made, the model is related to Eysenck's theorizing about cortical arousal (Eysenck, 1967, 1975). However, because there seem to be some differences of opinion as to the nature of the underlying neurophysiological structures and processes, these factors are not specified in the model. Instead, the general terms "alertness-regulating system" and "anxiety-regulating system" are used, thus leaving open the issue of the exact neurophysiological mechanisms involved.

To my knowledge, an analysis along the lines developed here has not been made previously with reference to adrenaline excretion. However, the idea of two different arousal systems, as proposed by Eysenck, has also been put forth and documented by other researchers (e.g., Gellhorn and Longbourrow, 1963; Routtenberg, 1968). This conceptualization is central to Schalling's view of impulsiveness and anxiety proneness as two important personality dimensions (Schalling, 1977).

The basic idea of the model is that there are two partly independent, partly dependent pathways to cortical arousal. One is via the alertness-regulating system (upper pathway), with little or perhaps no participation from the anxiety-regulating system. The other is via the anxiety-regulating system (lower pathway), in which case the alertness-regulating system also becomes involved (see arrow connecting the lower and upper pathways). Furthermore, it is assumed that the amount of adrenaline output is monotonically related to level of cortical arousal. However, because cortical arousal can be produced via two different pathways, the processes involved should be reflected in the measure of adrenaline excretion. In the case of upper-pathway involvement, the adrenaline measure should correlate predominantly with indices of the alertness-regulating system. In contrast, when the anxiety-regulating system is activated, adrenaline output should be related both to indices of this system and to those of the alertness-regulating system. Thus, under conditions of emotional involvement, adrenaline level should cover (at least) two different components (state anxiety and state alertness), whereas in cases of primarily cognitive alertness or involvement, output of adrenaline should reflect mainly the alertness component (state alertness and possibly other components not considered here).

Expanding somewhat on the previous formulation, it is assumed that situations involving demands on cognitive alertness and vigilance and on attention and effort but that are not threatening or emotionally disturbing produce cortical arousal via the alertness-regulating system (the upper pathway). This kind of stimulation thus has no or only weak effects on the anxiety-regulating system. Higher levels of cortical arousal produced in this way are experienced as a state of alertness or cognitive involvement.

It is furthermore postulated that individuals differ markedly both in thresholds and habitual level of activation of the alertness-regulating system. Well-controlled, nonaggressive individuals are assumed to have low thresholds and high habitual levels, whereas the opposite is true of aggressive, acting-out individuals. An individual's predisposition to react to stimuli of various intensities and with high or low levels (trait alertness) in the alertness-regulating system and the ensuing state of cortical arousal (state alertness) are indexed in the present study by the composite of controlled, nonaggressive versus unprovoked aggressive behavior and introversion versus extraversion (the previously discussed composite with reversed scoring).

In contrast, situations that are emotionally taxing ("stressful") will activate the anxiety-regulating system. However, this activation is also assumed to affect the alertness-regulating system. The basis for this assumption is behavioral and introspective observations as well as knowledge of the probable neurophysiological mechanisms involved in these processes (Eysenck, 1975; Gale, 1973). Thus the cortical arousal produced in this way will have two components, one related to the anxiety-regulating system and one to the alertness-regulating system. The emotionally activated individual will be both anxious and alert (state anxiety plus state alertness).

Also with regard to the anxiety-regulating system, individuals are assumed to differ substantially in thresholds and habitual levels. The individual's predisposition to react to stimuli of various intensities and with high or low levels (trait anxiety) in the anxiety-regulating system and the anxiety component of the ensuing state of cortical arousal (state anxiety) are indexed in the present study by the composite of psychic anxiety versus low psychic anxiety and situational anxiety versus low situational anxiety. It can be assumed that a certain minimum level of stimulation is required for this composite or its component variables to reflect individual differences in the predisposition to alertness reactions. Accordingly, adrenaline levels under "resting conditions" may not be systematically related to individual differences in these indices.

Because an interaction was empirically found between the two composites in their relation to adrenaline (see the section on determining adrenaline level), an interaction between the two arousal systems might be tentatively included as part of the model: The positive relation between indices of the alertness-regulating system and adrenaline is assumed to become increasingly strong with higher levels of indices of the anxiety-regulating system. It is understood that this interaction will be present only or mainly when the stimulus situation leads to an activation of the anxiety-regulating system (i.e., is emotionally taxing).

Parenthetically it might be mentioned that, in the two arousal systems previously referred to (e.g., Eysenck, 1967, 1975; Routtenberg, 1968), what seems to correspond to the alertness-regulating system and the upper pathway is chiefly identified with the brainstem reticular activation structures. Similarly, the neurophysiological basis for the lower pathway and the anxiety-regulating system is assumed to be some of the limbic structures, the hypothalamus, and the autonomic system. It should be noted, however, that the overlapping of the present model with previous two-arousal systems is not quite complete with regard to concepts used and operationalization of concepts.

Though there are certain advantages in having "cortical arousal" as a link in the process diagram (Figure 14.3), it may also create some problems. In particular, cortical arousal is not a unitary concept (which, by the way, is not implied in the previous analyses), and different psychophysiological indices of it have shown relatively little covariation (see, e.g., Lacey, 1967). Accordingly, in interpreting the term "cortical arousal" in the model, it is probably useful to place more emphasis on experiential aspects of the concept than on psychophysiological ones.

Some implications

Some correlational consequences of the preceding analyses have already been pointed out, for situations with or without emotional involvement. In addition, it should follow that, in emotionally taxing situations, the individual's adrenaline level should be more completely determined (R should be higher) than in relatively nonemotional situations. The reason for this inference is that indices of the anxiety-regulating system should have more predictive power in stressful than in nonstressful situations. In the present study, this prediction can be tested by contrasting the multiple regressions for adrenaline measures collected on the first (more taxing emotionally) and second examination days. Furthermore, considering the suggestion of an interaction between the two arousal systems, one would expect a larger (more significant) contribution to R from the interaction term in emotionally activating situations. This could again be examined through a comparison of the results for the first and the second examination days. Finally, a general consequence of the model is that an individual's adrenaline level cannot generally be construed as an indicator of the emotional impact or stressfulness of the stimulus situation. The previous analyses suggest that, depending on the situation, the adrenaline level reflects either mainly an alertness component of cortical arousal (or adrenal–medullary activity) or a combination of alertness and anxiety ("stress") components. This view of adrenaline would seem to run counter to much current thinking in this area.

Some empirical tests

The previously reported empirical analyses (see the section on determining adrenaline level) showed that each of the composite indices of the alertness-regulating system and the anxiety-regulating system correlated substantially with the composite measure of adrenaline level. In addition, each composite index gave a significant contribution to explained variance over and above the contribution from the other composite. These composite indices were thus partly independent. To some extent, these findings constituted the starting point for the subsequent theoretical formulation. However, these analyses can be carried farther, taking the variation in stressfulness of the two examination days into account. In this context it is useful to report results separately for each of the two component variables making up the two composites (Figure 14.3).

First, looking at the zero-order correlations, it is obvious that the two alertness indices (controlled, nonaggressive behavior and introversion) correlated about as strongly with adrenaline level derived from the first as from the second examination days (average $r = .381$ for the first day and .406 for the second). This is in contrast with the results for the two anxiety indices, the average r being .388 for the first day and .260 for the second. A difference of this magnitude was obtained not only for the situational anxiety variable, which specifically referred to the first day, but, more important, also for the psychic anxiety scale. This finding of a higher correlation between anxiety indices and adrenaline level for the first, emotionally more taxing day is certainly in agreement with the prediction derived from the theoretical model.

From a slightly different point of view, it was found that the multiple regressions for the four combinations of alertness and anxiety indices (one alertness index and one anxiety index) were consistently higher for adrenaline levels from the first than for levels from the second examination day. Though the average difference was not great ($\bar{R} = .482$ and .436, respectively), the results showed that the anxiety indices had better predictive power for the adrenaline measure that referred to the emotionally more disturbing situation.

This was also evident from a comparison of the β weights for the anxiety indices in the equations (each with two independent variables) predicting adrenaline level for the first and the second examination days. In three of four equations for the first day, the β weights for the two anxiety indices were significant (and p was .06 for the β weight in the fourth equation). This contrasts with the situation for the second day, where none of the four β weights for the anxiety variables were nonsignificant. They were all positive ($\bar{r} = .260$), indicating that the adrenaline measure for the second day also contained an anxiety component, though reduced in size, as expected. By comparison, all the β weights for the two alertness indices were significant in these eight equations.

Considering possible interactions between alertness and anxiety indices, the results were clearly different for the two alertness variables. The peer measure of controlled, nonaggressive (vs. unprovoked aggressive) behavior showed significant interactions with the psychic anxiety scale as well as the situational anxiety scale in predicting adrenaline level for the first examination day. This was in marked contrast with the introversion versus extraversion scale, which did not even show a trend in that direction. For the adrenaline measure referring to the second day, there were no significant interactions whatsoever, as was expected on theoretical grounds.

It can be tentatively concluded that these results provide some support for the idea that the alertness-regulating system and the anxiety-regulating system interact (in the statistical sense, see Olweus, 1977) with one another in emotionally taxing situations. The present data suggest, however, that the two indices of the alertness-regulating system function differently in this respect. This discrepancy merits further study.

Overall, the results presented here are in general agreement with the predictions derived from the theoretical analyses. The results from the interaction analyses and the pattern of correlations between the alertness and anxiety indices suggest that the peer measure of controlled, nonaggressive versus unprovoked aggressive behavior was the purer indicator of the alertness-regulating system in this study.

Adrenaline and unprovoked aggressive behavior

Up to now, the main focus has been on the factors and processes that determine an individual's level of adrenaline excretion. It is now appropriate to change the perspective and see if the previous analyses and findings can be of help in predicting aggressive behavior and explaining its development.

With regard to prediction, three of the four childhood variables (farthest to the left in Figure 14.2) that were found to be important in determining unprovoked aggressive behavior (Olweus, 1980) correlated very weakly with average adrenaline level ($r < .100$). The exception was mother's permissiveness, which correlated $-.360$. Moreover, the grade 6 variables in Figure 14.2 correlated in the .30s with adrenaline level, but there also remained a substantial negative relation between adrenaline level and unprovoked aggressive behavior at grade 9 when the grade 6 variables and the four childhood variables were controlled for. Thus it is very likely that adding adrenaline level to a regression equation with unprovoked aggressive behavior (or similar dimensions) as the dependent variable will increase predictability in many situations.

In the previous analyses, an individual with a high level of habitual aggressive behavior and a low level of adrenaline as measured in nonstressful situations was assumed to have typically low cortical arousal. Partly following Eysenck (1967, 1975) and others, we can briefly pursue the following lines of reasoning. A boy with a typically low level of cortical arousal often experiences a kind of stimulus hunger or craving. He becomes easily habituated and bored and has a desire for new and varied stimuli, for sensations and thrills. Strong stimuli are not experienced as aversive or disturbing, as they would be for a boy with a typically high level of cortical arousal. Rather, they can be engaging and exciting. In this way, a boy with a low level of cortical arousal who has been exposed to childhood conditions that predispose him to habitually aggressive behavior – conditions of the kind shown in the left part of Figure 14.2 – may feel aroused and excited when he is provoked and engages in aggressive behavior when he feels strong anger. Such behavior may thus be reinforcing to him. He also seeks out situations in which there is a high probability of his behaving aggressively.

In contrast, a boy with a typically low level of cortical arousal who has not experienced the above predisposing conditions (or fewer of them) shows a good deal of outgoing, extraverted behavior patterns, but he himself initiates less aggressive behavior than the boy discussed in the preceding paragraph. However, when provoked, he tends to respond with aggression.

Finally, a boy with a typically high level of cortical arousal often experiences aggressive behavior and strong anger of his own as aversive and unpleasant. Generally, he is not inclined to seek out situations that easily lead to aggressive interactions. When provoked, he tries to use nonaggressive response modes of a submissive or constructive nature.

It should be emphasized that the above formulations should not be construed as precise predictions of behavior in particular situations. Rather, broad predispositions are assumed to increase or decrease the probability of certain behavior patterns in a range of situations. Thus these behavioral tendencies are posited to affect the developmental course of an individual in a general way. For more specific predictions, however, other factors must also be taken into account.

An analysis somewhat parallel to the above can be performed for antisocial behavior patterns. The previously mentioned self-report scale of antisocial behavior at grade 9 correlated $-.360$ with average adrenaline level.

Some related findings

Two other studies have revealed a negative relation between adrenaline level and aggressive acting-out behavior. Johansson, Frankenhaeuser, and Magnusson (1973) found a correlation of $-.25$ between teacher ratings of aggressiveness and level of adrenaline as measured during a 1-hour performance on arithmetic tests. The relation of teacher-rated motor restlessness to adrenaline was $-.34$. The subjects in this study were 98 boys, aged 13, being a largely representative sample of sixth graders from a medium-sized Swedish town. The adrenaline values for this active period were based on only one urine sample. Adrenaline was also measured during a passive period when the subjects viewed a relaxing film. The correlation pattern for the latter adrenaline variable was similar to that for the active period, but the relations were generally weaker.

Also, Woodman and his associates in England have produced several reports (e.g., Woodman, 1979; Woodman & Hinton, 1978) on a group of 58 maximum-security hospital patients who were socially highly deviant. Among these patients, a subgroup was isolated with low adrenaline and high noradrenaline excretion in anticipation of a mildly stressing situation. Thus their noradrenaline-to-adrenaline ratios were clearly higher than for the remaining group of patients. This subgroup was characterized by a history of convictions for extreme physical violence.

Due to some procedural problems, it is difficult to determine the reliability and generalizability of the findings of this study. Among other things, as many as two-thirds of the patients were labeled "mentally ill," and it is unclear to what extent mental illness affected the patients' perception of the situation and hence their catecholamine excretion. Nevertheless, these results, too, suggest a negative relation between habitually aggressive, acting-out behavior and adrenaline level.

Acknowledgments

The research reported in this chapter was supported by grants from the Sweden Bank Tercentenary Foundation, the Swedish Ministry of Health and Social Affairs, Delegation for Social Research (Project No. DSF 82/13), the Norwegian Research Council for Science and the Humanities, and the W. T. Grant Foundation.

References

Andersson, B., Hovmöller, S., Karlsson, C.-G., & Svensson, S. (1974). Analysis of urinary catecholamines: An improved auto-analyzer fluorescence method. *Clinica Chimica Acta, 51,* 13–28.

Eysenck, H. J. (1967). *The biological basis of personality.* Springfield, IL: Thomas.

Eysenck, H. J. (1975). The measurement of emotion: Psychological parameters and methods. In L. Levi (Ed.), *Emotions: Their parameters and measurement.* New York: Raven Press.

Eysenck, H. J., & Eysenck, S. (1975). *Manual of the Eysenck Personality Questionnaire.* London: Hodder & Stoughton.

Frankenhaeuser, M. (1971). Behavior and circulating catecholamines. *Brain Research, 31,* 241–62.

Frankenhaeuser, M. (1979). Psychoendocrine approaches to the study of emotion as related to stress and coping. In H. E. Howe & R. A. Dienstbier (Eds.), *Nebraska symposium on motivation 1978.* Lincoln: University of Nebraska Press.

Gale, A. (1973). The psychophysiology of individual differences: Studies of extraversion and the EEG. In P. Kline (Ed.), *New approaches in psychological measurement.* New York: Wiley.

Gellhorn, E., & Longbourrow, G. N. (1963). *Emotions and emotional disorders.* New York: Harper & Row.

Johansson, G., Frankenhaeuser, M., & Magnusson, D. (1973). Catecholamine output in school children as related to performance and adjustment. *Scandinavian Journal of Psychology, 14,* 20–8.

Lacey, J. I. (1967). Somatic response patterning and stress: Some revisions of activation theory. In M. H. Appley & R. Trumbull (Eds.), *Psychological stress: Issues in research.* New York: Appleton-Century-Crofts.

Levi, L. (1972). Stress and distress in response to psychosocial stimuli: Laboratory and real life studies on sympathoadrenomedullary and related reactions. *Acta Medica Scandinavica,* Suppl. 528.

Moyer, K. E. (1976). *The psychobiology of aggression.* New York: Harper & Row.

Olweus, D. (1977). A critical analysis of the "modern" interactionist position. In D. Magnusson & N. S. Endler (Eds.), *Personality at the cross-roads: Current issues in interactional psychology.* Hillsdale, NJ: Erlbaum.

Olweus, D. (1978). *Aggression in the schools: Bullies and whipping boys.* Washington, DC: Hemisphere.

Olweus, D. (1979). Stability of aggressive reaction patterns in males: A review. *Psychological Bulletin, 86,* 852–75.

Olweus, D. (1980). Familial and temperamental determinants of aggressive behavior in adolescent boys: A causal analysis. *Developmental Psychology, 16,* 644–60.

Olweus, D. (1983). The role of testosterone in the development of aggressive, antisocial behavior in human adolescents. In K. T. Van Deusen & S. A. Mednick (Eds.), *Prospective studies of crime and delinquency.* Boston: Klüwer–Nijhoff.

Olweus, D. (1984). Development of stable aggressive reaction patterns in males. In R. Blanchard & C. Blanchard (Eds.), *Advances in the study of aggression* (Vol. 1). New York: Academic Press.

Olweus, D., Mattsson, A., Schalling, D., & Löw, H. (1980). Testosterone, aggression, physical, and personality dimensions in normal adolescent males. *Psychosomatic Medicine, 42,* 253–69.

Rose, R. M. (1975). Testosterone, aggression, and homosexuality: A review of the literature and implications for future research. In E. J. Sachar (Ed.), *Topics in endocrinology.* New York: Grune & Stratton.

Routtenberg, A. (1968). The two-arousal hypotheses: Reticular formation and limbic system. *Psychological Review, 75,* 51–80.

Schalling, D. (1977). The trait-situation interaction and the physiological correlates of behavior. In D. Magnusson & N. S. Endler (Eds.), *Personality at the crossroads: Current issues in interactional psychology.* Hillsdale, NJ: Erlbaum.

Schalling, D., Cronholm, B., & Åsberg, M. (1975). Components of state and trait anxiety as related to personality and arousal. In L. Levi (Ed.), *Emotions: Their parameters and measurement.* New York: Raven Press.

von Euler, U. S., & Lishajko, F. (1961). Improved technique for the fluorimetric estimation of catecholamines. *Acta Physiologica Scandanavia, 51,* 348–55.

Woodman, D. D. (1979). Urinary catecholamines and test habituation in maximum security hospital patients. *Journal of Psychosomatic Research, 23,* 263–6.

Woodman, D. D., & Hinton, J. (1978). Catecholamine balance during stress anticipation: An abnormality in maximum security hospital patients. *Journal of Psychosomatic Research, 22,* 477–83.

15   Personality correlates of plasma testosterone levels in young delinquents: an example of person–situation interaction?

Daisy Schalling

Studies of the influence of male sex hormones on aggression and violence have had inconsistent results (for reviews see Meyer-Bahlburg, 1981; Rose, 1975; Rubin, Reinisch, & Haskett, 1981). The empirical bases are rather weak for two commonly held assumptions: that aggressive behavior in animals is determined by testosterone level and that testosterone also activates violent and aggressive behavior in humans.

The animal research gives little evidence for a direct effect of sex hormones on fighting but indicates a relation between changes in social rank or status and dominant–submissive behavior and changes in testosterone levels, at least in monkeys (Rose, Holaday, & Bernstein, 1971) and mice (Henry & Stephens, 1978). Keverne, Meller, and Eberhart (1982) found that high-rank monkeys had a 300–500% increase in testosterone when introduced into a mixed-sex group. They displayed (as expected) higher sexual activity than the low-rank animals, who had only a slight increase in testosterone. Although they did not show more aggressive behavior, the high-rank, high-testosterone monkeys were the objects of significantly less aggression by other males. When placed again in single cages, they no longer differed in testosterone level from the low-rank monkeys. Nor were there any differences between high- and low-rank monkeys when they were separately introduced to females, with no other males present. In the latter situation, the only endocrine difference observed was higher "stress" hormone (cortisol and prolactin) levels in the low-rank animals. High testosterone secretion was thus associated with high social rank but only in a challenging group situation.

Studies of relations between testosterone levels and human behavior have been concerned mainly with kinds of aggression different from those behaviors studied in animals, although a few have also included ratings of dominance (Ehrenkranz, Bliss, & Sheard, 1974). The results have varied, depending on the type of subjects and methods used (reviewed by Rose, 1975; Rubin et al., 1981). Investigations on normal adult subjects have had

283

largely negative results. There are many difficulties in such research, one of the main problems being that overt aggressive behavior such as fighting is relatively rare in normal adults. Furthermore, the terminology is confused in this field, and the borders between aggression, violence, and hostility are not clear (Valzelli, 1981). The measurement of "aggressive" attitudes and feelings and other indirect manifestations of aggression or hostility offer special methodological difficulties. They require valid self-report, which is not easy to obtain, or they require sophisticated indirect methods like projective tests (Rydin, Schalling, & Åsberg, 1982). It is thus not surprising that the relations between testosterone levels and measures of aggression have been mainly weak and nonsignificant, both in normal adults and in prisoners. As pointed out by Rose (1975) one might find more sex hormone–behavior relations if measures were taken more proximally to puberty. Furthermore, it can be argued that studies of groups of institutionalized offenders could give more information on such relations, because there is a greater range of behaviors and better records of overt aggressive behavior (Kreuz & Rose, 1972).

In view of the animal research described above, it appears that the targets of research on relations between testosterone and human male behavior and personality should be broadened. Perhaps variables like social dominance, assertiveness, sociability, and sensation seeking would be more interesting as correlates to testosterone than the commonly studied aggression–hostility variables (e.g., the Buss–Durkee Inventory scales).

In the following, a psychoendocrinological study will be described that was based on such considerations. It was performed on adolescent institutionalized offenders and included several personality variables assumed to be relevant. Subjects were 40 male delinquents, 14–19 years, who were residents in a Swedish Borstal school for serious recidivist offenders. A detailed report of the group and the various measures used has been published (Mattsson, Schalling, Olweus, Löw, & Svensson, 1980). Briefly, plasma testosterone levels were analyzed from three morning blood samples by a reliable radioimmunoassay method. A series of self-report inventory scales were given, and staff and psychiatric ratings were performed (for details, see Mattsson et al., 1980). A comparison group of 58 age-similar normal schoolboys was obtained (described in Olweus, Mattsson, Schalling, & Löw, 1980). Mean age was 16 years both for the delinquents and the comparison group. Several aspects of aggression were measured in both groups by scales taken from two self-report inventories, the Olweus Aggression Inventory (OAI) and the Olweus Q-Inventory (OQI), which have been validated for schoolboys by comparisons with peer and teacher ratings (Olweus, 1978). Other relevant personality scales were taken from the Eysenck Personality Questionnaire (EPQ) and the Karolinska Scales of Personality (KSP) (see Schalling, Edman, & Åsberg, 1983).

Pubertal stage was assessed by inspection of pubic hair development. Maturity (Tanner Stage 5) had been attained by 20 (50%) of the delinquents and 43 (77%) of the nondelinquents. In spite of this difference, the delinquents had slightly higher testosterone levels (587 ng/100 ml in the delinquent vs. 544 ng/100 ml in the comparison group). The delinquents with Tanner stages below 5 (4 in Stage 3, 15 in Stage 4) had significantly higher testosterone levels than the normal boys in these stages (3 in Stage 3, 9 in Stage 4). Testosterone levels were associated with Tanner stages in the nondelinquent group but not in the delinquent group. The seven inmates (3 in Stage 5, 3 in Stage 4, and 1 in Stage 2) who had committed the most violent crimes (armed robbery) had higher mean testosterone levels ($p < .05$, one-tailed), but there were no significant differences between those who had a history of property offenses only and the remaining delinquents.

The relations between testosterone and personality in the delinquents were analyzed by comparing personality scores in two extreme groups, each of eight boys selected for mean testosterone levels and by product moment correlations. High testosterone levels were associated with high scores in one of the OAI-derived scales, the verbal aggression scale, but not with high scores in physical aggression. They were also associated with high scores in a scale of preference for physical sports. Furthermore, high testosterone levels were associated with high extraversion, low neuroticism and low lie scores in the EPQ and with high scores in monotony avoidance (sensation seeking) in the KSP (for details, see Mattsson, et al., 1980).

However, these relations were all rather weak, with correlations mostly around .30. There are, of course, many potentially attenuating sources of error in a study of this type. Several factors that may influence testosterone levels are left uncontrolled (e.g., many subjects were heavy smokers), and there were occasional stressful events (escapes, conflicts) in the school, both of which could influence testosterone levels. There are cyclic fluctuations in testosterone production, which may partly explain the rather large intraindividual variance (the mean coefficient of variation was 23%). Despite the uniform blood sampling (between 8 and 10 a.m.) circadian rhythms may be of importance for the testosterone variation.

The fact that half of the boys had not attained pubertal maturity may be a confounding factor in the relations between testosterone levels and personality scores. Testosterone levels are probably not associated with behavior in the same way before pubertal maturity as they are after maturity. It was therefore decided to perform a separate personality–testosterone analysis on the 20 boys who had attained Tanner Stage 5 as assessed by pubic hair development (Schalling, Mattson, Olweus, Edman, Levander, & Löw, 1983). There was a significant age difference, as expected. The mean age in the immature subgroup was 15.4 (range 14–17), and that in the mature (Tanner Stage 5) group 16.9 (range 15–19). However, there were no significant differences in testosterone levels; for the immature subgroup, the mean level was 595.4 (range 407–860 ng/100 ml), and for the mature group 593.1 (range 420–820 ng/100 ml).

In the remainder of the chapter, a short description will be given of the results of this analysis, expressed as correlations between personality scores and testosterone levels for the Tanner 5 subgroup. The effects of excluding the immature boys were dramatic. Most correlations were markedly higher in the mature subgroup, whereas the general pattern and directions of correlations remained unchanged. The main results are illustrated in Table 15.1. For comparison purposes, the correlations are also given for the total group.

The relations between testosterone and the OAI aggression scales in the subgroup showed the same pattern as in the total group. High testosterone levels were not associated with scores in the physical aggression scale (fighting with peers) but were strongly associated with high scores in the so-called verbal aggression scale ($r = .65$, $p < .01$). This scale consisted of two items (rating format 1–6) taken from the corresponding OAI scale: "When a teacher has promised that we will have some fun but then changes his (her) mind, I protest," and "When an adult tries to boss me around, I resist strongly." The items are concerned with defense of status or assertive behavior and with protesting upon provocation or unfair treatment. The remaining scales in the OAI inventory – aggressive attitudes and impulses and aggressive inhibitory responses – did not correlate significantly with testosterone levels, either in the total group or in the subgroup. An additional aggression scale, taken from the OQI (Olweus et al., 1980), was weakly associated with testosterone in the total group ($r = .24$) but showed a significant correlation in the subgroup ($r = .56$, $p < .01$). This scale has seven items, of which the four items with the highest testosterone correlations are concerned with showing anger openly and telling people off rather than avoiding conflict and keeping silent. Thus, again, defenses of status (not allowing oneself to be "bossed" by others) is characteristic of the high-testosterone boys.

Included in the OAI inventory is a scale with items referring to liking for various sports (swimming, ice hockey, boxing). As in the total group

Table 15.1. *Correlations between mean testosterone levels and personality inventory scales in male delinquents (14–19 years)*

Inventory scale	Total group ($N = 38–40$)	Pubertal maturity subgroup[a] ($N = 18–20$)
Olweus Aggression Inventory		
Physical aggression (against peers)	.03	.18
Verbal aggression (against adults)	.38*	.65**
Aggressive attitude and impulses	.10	.28
Aggression inhibitory responses	−.18	.18
Preference for physical sports	.33*	.61**
Olweus Q-Inventory		
Aggression	.24	.56**
Eysenck Personality Questionnaire		
Extraversion – impulsivity subscale	.14	.14
Extraversion – sociability subscale	.36*	.61**
Extraversion (total scale)	.31*	.48*
Neuroticism	−.30	−.27
Psychoticism	.13	.21
Lie (conformity)	−.46**	−.67**
Karolinska Scales of Personality		
Impulsiveness	.05	.11
Monotony avoidance	.24	.50*

[a] This subgroup consisted of delinquents who had attained pubertal maturity (Tanner Stage 5, assessed by pubic hair development).
* = $p < .05$.
** = $p < .01$.

there was a significant positive correlation with testosterone level in the subgroup for this scale. High-testosterone boys apparently enjoy physical exhaustion and competition in sports.

The extraversion scale from the EPQ was divided into two subscales: impulsivity and sociability. As seen from Table 15.1, the sociability component of extraversion was positively associated with testosterone, again most strongly in the subgroup ($r = .61$, $p < .01$). There was also a highly significant relation between high testosterone and low lie scores. The implication, according to some interpretations of this scale (Schalling, 1978), is that high-testosterone subjects are less conforming than and do not care as much for conventional rules for behavior as low-testosterone subjects.

The two aspects of impulsivity from the KSP scales, impulsiveness and monotony avoidance, differ as to their association with testosterone.

There was no relation to the impulsiveness scale, but in the subgroup there was a significant positive correlation between testosterone level and monotony avoidance. As expected, there were no relations between testosterone and scores in various anxiety scales from the KSP.

The pattern of self-description among the high-testosterone delinquents, as opposed that among the low-testosterone delinquents, is coherent and interpretable. It cannot be ascribed to the intercorrelations among the personality variables (Schalling, Edman, & Åsberg, 1983). It should be emphasized that the personality profile is not that commonly obtained with psychopaths (Schalling, 1978), who tend to have high impulsiveness and low sociability scores. The picture is rather one of a highly assertive and self-assured boy who is able to defend himself when provoked and who can show anger when necessary, that is, has "anger arousability" (Meyer-Bahlburg, 1981). The analysis of the relations between testosterone levels and corresponding scales in the group of normal adolescents made by Olweus et al. (1980) is congruent with the present interpretation. Olweus (in press) emphasized that the high-testosterone boys tend to respond to provocation, including threat or unfair treatment. Both in the delinquent and in the normal group, the testosterone levels showed positive correlations, on the item level, with items concerning protesting against being "bossed."

In the present study there are some staff-rating and self-rating items (Schalling, Mattsson, Olweus, Edman, Levander, & Löw, 1983) indicating that high-testosterone delinquents are less likely to be targets of aggression by others than are low-testosterone subjects, which is consistent with the data on monkeys reported by Kaverne et al. (1982). There were, however, no peer ratings and thus no direct evidence of the status of the high-testosterone boys in the eyes of the other boys, but self-ratings and staff ratings (Schalling, Mattsson, Olweus, Edman, Levander, & Löw, 1983) suggest that they are "high-rank" individuals in their group. It is possible, as suggested by Meyer-Bahlburg (1981), that testosterone may modify the subtle cues for agonistic (aggressive, submissive, or defensive) reactions from others. High-testosterone boys appear to be sensation seeking, to enjoy the company of the other boys, and not to submit to conventional rules of behavior. Their liking for strenuous sports seems to fit this picture. Their behavior can be said to represent the stereotype of masculinity. The findings are quite consistent with those reported by Daitzman and Zuckerman (1980), who found that high testosterone levels in students were associated with sensation seeking, sociability, and dominance.

There was in the present study no relation between testosterone levels and psychoticism in the EPQ, a scale that has been assumed by Eysenck to be particularly associated with male sex hormones. The assumption was based on studies showing consistently higher psychoticism scores in male subjects and in many clinical groups with a male predominance, for example, psychopaths and criminals (Eysenck & Eysenck, 1976). However, the lack of a relation between psychoticism and concurrently measured testosterone levels does not, of course, rule out the possibility that there may have been a fetal testosterone influence contributing to the organization of the CNS and thereby to certain behavioral traits.

The interpretation of the present findings must remain tentative until more is known about the biosocial bases of the personality variables that were found to be associated with testosterone levels. There is increasing evidence for a biological basis for some of these variables, for example, for sensation seeking or monotony avoidance (Schalling, Edman, & Åsberg, 1983) and for sociability (Buss & Plomin, 1975). The biological factors are certainly complex, including genetic (e.g., monoamine transmitter systems, possibly interacting with testosterone) and perinatal factors having organizing effects on the developing brain. The personality picture derived from the self-descriptions of high-testosterone boys is similar in several respects to that obtained in studies of low-monoamine oxidase (MAO) subjects (Schalling, Edman, & Åsberg, 1983; Zuckerman, Buchsbaum, & Murphy, 1980). It is therefore noteworthy that MAO levels vary inversely with gonadal hormone levels in monkeys (Redmond, Murphy, & Baulu, 1976).

As pointed out above, the animal literature indicates that testosterone levels vary with changes in social situation. This can easily be demonstrated in monkey experiments in which defeats and victories can be artificially manipulated by various cage arrangements – for example, moving the animal from an isolated cage to a mixed cage and introducing other males of high or low rank. Everyday life for delinquents living together in a closed institution provides frequent experiences of interpersonal interactions, rivalry, conflicts, defeats, and victories. However, in this case it is the personality of the individual that is to a great extent decisive for his winning or losing in group interactions. It is possible that the unusually strong correlations between testosterone and personality in the present study are due partly to the person–situation interactions in the institution. It could be argued that high-testosterone boys are perhaps habitual "winners" in the daily life of the institution, as their self-descriptions would suggest. It has been shown by a study of pairs of wrestlers (Elias, 1982) that human winners also have a greater increase in testosterone levels than losers. High-testosterone boys seem able to defend their status by showing their anger and protesting against unfair treatment in an efficient way. They may enforce their will in more subtle ways than fighting by providing proper agonistic cues for submission to the other boys. There would thus be more frequent increases in testosterone associated with successful interactions for these subjects, and this frequency might contribute to the correlations between personality and testosterone seen in the present study. This hypothesis could be tested by carefully observing the ongoing social interactions while performing repeated measurements of testosterone in institutionalized subjects.

The present findings can be interpreted in terms of the state–trait distinction. A tentative conclusion is that the level of testosterone at a given time is a state phenomenon and susceptible to change when the situation changes. However, the *proneness* to secrete a large amount of testosterone in challenging interpersonal situations may be a *trait* and closely associated with the traits of assertiveness and sensation seeking.

Acknowledgments

This work was supported by grants from the Swedish Council for Research in the Humanities and Social Sciences (582/82) and the Swedish Medical Research Council (4545).

References

Buss, A. H., & Plomin, R. (1975). *A temperament theory of personality*. New York: Wiley.

Daitzman, R., & Zuckerman, M. (1980). Disinhibitory sensation seeking, personality and gonadal hormones. *Personality and Individual Differences, 1,* 103–10.

Ehrenkranz, J., Bliss, F., & Sheard, M. H. (1974). Plasma testosterone correlation with aggressive behavior and social dominance in man. *Psychosomatic Medicine, 36,* 469–75.

Elias, M. (1982). Serum cortisol, testosterone and testosterone-binding globulin responses to competitive fighting in human males. *Aggressive Behavior, 7,* 215–24.

Eysenck, H. J., & Eysenck, S. B. G. (1976). *Psychoticism as a dimension of personality.* London: Hodder & Stoughton.

Henry, J. P., & Stephens, P. M. (1978). *Stress, health and the social environment.* New York: Springer-Verlag.

Keverne, E. B., Meller, R. E., & Eberhart, J. A. (1982). Social influences on behavior and neuroendocrine responsiveness in Talapoin monkeys. *Scandinavian Journal of Psychology,* Suppl. 1, 37–47.

Kreuz, I. F., & Rose, R. M. (1972). Assessment of aggressive behavior and plasma testosterone in a young criminal population. *Psychosomatic Medicine, 34,* 321–32.

Mattsson, Å., Schalling, D., Olweus, D., Löw, H., & Svensson, J. (1980). Plasma testosterone, aggressive behavior, and personality dimensions in young male delinquents. *Journal of the American Academy of Child Psychiatry, 19,* 476–90.

Meyer-Bahlburg, H. F. L. (1981). Androgens and human aggression. In P. F. Brain & D. Benton (Eds.), *The biology of aggression* (pp. 263–76). Rockville, MD: Sijthoff & Noordhoff.

Olweus, D. (1978). *Aggression in the schools.* Washington DC: Hemisphere.

Olweus, D. (in press). The role of testosterone in the development of aggressive, antisocial behavior in human adolescents. In K. T. Van Deusen & S. A. Mednick (Eds.), *Antecedents of antisocial behavior*. Boston: Klüver–Nijhoff.

Olweus, D., Mattsson, Å., Schalling, D., & Löw, H. (1980). Testosterone, aggression, physical and personality dimensions in normal adolescent males. *Psychosomatic Medicine, 42,* 253–69.

Redmond, D. E., Murphy, D. L., & Baulu, J. (1979). Platelet monoamine oxidase activity correlates with social affiliative and agonistic behaviors in normal rhesus monkeys. *Psychosomatic Medicine, 41,* 87–100.

Rose, R. M. (1975). Testosterone, aggression, and homosexuality: A review of the literature and implications for future research. In E. J. Sachar (Ed.), *Topics in psychoendocrinology* (pp. 83–103). New York: Grune & Stratton.

Rose, R. M., Holaday, J. W., & Bernstein, I. S. (1971). Plasma testosterone, dominance rank and aggressive behavior in male rhesus monkeys. *Nature, 231,* 366–8.

Rubin, R. T., Reinisch, J. M., & Haskett, R. F. (1981). Postnatal gonadal steroid effects on human behavior. *Science, 211,* 1318–24.

Rydin, E., Schalling, D., & Åsberg, M. (1982). Rorschach ratings in depressed and suicidal patients with low levels of 5-hydroxyindoleacetic acid in cerebrospinal fluid. *Psychiatry Research, 7,* 229–43.

Schalling, D. (1978). Psychopathy-related personality variables and the psychophysiology of socialization. In R. D. Hare & D. Schalling (Eds.), *Psychopathic behaviour: Approaches in research* (pp. 85–106). New York: Wiley.

Schalling, D., Edman, G., & Åsberg, M. (1983). Impulsive cognitive style and inability to tolerate boredom: Psychobiological studies of temperamental vulnerability. In M. Zuckerman (Ed.), *Biological bases of sensation, impulsivity and anxiety* (pp. 123–45). Hillsdale NJ: Erlbaum.

Schalling, D., Mattsson, Å., Olweus, D., Edman, G., Levander, S., & Löw, H. (1983). Personality and behavioral correlates of plasma testosterone levels in young offenders. Manuscript in preparation.

Valzelli, L. *Psychobiology of aggression and violence*. New York: Raven Press.

Zuckerman, M., Buchsbaum, M. S., & Murphy, D. L. (1980). Sensation seeking and its biological correlates. *Psychological Bulletin, 88,* 187–214.

16   Metabolic dysfunctions among habitually violent offenders: reactive hypoglycemia and cholesterol levels

Matti Virkkunen

Introduction

Hypoglycemia

There is some evidence that hypoglycemia could be connected to criminal and violent behavior (Bolton, 1973, 1976; Bovill, 1973; Groesbeck, D'Asaro & Nigro, 1975; Hill & Sargant, 1943; Neziroglu, 1979; Wilder, 1947; Yarura-Tobias & Neziroglu, 1975, 1981). Hill and Sargant (1943) described a murderer whose EEG showed paroxysmal features only when he became hypoglycemic. Yarura-Tobias and Neziroglu (1975) described a behavioral glucodysrhythmic syndrome among men with explosive behavior who had abnormal EEG tracings and 5-hour oral glucose tolerance tests (GGTs). EEG abnormalities and psychological changes, including temper tantrums, have also been described in patients suffering from labile diabetes or diabetes mellitus (Fabrykant & Pacella, 1948; Wilson, 1951).

Dietary differences between a group of chronic juvenile offenders and a group of behaviorally disordered students were noted by Schauss and Simonsen (1979). There is preliminary evidence that by lowering daily sucrose intake it may be possible to reduce antisocial acts among juvenile delinquents living in detention homes (Schoenthaler, 1982). At least among some hyperactive children the amount of sugar products added to nutritional foods and the ratio of carbohydrates to protein are associated with the amount of destructive aggressive behavior observed during free

292

play at ages 4 to 7 years (Prinz, Roberts, & Hantman, 1980). In a prospective study 30–60% of hyperactive (attention-deficit disorder) children committed crimes during later years (Satterfield, Hoppe, & Schell, 1982).

Cholesterol

There have been only a few hints that low cholesterol level is somehow connected to criminal behavior. Low serum cholesterol levels have been found to be related to poorly internalized social norms, irresponsibility, and self-criticism (Jenkins, Hames, Zyzanski, Rosenman, & Friedman, 1969). The psychological traits were assessed by means of the California Psychological Inventory. Hatch et al. (1966) used prisoners as a control group in a study of coronary heart disease and found, surprisingly, that the prisoners had very low cholesterol levels and small variance in cholesterol level.

It is well known that low cholesterol level is more typical among persons with some particular personality dimensions than among normal persons. Cholesterol level is lower among "field-independent" than among "field-dependent" persons (Flemenbaum & Anderson, 1978; Flemenbaum & Flemenbaum, 1975; McCarnie, Simpson & Stevens, 1981). Field-independent individuals function independently of external frames of reference in perceiving and processing environmental stimuli and are less attentive to the social cues and information provided by others. There is also evidence that low cholesterol level is related to poor motivation and higher cholesterol level is associated with unpleasant feelings such as depression (Rahe, Rubin, & Gunderson, 1972).

The author's interest in cholesterol levels arose during work in the 1970s as a senior doctor in a special ward that conducted some 150 mental examinations of criminals for the Finnish courts per year. There it was routine to take cholesterol measurements, and it seemed that these values were often quite low, though cholesterol levels in the general Finnish population have usually been considered to be among the highest in the world (Aromaa et al., 1975). Five-hour GTTs were performed to determine whether some personality features were related to reactive hypoglycemic factors among habitually violent offenders. The criteria for antisocial personality were very soon found to be connected to these two metabolic factors. The following summary of five papers presents findings obtained from habitually violent and recidivistic male offenders seen in the Mental Examination Department of Helsinki University Central Hospital. We found that there were metabolic dysfunctions among these offenders (Virkkunen, 1979a; 1982; 1983a,c; Virkkunen & Huttunen, 1982).

Cholesterol levels among habitually violent offenders

The criteria for antisocial personality presented by Feighner et al. (1972) were applied to the selection of subjects in the first study (Virkkunen, 1979a). The data were collected from offenders who on court order were subjected to mental examination in a special ward of the psychiatric clinic at Helsinki University Central Hospital. On admission to the hospital efforts were made to distinguish by interview those who fulfilled the criteria for antisocial personality from those with other personality disorders. Those who had other personality disorders were included as controls. Possible psychotics or intellectually deficient persons were excluded, as were offenders over the age of 50, because those with antisocial personality were generally young. The subjects and the controls were matched for age as closely as possible.

The present study involved 139 subjects with antisocial personality and 135 controls. Those with antisocial personality tended to be habitually violent under the influence of alcohol. Nearly all subjects had committed property crimes and over half had committed crimes of violence. Three-fourths of the controls had committed crimes of violence.

On the day after admission, serum sampling was carried out on the subjects, after a minimum of 12 hours of fasting, to determine the cholesterol level enzymatically. The results clearly demonstrated that the serum cholesterol level was lower in the antisocial subjects than in the controls. The differences were particularly clear in the younger age groups – 15–19 and 20–29. When the mean cholesterol values for the Finnish male population were taken into account (Aromaa et al., 1975), the low cholesterol values described above were further emphasized, because the Finnish population values were even somewhat higher than those in the control group with other personality disorders.

Because it was possible that low cholesterol level was related to a tendency to behave violently under the influence of alcohol, the relation between cholesterol and intermittent explosive disorder was examined in the next study of 280 homicidal offenders (Virkkunen, 1983b). The writer himself made or supervised the mental examinations and observed all the offenders, checking the criteria personally.

Three groups of homicidal subjects and one group of nonhomicidal controls were examined. Seventy-three of the homicidal subjects who were diagnosed as having an antisocial personality formed the first group. One-hundred homicidal subjects with intermittent explosive disorder formed the second group. Both of these groups had been habitually violent under the influence of alcohol. To fulfill the criteria for intermittent explosive disorder, subjects had to have displayed several discrete episodes of loss of control of aggressive impulses (grossly out of proportion to any precipitating psychosocial stressor) resulting in serious assault or destruction of property. Offenders whose habitual violence had been directed against their wives in family quarrels were not included if they had not also committed violent acts against other people or property. The third group contained 107 homicidal offenders who had not shown habitually violent behavior under the influence of alcohol. Among these were 18 schizophrenics, 3 persons with paranoid psychoses, 4 with organic psychoses, 53 with paranoid personality, 21 with passive–aggressive personality, and 3 with dependent personality. Five of these 107 persons had diagnoses of antisocial personality disorder and had committed "accidental" homicides. The controls were 50 persons with antisocial personality who had not behaved violently under the influence of alcohol. They had usually committed only various property crimes. All final diagnoses were made using criteria from the DSM-III (Task Force on Nomenclature and Statistics of the American Psychiatric Association, 1980). There were no significant statistical differences in weight, height, or intelligence between the groups.

Among those homicidal offenders with antisocial personality (Group 1) or intermittent explosive disorder (Group 2) all had committed the capital offenses after a long drinking period. In the period before the homicide, these persons typically had a very poor appetite or no appetite at all. Those in Group 1 had been drinking an average of 7.6 (± 2.3) hours before the offense; those in Group 2 for 7.4 (± 2.2) hours. The period of drinking had been much shorter among the other homicidal offenders: Group 3, 2.9 (± 2.5) hours.

Serum cholesterol measurements were made enzymatically as in the study reported above (Trinder, 1969). Tables 16.1 and 16.2 show that both Group 1 and Group 2 subjects at two age levels (under 20 and 21–30 years) had lower cholesterol levels than Group 3 homicidal offenders and controls. In Group 2 (intermittent explosive disorder) the cholesterol level differences were significant when compared with Group 3 in the three older age groups as well. These results suggest that there may be two subgroups in the diagnostic category of antisocial personality disorder, persons with a habitually violent response to alcohol consumption and persons without such a pattern. These subgroups can be discriminated by their differing serum cholesterol levels as well as by the clinical histories of their antisocial acts. In addition to this hypothesis, the similarity in cholesterol levels between the two diagnostic categories – antisocial personality and intermittent explosive disorder – when subjects in each cate-

Table 16.1. *Serum cholesterol values by age among homicidal offenders and a control group*

Age of Subjects	Group 1[a]			Group 2[b]			Group 3[c]			Group 4[d]		
	N	Mean	S.D.	N	Mean	S.D.	N	Mean	S.D.	N	Mean	S.D.
Under 20	14	4.19	0.62	7	4.01	0.49	9	5.60	0.41	10	5.25	0.61
21–30	26	4.92	0.61	27	4.85	0.67	19	6.18	0.66	32	6.06	0.84
31–40	13	6.05	0.86	34	5.63	1.29	30	6.66	0.89	8	6.21	0.63
41–50	9	6.06	0.93	13	5.52	0.64	30	6.74	1.09	0	—	—
Over 50	11	6.25	1.16	19	5.37	0.92	19	6.44	0.64	0	—	—
Total	73	5.32	1.09	100	5.24	1.05	107	6.47	0.90	50	5.92	0.83

Note: Values represent millimoles per liter.

[a] Homicidal offenders with antisocial personality and habitual violence under the influence of alcohol.

[b] Homicidal offenders with intermittent explosive disorder and habitual violence under the influence of alcohol.

[c] Other homicidal offenders without habitual violence under the influence of alcohol.

[d] Controls: persons with antisocial personality without habitual violence under the influence of alcohol.

Source: Virkkunen (1983c).

Table 16.2. *Comparison of group mean serum cholesterol values by age among three groups of homicidal offenders and a control group*

| | t Values of comparisons | | | |
Age of subjects	Group 1/ Group 2	Group 1/ Group 3	Group 1/ Group 4	Group 2/ Group 3
Under 20	0.67	6.03*	4.17*	7.10*
21–30	0.43	6.66*	5.78*	6.71*
31–40	1.06	2.10	0.47	3.67*
41–50	1.57	1.74	—	3.75*
Over 50	2.28	0.59	—	4.16*
Total	0.46	7.71*	3.28*	9.04*

Note: Values represent millimoles per liter. For a definition of Groups 1–4, see Table 16.1.
*T Value is significant at $p < 0.01$.

Source: Virkkunen (1983c).

gory respond violently to alcohol consumption suggests that etiological factors in these two disorders may be partially the same.

Supplementary results from a subgroup of the homicidal offenders are also of interest. Low cholesterol level and the tendency toward habitual violence under the influence of alcohol were found among the fathers of 115 subjects. Low cholesterol level was also related to violence against oneself, such as suicidal attempts and slashings.

Reactive hypoglycemia among habitually violent offenders

A subsequent study demonstrated that among habitually violent and recidivistic males with antisocial personality in the middle age group (average age 30 years) there is an enhanced reactive hypoglycemia during the GTT (Virkkunen & Huttunen, 1982). Sixty successive males who had committed one or more severe violent crimes were investigated. Most of them had committed other kinds of crime as well. Subjects were excluded who had been convicted of robbery only, sexual crimes without violence, or arson. Violent offenders more than 50 years of age, those who were mentally retarded, or those who had a chromosome abnormality were also excluded.

Thirty-two of the subjects were diagnosed as antisocial personality using research diagnostic criteria (Spitzer, Endicott, & Robins, 1975). They usually also fulfilled the criteria for borderline personality disorder. Four uncertain cases with explosive features were excluded. The remaining 24 subjects (usually first-time violent offenders with depressive and paranoid features) served as controls. There were no significant statistical differences between the groups in age, weight, or IQ. The study compared the (GTTs) of violent offenders with a diagnosis of antisocial personality with the GTTs of control violent offenders. In addition, a second control group was composed of 20 male employees of the psychiatric clinic of Helsinki University Central Hospital. They were also matched for age and weight with the subjects.

All participants underwent a 5-hour GTT that was preceded by an overnight fast of at least 12 hours but in no case more than 16 hours. Stress was avoided the night before and during the test, and no other examinations were done on the test day. No medications were taken during the test or during the three previous days. All the participants were in identical, stable metabolic states with normal appetite before the GTT. All had been healthy, and there were no diabetics. All the participants kept to their normal diet during the three days preceding the GTT. On the morning of the examination, after a fasting blood sample had been taken, all the participants were given glucose (Glycodyn^R), 1 g/kg (4 ml/kg) body weight, which was taken orally as quickly as possible, and blood samples were then collected after 0.5, 1, 2, 3, 4, and 5 hours. Blood glucose was assessed enzymatically, and the analyses were made in the clinical laboratory of the University Central Hospital of Helsinki.

There was a tendency for blood glucose to fall to a very low level in subjects with antisocial personality, and this "hypoglycemic" phase after the initial rise in blood glucose was longest among subjects with antisocial personality. The difference between this group and the controls was statistically significant ($t = 4.75$; d.f. 54; $p < 0.001$). Half of the patients with antisocial personality had not yet regained the original basal level at the end of the 5-hour GTT. There were no such cases among the violent controls or among the psychiatric personnel. Hypoglycemia with blood glucose concentrations of less than 2.6 mmol/liter was found in 25 (78.1%) of those with an antisocial personality but in only 8 (33.3%) of the controls ($\psi^2 = 9.59$; d.f. 1; $p < 0.001$). There were 4 men (20.0%) with 2.6 mmol/liter or less among the psychiatric personnel.

A second study was done to clarify whether the GTT differed between violent subjects with antisocial personality and violent subjects with intermittent explosive disorder (Virkkunen, 1982). The criteria for the exclusion of subjects from the study, the GTT procedures, and the data for 20 hospital employee controls (Group 3) were the same as in the first study. Thirty-seven subjects formed an antisocial personality group (Group 1), and 31 an intermittent explosive disorder group (Group 2). All the violent acts in both the antisocial and explosive groups had been committed while

Table 16.3. *Glucose tolerance test values in two groups of habitually violent offenders and a control group*

	Group 1[a]		Group 2[b]		Group 3[c]	
Glucose tolerance test	Mean	S.D.	Mean	S.D.	Mean	S.D.
A. Basal level of glucose (mmol/liter)	3.93	0.44	3.65	0.41	4.00	0.51
B. Hyperglycemic level (mmol/liter)	6.84	1.60	6.60	1.83	6.17	1.69
C. Hypoglycemic level (mmol/liter)	2.41	0.54	2.27	0.36	3.09	0.50
D. Difference between hyper- and hypoglycemic levels (mmol/liter)	4.47	0.19	4.43	0.21	3.19	0.10
E. Duration of hypoglycemic phase (min)	195.4	44.4	125.8	48.3	165.0	39.1

Note: The following comparisons were significant, using two-tailed t test: A, 1 vs. 2 (d.f. 66, $t = 2.67$, $p < 0.01$), 2 vs. 3 (d.f. 49, $t = 2.70$, $p < 0.01$). C, 1 vs. 3 (d.f. 55, $t = 4.63$, $p < 0.001$), 2 vs. 3 (d.f. 49, $t = 6.79$, $p < 0.001$). D, 1 vs. 3 (d.f. 55, $t = 2.77$, $p < 0.01$), 2 vs. 3 (d.f. 49, $t = 2.46$, $p < 0.05$). E, 2 vs. 3 (d.f. 49, $t = 3.45$, $p < 0.001$).
[a] Habitually violent offenders with antisocial personality ($N = 37$).
[b] Habitually violent offenders with interintermittent explosive disorder ($N = 31$).
[c] Controls: psychiatric personnel ($N = 20$).

Source: Virkkunen (1982), Table II.

the individual was under the influence of alcohol, usually very impulsively. There were no statistical differences between the groups in age, weight, or IQ.

The mean basal levels of glucose, as well as hyperglycemic and hypoglycemic levels, can be seen in Table 16.3. Blood glucose fell below the basal level to a very low standard both in the intermittent explosive disorder and in the antisocial personality group. The reactive hypoglycemic phase, following the initial rise in blood glucose, lasted a relatively long time among those who had an antisocial personality. In the intermittent explosive disorder group it lasted a shorter time, even shorter than in the psychiatric personnel group.

Low reactive hypoglycemic levels were connected to two important facts in the two violent groups combined (Tables 16.4 and 16.5). First, subjects with low levels reported disturbances of memory about their violent acts. Second, in the opinion of their relatives, the low-level subjects were quarrelsome and aggressive under the influence of alcohol.

Several other characteristics that are especially typical of antisocial personality were significantly related to a long hypoglycemic phase. For example, truancy, low verbal IQ, low Kahn value, tatoos, slashings, stealing from one's own home in childhood, and more than two criminal

Table 16.4. *Relation of reactive hypoglycemic level and duration of hypoglycemic phase to psychosocial variables among habitually violent offenders*

Psychosocial variable	Variable present	Reactive hypoglycemic level (mmol/liter)			Duration of the hypoglycemic phase (min)		
		Mean	S.D.	t Value	Mean	S.D.	t Value
Quarrelsome and ag-gressive under the influence of alcohol (N = 58)	Yes	2.26	0.44	4.20**	195.5	44.6	1.93
	No	2.86	0.28	—	158.2	58.2	—
Loss of memory about violent acts (N = 52)	Yes	2.25	0.43	3.39**	165.0	58.8	0.34
	No	2.67	0.44	—	159.4	55.1	—
Verbal IQ less than performance IW (N = 31)	Yes	2.37	0.54	0.44	182.3	61.1	2.53*
	No	2.32	0.40	—	148.1	50.2	—
Kahn value under 80 (N = 38)	Yes	2.30	0.50	0.37	178.2	52.0	2.51*
	No	2.35	0.42	—	141.2	63.0	—
Tatoos (N = 31)	Yes	2.40	0.50	0.80	181.4	58.0	2.41*
	No	2.31	0.44	—	148.8	53.7	—
Slashing scars (N = 17)	Yes	2.54	0.49	1.98	192.9	49.1	2.52*
	No	2.28	0.45	—	153.9	57.4	—
Behavioral problems and sleeping difficul-ties in the hospital (N = 27)	Yes	2.29	0.49	0.72	185.6	49.7	2.65*
	No	2.38	0.46	—	149.3	58.5	—

* $p < 0.05$.
** $p < 0.01$.

Source: Virkkunen (1982).

sentences were associated with this long period, as was the violence of the subjects' fathers under the influence of alcohol (see Tables 16.4 and 16.5).

In the last study to be reported here (Virkkunen, 1983a) insulin secretion during the GTT among 23 habitually violent offenders between ages 16 and 30 with antisocial personality was investigated. The purpose of the study was to compare insulin secretion during a GTT in the adult subject with antisocial personality who had also had an unsocialized aggressive conduct disorder as a boy with the secretion in antisocial personality disordered adult subjects who had not had early aggressive conduct disorder. The subjects were divided into two groups. Group 1 contained the 16

Table 16.5. *Relations of reactive hypoglycemic level and duration of hypoglycemic phase to psychosocial variables among habitually violent offenders*

Psychosocial variable	Variable present	Reactive hypoglycemic level (mmol/liter)			Duration of the hypoglycemic phase (min)		
		Mean	S.D.	*t* Value	Mean	S.D.	*t* Value
Father violent under the influence of alcohol ($N = 39$)	Yes	2.31	0.50	0.58	178.7	53.1	3.40**
	No	2.38	0.43	—	129.3	56.9	—
Criminality of fathers ($N = 13$)	Yes	2.09	0.52	2.25*	174.2	58.9	0.73
	No	2.41	0.44	—	161.2	57.6	—
Father absent (death or separation) in puberty ($N = 22$)	Yes	2.53	0.47	2.27*	175.0	51.8	1.12
	No	2.26	0.45	—	158.3	60.0	—
Truancy ($N = 37$)	Yes	2.37	0.51	0.50	188.9	45.0	4.47**
	No	2.32	0.41	—	133.5	57.0	—
Stealing, including theft at home in childhood ($N = 29$)	Yes	2.40	0.47	0.86	180.2	53.8	2.23*
	No	2.31	0.46	—	150.6	57.5	—
Property crimes ($N = 46$)	Yes	2.35	0.50	0.18	175.7	56.5	2.58*
	No	2.33	0.39	—	138.6	52.8	—
More than two sentences for crimes of any kind ($N = 38$)	Yes	2.38	0.47	0.74	182.4	51.9	3.21**
	No	2.30	0.46	—	140.0	56.6	—

* $p < 0.05$.
** $p < 0.01$.

Source: Virkkunen (1982).

subjects who had clearly met DSM-III criteria for unsocialized aggressive conduct disorder before age 18. Group 2 was composed of the 7 remaining subjects for whom an insufficient number of criteria had been recorded to meet the adolescent diagnosis. Ten hospital employees served as a third comparison group. No subjects who were retarded (IQ under 68) or had a chromosome abnormality (XYY or XXY) were included. It should be noted that all 23 subjects had evidence of previous childhood attention-deficit disorder (ADD).

Retrospective diagnoses of aggressive conduct disorder and ADD were performed with the following materials. Near relatives were sent a questionnaire in which they were asked to give details concerning any behavioral problems the subject had experienced in adolescence and early childhood. School authorities and teachers were asked to give any account of any problems in school and also supply photostatic copies of school reports. Relevant documents were obtained from juvenile reformatories and from child and adolescent psychiatric hospitals and outpatient centers. The documents were analyzed for behaviors meeting the DSM-III criteria for unsocialized aggressive conduct disorder and/or ADD. The criteria were further confirmed by means of personal interviews, and if anything remained unclear close relatives were also interviewed.

The groups were well matched on weight. However, Group 1 individuals had a mean age of 20.6 years, Group 2 individuals a mean age of 25.3 years, and the hospital employees a mean age of 23 years. All 23 antisocial personality subjects fulfilled the criteria of DSM-III for alcohol abuse, but physical dependence with withdrawal symptoms had developed in only 8 persons. Of these, 7 were the antisocial subjects without an unsocialized aggressive conduct disorder. These persons were also the oldest subjects, having a mean age of 26.6 ± 3.1 years.

All 33 subjects underwent a 4-hour GTT with insulin measurements. The last insulin sample was taken after 3 hours because the basal level is usually reached by then. The glucose and insulin values can be seen in Tables 16.6 and 16.7. Insulin secretion was more enhanced in those who had had an early unsocialized aggressive conduct disorder than in the other two groups. The differences were very clear in the 60-, 90-, and 120-min values. The glucose values, however, did not differ much between groups.

Mean individual peak values in insulin secretion were significantly higher among subjects with an early onset (12–14 years of age) of alcohol abuse than in subjects without such early alcohol abuse ($t = 3.82$, $p < 0.01$). Also, subjects who experienced a continuation of attention problems into late adolescence had higher peak values than subjects whose ADD diminished earlier ($t = 3.30$, $p < 0.01$). Day–night rhythm disturbances, sleeping difficulties, and increasing behavioral problems, observed during the average 1-month observation period in the psychiatric ward were characteristic of subjects with high individual peak values.

It is notable that low cholesterol values were correlated with enhanced insulin secretion in this study ($r = 0.575$, $N = 23$, $p < 0.01$). Among subjects with a prior unsocialized aggressive conduct disorder, cholesterol was only 4.0 ± 0.35 mmol/liter. Among the other subjects with antisocial personality it was 5.9 ± 0.20 mmol/liter. The latter mean value corresponded to the values that have been found in these age groups in a normal male population in Finland (Aromaa et al., 1975).

Enhanced and long-lasting insulin secretion seems to be related to the

Table 16.6. *Mean glucose levels and insulin secretion values of two groups of adult antisocial subjects, and a control group*

Test value	Group 1[a]		Group 2[b]		Group 3[c]	
	Mean	S.D.	Mean	S.D.	Mean	S.D.
Glucose (mmol/liter)						
0 hours	4.20	0.40	4.07	0.37	4.38	0.46
15 min	5.88	1.03	5.71	0.89	6.12	0.84
30 min	7.37	1.35	6.40	1.19	7.42	1.61
60 min	7.08	1.91	4.93	1.11	6.25	2.23
90 min	5.63	1.76	4.66	1.29	5.66	1.80
120 min	4.74	1.54	4.23	1.09	4.96	1.62
180 min	3.52	0.67	3.41	0.44	4.12	0.86
240 min	3.67	0.51	3.76	0.32	4.01	0.70
Food glucose nadir	2.99	0.46	3.11	0.50	3.47	0.52
Insulin (mU/liter)						
0 hours	8.59	3.60	4.56	2.56	6.49	4.20
15 min	36.09	17.21	23.99	12.52	23.40	14.71
30 min	54.78	21.45	36.77	10.50	36.22	23.38
60 min	60.19	23.52	22.36	7.81	29.22	23.69
90 min	49.61	17.90	21.49	10.87	24.92	11.88
120 min	32.58	17.05	10.01	5.90	21.44	11.73
180 min	10.38	3.74	3.74	1.68	9.27	8.87
Mean of the individual peak values	68.33	20.71	37.99	9.86	45.65	21.89

[a] Antisocial personality with unsocialized aggressive conduct disorder ($N = 16$).
[b] Antisocial personality without unsocialized aggressive conduct disorder ($N = 7$).
[c] Controls: psychiatric personnel ($N = 10$).

Source: Virkkunen (1983a).

diagnosis of antisocial personality when it is preceded by early unsocialized aggressive conduct disorder. The age at which enhanced insulin secretion first appears in this group is not known. The finding was present among the youngest subjects in this study (two persons 16–17 years old). In spite of the enhanced insulin secretion found among most of the antisocial personalities in this last study, the subjects' reactive hypoglycemic values did not drop to the low level previously found in violent offenders with antisocial personality who were in the middle age group in the earlier two studies. The reason for this is not clear. On the basis of these three studies it is possible to hypothesize that the reactive hypoglycemic reaction to enhanced insulin secretion tends to become more pronounced with age. It is notable that alcohol abuse tends to become increasingly severe across the time span from adolescence to middle age.

Table 16.7. *Comparison of group mean glucose levels and insulin secretion values among two groups of adult antisocial subjects and a control group*

	T Values of comparisons		
Test value	Group 1/ Group 2	Group 1/ Group 3	Group 2/ Group 3
Glucose (mmol/liter)			
0 hours	0.72	1.05	1.46
15 min	0.37	0.61	0.95
30 min	1.64	0.09	1.42
60 min	2.75*	1.00	1.44
90 min	1.31	0.04	1.26
120 min	0.80	0.34	1.04
180 min	0.37	2.00	1.98
240 min	0.42	1.44	0.89
Food glucose nadir	0.56	2.43*	1.41
Insulin (mU/liter)			
0 hours	2.67*	1.36	1.08
15 min	1.67	1.93	0.09
30 min	2.09*	2.07*	0.06
60 min	4.11**	3.26**	0.73
90 min	3.83**	3.85**	0.61
120 min	3.37**	1.81	2.36*
180 min	3.19**	0.40	1.61
Mean of the individual peak values	3.99**	2.66*	0.86

Note: For a definition of Groups 1–3, see Table 16.6.
* $p < 0.05$.
** $p < 0.01$.

Source: Virkkunen (1983a).

Summary

The studies described above provide evidence that, among habitually violent and recidivistic males with antisocial personality, those in the younger age groups tend to have a very low cholesterol level. The same finding has been demonstrated among habitually violent males with intermittent explosive disorder.

It has also been found that habitually violent and recidivistic persons with antisocial personality have in middle age, and often earlier, enhanced reactive hypoglycemia during the GTT. The last-mentioned finding is also typical of those with intermittent explosive disorder. There is evidence that, at least among those with adult antisocial personality preceded by unsocialized aggressive conduct disorder in puberty, there is enhanced and long-lasting insulin secretion during the GTT.

Discussion

It is well known that habitual violence and alcohol abuse are connected (Coid, 1982; Evans, 1980). In studies of murder (Virkkunen, 1974; Wolfgang & Strohm, 1956), rape (Gebhard, Gagnon, Pomeroy & Christianson, 1965; Johnson, Gibson, & Linden, 1978; Rada, 1975), assault (Mayfield, 1976; Virkkunen, 1979b), wife and child abuse, and beating (Byles, 1978; Hanks & Rosenbaum, 1977), alcohol has been found to be a factor in the majority of cases.

The so-called alcohol-induced fasting hypoglycemia characteristically develops in chronically malnourished or, more acutely, food-deprived individuals within 6 to 36 hours of ingesting a moderate to large amount of alcohol (Marks, 1978). In such cases the ethanol induces hypoglycemia by inhibiting hepatic glucose production (Wilson, Brown, Juul, Prestwich, & Sönksen, 1981). In the studies described in this chapter, the offenders with an antisocial personality or an intermittent explosive disorder had usually been drinking for many hours, and they had had a very poor appetite or no appetite at all during this period. Moreover, alcohol increases still more the insulin secretion caused by low glucose level (alcohol-induced reactive hypoglycemia) (Marks, 1978). So it is possible that the habitually violent offenders were in a reactive hypoglycemic state when their violent acts were committed.

Mednick, Pollock, Volavka, and Gabrielli (1982) proposed that hypoglycemia exerts some of its behavioral effects by means of epilepsy-like mechanisms. Lewis, Pincus, Shanok, and Glaser (1982) suggested criteria for making the diagnosis of psychomotor epilepsy in violent adolescents as "well documented episodes of lapses of fully conscious contact with reality observed by others," "episodes followed by confusion, fatigue or sleep," and "impaired or absent memory for these episodes." These criteria can be understood as neuroglycopenic symptoms under certain circumstances (Virkkunen, 1983b). Cloninger, Bohman, and Sigvardsson (1981) and Bohman, Cloninger, Sigvardsson, and von Knorring (1982) noticed in their studies of inheritance of criminal behavior that alcoholic criminals often commit repetitive violent offenses, whereas nonalcoholic criminals characteristically commit a small number of petty property offenses. They emphasized that it is crucial to distinguish antisocial personality disorders from criminality symptomatic of alcohol abuse in future etiological studies. These findings are consistent with the results of studies reported in this chapter. There may be two groups of antisocial personality disorders: one with habitual violence under the influence of alcohol and the other without alcohol effects. An association between alcohol and violent behavior in the fathers of the subjects was also noted in the writer's earlier study (Virkkunen, 1979b). A combination of constitutional predisposition and pharmacological effects of alcohol could imply that underlying organic factors predispose individuals to habitual violence, as Coid (1982) has proposed.

A possible reason for the fact that habitual violence is seen especially in individuals who are under the influence of alcohol and/or have low cholesterol levels could be the enhanced insulin secretion that occurs in both states. In one of the studies described above there was a clear correlation between enhanced insulin secretion and low cholesterol level. Insulin is related not only to carbohydrate metabolism but also to lipid metabolism. The greatest part of cholesterol in humans is low-density lipoprotein (LDL) cholesterol. The LDL cholesterol is catabolized in peripheral tissues, and the rapidity of this catabolism determines the LDL level in the plasma and thus the cholesterol level. How much LDL gets to the peripheral tissues depends on the so-called LDL receptors on the surfaces of cells (Brown & Goldstein, 1976, 1979). Insulin increases the number of LDL receptors and thus LDL degradation (Chait, Bierman, & Albers, 1979), but can also stimulate intracellular lysosomal enzyme activity (Henze & Chait, 1981). Insulin among habitually violent persons seems to be very effective. It is well known that in obese individuals there is enhanced insulin secretion but, at the same time, insulin resistance. Many obese people have severe glucose intolerance. The weights of the males with habitually violent behavior in the above studies, however, were in the normal range. Habitually violent offenders, especially with antisocial personality, are often athletic. Diminished insulin response has been found in highly trained athletes (Björntorp et al., 1972; Lohman, Liebold, Heilmann, Senger, & Pohl, 1978). This seems not to be true among athletic habitually violent offenders.

The differences in recovery from hypoglycemia between the habitually violent offenders with antisocial personality and those with intermittent explosive disorder might depend on the hormones released as counterregulatory response to hypoglycemia: epinephrine, norepinephrine, cortisol, growth hormone, and glucagon (DeFranzo et al., 1977; Santeusanio et al., 1981). Marks (1978) earlier speculated that abnormalities in these hormonal responses would not only predispose to the development of hypoglycemia but also delay recovery from it. However, it is important to note that enhanced insulin secretion also lasted longer in subjects with antisocial personality than in controls. There are preliminary findings that in intermittent explosive disorder this enhanced insulin secretion is of very rapid onset but of short duration (Virkkunen, in press), which may also explain the differences.

Some studies have suggested that habitual violence and impulsiveness are correlated with low cerebrospinal fluid levels of the serotonin metabolite 5-hydroxyindoleacetic acid (5-HIAA) (Brown, Goodwin, Ballenger, Goyer, & Major, 1979; Brown et al., 1982). Alcoholism can also be associated with these abnormal levels (Ballenger, Goodwin, Major, & Brown, 1979). The bulk of other evidence seems to indicate that, both in laboratory animals and in humans, reduced brain serotonergic control, either genetically predetermined or chemically or dietarily induced, is correlated with abnormal aggression and violence (Valzelli, 1981). There is also evidence that intracellular pancreatic B-cell serotonin acts as a tonic inhibitor of insulin release, at least among some laboratory animals (Feldman & Lebovitz, 1972; Pulido, Bencosme, de Bold, & de Bold, 1978; Wilson, Downs, Feldman, & Lebovitz, 1974). Serotonergic inhibition by p-chlorophenylalanine, a compound that blocks serotonin synthesis, causes increased insulin secretion after glucose in humans (DeLeiva et al., 1978). Also, drugs reported to be specific serotonin antagonists potentiate the release of glucose-induced insulin among normal human subjects (Pontiroli, Viberti, Tognetti, & Pozza, 1975). So low serotonin level and enhanced insulin secretion may be related in habitually violent offenders.

Additional studies of habitually violent offenders are needed to clarify the connections with low cholesterol level, insulin secretion, and serotonin metabolism. Because there is evidence that habitually violent persons are apt to behave violently under laboratory conditions when given alcohol (Maletzky, 1976), the exact mechanism must be clarified. Enhanced and long-lasting insulin secretion seems to be related to adult antisocial personality preceded by adolescent unsocialized aggressive conduct disorder. It may be possible by biochemical means to identify prospectively those conduct-disordered children with habitual violence and impulsiveness who have a poor adult prognosis. An especially low cholesterol level could be a good and easily measured indicator of dangerousness (habitual violence) among these children and adolescents. Preliminary findings have been acquired by this approach (Virkkunen & Penttinen, 1983). To verify the hypotheses suggested here, however, prospective follow-up studies are necessary.

References

Aromaa, A., Björketén, F., Eriksson, A., Fellman, A., Kirjarinta, M., Maatela, J., & Tamminen, M. (1975). Serum-cholesterol and triglyceride concentrations of Finns and Finnish Lapps: Basic data. *Acta Medica Scandinavica, 198,* 13–26.

Ballenger, J. C., Goodwin, F. K., Major, L. F., & Brown, G. L. (1979). Alcohol and central serotonin metabolism in man. *Archives of General Psychiatry, 36,* 224–7.

Björntorp, P., Fahlén, M., Grimby, G., Gustafson, A., Holm, J., Renström, P., & Scherstén, T. (1972). Carbohydrate and lipid metabolism in middle-aged, physically well trained men. *Metabolism, 23,* 1037–44.

Bohman, M., Cloninger, C. R., Sigvardsson, S., & von Knorring, A.-L. (1982). Predisposition to petty criminality in Swedish adoptees: I. Genetic and environmental heterogeneity. *Archives of General Psychiatry, 39,* 1233–41.

Bolton, R. (1973). Aggression and hypoglycemia among the Qolla: A study in psychobiological anthropology. *Ethnology, 12,* 227–57.

Bolton, R. (1976). Hostility in fantasy: A further test of the hypoglycemia–aggression hypothesis. *Aggressive Behavior, 2,* 257–74.

Bovill, D. (1973). A case of functional hypoglycaemia: A medicolegal problem. *British Journal of Psychiatry, 123,* 353–8.

Brown, G. L., Ebert, M. H., Goyer, P. F., Jimerson, D. C., Klein, W. J., Bunney, W. E., & Boodwin, F. K. (1982). Aggression, suicide and serotonin: Relationships to CSF amine metabolites. *American Journal of Psychiatry, 139,* 741–6.

Brown, G. L., Goodwin, F. K., Ballenger, J. C., Goyer, P. F., & Major, L. F. (1979). Aggression in humans correlates with cerebrospinal fluid amine metabolites. *Psychiatry Research, 1,* 131–9.

Brown, M. S., & Goldstein, J. L. (1976). Familial hypercholesterolemia: A genetic defect in the low-density lipoprotein receptor. *New England Journal of Medicine, 294,* 1386–90.

Brown, M. S., & Goldstein, J. L. (1979). Receptor-mediated endocytosis: Insight from the lipoprotein receptor system. *Proceedings of the National Academy of Sciences, 76,* 3330–7.

Byles, J. A. (1978). Violence, alcohol problems and other problems in disintegrating families. *Journal of Studies on Alcohol, 39,* 551–3.

Chait, A., Bierman, E. L., & Albers, J. J. (1979). Low-density lipoprotein receptor activity in cultured human skin fibroblasts: Mechanism of insulin-induced stimulation. *Journal of Clinical Investigation, 64,* 1309–19.

Cloninger, C. R., Bohman, M., & Sigvardsson, S. (1981). Inheritance of alcohol abuse: Cross-fostering analysis of adopted men. *Archives of General Psychiatry, 38,* 861–8.

Coid, J. (1982). Alcoholism and violence. *Drug and Alcohol Dependence, 9,* 1–13.

DeFranzo, R. A., Andres, R., Bledsoe, T. A., Boden, G., Falona, G. A., & Tobin, J. D. (1977). A test of the hypothesis that the rate of fall in glucose concentration triggers counterregulatory hormonal responses in man. *Diabetes, 26,* 445–52.

DeLeiva, A., Tanenberg, R. J., Anderson, G., Greenberg, B., Senske, B., & Goetz, F. C. (1978). Serotoninergic activation and inhibition: Effects of carbohydrate tolerance and plasma insulin and glucagon. *Metabolism, 28,* 511–20.

Evans, C. M. (1980). Alcohol, violence and aggression. *British Journal of Alcohol and Alcoholism, 15,* 104–17.

Fabrykant, M., & Pacella, B. (1948). Labile diabetes: Electroencephalographic status and effect of anticonvulsive therapy. *Annals of Internal Medicine, 29,* 860–77.

Feighner, J. P., Robins, E., Guze, S. B., Woodruff, R. A., Winokur, G., & Munoz, R. (1972). Diagnostic criteria for use in psychiatric research. *Archives of General Psychiatry, 26,* 57–63.

Feldman, J. M., & Lebovitz, H. E. (1972). A serotonergic mechanism for the control of insulin secretion. *Transactions of the Association of American Physicians, 85,* 279–94.

Flemenbaum, A., & Anderson, R. P. (1978). Field dependence and blood cholesterol: An expansion. *Perceptual and Motor Skills, 46,* 867–74.

Flemenbaum, A., & Flemenbaum, E. (1975). Field dependence, blood uric acid and cholesterol. *Perceptual and Motor Skills, 41,* 135–41.

Gebhard, P. H., Gagnon, J. H., Pomeroy, W. B., & Christenson, C. V. (1965). *Sex offenders: An analysis of types.* New York: Harper & Row.

Groesbeck, D., D'Asaro, B., & Nigro, C. (1975). Polyamine levels in jail inmates. *Journal of Orthomolecular Psychiatry, 4,* 149–152.

Hanks, S. E., & Rosenbaum, C. P. (1977). Battered women: A study of women who live with violent alcohol-abusing men. *American Journal of Orthopsychiatry, 47,* 291–306.

Hatch, F. T., Reisell, P. K., Poon-King, T. M. W., Canellós, G. P., Lees, R. S., & Hagopian, L. M. (1966). A study of coronary heart disease in young men: Characteristics and metabolic studies of patients and comparison with age-matched healthy men. *Circulation, 33,* 679–703.

Henze, K., & Chait, A. (1981). Lysosomal enzyme activities and low-density lipoprotein receptors in circulating mononuclear cells: Effect of insulin therapy in diabetic patients. *Diabetologia, 20,* 625–9.

Hill, D., & Sargant, W. (1943). A case of matricide. *Lancet, 1,* 526–7.

Jenkins, C. D., Hames, C. G., Zyzanski, S. J., Rosenman, R. H., & Friedman, M. (1969). Psychological traits and serum lipids. *Psychosomatic Medicine, 31,* 115–28.

Johnson, S. D., Gibson, L., & Linden, R. (1978). Alcohol and rape in Winnipeg, 1966–1973. *Journal of Studies on Alcohol, 39,* 1887-98.

Lewis, D. O., Pincus, J. H., Shanok, S. S., & Glaser, G. H. (1982). Psychomotor epilepsy and violence in a group of incarcerated adolescent boys. *American Journal of Psychiatry, 139,* 882–7.

Lohman, D., Liebold, W., Heilmann, W., Senger, H. & Pohl, A. (1978). Diminished insulin response in highly trained athletes. *Metabolism, 27,* 521–4.

Maletzky, B. M. (1976). The diagnosis of pathological intoxication. *Journal of Studies on Alcohol, 37,* 1215–28.

Marks, V. (1978). Alcohol and carbohydrate metabolism. *Clinics in Endocrinology and Metabolism, 7,* 333–48.

Mayfield, D. G. (1976). Alcoholism, alcohol, intoxication and assaultive behavior. *Diseases of the Nervous System, 37,* 288–91.

McCranie, E. W., Simpson, M. E., & Stevens, J. S. (1981). Type A behavior, field dependence, and serum lipids. *Psychosomatic Medicine, 43,* 107–16.

Mednick, S. A., Pollock, V., Volavka, J., & Gabrielli, W. F., Jr. (1982). Biology and violence. In M. E. Wolfgang & N. A. Weiner (Eds.), *Criminal violence* (pp. 21–80). Beverly Hills, CA: Sage.

Neziroglu, F. (1979). Behavioral and organic aspects of aggression. In J. Obiols, C. Ballus, E. Gonzales-Monhus, & J. Pujol (Eds.), *Biological psychiatry today* (pp. 1215–22). Amsterdam: Elsevier.

Pontiroli, A. E., Viberti, G. C., Tognetti, A., & Pozza, G. Effect of metergoline, a powerful and long-acting antiserotonergic agent, on insulin secretion in normal subjects and in patients with chemical diabetes. *Diabetologia, 11,* 165–7.

Prinz, R. J., Roberts, W. A., & Hantman, E. (1980). Dietary correlates of hyperactive behavior in children. *Journal of Consulting and Clinical Psychology, 48,* 760–9.

Pulido, O. M., Bencosme, S. A., de Bold, M. L., & de Bold, A. J. (1978). Intracellular pancreatic B cell serotonin and the dynamics of insulin release. *Diabetologia, 15,* 197–204.

Rada, R. T. (1975). Alcoholism and forcible rape. *American Journal of Psychiatry, 132*, 444–6.

Rahe, R. H., Rubin, R. T., & Gunderson, E. K. E. (1972). Measures of subjects' motivation and affect correlated with their serum uric acid, cholesterol and cortisol. *Archives of General Psychiatry, 26*, 357–9.

Santeusanio, F., Bolli, G., Massi-Benedetti, M., DeFeo, P., Angeletti, G., Compagnucci, P., Calbrese, G., & Brunetti, P. (1981). Counterregulatory hormones during moderate, insulin-induced blood glucose decrements in man. *Journal of Clinical Endocrinology and Metabolism, 52*, 477–82.

Satterfield, J. H., Hoppe, C. M., & Schell, A. M. (1982). A prospective study of delinquency in 110 adolescent boys with attention deficit disorder and 88 normal adolescent boys. *American Journal of Psychiatry, 139*, 795–8.

Schauss, A. G., & Simonsen, C. E. (1979). A critical analysis of the diets of chronic juvenile offenders (Part 1). *Journal of Orthomolecular Psychiatry, 8*, 149–57.

Schoenthaler, S. J. (1982). The effect of sugar on the treatment and control of antisocial behavior: A double-blind study of an incarcerated juvenile population. *International Journal for Biosocial Research, 3*, 1–9.

Spitzer, R., Endicott, J., & Robins, E. (1975). *Research diagnostic criteria: Biometrics research*. New York: New York State Department of Health.

Task Force on Nomenclature and Statistics of the American Psychiatric Association. (1980). *Diagnostic and statistical manual of mental disorders*. Washington, DC: American Psychiatric Association.

Trinder, P. (1969). Determination of cholesterol in blood using cholesterol oxidase with alternative oxygen acceptor. *Annals of Clinical Biochemistry, 6*, 24–7.

Valzelli, L. (1981). Aggression and violence: A biological essay of the distinction. In L. Valzelli, & I. Morgese (Eds.), *Aggression and violence: A psychobiological and clinical approach* (pp. 39–60). Saint Vincent, Italy: Edizioni centro culturale e congressi.

Virkkunen, M. (1974). Alcohol as a factor precipitating aggression and conflict behavior leading to homicide. *British Journal of Addiction, 69*, 149–54.

Virkkunen, M. (1979a). Serum cholesterol in antisocial personality. *Neuropsychobiology, 5*, 27–30.

Virkkunen, M. (1979b). Alcoholism and antisocial personality. *Acta Psychiatrica Scandinavica, 59*, 493–501.

Virkkunen, M. (1982). Reactive hypoglycemic tendency among habitually violent offenders: A further study by means of the glucose tolerance test. *Neuropsychobiology, 5*, 35–40.

Virkkunen, M. (1983a). Insulin secretion during the glucose tolerance test in antisocial personality. *British Journal of Psychiatry, 142*, 598–604.

Virkkunen, M. (1983b). Psychomotor epilepsy and violence (Letter to the Editor). *American Journal of Psychiatry, 140*, 646–7.

Virkkunen, M. (1983c). Serum cholesterol levels in homicidal offenders: A low cholesterol level is connected with a habitually violent tendency under the influence of alcohol. *Neuropsychobiology, 10*, 65–9.

Virkkunen, M., & Huttunen, M. O. (1982). Evidence for abnormal glucose tolerance test among violent offenders. *Neuropsychobiology, 8*, 30–4.

Virkkunen, M., & Penttinen, H. (1984). Serum cholesterol in aggressive conduct disorder: A preliminary study. *Biological Psychiatry 19*, 435–9.

Virkkunen, M. (in press/1986). Insulin secretion during the glucose tolerance test among habitually violent and impulsive offenders. *Aggressive Behavior 12*, 303–10.

Wilder, J. (1947). Sugar metabolism and its relation to criminology. In S. Linder & R. Selinger (Eds.), *Handbook of correctional psychology* (pp. 98–129). New York: Philosophical Library.

Wilson, D. R. (1951). Electroencephalographic studies in diabetes mellitus. *Canadian Medical Association Journal, 65,* 462–5.

Wilson, J. P., Downs, R. W., Jr., Feldman, J. M., & Lebovitz, H. E. (1974). Beta cell monoamines: Further evidence for their role in modulating insulin secretion. *American Journal of Physiology, 227,* 305–12.

Wilson, N. M., Brown, P. M., Juul, S. M., Prestwich, S. A., & Sönksen, P. H. (1981). Glucose turnover and metabolism and hormonal changes in ethanol-induced hypoglycaemia. *British Medical Journal, 282,* 849–53.

Wolfgang, M. E., & Strohm, R. B. (1956). The relationship between alcohol and criminal homicide. *Quarterly Journal of Studies on Alcohol, 17,* 411–25.

Yarura-Tobias, J. A., & Neziroglu, F. A. (1975). Violent behavior, brain dysrythmia, and glucose dysfunction: A new syndrome. *Journal of Orthomolecular Psychiatry, 4,* 182–8.

Yarura-Tobias, J. A., & Neziroglu, F. A. (1981). Aggressive behavior, clinical interfaces. In L. Valzelli & I. Morgese (Eds.), *Aggression and violence: A psychobiological and clinical approach* (pp. 195–210). Saint Vincent, Italy: Edizioni centro culturale e congressi.

17 The role of psychosurgical studies in the control of antisocial behavior

Mark A. J. O'Callaghan and Douglas Carroll

Introduction

Although brain surgery for the control of explicitly antisocial behavior comprises a tiny fraction of all psychosurgical operations, it nevertheless occupies a central place in the fierce controversy surrounding what Breggin (1972) called the "second wave" of psychosurgery. In our analysis of published reports, encompassing some 15,000 psychosurgical cases, about 2½% of the operations were for the control of antisocial behavior (O'Callaghan & Carroll, 1982). In this chapter, we shall present a more detailed review of these, concentrating on the control of sexual "disorders" and aggressive behavior.

Genesis of psychosurgical procedures for the control of antisocial behavior

Aggressive behavior

Although psychosurgery can be briefly defined as the interruption of histologically normal brain tissue for the control of behavior, there are those who suggest that there is indeed some abnormality of brain function that gives rise to antisocial behavior. Mark and his colleagues, for example, proposed that some acts of aggression reflect behavioral dyscontrol arising from an amygdala-based pathology. For evidence they relied heavily on the existence of an orderly relation between episodic aggressive behavior and temporal lobe epilepsy (Mark & Ervin 1970; Mark & Ordia, 1976), although it must be noted that it is the aggressive behavior and not the epilepsy that affords the major impetus for surgery (Mark, Sweet, & Ervin, 1972). In addition, it is perhaps worth noting that not everyone is convinced of this epilepsy–aggression link (Rodin, 1973).

However, the main impetus for amygdalectomy in the context of aggressive behavior arose out of the animal research that followed Klüver

312

and Bucy's initiative. Klüver and Bucy (1938) described a syndrome of behavioral changes in monkeys following bilateral temporal lobotomy; these included compulsive orality, hypersexuality, failures in recognition, deficits in avoidance behavior, and docility. Subsequent research (e.g., Schreiner & Kling, 1953) revealed that much of this Klüver–Bucy syndrome could be produced by lesions restricted to the amygdaloid nucleus. However, it was primarily the sedative effects of surgery that attracted the interest of psychosurgeons.

Psychosurgeons have always been guilty of a certain selectivity of perception when it comes to animal brain–behavior research. This is nowhere more evident than in the lessons drawn from the amygdala lesion studies. For example, when surgery was initiated at the site of the amygdala, psychosurgeons had no independent grounds for suspecting only fractional Klüver–Bucy effects, that is, only docility. Furthermore, more recent animal research (e.g., Kling, 1972), indicating the pervasive influence of postoperative social context, has yet to be incorporated into psychosurgical theory. Kling's studies reveal that Klüver–Bucy effects, including docility, are present only in restrictive, laboratory environments. When amygdalectomized monkeys were returned to a free-ranging colony, they displayed a strikingly different set of deficits. Operated animals seemed no longer able to comprehend established social norms. They failed to respond appropriately to social communications and continuously appeared confused and fearful. Frequently, when approached by a monkey in a nonthreatening way, they would respond by cowering or fleeing. Alternatively, operated animals would, on occasion, react provocatively when threatened by a dominant colony member. A severe beating was the price of such social incompetence. In adult monkeys the failure to resocialize postoperatively was total. Complete social isolation was invariably followed by death from starvation or from attacks by predators.

Sexual "disorders"

The biological foundations for the surgical control of sexual "disorders" have received even less formal elaboration. Rationales have again relied heavily on extrapolation from animal research. Indeed, it must be noted that early psychosurgical studies appeared to contraindicate the use of brain surgery for the control of sexual "disorders." Although a favorable outcome was claimed by both Motta (1953) in the case of a homosexual treated by transorbital leucotomy and by Bailey, Dowling, and Davies (1977) for psychosexual exhibitionism by cingulotractotomy, larger scale operative series have failed to produce benefit. Freeman (1952), for example, the most prolific of psychosurgeons, stated that in his experience sexual "disorders" were poorly indicated. Scoville (1972) drew similar conclusions about the utility of orbital undercutting in this context. His conclusions, based on his own large series, are worth noting:

Constitutional psychopathy, sex perversion, and criminal behavior are not benefitted by selective lobotomy because of a constitutional lack of a moral sense, conscience or guilt. Such traits must be overly developed rather than absent in order to benefit from lobotomy. Actually lobotomy may make such cases worse. As Walter Freeman pointed out after operating on a "peeping Tom," the only change he could see was that the patient transferred his peeping from a hidden back alley before, to the front sidewalk, after operation. (P. 7)

It should be emphasized, however, that none of the early surgical procedures mentioned above were specifically developed to control sexual "disorder." They were undertaken for much more general disturbances of behavior. In contrast, the newer, "second-wave" operations are decidedly specific in their behavioral aspirations, as well as in their anatomical foci. The main impetus for the application of hypothalamotomy to sexual "disorders" came, as indicated, not from human but from animal research. As Kiloh (1977a) noted:

Experimental work on cats suggested to Roeder (1966) that hypersexuality might respond to centromedial hypothalamotomy. The argument was extended to sexual deviations for reasons which are not clear. (Pp. 46–47)

Kiloh was clearly skeptical. Indeed, few conceptual leaps from animals to humans can have been so ill-considered and cavalier (Carroll & O'Callaghan, 1983). As the main proponents of human hypothalamotomy themselves admitted (Roeder, Orthner, & Müller, 1972), two films – one of Schreiner and Kling's (1956) amygdalectomized cats and another of Dörner's (1971) hormonal work – provided the theoretical inspiration:

This film, exhibited by Schreiner and Kling at the International Neurologic Congress in Brussels (1957), was a mine of information for human sexual pathology. Without going into more specific details, much of what was observed in the behavior of male cats after lesions in the region of the amygdaloid nucleus resembles human perversions. Already this film convinced us that there were solid reasons for undertaking a therapeutic stereotaxic procedure. Synchronous with our work, Dörner reported on experimental homosexuality through hormonal influences. He showed a very instructive film during the Symposion der Deutschen Neurovegetativen Gesellschaft Göttingen in 1969. (P. 88)

It is important to emphasize that no causal cerebral abnormality was ever clearly established in the operatees (mainly male pedophilic homosexuals) subjected by Roeder et al. (1972) to hypothalamotomy. Surgery (by electrocoagulation) was performed on the basis of animal research that had indicated that intervention in the ventral medial hypothalamus

eliminated the worst excesses of hypersexuality displayed by amygdalectomized animals. Dieckmann and Hasler (1975), the other major proponents of hypothalamotomy, also made much of Dörner's work. Psychosurgery (also by electrocoagulation) was regarded as addressing the
balance between the two sex centers whose dynamics dictated the character of an individual's sexual deportment:

Both centers are capable of influencing sexual behavior as well. The center within
the anterior hypothalamic area is assumed by Dörner (Döcke & Hinz, 1969;
Dörner, Döcke, & Moustafa, 1968) to be a male sex-behavior center and the other
to be the female sex-behavior center. (P. 179)

Four points should be made here. First, Dörner's deployment of research evidence to support single and separate "sex-behavior centers"
regulating the behavior of each sex would find few unreserved supporters
(see Valenstein, 1973). Second, as Valenstein noted, there is now a wide
variety of research data that implicate the ventromedial hypothalamus in
a range of biological functions in addition to sex. Third, there is compelling evidence that, although structural and hormonal influences may dom-
inate with regard to the intensity of sexual interest, learning and social
context play a crucial role in the mode of expression of that interest, that
is, its direction, especially in humans (see Zuckerman, 1972). Finally, the
hypersexuality that appeared in animal species following amygdalectomy
may be exclusive of particular unnatural postoperative environments
(Kling, 1972). Thus the social dynamics, as well as the precise character
of animal sexual excesses following amygdalectomy, make a pitifully poor
metaphor for human sexual disorder.

Empirical evaluation of psychosurgery for the control of antisocial behavior

Clearly, the use of psychosurgery for the control of antisocial behavior is
without an adequate theoretical foundation. However, psychosurgeons
have generally placed greater emphasis on empirical rather than theoretical considerations. It is often the case that theory lags behind practice in
therapeutic settings. Accordingly, let us now examine the empirical case.

At the outset of any such empirical evaluation, however, it must be
appreciated that psychosurgical studies are of a notoriously poor quality.
Valenstein (1977) assigned English-language reports of psychosurgery
published between 1970 and 1975 to one of six categories of a scientific
merit schemata based on the work of May and van Putten (1974). More
than 90% of these studies were allocated to the lowest scientific merit
category, with over half being relegated to the lowest category of all.

Table 17.1. *Summary of results of amygdalectomy in the treatment of aggressive behavior and conduct disorders*

N	Outcome classification				
	1. Marked improvement (%)	2. Some improvement (%)	3. No improvement (%)	4. Worse (%)	Reference
40	45	33	22	—	Narabayashi & Uno (1966)
115	38	37	17	8	Balasubramaniam, Kanaka, & Ramamurthi (1970)
12	67	25	8	—	Vaernet & Madsen (1970)
18	22	28	50	—	Kiloh, Gye, Rushworth, Bell, & White (1974)

Articles reporting the results of amygdalectomy and hypothalamotomy for the control of aggressive behavior and sexual "disorders" are no exception. These procedures have not been subjected to a properly conducted, prospective-controlled trial with sophisticated and independent assessment. Instead, researchers have relied exclusively on brief and causal case reports.

As part of an analysis of psychosurgical procedures in general, data from the major studies were summarized in tabular form (O'Callaghan & Carroll, 1982). Four amygdalectomy studies lending themselves to this sort of treatment are presented in Table 17.1, and four hypothalamotomy studies appear in Table 17.2. To facilitate these presentations, operatees have been assigned to one of four categories of improvement, based on original outcome classifications. Obviously such categories are somewhat arbitrary in that they do not represent objective divisions along a continuum of outcome. Nevertheless, we have adopted such a system because contemporary psychosurgical data are usually presented in this form and it does provide some basis for comparison among studies and among operative procedures. The categories employed in Tables 17.1 and 17.2 are as follows:

1. *Marked improvement.* Patient has either completely recovered or markedly improved, is on little or no medication, occasionally or never consults psychiatrists, and generally functions at 75% to 100% of ability.
2. *Some improvement.* Patient has shown some improvement, takes medi-

Table 17.2. *Summary of results of hypothalamotomy in the treatment of sexual "disorders"*

		Outcome classification					
N	Diagnosis	1. Marked improvement (%)	2. Some improvement (%)	3. No improvement (%)	4. Worse (%)	Original categories	Reference
11	Sexual deviations[a] (p. 87)	60	10	30	—	1, ++++ 2, ++ (fair) 3, + (poor) (p. 102)	Roeder et al. (1972)
20[b]	Sexual deviations[c]	75	15	5	5[d]	1, Good 2, Fair 3, Poor (p. 121)	Müller, Roeder, & Orthner (1973)
6	Sexual deviations[e]	83	17	—	—	1, Good 2, Fair (p. 183)	Dieckmann & Hassler (1975)
47[f]	Sexual violence[g]	100	—	—	—	1, Marked reduction of sex drive (p. 460)	Dieckmann & Hassler (1977)

[a] Mainly "pedophilia" and "homosexual" (p. 102).

[b] Includes patients of first series.

[c] Mainly "homosexual deviations."

[d] One patient died 6 days after operation.

[e] All imprisoned: 3 homosexuals (2 with pedophilia), 2 "violent hypersexuality," and 1 hypersexual "pyromanic perversity" (p. 183).

[f] Includes 3 patients of first series.

[g] All convicted of sexual violence, 3 for "severe heterosexual rapes"; 1 because of "repeated sexually motivated arson" (p. 452).

cation regularly, consults psychiatrists regularly, and generally functions at 25% to 75% of ability.

3. *No improvement.* Patient's condition is not (or only very minimally or temporarily) improved; patient is under constant psychiatric care and generally functions at below 25% of ability.

4. *Worse.* Patient's psychiatric disorder has worsened or general condition has deteriorated due to adverse operative sequelae; includes patients whose deaths can in some way be attributed to operation and patients who have committed suicide.

As can be seen from Table 17.1 the results for amygdalectomy in the control of aggressive behavior are decidedly unremarkable. Overall, the procedure has an improvement rate no greater than that for the now largely discredited prefrontal operations of the past (O'Callaghan & Carroll, 1982).

Table 17.2 indicates that the results of hypothalamotomy for the treatment of sexual "disorders," taking the authors' assessments at face value, appear to be much more favorable. However, in the absence of adequately controlled methodology, doubts must remain; beneficial outcomes could merely reflect remission over time or placebo and expectancy effects. The target population for frontal lobe surgery was gauged to present an untreated symptom remission rate of around 40% (Staudt & Zubin, 1957). Although no estimates are available for amygdalectomy or hypothalamotomy candidates, there is no reason to suspect a lower remission rate. In addition, there is evidence of sizable placebo effects with surgery in other contexts (Beecher, 1961).

It should also be appreciated that the criteria for allocating patients to improvement categories are frequently applied in a less than rigorous fashion. For example, as Dieckmann and Hassler (1975) admitted, in the majority of their cases the "deviant" sexual symptoms were reduced but not fully eliminated; this was true even of those who attracted a "good" (i.e., Category 1) postoperative classification. Similarly, the reduction in aggressive behavior following amygdalectomy was not always complete or, if it was, it was bought at the cost of a more general dampening of function, as will be discussed later.

Another difficulty with these procedures is that the durability of the operative effects have yet to be satisfactorily established. Follow-ups are insufficiently protracted to allow a determination. However, evidence from amygdalectomy studies indicates a dramatic change in improvement rates between short- and long-term follow-up (Table 17.3). With regard to the Heimburger et al. studies (Heimburger, Small, Small, Milstein, & Moore, 1978; Heimburger, Whitlock, & Kalsbeck, 1966), it would seem that with longer term follow-up, the observed efficacy of the procedure

Table 17.3. Comparison of short- and long-term results of amygdalectomy

N	Outcome classification				Follow-up	Reference
	1. Marked improvement (%)	2. Some improvement (%)	3. No improvement (%)	4. Worse (%)		
25	64	28		8	1–3 years	Heimburger et al. (1966)
58	45		48	7	1–11 years (average 6 years)	Heimburger et al. (1978)
18	61	17	22	—	"Immediate"	Narabayashi (1979)
18	39	22	39	—	5–17 years	Narabayashi (1979)

declines markedly. Although this decline could reflect the subsequent inclusion of patients with a generally poorer prognosis, this would seem unlikely. In any case, Narabayashi's data are not confounded in this manner; they clearly depict a marked reduction in substantive postoperative improvement over time (Narabayashi, 1979; Narabayashi & Uno, 1966). Although such precise data are lacking with regard to hypothalamotomy, there are some hints of an analogous trend in sexual "disorder" patients; an increase in such sexual activity with time was witnessed in some cases (Dieckmann & Hassler, 1975; Schneider, 1977).

Adverse sequelae

In any evaluation of efficacy, it is important to establish whether the effects of surgery are specific or whether they are embedded in a complex matrix of psychological changes, many of them undesirable. Unfortunately, as Tables 17.4 and 17.5 reveal, there is a woeful lack of information on side effects of these procedures. The presence or absence of adverse sequelae are rarely indicated in the reports (blank space in Tables 17.4 and 17.5), or often researchers merely mention that there was some problem in a particular sphere (e.g., a check mark in the tables) without revealing its precise frequency. However, disastrous outcomes such as death after hypothalamotomy as well as seizures and clinical deterioration after amygdalectomy have been reported. Let us now examine the matter of specificity in more detail.

Specificity of lesion effects

The unconvincing theoretical rationales offered for both amygdalectomy and hypothalamotomy would certainly lead us to suspect claims that surgery addressed only some specific target disorder. In addition, it is worth noting in this context that a very limited class of operations is applied to a wide variety of sexual "disorders" appearing either singly or in combination; hypersexuality, homosexuality, pedophilia, sexual violence (e.g., rape), exhibitionism, and sexually motivated arson have all been treated by the same procedure. The same is true for amygdalectomy; it has been applied to a wide range of conduct disorders (see O'Callaghan & Carroll, 1982).

More tellingly, there is evidence that what surgery achieves is a general change rather than the elimination of a specific "deviation." The nonspecific effects of amygdalectomy are particularly apparent in Andersen's (1972) fairly thorough assessment of Vaernet and Madsen's (1970) opera-

Table 17.4. *Summary of adverse sequelae of amygdalectomy*

N	Worse	Dead	Surgical/ neurological complications	Seizures	Incontinence	Weight	Personality social behavior disorders	Memory	Cognitive/ abstract impairment	Remarks	Reference
40	0									One of 13 nonepileptic patients	Narabayashi & Uno (1966)
115	8					0		0	0		Balasubramaniam et al. (1970)
12	0							0	0		Vaernet & Madsen (1970)
18	0	0	6	31					0		Kiloh et al. (1974)

Note: Values represent percentages of operatees.

Table 17.5. *Summary of adverse sequelae of hypothalamotomy*

N	Worse	Dead	Surgical/ neurological complications	Seizures	Incontinence	Weight	Personality social behavioral disorders	Memory	Cognitive/ abstract impairment	Reference
11	0	0							0	Roeder et al. (1972)
22	5	5	5			5	✓			Müller et al. (1973)
6	0	0				✓	✓			Dieckmann & Hassler (1975)
4	0	0	25			50				Dieckmann & Hassler (1977)

Note: Values represent percentages of operatees.

tees. It is highly likely that, when aggressive behavior has declined, it has done so in the context of a general dampening of function (O'Callaghan & Carroll, 1982). Similarly, in the case of hypothalamotomy, it appears that there is a general reduction in libido. As Kiloh (1977b) admitted,

As far as operations for sexual problems are concerned I think it is very likely that these too are effective as far as reducing the strength of libido is concerned, though I remain sceptical of their ability to change sexual orientation. (P. 160)

At least half of the patients in Roeder et al.'s (1972) series and all of Dieckmann and Hassler's (1977) patients (see also Dieckmann, Horn, & Schneider, 1979) reported a reduction of overall sexual activity along with a diminution of "deviancy." Indeed, in some cases the decreases in "normal" sexual activity were severe. Schneider (1977) revealed a markedly reduced response to sexual stimuli of various sorts:

All patients complained of such reduction not only with respect to sexual stimuli arising out of a concrete sexual encounter with a partner but also such stimuli that occurred within the course of everyday ordinary activity. (P. 464)

Similarly, one of Dieckmann and Hassler's (1977) patients reported:

I concretely ascertain that my sexual drive has been drastically reduced. Sexual pressures, as I felt them before the operation, do not exist any more. The need of masturbation showed itself once or twice a few weeks after the intervention; another time on probation I tried it. During the last three months I have had no desire for sexual activity. During the visits of my wife, I ascertained that body touches don't excite me any more. (P. 458)

Another of their earlier operatees (Dieckmann & Hassler, 1975, p. 183) indicated that he had become completely impotent 2.5 years after the operation. One of Roeder et al.'s (1972) patients experienced a similar general decrease in libido:

Followed up for 23 months. Greatly reduced sex drive. Erections only every third or fourth morning. Having intercourse with his wife, but had no ejaculation, no orgasm. His wife had full satisfaction. The homosexual drives had disappeared, sexual ideas may come but scarcely influence him. Patient was very satisfied with the effect of hypothalamotomy at first. Now again troubled by homosexual libido. (P. 95)

Reports such as these not only cast grave doubts on the specificity of operative effects but, to return to earlier issues, also raise questions about the durability of outcome and the criteria for success adopted. General concerns regarding assessment and attributions of success have been expressed elsewhere (O'Callaghan & Carroll, 1982). The following remarks by Balasubramaniam, Kanaka, Ramanujam, and Ramamurthi (1971) of their outcome criteria for hypothalamotomy on "patients who are restless or exhibit destructive tendencies" (p. 227) are illustrative:

In assessing the usefulness of an operation like hypothalamotomy what should be taken into consideration is the manageability of the patient. Whereas previously the patient had to be tied to a post or kept in a cell, post operatively even a small relief is welcome. (P. 230)

It is clear that the history of psychosurgery is full of instances in which specific control has been bought at the expense of a general reduction effect (O'Callaghan & Carroll, 1982). For example, Freeman and Watts's (1950) account of a woman of gigantic proportions who for years was confined to a strong room and for whom "five attendants were required to restrain her while the nurse gave her the hypodermic" (p. 406) illustrates this emphasis on sedation and manageability. They reported that following surgery the woman's behavior was noticeably subdued:

. . . from the day after operation (and we demonstrated this repeatedly to the timorous ward personnel) we could playfully grab Oretha by the throat, twist her arm, tickle her in the ribs and slap her behind without eliciting anything more than a wide grin or a hoarse chuckle. (Pp. 406–7)

On occasions in which independent investigations of postoperative status have been carried out, further doubts are raised regarding the thoroughness of the psychosurgeon's original evaluations. Mark and Ervin's (1970) report offers an example. They conclude about their "Thomas R" case:

Four years have passed since the operation, during which time Thomas has not had a single episode of rage. He continues, however, to have an occasional epileptic seizure with periods of confusion and disordered thinking. (Pp. 96–7)

However, this picture of postoperative success is not supported by other assessments (Breggin, 1973; Chorover, 1974; Scheflin & Opton, 1978). Scheflin and Opton (1978) offered the following summary:

After seven months, Dr. Mark removed the electrodes and released Thomas in the custody of his mother. She found him "sickly, pale and weak." His life subsequently has been a phantasmagoria of confusion, violence, delusion and incarceration. He never worked again, but drifted back and forth between police lock-ups and mental hospitals. The Veterans Administration declared him "totally disabled" on October 26th, 1968, although his surgeons were still citing him as a success much later. (P. 300)

Conclusions

Not only is the psychosurgical treatment of sexual offenders without solid theoretical foundation, but examination of the empirical cases indicates that what appears, at first glance, to be evidence of efficacy does not survive close scrutiny. Aside from the obvious and necessarily compromising shortcomings of experimental design and control, postoperative assessment practices betray a somewhat idiosyncratic appreciation of what constitutes a successful outcome. Operatees classified as markedly improved are often inadvertently revealed as having gained only partial and/or temporary benefit. In addition, there is little concrete evidence that operative effects are specific. Reductions in sexual deviance are almost invariably embedded in a general decline in sexual interest and activity. Although general deficits are often alluded to, they rarely temper conclusions regarding efficacy.

The application of amygdalectomy for the control of violent and aggressive behavior is similarly without a compelling physiological rationale. Furthermore, there are few superficial indications of improvement with this sort of procedure. Where success has been claimed, it can be shown to be shortlived or contradicted by independent assessment. There is little concrete evidence of specificity, and operatees would appear to run the real risk of harmful neurological side effects.

The social context of psychosurgical intervention in sexual "deviance" and violent behavior has attracted only passing reference. However, it is important to appreciate that court referrals and prisoners comprise a large proportion of the surgical candidates. Presented with the choice between psychosurgery and imprisonment or even castration in some cases of sexual "deviance," it is not surprising that consent for amygdalectomy or hypothalamotomy is readily forthcoming. Furthermore, such singular motivational dynamics are not without serious implications for self-reports of operative efficacy (see Dieckmann, Horn, & Schneider, 1979, pp. 190–1). Clearly, both moral and scientific propriety demand the introduction of external regulation (Carroll & O'Callaghan, 1984).

The biology of antisocial behavior is without question a legitimate area of inquiry; it promises not only a deeper understanding of the circumstances of deviance but practical remedies as well. However, the particular biological solution of antisocial behavior examined here should caution us against shoddy scholarship and hasty application. Furthermore, cost–benefit arguments (see, e.g., Ervin, 1970; Roeder et al., 1972) should never be allowed to override considerations of scientific merit and patient welfare. Socially pernicious and ultimately ineffective therapeutic adventures such as psychosurgery might then be avoided.

References

Anderson, R. (1972). Differences in the course of learning as measured by various memory tasks after amygdalotomy in man. In E. Hitchcock, L. Laitinen, & K. Vaernet (Eds.), *Psychosurgery*. Springfield, IL: Thomas.
Bailey, H. R., Dowling, J. L., & Davies, E. (1977). Studies in depression: IV. Cingulotractotomy and related procedures for severe depressive illness. In W. H. Sweet, S. Obrador, & J. G. Martín-Rodríguez (Eds.), *Neurosurgical treatment in psychiatry, pain, and epilepsy*. Baltimore, MD: University Park Press.

Balasubramaniam V., Kanaka, T. S., & Ramamurthi, B. (1970). Surgical treatment of hyperkinetic and behavior disorders. *International Surgery, 54,* 18–23.

Balasubramaniam, V., Kanaka, T. S., Ramanujam, P. B., & Ramamurthi, B. (1971). Stereotaxic hypothalamotomy. *Indian Journal of Surgery, 33,* 227–30.

Beecher, H. K. (1961). Surgery as placebo: A quantitative study of bias. *Journal of the American Medical Association, 176,* 1102–7.

Breggin, P. R. (1972). The return of lobotomy and psychosurgery. *Congressional Record, 118*(26), 5567.

Breggin, P. R. (1973). The second wave. *Mental Health, 57,* 10–13.

Carroll, D., & O'Callaghan, M. A. J. (1982). Psychosurgery and the control of aggression. In P. F. Brain & D. Benton (Eds.), *The biology of aggression.* The Hague, Netherlands: Sijthoff & Noordhoff.

Carroll, D., & O'Callaghan, M. A. J. (1983). Psychosurgery and brain–behavior relationships in animals. In G. C. L. Davey (Ed.), *Animal models of human behavior.* New York: Wiley.

Carroll, D., & O'Callaghan, M. A. J. (1984). Controlling psychosurgery. In D. J. Müller, D. E. Blackman, & A. J. Chapman (Eds.), *Psychology and law.* New York: Wiley.

Chorover, S. L. (1974). The pacification of the brain. *Psychology Today, 7,* 59–69.

Dieckmann, G., & Hassler, R. (1975). Unilateral hypothalamotomy in sexual delinquents. *Confinia Neurologica, 37,* 177–86.

Dieckmann, G., & Hassler, R. (1977). Treatment of sexual violence by stereotactic hypothalamotomy. In W. H. Sweet, S. Obrador, & J. G. Martín-Rodríquez (Eds.), *Neurosurgical treatment in psychiatry, pain and epilepsy.* Baltimore, MD: University Park Press.

Dieckmann, G., Horn, H. J., & Schneider, H. (1979). Long-term results of anterior hypothalamotomy in sexual offences. In E. R. Hitchcock, H. T. Ballantine, Jr., & B. A. Meyerson (Eds.), *Modern concepts in psychiatric surgery.* Amsterdam: Elsevier.

Ervin, F. R. (1970, November 29). Violence: As likely from faulty brain as faulty upbringing. *Boston Globe,* p. 4.

Freeman, W. (1952). Psychosurgery: Survey after fifteen years. *Rocky Mountain Medical Journal, 49,* 587–9.

Freeman, W., & Watts, J. W. (1950). *Psychosurgery* (2nd ed.). Springfield, IL: Thomas.

Heimburger, R. F., Whitlock, C. C., & Kalsbeck, J. E. (1966). Stereotaxic amygdalotomy for epilepsy with aggressive behavior. *Journal of the American Medical Association, 198,* 741–5.

Heimburger, R. F., Small, I. F., Small, J. G., Milstein, V., & Moore, D. (1978). Stereotactic amygdalotomy for convulsive and behavioral disorders. *Applied Neurophysiology, 41,* 43–51.

Kiloh, L. G. (1977a). The treatment of anger and aggression and the modification of cerebral deviation. In J. S. Smith & L. G. Kiloh (Eds.), *Psychosurgery and society.* Oxford: Pergamon.

Kiloh, L. G. (1977b). Overview of symposium: Psychosurgery and society. In J. S. Smith & L. G. Kiloh (Eds.), *Psychosurgery and society.* Oxford: Pergamon.

Kiloh, L. G., Gye, R. S., Rushworth, R. G., Bell, D. S., & White, R. T. (1974). Stereotactic amygdaloidotomy for aggressive behaviour. *Journal of Neurology, Neurosurgery and Psychiatry, 37,* 437–44.

Kling, A. (1972). Effects of amygdalectomy on social-affective behavior in non-human primates. In B. E. Eleftheriou (Ed.), *The neurobiology of the amygdala.* New York: Plenum.

Klüver, H., & Bucy, P. C. (1938). An analysis of certain effects of bilateral temporal lobectomy in rhesus monkeys with special reference to "psychic blindness." *Journal of Psychology, 5,* 33–54.

Mark, V. H., & Ervin, F. R. (1970). *Violence and the brain.* New York: Harper & Row.

Mark, V. H., & Ordia, I. J. (1976). The controversies over the use of neurosurgery in aggressive states and an assessment of the critics of this kind of surgery. In T. P. Morley (Ed.), *Current controversies in neurosurgery.* Philadelphia: Saunders.

Mark, V. H., Sweet, W. H., & Ervin, F. R. (1972). The effect of amygdalotomy on violent behavior in patients with temporal lobe epilepsy. In E. Hitchcock, L. Laitinen, & K. Vaernet (Eds.), *Psychosurgery.* Springfield, IL: Thomas.

May, P. R. A., & Van Putten, T. (1974). Treatment of schizophrenia, II: A proposed rating scale of design and outcome for use in literature surveys. *Comprehensive Psychiatry, 15,* 267–75.

Motta, E. (1953). Trattamento di caso di omosessualità con la leucotomia transorbitale. *Giornale di Psichiatria e di Neuropatologia, 81,* 291–306.

Müller, D., Roeder, F., & Orthner, H. (1973). Further results of stereotaxis in human hypothalamus in sexual deviations: First use of this operation in addiction to drugs. *Neurochirugia, 16,* 113–26.

Narabayashi, H. (1979). Long-range results of medial amygdalotomy on epileptic traits in adult patients. In T. Rasmussen & R. Marino (Eds.), *Functional neurosurgery.* New York: Raven Press.

Narabayashi, H., & Uno, M. (1966). Long-range results of stereotaxic amygdalotomy for behaviour disorders. *Confina Neurologica, 27,* 168, 171.

O'Callaghan, M. A. J., & Carroll, D. (1982). *Psychosurgery: A scientific analysis.* Lancaster: Medical & Technical Publishing.

Rodin, E. A. (1973). Psychomotor epilepsy and aggressive behavior. *Archives of General Psychiatry, 28,* 210–13.

Roeder, F., Orthner, H., & Müller, D. (1972). The stereotaxic treatment of paedophilic homosexuality and other sexual deviations. In E. Hitchcock, E. Laitinen, & K. Vaernet (Eds.), *Psychosurgery.* Springfield, IL: Thomas.

Scheflin, A. W., & Opton, E. M., Jr. (1978). *The mind manipulators.* New York: Paddington Press.

Schneider, H. (1977). Psychic changes in sexual delinquency after hypothalamotomy. In W. H. Sweet, S. Obrador, & J. G. Martín-Rodríguez (Eds.), *Neurosurgical treatment in psychiatry, pain, and epilepsy.* Baltimore, MD: University Park Press.

Schreiner, L., & Kling, A. (1953). Behavioral changes following rhinencephalic injury in cat. *Journal of Neurophysiology, 16,* 643–59.

Schreiner, L., & Kling, A. (1956). Rhinencephalon and behavior. *American Journal of Physiology, 184,* 486–90.

Scoville, W. B. (1972). Psychosurgery and other lesions of the brain affecting human behavior. In E. Hitchcock, L. Laitinen, & K. Vaernet (Eds.), *Psychosurgery.* Springfield, IL: Thomas.

Staudt, V. M., & Zubin, J. (1957). A biometric evaluation of the somatotherapies in schizophrenia. *Psychological Bulletin, 54,* 171–96.

Vaernet, K., & Madsen, A. (1970). Stereotaxic amygdalotomy and basofrontal tractotomy in psychotics with aggressive behaviour. *Journal of Neurology, Neurosurgery and Psychiatry, 33,* 858–63.

Valenstein, E. S. (1973). *Brain control: A critical examination of brain stimulation and psychosurgery.* New York: Wiley.

Valenstein, E. S. (1977). The practice of psychosurgery: A survey of the literature (1971–

1976). In *National Commission for the Protection of Human Subjects of Biomedical and Behavioral Research: Appendix*. Washington DC: Department of Health, Education and Welfare.

Zuckerman, M. (1972). Physiological measures of sexual arousal in the human. In N. S. Greenfield & R. A. Sternbeck (Eds.), *Handbook of psychophysiology*. New York: Holt, Rinehart & Winston.

18   Pharmacological approaches to the treatment of antisocial behavior

C. R. Cloninger

Introduction

Drug therapy of antisocial behavior has yielded limited and inconsistent benefits in the past, but recent advances in diagnosis, neurophysiology, and neuropharmacology now offer considerable promise. Antisocial behavior syndromes are developmentally complex and composed of heterogeneous symptoms. Knowledge of the underlying neurophysiological and neurochemical processes has been limited, so that drug treatment for one target symptom has often led to a worsening of other parts of the clinical picture. Clinical drug trials have been carried out mainly with highly heterogeneous patient populations, so that results have usually been difficult to interpret and to replicate. Recent advances that will be described here make it possible now to specify drug-responsive target symptoms and more homogeneous clinical subgroups and to approach drug choice with rational guidance from knowledge of how to match the neuropharmacological properties of drugs with what is known about the neurochemical and neurophysiological basis of the target symptoms.

Despite optimism about recent advances, two points must be emphasized. First, antisocial behavior is developmentally complex with many different genetic and environmental determinants (1–6), so drugs are always merely an adjunct in a comprehensive treatment program. Second, all available treatment recommendations must be considered preliminary and tentative until long-term, double-blind, controlled trials are conducted that take into account available knowledge. Nevertheless, the recommended diagnostic and treatment procedures should both help clinicians refine their treatment strategy and stimulate further research in this important and challenging area.

329

The patient population

Antisocial behavior is defined to include any deviation from accepted social conventions. Such behavior, broadly defined, occurs in the absence of mental disorders and in the context of a wide variety of psychopathology. In this chapter I shall consider only the treatment of patients with disability from chronic or recurrent antisocial behavior that is considered a primary personality disorder in late adolescence and adulthood or a primary conduct disorder in childhood and early adolescence. According to the third edition of the *Diagnostic and Statistical Manual* (DSM-III) of the American Psychiatric Association (7), adults under consideration have antisocial personality or histrionic personality (8, 9) alone or possibly in combination with intermittent explosive disorder. The juvenile patients considered have conduct disorder alone or in combination with attention-deficit disorder, formerly called hyperkinetic child syndrome. In this chapter, these disorders will collectively be referred to as primary antisocial behavior disorders because follow-up and family studies indicate they are etiologically related (8, 9, 10). Criteria for these disorders are described in detail elsewhere (7) and will not be reviewed here because they do not define subgroups that are sufficiently homogeneous for effective drug choice. A more fine-grained subclassification scheme and its clinical, neurophysiological, and neuropharmacological basis will be described herein.

Overview of treatment

The primary antisocial behavior disorders begin in childhood and run a chronic course with the peak of antisocial behavior in late adolescence. The long-term prognosis is variable, with about 2% remitting their antisocial behavior each year after age 21 (1). When "remitted" antisocials are questioned, they nearly always attribute their improvement to a good marriage, membership in formal or informal self-help peer groups, a good job, or simply "growing up" (1, 11). Psychosocial or neurobiological treatment by professionals is rarely reported to have been useful. Many of the hyperkinetic children who seemed to have responded best to stimulants like methylphenidate as children discontinue treatment and manifest severe criminal behavior in adolescence and adulthood (12, 14). Attention to educational and vocational needs (15), psychological help with cognitive and interpersonal problems (16), and participation in self-help groups or therapeutic communities (1) may prove crucial to sustained improvement in multimodal treatment programs. Psychotherapy alone is seldom helpful: in the words of the late Samuel Yochelson, it produces "criminals with insight – but criminals nonetheless." Thus drug treatment may often be needed to improve underlying deficits before patients are amenable to psychosocial treatment. A thorough initial assessment is required in order to prescribe drugs that are appropriate for the constellation of symptoms manifested by a particular patient. This should include a psychiatric, medical, and social history as described by Guze (10), psychometric ratings of psychopathy-related traits as described by Schallings (33), electroencephalography (13, 17, 18) and ideally other neurophysiological tests, such as event-related brain potentials (19), and pharmacobehavioral tests, as described later. Such comprehensive evaluations are needed to identify subtypes of antisocial individuals who respond to particular psychoactive drugs.

Both drug abuse and lack of compliance with prescribed medication schedules are major obstacles to beneficial drug therapy. These problems, together with the needs for comprehensive initial assessment and close monitoring for adverse drug reactions, are indications for initiating treatment in a controlled setting like that available to patients in a hospital. Some patients who are highly motivated with good social support from family, friends, or probation officers may be treated as outpatients even initially, but they are exceptional.

Any drug therapy may be harmful in several ways. First, drug abuse of euphoriants and minor tranquillizers may lead to addiction and/or worsening of behavior. Second, adverse reactions, such as increased violence or agitation, may occur. Third, prescription of drugs may provide another excuse for manipulative patients to deny responsibility for their behavior. Accordingly, the clinician must avoid drugs with high abuse potential and must emphasize the empirical and adjunctive nature of any drug trial. Change in interpersonal behavior patterns of long standing will require that the patient feel responsible and motivated for such change. Also, if the physician approaches treatment with this attitude, he or she is less likely to become frustrated and more likely to maintain a positive therapeutic alliance.

Target symptoms for treatment

The target symptoms for the treatment of antisocial behavior syndromes can be divided into four major types of phenomena (Table 18.1): (a) aggression, (b) deficits in operant conditioning and social learning, (c) deficits in attention and impulse controls, and (d) electrocerebral or electroencephalographic (EEG) abnormalities. Some of these features are

Table 18.1. *Target symptoms in the treatment of primary antisocial syndromes*

Aggression
Low frustration tolerance (hyperirritability)
Predatory violence (cruel bullying)
Impulsive assaults
Instrumental assaults with social detachment
Dyssocial assaults

Deficits in operant conditioning and social learning
Poor avoidance learning
Marked egocentricity (social detachment)
Reinforcement of dyssocial behavior

Deficits in attention and impulse control
Novelty seeking
Inattention
Impulsivity
Hyperactivity

Electrocerebral abnormalities
Low seizure threshold
Immaturely slow EEG

---

moderately correlated; for example, many impulsive antisocial subjects have low frustration tolerance, poor avoidance learning, stimulation seeking, and immature EEGs. However, any population is heterogeneous and includes individuals with these symptoms in different constellations that require distinct pharmacological approaches. First I shall describe the target symptoms and available information about neurochemistry and neurophysiology that is relevant to drug treatment. Then I shall describe seven antisocial subtypes that are useful to distinguish for drug therapy.

Aggression

Aggressive behavior is broadly defined to include any acts that injure or intimidate others. It is useful for descriptive and treatment purposes to differentiate among different forms of criminal violence (20), hostility (21, 22), and bullying (23).

Five types of aggression behavior are distinguished in Table 18.1. The most frequent basis for chronic or repetitive aggressive behavior is a low frustration tolerance; such individuals are "hot-tempered" or "hot-blooded," easily provoked, or hyperirritable. Often, they are later distressed by their rages or temper tantrums but seem unable to exert self-control after minor provocation. Such individuals do poorly in crowded

Table 18.2. *Neurotransmitter roles in aggression*

	Type of aggressive behavior		
Neurotransmitter	Affective aggression	Sexual aggression	Predatory aggression
Catecholamines			
Dopamine	↑ ↑	↑ ↑	↓ (?)
Norepinephrine	↑	↑	↓
Epinephrine	?	↓	↓
Acetylcholine	↑	↑	↑ ↑
Serotonin	↓ ↓	↓ ↓	↓

Key: ↑ = facilitate; ↓ = inhibit.

Source: Modified from Hamburg and Trudeau (1981).

quarters and often prefer or demand wide personal territorial boundaries. Such behavior is sometimes described as "affective aggression" because of the highly emotional or excited aspects that are distressing to all involved.

In contrast, habitual bullies are predatory and seem to enjoy victimizing their prey. Such individuals are often described as "cold and cruel" because of their sadistic meanness. This may begin at an early age with cruelty to animals. Other forms of aggression are less often chronic. Some assaults and even homicides, described here as "impulsive," are unpremeditated or inadvertent acts that occur when criminals are frightened or surprised, for example, during the course of a robbery. They are largely the result of poor planning and unfortunate availability of weapons (20).

Other "instrumental" forms of violence are planned by egocentric, socially detached ("cold-blooded") individuals motivated by a calculated decision. Professional assassinations and terrorism with a basis in overvalued political, social, or racial ideas are examples of such aggression.

Finally, some types of fighting are determined largely by peer pressures to conform to violent social customs of a gang or ghetto or larger social group. Such dyssocial behavior requires treatments that undermine the maintenance of such operantly conditioned behavior.

Some human data about the neurochemical correlates of these different types of aggression and extensive animal studies reveal marked differences in the neuroregulation of different types of aggression (Table 18.2). Specifically, the adrenergic and dopaminergic systems facilitate affective aggression, such as fighting induced by painful shocks or isolation, and inhibit predatory aggression. In contrast, activation of the cholinergic system induces both these classes of aggression, and the serotonergic system inhibits both classes. Supporting human data are described later. This provides a theoretical basis for chemotherapy of affective and predatory aggression (24, 25). Other forms of aggression are considered in reference to deficits in operant conditioning and in impulse control.

Deficits in operant conditioning and social learning

One of the most consistent empirical observations about antisocial individuals is that criminals who are impulsive and stimulation seeking (i.e., sociopaths or psychopaths) are as capable of learning positively reinforced tasks as normal individuals but learn poorly to avoid aversive stimuli (26–29). Sociopathic criminals show little increase in electrodermal activity in anticipation of an aversive stimulus but are readily able to learn anticipatory heart rate and digital vasomotor responses. In addition recovery time for skin conductance responses is inversely correlated with severity of delinquency. The slow recovery time of sociopaths has been interpreted as indicative of slow fear reduction when making avoidance responses to conditioned noxious stimuli; whenever reinforcement by fear reduction is delayed, avoidance learning is diminished (31). Furthermore, the combination of a large heart rate increase in the presence of low skin conductance before aversive stimuli may be related to a capacity to ignore, "repress," or "gate out" aversive stimuli (30).

The clinical features correlated with poor avoidance learning among antisocial subjects are low anticipatory anxiety (i.e., worry, rumination, and concern about future misfortune, harm, or punishment) and high impulsivity (i.e., acting on the spur of the moment, lack of reflectiveness, rapid decision making and action, lack of planning, carefreeness, and carelessness) (33). It should be emphasized that low anticipatory anxiety does not imply lack of other types of somatic anxiety. The cardiovascular responsiveness of impulsive antisocials is not diminished; many also experience high somatic anxiety with panic and cardiovascular symptoms such as palpitations and dyspnea (33). Many also experience muscular tension and motor restlessness or hyperactivity, as discussed in the next section on attention deficits.

Schachter and Latane (27) showed that impulsive sociopaths improve their avoidance learning dramatically when injected with epinephrine but not placebo. In contrast, normal individuals do not learn as well after epinephrine injection (27). Furthermore, chlorpromazine disinhibits some

Table 18.3. *Drug effects on operant conditioning*

Drug	Type of conditioning schedule[a]	
	Avoidance	Maintenance
Minor tranquillizers		
Benzodiazepines	↓ ↓	—
Mepropamate	↓ ↓	—
Barbiturates	↓ ↓	—
Alcohol	↓ ↓	—
Major tranquillizers		
Phenothiazines	↓ [b]	↓ ↓
Butyrophenones	↓ [b]	↓ ↓
Amphetamine	↑	↑
Imipramine	—	↑ (?)
Morphine	—	?
Lithium	↑ (?)	↓ (?)

[a] Avoidance refers to inhibition by punishment or nonreward; maintenance refers to facilitation by positive or negative reinforcement. Reduced (↓) avoidance indicates increase in previously suppressed behavior. Reduced maintenance indicates decrease in a previously manifest behavior. Dashes (—) indicate no substantial change.
[b] Neuroleptic effects on conditional avoidance may be blocked by anticholinergics.

Source: Based largely on Goodman and Gilman (1980) and Stein (1981).

types of antisocial impulses so that subjects cheat more in experimental tests (34).

Other drug effects on operant conditioning are summarized in Table 18.3. Minor tranquillizers dramatically diminish conditioned avoidance. The reduced avoidance behavior resulting from benzodiazepines is highly correlated with their clinical anxiolytic effects (35). Thus it would be predicted that alcohol and other minor tranquillizers act to impair avoidance conditioning of impulsive antisocials further. In contrast, neuroleptics have little effect on avoidance conditioning but weaken maintenance of operantly conditioned behavior regardless of the type of reinforcement (positive or negative) (35). Stein has summarized extensive evidence that benzodiazepines disinhibit avoidance conditioning by γ-aminobutyric acid-ergic reduction of the activity of serotonin neurons in the brain's "punishment" system. Conversely, the behavior-facilitating effects of both positive and negative reinforcement are thought to be mediated by a catecholaminergic mechanism (35). This provides a theoretical basis for drug choices to improve avoidance learning with serotonergic drugs and to reduce the maintenance of positively reinforced "dyssocial" behavior with catecholamine antagonists like the phenothiazines.

Because clinical symptoms may sometimes be difficult to assess, some (27) have suggested that reactivity to epinephrine or other neurophysiological and pharmacobehavioral tests (29, 30) may be better predictors of avoidance learning ability than observed or reported behavior.

Deficits in attention and impulse control

A substantial proportion of impulsive antisocials are noted to be stimulus bound and novelty seeking, much like patients with frontal brain lesions. They are hypovigilant, distractible, and inattentive, and their intentions quickly lose regulating influence on behavior. In addition, many impulsive antisocials recurrently experience somatic anxiety with panic and many cardiorespiratory symptoms, especially in acutely stressful situations. They also experience muscular tension and motor restlessness. This combination of novelty seeking, easy distractibility, somatic reactivity, and hyperactivity is thought to be related to low cortical arousal and lowered inhibitory control of the reticular system and frontal cortex over autonomic and skeletomuscular systems (8, 33).

Satterfield (13, 14) has presented evidence that a substantial subgroup (about 25–30%) of children with attention-deficit disorder (i.e., hyperactivity, inattention, and impulsivity) have conduct disorders in adolescence and antisocial personality as adults. The biological, but not adoptive, parents of antisocial hyperkinetic children have an excess of antisocial personality and somatization disorder (36, 37). Not all hyperkinetic inattentive children have these features; some are hyperaroused (often with no personal or family history of antisocial behavior) and respond poorly to catecholamine agonists. Satterfield has shown that children with low arousal, as measured by low electrodermal activity and a large N2 component of auditory evoked potentials, respond well to catecholamine agonists like methylphenidate. Others with hyperarousal may respond better to cholinergic drugs such as deanol or dietary lecithin.

Several investigators have documented the persistence of hyperkinetic childhood syndrome into adulthood. Inattention and impulsivity are often persistent and hyperactivity may be diminished, but chief complaints are usually low frustration and stress tolerance with hyperirritability and somatic anxiety. Using DSM-III criteria, Wender's subjects included a predominance of subjects with antisocial personality, somatization disorder (Briquet's syndrome), and abuse of alcohol and other drugs. These patients reportedly respond well to catecholamine agonists such as low doses of imipramine (especially for somatic anxiety with dysphoria and panic attacks) and psychostimulants like methylphenidate or pemoline (38, 40). This provides a basis for identification of a subgroup of impulsive antisocials most likely to respond well to catecholamine agonists and poorly to serotonin antagonists such as minor tranquillizers.

Electrocerebral abnormalities

Electroencephalographic (EEG) evaluations have consistently found that the EEG is abnormal in 50% to 60% of antisocials, particularly in unusually aggressive or hospitalized patients; this literature has been reviewed elsewhere (18, 29, 41). Mednick et al. (42) reported that slow α activity is predictive of later delinquency. An excess of posterior temporal slow waves (usually 3–5 Hz) in antisocials has been interpreted as evidence of delayed maturation (43). However, these slow-wave abnormalities are not correlated with clinical differences or prognosis.

A more useful approach to EEG for treatment has been described by Monroe (17, 44). Individuals with intermittent explosive disorder (i.e., repeated discrete episodes of sudden unprovoked outbursts of uncontrollable rage) have a high incidence of subcortical ictal phenomena in the limbic area. These can be demonstrated by special activation procedures using α-chlorolase. Neuroleptics aggravate this nervous system instability, whereas benzodiazepines and other anticonvulsants ameliorate it. Screening patients for evidence of a low seizure threshold is indicated to identify those likely to benefit from anticonvulsants or to be harmed by drugs that further lower seizure thresholds. This should be considered even if a seizure diathesis is not a sufficient explanation for the total clinical picture.

Antisocial subtypes for drug therapy

Different constellations of target symptoms require different drugs, but little work has been carried out to develop and validate a clinically useful subclassification scheme. A tentative typology for drug treatment is depicted in Figure 18.1. Recommendations for drug treatment of these seven subtypes are summarized in Table 18.4 on the basis of available neurochemical and neurophysiological data and relevant clinical trials. In this section I shall describe the constellation of target symptoms in each sub-

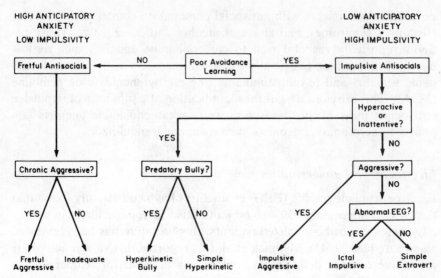

Figure 18.1. Tentative decision tree for subclassification of antisocial behavior syndromes.

type and the general pharmacological strategy I recommend. In the next section, individual drugs and their use will be described in more detail.

Fretful antisocials

Two antisocial syndromes are differentiated in which the individuals are presumed to have no defect in avoidance learning. Both are high in anticipatory anxiety and low in impulsivity (hence the term "fretful"). Both are presumed to be aggravated by catecholaminergic drugs, so psychostimulants are contraindicated. Further choice of drugs depends on the presence or absence of chronic aggression.

"*Fretful aggressive*" subjects are characterized by their intense anger, suspiciousness, and feelings of resentment. Although not delusional, they are ruminative and concerned about current and future misfortune. They tend to see themselves as innocent victims rather than predators or provocateurs. They are often tense and dysphoric, distressed by their aggression and their rejection by others. Such aggressive behavior in resentful paranoid individuals is reported to be responsive to lithium (45). Neuroleptics are indicated for such aggressiveness and may help to diminish antisocial behavior being operantly maintained by positive or negative reinforcement.

Table 18.4. *Choice of drugs according to antisocial subtype: Tentative recommendations*

Antisocial subtype	Drugs of choice	Contraindicated drugs
Fretful antisocials		
Fretful aggressive	1. Lithium 2. Neuroleptics	Psychostimulants
Inadequate (schizoid/asocial or dyssocial)	1. Neuroleptics (especially if EEG normal) 2. Benzodiazepines (especially if EEG abnormal)	Psychostimulants, lithium (?) (especially if schizoid)
Impulsive antisocials		
Hyperkinetic bully	1. Pemoline 2. Lithium	Minor tranquillizers, neuroleptics (?)
Impulsive aggressive	1. Lithium 2. Serotonergics	Minor tranquillizers, antiserotonergics, cholinergics, neuroleptics (?)
Simple hyperkinetic	1. Methylphenidate *d*-amphetamine (if no drug abuse) 2. Pemoline 3. Imipramine (especially if high somatic anxiety)	Minor tranquillizers, neuroleptics (?)
Ictal impulsive	1. Phenytoin 2. Carbamazepine 3. Benzodiazepines (?)	Neuroleptics, psychostimulants, antidepressants
Simple extravert	Neuroleptics	Minor tranquillizers

Other nonaggressive antisocials with anticipatory anxiety include both dyssocial and schizoid (cold, aloof, asocial) individuals. These could be differentiated further clinically, but may be treated with the same drugs. The dyssocial individuals may be normal in mental status and physiological studies, except that they are distressed by the conflict between peer pressures and their own anticipation of the long-term consequences of their behavior. If the EEG is normal, treatment with neuroleptics may help diminish their positively reinforced dyssocial behavior. If the EEG suggests a low seizure threshold, trial of a benzodiazepine may be useful for its anticonvulsant activities. Lithium is not indicated in the absence of aggression and impulsivity because it does not diminish other antisocial conduct (45, 46, 47) and is often poorly tolerated in anxious schizoid individuals (46).

Impulsive antisocial syndromes

Five subtypes of individuals with antisocial syndromes who are presumed to have poor avoidant conditioning are differentiated according to the presence or absence of evidence of low reticular inhibition, aggression, and EEG abnormalities. In all cases minor tranquillizers and other anti-serotonergic drugs are presumed to be contraindicated because they reduce avoidant conditioning.

Two types of impulsive subjects are distinguished who have other presumptive evidence of low reticular inhibition such as prominent inattention or distractibility, hyperactivity, or marked emotional lability associated with high somatic anxiety including overreactions to minor stressful events. Catecholaminergic drugs are presumed to be indicated except in the presence of predatory aggression.

In the latter case "hyperkinetic bullies" can be treated with dopaminergic drugs, which reduce predatory aggression (see Table 18.2) as well as increase cortical arousal. Alternatively, lithium may be indicated because it is serotonergic and benefits at least some (25–33%) impulsive aggressive subjects (45, 46, 47). Cholinergic and antidopaminergic drugs are presumed to be contraindicated in hyperkinetic bullies.

In "simple hyperkinetics" who are not predatory bullies the chief complaints are inattention, impulsivity, hyperactivity, and emotional lability with high somatic anxiety to minor events. These same symptoms occur in varying intensity in both children and adults, as discussed earlier. The most consistent evidence for beneficial drug effects has been reported for catecholaminergic drugs, such as amphetamine, methylphenidate, and pemoline. The former two drugs are euphoriants for some individuals and have a high potential for abuse that rules out their routine use. In patients with prominent somatic anxiety, including panic attacks, who are sometimes diagnosed as having histrionic personality or somatization disorder, low doses of imipramine (38, 48) and psychostimulants (39) have been found beneficial. However, some patients with a similar clinical picture are cortically hyperaroused, rather than having low reticular inhibition; such patients may respond preferentially to cholinergic drugs, like deanol, or dietary manipulation with lecithin, which leads to increased cholinergic activity (49). However, cholinergic drugs probably should be avoided if hyperirritability is a prominent problem because such aggression is expected to be aggravated (Table 18.2).

Serotonin agonists are recommended for "impulsive aggressive" subjects without somatic anxiety, inattention, or hyperkinesis. They are recommended for their effect on aggression (see Table 18.2) and also their predicted improvement of avoidance conditioning (see Table 18.3). This is supported by findings of reduced serotonin metabolites (5-hydroxyindoleacetic acid) in the cerebrospinal fluid of impulsive aggressive personality disorders (50) and the XYY syndrome (51). Thus lithium, which enhances serotonergic activity, would be expected to be a drug of choice for such patients. This is supported by Sheard's finding of improvement in mesomorphic aggressive criminals (46, 47) and Tupin's finding that such patients report reduced anger and increased reflectiveness (45). Trials with the serotonin precursor tryptophan have also been found beneficial in XYY subjects with reduced serotonin metabolites in their cerebrospinal fluid (51). It is possible that amitriptyline may also be useful, because it has both serotonergic and anticholinergic effects. Serotonin antagonists, such as minor tranquillizers, and cholinergics, such as deanol, are not recommended for the impulsive aggressive subtype.

"Ictal impulsive" patients are identified by the correlation between EEG evidence of seizure activity and clinical episodes of unprovoked aggressive outbursts. When patients have evidence of chronic or recurrent antisocial behavior or impulsivity, a diagnosis of intermittent explosive disorder cannot be made. Nevertheless, even in the absence of classical seizures a trial of anticonvulsants may be considered. If benzodiazepines are used the patients must be closely observed because they may disinhibit suppressed antisocial impulses. Also if improvement does occur, tolerance develops to the anticonvulsant effects of benzodiazepines (52).

The uncomplicated "simple extravert" is identified by impulsivity unassociated with aggression, hyperactivity, or EEG abnormalities. Some may be successful as "confidence" men. Most subjects with such benign features who do have extensive antisocial behavior are likely to be abusers of alcohol, minor tranquillizers, or other drugs. Treatment for such drug abuse is the most important treatment in all such cases. No other drugs may be required. Alternatively, low doses of neuroleptics may be used briefly to reduce antisocial behavior that is being maintained by positive or negative reinforcement.

Results of clinical use

Lithium

Clinical trials of lithium salts have been reported for a variety of settings and types of patient (24, 25, 45–47, 54, 55). There have been many anecdotal reports and nonblind trials (45, 53, 55), a single-blind trial of 12 aggressive delinquents (46), and a double-blind trial of 66 impulsive aggressive convicts (47). The target symptoms in antisocial patients are reduction in anger and aggressive behavior and increased capacity to reflect on consequences of behavior (i.e., decreased impulsivity, increased anticipatory avoidant behavior). Benefit has been observed in violent criminals who were anxious and paranoid (45) and in aggressive criminals who were hyperactive, overtalkative, and muscular (mesomorphic) or emotionally labile and volatile (46). Roughly 25–33% of such criminals have improved substantially. Reports of response to lithium in the presence of full hyperkinetic syndrome in aggressive children have not been consistent (53). Improvement in aggression due to low frustration tolerance and impulsivity is accepted well by patients, but bullies (in whom aggression is egosyntonic) tolerate diminution of their aggressiveness poorly, even though many do respond to the drugs as long as they comply with treatment (45, 54). Anxious schizoid subjects also tolerate lithium therapy poorly (46). Antisocial behavior unrelated to aggression and impulsivity, such as lying, extortion, and "conning," are seldom benefited.

Lithium's known pharmacological effects (24) include enhancement of serotonergic activity by increasing blood and brain levels of the serotonin precursor tryptophan and serotonin production in brain neurons. It also has anticholinergic effects, decreasing acetycholine turnover and synthesis. Lithium also has many effects on catecholaminergic systems, including inhibition of tyrosine hydroxylase and decreasing the release of catecholamines at the synaptic cleft (24).

In the treatment of aggressive criminals, the therapeutic range for lithium has been reported to be 0.6–1.5 mEq/liter (46). Tupin reported benefits over a mean of 10 months with mean serum levels of 0.82 ± 0.18 mEq/liter. A slow increase in serum level is recommended to avoid poor compliance due to unpleasant side effects (46). Individual titration of dosage is indicated, but levels below 1 mEq/liter seem to be beneficial in most cases.

Neuroleptics

A wide variety of neuroleptics have been used to treat antisocial personality and conduct disorders, including piperidine (especially periciazine and thioridazine), piperizine (especially fluphenazine), and aliphatic phenothiazines (especially chlorpromazine), butyrophenones (especially haloperidol), and thioxanthenes (especially chlorprothixene). In addition to aggressiveness and impulsiveness, target symptoms include, to a lesser extent, mood lability and other types of antisocial behavior that may be maintained by positive or negative reinforcement, such as stealing, lying, and lack of industry.

The piperidine phenothiazines with low extrapyramidal side effects have been recommended as superior to other neuroleptics in adult personality disorders. In the United States thioridazine is recommended (56). Periciazine or propericiazine is not marketed in the United States but has been extensively used in Europe, especially in France (56, 57). It does not have the inhibiting effect on drive and avoidant conditioning or the extrapyramidal action of the piperizines. Long-acting preparations such as fluphenazine enanthate are reported to be effective in some aggressive antisocials (56). The piperidines and chlorprothixene are also recommended in children (56). When patients are epileptic or have abnormal EEG, neuroleptics (especially sedative ones) should be avoided, since they increase cerebral excitability; the piperazines and thioxanthenes are least likely to do this. In patients with hyperkinetic features, phenothiazines, including thioridazine, are much less effective than psychostimulants (19, 57).

The effects of neuroleptics on avoidance conditioning are correlated with extrapyramidal effects and may be blocked by anticholinergics. In treating antisocial subjects good control of extrapyramidal symptoms is important for both compliance and conditioning purposes.

The doses of neuroleptics used in personality disorders are much lower than in psychosis. For example, periciazine has been recommended in doses of 10 to 30 mg in average adults, and thioridazine is recommended in doses of less than 100 mg (58).

Minor tranquillizers

The use of minor tranquillizers in antisocial subjects is highly controversial. It is well known that alcohol has a disinhibiting effect and often is associated with violence and other criminal behavior (10, 20). However, the use of benzodiazepines has been associated with inconsistent recommendations due to observations of both increased and decreased aggressive and antisocial behavior, depending on the particular drug, initial levels of anxiety and hostility, and personality (59, 60, 61). A recent review suggested that increased antisocial behavior is associated only with excessive dosage or abuse (62). Oxazepam has been associated with less hostile reactions than other benzodiazepines (59, 60, 63). The high potential for drug abuse is a major problem with minor tranquillizers that limits their use in antisocial subjects. Impulsive antisocials with poor avoidance conditioning are expected to be worsened on theoretical grounds (Table 18.3). Thus they are recommended here only when anticipatory anxiety is prominent and impulsivity is low or EEG abnormalities warrant a trial as an anticonvulsant. In the latter case, subjects must be monitored closely to adjust dosage if impulsivity is exacerbated and as tolerance develops to the anticonvulsant actions (52).

Psychostimulants

Consistently beneficial results in the treatment of antisocial children and adults with catecholamine agonists, such as amphetamine, methylphenidate, and pemoline, have been reported only in patients with features of inattention, impulsivity, and hyperactivity beginning in childhood (39, 64, 65). Other patients often tolerate the stimulatory effects poorly or abuse the drugs for euphoriant properties (24, 64). Although the most consistent benefit has been obtained with amphetamine and methylphenidate, pemoline is a noneuphoriant drug with low potential for abuse and has been found effective in some adult hyperkinetics with antisocial personality and somatization syndrome (39).

Deanol (dimethylaminoethanol) is a stimulant that has been regarded as a precursor of acetylcholine. However, it competes with choline for uptake at the blood–brain barrier (66), and some experiments have shown no intraneuronal increase in brain acetylcholine (67). In brain-damaged adults deanol is well tolerated and leads to increased alertness (57), but further investigation of its use in younger and antisocial patients is required. An alternative approach to increased acetylcholine activity is increased ingestion of dietary sources of choline, such as soybeans, liver, eggs, choline itself, or phosphatidylcholine (lecithin) (49).

Antidepressants

The only antidepressants that have been recommended for treatment of antisocial subjects are tranylcypromine and imipramine. Tranylcypromine is structurally similar to amphetamine and has pharmacological properties related both to amphetamine and to its potent inhibition of monoamine oxidase (57, 68). It produces psychomotor stimulation by releasing norepinephrine and inhibiting its reuptake at the synaptic cleft (68). It is more effective in some dysphoric states associated with somatic anxiety and hostility than in retarded depressions (57). Because of its beneficial effect on depression, somatic anxiety, and its stimulant properties, it has been recommended in adult hyperkinetics with such symptoms (39). The risk of hypertensive crises requires compliance with diets low in tyramine; many antisocial subjects are irresponsible in such strict dietary compliance, so the use of tranylcypromine must be considered with caution.

Similarly, imipramine has been recommended in adult hyperkinetics with prominent somatic anxiety, including panic attacks (38). It should be noted that neurochemical heterogeneity may be present in patients with similar clinical pictures: Underactivity of dopaminergic or noradrenergic systems may be responsive to pemoline or imipramine, respectively, and both may respond to tranylcypromine.

Doses of imipramine beneficial for panic attacks are much lower than usually required in primary major depressive disorders; rapid improvement on 25 to 50 mg of imipramine has been described by Mann and Greenspan (38). Similarly, Liebowitz and Klein reported that some patients with panic attacks experience immediate beneficial effects on oral doses as low as 5 mg with plasma levels between 15 and 60 ng/ml. In contrast depression seldom responds to plasma levels below 180 ng/ml (48). Thus the recommended starting dose of imipramine for hyperkinetic patients with prominent somatic anxiety is 25 mg/day.

Conclusion

Recent advances in the study of the neurochemical and neurophysiological basis of different types of antisocial behavior offer much promise for neuropharmacological treatment as an adjunct to treatment. The major limitation to rational drug therapy is the lack of a validated subclassification of antisocial behavior. Without this, clinical trials of available drugs will continue to produce the inconsistent and limited success that characterize past efforts. Even the most impressive current trials (namely, those with lithium salts and stimulants) yield substantial improvement in only a minority of subjects.

The differentiation of seven subtypes of antisocial behavior for drug treatment is a preliminary attempt to integrate available knowledge and to stimulate a more comprehensive approach to clinical assessment. It is hoped that clinical assessments can also be supplemented with pharmacobehavioral tests in some clinical investigations (54).

The clinician now has available a wide range of drug treatment strategies. This justifies much greater optimism and medical interest in the treatment of antisocial behavior disorders.

Acknowledgment

This work was supported in part by Grant MH-31302, AA-03539 and Research Scientist Development Award MH-00048.

References

1. Valliant, G. E., & Perry, J. C. (1980). Personality disorders. In H. I. Kaplan, A. M. Freedman, & B. J. Suddock (Eds.), *Comprehensive textbook of psychiatry* (3rd ed., pp. 1579–82). New York: Williams & Wilkins.
2. Tucker, G. J., & Pincus, J. H. (1980). Child, adolescent, and adult antisocial and dyssocial behavior. In H. I. Kaplan, A. M. Freedman, & B. J. Sadock (Eds.), *Comprehensive textbook of psychiatry* (3rd Ed., pp. 2816–26). New York: Williams & Wilkins.
3. Cloninger, C. R., & Reich, T. (1983). Genetic heterogeneity in alcoholism and sociopathy. In S. S. Kety (Ed.), *Genetics of neurological and psychiatry disorders*. New York: Raven Press.
4. Bohman, M., Cloninger, C. R., & Sigvardsson, S. (in press). Predisposition to petty criminality in Swedish adoptees: I. Genetic and environmental heterogeneity. *Archives of General Psychiatry*.
5. Cloninger, C. R., Sigvardsson, S., & Bohman, M. (in press). Predisposition to petty criminality in Swedish adoptees: II. Cross-fostering analysis of gene–environment interaction. *Archives of General Psychiatry*.
6. Sigvardsson, S., Cloninger, C. R., & Bohman, M. (in press). Predisposition to petty criminality in Swedish adoptees: III. Sex differences and validation of the male typology. *Archives of General Psychiatry*.
7. American Psychiatric Association (1980). *Diagnostic and statistical manual* (3rd ed). Washington, DC: Author.
8. Cloninger, C. R. (1978). The link between hysteria and sociopathy. In H. S. Akiskal & W. L. Webb (Eds.), *Psychiatric disorders: Exploration of biological predictors* (pp. 189–218). New York: Spectrum.
9. Cloninger, C. R., (1985). Somatoform and associative disorders. In G. Winokur and P. J. Clayton (Eds.), *Medical basis of psychiatry*. Philadelphia: Saunders.
10. Guze, S. B. (1976). *Criminality and psychiatry disorders*. New York: Oxford University Press.
11. Robins, L. N. (1966). *Deviant children grown up: A sociological and psychiatric study of sociopathy personality*. Baltimore, MD: Williams & Wilkins.
12. Satterfield, J. H., Satterfield, B. T., & Cantwell, D. P. (1981). Three-year multimodality treatment of 100 hyperactive boys. *Journal of Pediatrics, 98,* 650.
13. Satterfield, J. H. (1978). The hyperactive child syndrome: A precursor of adult psychopathy? In R. Hare & D. Schallings (Eds.), *Psychopathic behavior: Approaches to research*. New York: Wiley.
14. Satterfield, J. H., Hoppe, C. M., & Schell, A. M. (in press). A prospective study of delinquency in 110 attention deficient disorder and 88 normal adolescent boys. *American Journal of Psychiatry*.
15. Shore, M. R., & Massimo, J. L. (1973). After ten years: A follow-up study of comprehensive vocationally oriented psychotherapy. *American Journal of Orthopsychiatry, 43,* 128.
16. Horowitz, M. J. (Ed.). (1977). *Hysterical personality*. New York: Aronson.
17. Monroe, R. R. (1975). Anticonvulsants in the treatment of aggression. *Journal of Nervous and Mental Disorders, 160,* 119.

18. Syndulko, K. (1978). Electrocortical investigations of sociopathy. In R. D. Hare & D. Schallings (Eds.), *Psychopathic behavior: Approaches to research* (pp. 145–56). New York: Wiley.

19. Saletu, B., Saletu, M., Simeon, J., Viamontes, G., & Itil, M. (1975). Comparative symptomatology and evoked potential studies with *d*-amphetamine, thioridazine, and placebo in hyperkinetic children. *Biological Psychiatry, 10,* 253.

20. Tinklenberg, J. R., & Ochberg, F. M. (1981). In D. A. Hamburg & M. B. Trudeau, *Biobehavioral aspects of aggression* (pp. 121–40). New York: Liss.

21. Buss, A. H., & Durkee, A. (1957). An inventory for assessing different kinds of hostility. *Journal of Consulting Psychology, 21,* 343.

22. Buss, A. H. (1961). *The psychology of aggression.* New York: Wiley.

23. Olweus, D. (1979). Stability of aggressive reaction patterns in males: A review. *Psychological Bulletin, 86,* 852.

24. Leventhal, B. L., & Brodie, H. K. H. (1981). The pharmacology of violence. In D. A. Hamburg & M. B. Trudeau (Eds.), *Biobehavioral aspects of aggression* (pp. 85–106). New York: Liss.

25. Eichelman, B., Elliot, G. R., & Barchas, J. D. (1981). Biochemical, pharmacological, and genetic aspects of aggression. In D. A. Hamburg & M. B. Trudeau (Eds.), *Biobehavioral aspects of aggression* (pp. 51–84). New York: Liss.

26. Lykken, D. T. (1957). A study of anxiety in the sociopathic personality. *Journal of Abnormal Sociology and Psychology, 55,* 6.

27. Schachter, S., & Latane, B. (1964). Crime, cognition, and the autonomic nervous system. In M. R. Jones (Ed.), *Nebraska symposium on motivation* (pp. 221–75). Lincoln: University of Nebraska.

28. Eysenck, H. J. (1964). *Crime and personality.* Boston: Houghton Mifflin.

29. Hare, R. D., & Schallings, D. (Eds.). (1978). *Psychopathy behavior: Approaches to research.* New York: Wiley.

30. Hare, R. D. (1978). Electrodermal and cardiovascular correlates of psychopathy. In R. D. Hare & D. Schallings (Eds.), *Psychopathic behavior: Approaches to research* (pp. 107–44). New York: Wiley.

31. Mednick, S. A. (1975). Autonomic nervous system recovery and psychopathology. *Scandanavian Journal of Behavioral Therapy, 4,* 55.

32. Venables, P. (1975). Progress in psychophysiology: Some applications in a field of abnormal psychology. In P. Venables & M. Christie (Eds.), *Research in psychophysiology* (pp. 418–37). New York: Wiley.

33. Schallings, D. (1978). Psychopathy-related personality variables and the psychophysiology of socialization. In R. D. Hare & D. Schallings (Eds.), *Psychopathic behavior* (pp. 85–106). New York: Wiley.

34. Schachter, S., & Wheeler, L. (1962). Epinephrine, chlorpromazine, and amusement. *Journal of Abnormal Sociology and Psychology, 65,* 121.

35. Stein, L. (1981). Behavioral pharmacology of benzodiazepines. In D. F. Klein & J. G. Rabkin (Eds.), *Anxiety: New research and changing concepts* (pp. 201–14). New York: Raven Press.

36. Morrison, J. R., & Stewart, M. A. (1973). The psychiatric status of the legal families of adopted hyperactive children. *Archives of General Psychiatry, 28,* 888.

37. Stewart, M. A., Cummings, C., Singer, S., & DeBlois, C. S. (1981). The overlap between hyperactive and unsocialized aggressive children. *Journal of Child Psychology and Psychiatry, 22,* 35.

38. Mann, H. B., & Greenspan, S. I. (1976). The identification and treatment of adult brain dysfunction. *American Journal of Psychiatry, 133,* 1013.

39. Wender, P. H., Reimherr, F. W., & Wood, D. R. (1981). Attention deficit disorder

("minimal brain dysfunction") in adults: A replication study of diagnosis and drug treatment. *Archives of General Psychiatry, 38,* 449.

40. Quitkin, F., & Klein, D. F. (1969). Two behavioral syndromes in young adults related to possible minimal brain dysfunction. *Journal of Psychiatric Research, 7,* 131.

41. Cloninger, C. R. (1975). Recognizing and treating sociopathy. *Medical World News, 16,* 12.

42. Mednick, S. A., Volavka, J., Gabrielli, W. F., et al. (1981). EEG as a predictor of antisocial behavior. *Criminology, 19,* 219–22.

43. Hill, D. (1963). The EEG in psychiatry. In J. D. N. Hill & G. Parr (Eds.), *Electroencephalography: A symposium on its various aspects* (pp. 368–428). London: MacDonald.

44. Monroe, R. R. (1970). *Episodic behavioral disorders.* Cambridge, MA: Harvard University Press.

45. Tupin, J. P., Smith, D. B., Clanon, T. L., Kim, L. I., Nugent, A., & Groupe, A. (1973). The long-term use of lithium in aggressive prisoners. *Comprehensive Psychiatry, 14,* 311.

46. Sheard, M. H. (1975). Lithium in the treatment of aggression. *Journal of Nervous and Mental Disorders, 160,* 108.

47. Sheard, M. H., Marini, J. L., Bridges, C. I., & Wagner, E. (1976). The effect of lithium on impulsive aggressive behavior in man. *American Journal of Psychiatry, 133,* 1409.

48. Liebowitz, M. R., & Klein, D. F. (1981). Differential diagnosis and treatment of panic attacks and phobia states. *Annual Review of Medicine, 32,* 583.

49. Wurtman, R. J., & Growdon, J. H. (1978). Dietary enhancement of CNS neurotransmitters. *Hospital Practice, 13,* 71.

50. Brown, G. L., Ballinger, J. C., Minichiello, M. D., & Goodwin, F. K. (1979). Human aggression and its relationship to CSF 5-HIAA, MHPG, and HVA. In M. Sandler (Ed.), *Psychopharmacology of aggression* (pp. 131–48). New York: Raven Press.

51. Bioulac, B., Benezech, M., Renaud, B., Noel, B., & Roche, D. (1980). Serotonergic dysfunction in the 47,XYY syndrome. *Biological Psychiatry, 15,* 6.

52. Goodman, L. S., & Gilman, A. (Eds.). (1980). *The pharmacological basis of therapeutics* (6th ed). New York: Macmillan.

53. Whitehead, P., & Clark, L. (1970). Effect of lithium carbonate, placebo, and thioridazine in hyperactive children. *American Journal of Psychiatry, 127,* 824.

54. Marini, J. L., & Sheard, M. H. (1977). Antiaggressive effect of lithium ion in man. *Acta Psychiatrica Scandinavica, 55,* 269.

55. Tupin, J. P. (1972). Lithium use in non-manic-depressive conditions. *Comprehensive Psychiatry, 13,* 209.

56. Itil, T. M., & Wadud, A. (1975). Treatment of human aggression with major tranquillizers, antidepressants, and newer psychotropic drugs. *Journal of Nervous and Mental Disorders, 160,* 83.

57. Baldessarini, R. J. (1980). Drugs and treatment of psychiatric disorders. In L. S. Goodman & A. Gilman. (Eds.), *The pharmacological basis of therapeutics* (6th ed., pp. 391–447). New York: Macmillan.

58. Kalinowsky, L. B., & Hippius, H. (1969). *Pharmacological, convulsive and other somatic treatments in psychiatry.* New York: Grune & Stratton.

59. Azcarate, C. L. (1975). Minor tranquilizers in the treatment of aggression. *Journal of Nervous and Mental Disorders, 160,* 100.

60. Kalina, R. K. (1964). Diazepam: Its role in a prison setting. *Diseases of the Nervous System, 25,* 101.

61. Brown, C. R. (1978). The use of benzodiazepines in prison populations. *Journal of Clinical Psychiatry, 38,* 219.

62. Lader, M. H., & Petursson, H. (1981). Benzodiazepine derivatives: Side effects and dangers. *Biological Psychiatry, 16,* 1195.
63. Gardos, G., DiMascio, A., Salzman, C., & Shader, R. I. (1968). Differential actions of chlordiazepoxide and oxazepam on hostility. *Archives of General Psychiatry, 18,* 757.
64. Allen, R. P., Safer, D., & Covi, L. (1975). Effects of psychostimulants on aggression. *Journal of Nervous and Mental Disorders, 160,* 138.
65. Eisenberg, L., Lachman, R., Molling, P. A., Lockner, A., Mizelle, J. D., & Conners, C. K. (1963). A psychopharmacologic experiment in a training school for delinquent boys: Methods, problems, findings. *American Journal of Orthopsychiatry, 33,* 431.
66. Millington, W. R., McCall, A. L., & Wurtman, R. J. (1978). Deanol acetamidobenzoate inhibits the blood–brain transport of choline. *Annals of Neurology, 4,* 302.
67. Pepeu, G., Freedman, D. X., & Giarman, N. J. (1960). Biochemical and pharmacological studies of demethylamenoethanol (deanol). *Journal of Pharmacology and Experimental Therapeutics, 129,* 291.
68. Schildkraut, J. J. (1970). Tranylcypromine: Effects on norepinephrine metabolism in rat brain. *American Journal of Psychiatry, 126,* 925.

Author index

351

Subject index

361